Christian Social Ethics

D1571081

Christian Social Ethics
A Reader

Edited by
John Atherton

The Pilgrim Press
Cleveland, Ohio

Originally published
by the Society for Promoting Christian Knowledge,
London, as *Social Christianity: A Reader*.
Compilation and editorial matter © 1994 by John Atherton

Pilgrim Press edition published 1994
The Pilgrim Press, Cleveland, Ohio 44115

Printed in the United States of America on acid-free paper

99 98 97 96 95 94   5 4 3 2 1

Library of Congress Cataloging-in-Publication Data
Social Christianity.
Christian social ethics : a reader / edited by John Atherton.
         p.   cm.
Originally published: Social Christianity. London [England] :
Society for Promoting Christian Knowledge, 1994.
Includes bibliographical references.
ISBN 0-8298-0999-6
1. Sociology, Christian. 2. Christian ethics.
3. Social Ethics. 4. Social gospel.
I. Title.
BT738.S617   1994
261.8—dc20
94-6913
CIP

CONTENTS

Contents

Part II
LIBERATION THEOLOGY

Contents

Part III
CHRISTIAN CONSERVATISM

vii

The Author's Prayer

O Thou who art the light of my soul, I thank Thee for the incomparable joy of listening to Thy voice within, and I know that no word of Thine shall return void, however brokenly uttered. If aught in this book was said through lack of knowledge, or through weakness of faith in Thee or of love for men, I pray Thee to overrule my sin and turn aside its force before it harm Thy cause. Pardon the frailty of Thy servant, and look upon him only as he sinks his life in Jesus, his Master and Saviour. Amen.

Walter Rauschenbusch,
For God and the People: Prayers of the Social Awakening (1910)

Acknowledgements

The original suggestion that I should compile such a Reader was the idea of Ronald Preston. In fact, I owe far more than this to him, as my recent *Christianity in the Market* (1992) reveals. It has been a demanding, but creative, opportunity to link the two publications so closely. So many of the sources of this book, not surprisingly, are recognized in the first. In addition, I would like to acknowledge the help given to me by the John Rylands University Library of Manchester, and the Chetham's Library, Manchester.

The support of friends and colleagues is always a decisive factor in the production of a book such as this. I am very conscious of their toleration of my absence from meetings in the past few years. In particular, I owe much to the Board for Social Responsibility of the Diocese of Manchester, which I have had the privilege of chairing since 1980. My wife, Vannie, my secretary, Mrs Kathleen Petch, and my editor, Philip Law, continue to give me indispensable support.

I am grateful to the following for permission to include copyright material (full details of original publication are given in the text):

Brigadier C. G. V. Vyvyan CBE for Text 5 by R. H. Tawney

SCM Press, London, for Texts 6 and 7 by R. H. Preston; Text 14 by Philip Wogaman; and Text 16 by Gustavo Gutiérrez.

Charles Scribner's Sons, an imprint of Macmillan Publishing Co., New York, for Text 11 by Reinhold Niebuhr, © 1932 Charles Scribner's Sons; copyright renewed © 1960 Reinhold Niebuhr; and Text 13 by John C. Bennett, © 1946 Charles Scribner's Sons; copyright renewed © 1974 John C. Bennett.

World Council of Churches Publications, Geneva, for Text 12 by Reinhold Niebuhr.

Hodder & Stoughton Publishers, London, for Text 14 by Brian Griffiths.

Acknowledgements

The William Temple Foundation, Manchester, for Text 15 by
Ulrich Duchrow.

Sterling Lord Literistic, Inc., New York, for Text 19 by
Michael Novak, © 1982 Michael Novak.

John Atherton

Preface

The arrival of urban–industrial society in the nineteenth century transformed the world. It did so in terms of how people live and think and, as we are increasingly aware, in terms of the environment itself. It should not be surprising that a faith claiming a concern with the whole created order should have responded positively to the challenge of such a dramatic occurrence in world history. And so proved to be the case. The emergence of social Christianity in the second half of the nineteenth century initiated a series of developments in Christian social thought and practice which continue to influence the relationship between faith and society. It was an order of religious change that ranks with the Reformation.

This Reader seeks to trace significant strands in this history, concentrating on the growth of social Christianity, initially as Christian socialism in England and the social gospel in the United States in the nineteenth and early twentieth centuries. These early responses to the forces of urbanization and industrialization laid the foundations for many of the later developments in social Christianity. Yet as the social, economic and political contexts continued to change in Western society, so the Christian responses to them also evolved, often through a critical relationship with the earlier achievements. The work of Reinhold Niebuhr and John Bennett played a central part in these developments. It is out of this combined history that the contemporary exponents of social Christianity, like J. P. Wogaman in the United States and Ronald Preston in the United Kingdom, have emerged.

Any account of social Christianity cannot afford to ignore the contributions of liberation theology and Christian conservatism to modern Christian social thought and practice. With regard to the former, it can be argued that it has such strong connections with the radical strand of social Christianity that it should be included within that broad tradition. However, leading exponents – such as Gutiérrez – regard liberation theology as a new tradition quite different from the essentially Western phenomenon of social Christianity.[1] This claim is respected by this Reader, although the work of Ulrich Duchrow, a German theologian, is included in this category to link the Western and Latin American contexts through a European liberationist perspective.

The Christian conservative tradition, including the Christian political economists of the early nineteenth century, is an integral part of the Reader because it articulates a Christian commitment to the free market. It is an important argument in its own right, but also because social Christianity and liberation theology have been influenced by their opposition to this tradition and the economics it represents.

In the process of describing the ground that this Reader seeks to cover, it is helpful to recognize the material that is not included. The account of social Christianity does not address other significant strands in modern Christian social ethics, particularly those seeking to promote a radically distinctive Christian position in society. For example, the work of such post-liberal theologians as Stanley Hauerwas, with its emphasis on the role of character and narrative rather than ethical decision-making on moral quandaries, is not included. Nor is John Yoder's work on the peace tradition. Both are regarded as of subordinate importance in the elaboration of Christian involvement at the heart of urban-industrial life.

In this regard, the omission of Western political theology, as articulated by Jürgen Moltmann and Johannes Metz, is much more questionable. The argument of limited space could be used to justify the decision. However, a growing familiarity with the history and character of social Christianity in Britain and the United States does suggest that political theology is a separate tradition. In this sense, it was decided to use liberation theology as the preferred example of radical Christian social thought and practice independent of the tradition of social Christianity.

Why a Reader in Christian Social Ethics?

More clarity over what the Reader attempts to address can be gained by noting the reasons for its production.

First, and most important of all, it represents the central significance of the contemporary context for the development of Christian social thought and practice. Addressing the processes of industrialization and urbanization, and their social consequences, must surely occupy a priority place on the Christian agenda. They touch every aspect of human experience and the life of our environment. Not surprisingly, and recognized by Christians and Churches by the early part of the twentieth century, they also affect every area of the Churches' life, from biblical and doctrinal theology to liturgies and spirituality, from the education of Christians and citizens to the development of mission strategies in urban areas. Whatever position is taken on social, political or economic questions, the need for an informed understanding of the contemporary context cannot be ignored by any who wish to influence to good effect the development of Church and society in the light of Christian beliefs.

Secondly, because the context is so important for Christian life and witness, then we must become much more familiar with recognized Christian thinking on the emergence of modern contexts as advanced economies. Facing up to change effectively as Christians should never depend on following secular understandings alone. Nor can it depend on simple Christian imperatives like love, justice, and honesty. The extent and depth of change increasingly requires a substantial grasp of both secular understandings and the nature and relationship of Christian faith to them. This Reader seeks to provide detailed and inspirational support for such a task. It does this by illustrating the wealth of Christian social thought and practice by reference to some of the finest Christian contributions to the arguments over the development of the modern market economy,[2] from its earliest stages at the beginning of the nineteenth century to the 1980s. Because it has concentrated on the tradition of social Christianity, it emphasizes the contributions of thinkers in the United States and United Kingdom. Since these two nations and their Churches have played, and still do play, such a major part in the growth of the market economy and political democracy, their contributions to Christian social thought and practice should be given a rediscovered recognition in contemporary Christian debates on social, political and economic affairs. The World Council of Churches, in particular, would do well to heed such advice.[3] Even though market economies now appear to be the only realistic way of operating modern advanced economies, their continuing problems in the West, and the enormous difficulties facing societies in transition from command to market economies, make even more relevant the questioning of market economies, which social Christianity also powerfully represents. The sheer enormity of world poverty, and the liberation theology to which this has given rise, only confirm the need to take such judicious questioning seriously.

By introducing major thinkers in these debates to a wider public, it is hoped that an alarming gap in Christian resources for social witness will be filled. Astonishingly, I am not aware of the existence of any book that brings together such a wealth of Christian opinion on social affairs. As a result, for all involved in the leadership of the Churches, in the formation of church statements and action on social matters, and in theological education, this collection of the thinking of great Christian commentators on modern social, economic and political affairs should be of some relevance to their witness in and to society. Perhaps more importantly, it should inspire and guide clergy and laity who seek to be involved in contemporary life in realistic and therefore more hopeful ways.

Thirdly, in order to confirm and explain the appeal of such material to socially concerned Christians, the personal reasons for producing this Reader may be of some assistance. For most of my life and ministry I have been aware of the importance of the relationship between thought and practice for Christian life. Involvement in community and economic life feeds into the

Preface

development of Christian social thought, and the development of Christian social thought enriches involvement in community and economic affairs. The relationship between Christian social thought and practice should always be an ongoing interactive process.[4] As a young priest trying to make sense of the corporate realities that shaped life in the Gorbals in the late 1960s, I was driven to recognize the irrelevance of much traditional dogmatic and biblical theology, and church life, to that task.

Fortunately, I was then introduced to Reinhold Niebuhr's *Moral Man and Immoral Society*. From then on, I gradually came to see the astonishing richness and relevance of social Christianity for the development of contemporary Christian social thought and practice. I was stimulated and humbled by F. D. Maurice's criticisms, in the mid-nineteenth century, of the excesses of *laissez-faire* capitalism as a contradiction of beliefs about God and his purposes for human living. I was provoked by Walter Rauschenbusch's noble attempts, at the turn of this century, to argue for the Christianizing of an unchristian economic order. I have been guided by the wise and discerning judgements of Ronald Preston and J. P. Wogaman in their attempts to interpret today's market economy.

Of course, making creative sense of such an interaction between social Christianity and the contemporary task is helped by the *location* of one's involvement in life. The more I have ventured on this journey of interactive involvement, the more I have come to treasure where God has placed me for the last eight years as Canon Theologian of Manchester Cathedral. To work at the heart of one of the great conurbations where industrialization and urbanization originated, and which continues to undergo great economic and social change, is exactly the place to learn from the experiences of social Christianity. It is the most appropriate base for the great task of developing a Christian social thought in and for our times.

For me, it performs the same function as the LSE did for its founders, Sidney and Beatrice Webb, at the beginning of this century. For R. H. Tawney, 'The London School of Economics, the chief venture of their early years, was designed by them, not as a cloistered college, but as a mundane institution around which should eddy the full tide and roar of London life.'[5] It 'conveys a suggestion of workman-like realism', which

5

must surely lie at the heart of the witness to a God who took upon himself the realities of the world through and in the humanity of Jesus Christ. My book *Christianity and the Market* emerged out of this history, experience and insights in 1992. This present Reader is, in part, a complement to it, recording the actual contributions of the great Christians who stimulated and shaped that book. It can be read in conjunction with that first volume. More importantly, it should accompany, inspire, and inform us in our individual and communal journeyings through our society and history.

The shape of the Reader

After an introductory essay on the story and context of social Christianity, the material in this book is divided into three parts. The first and major section (Part I: Social Christianity) traces the historical development of Christian social thought through the writings of English contributors: F. D. Maurice, Brooke Foss Westcott, William Temple, R. H. Tawney and Ronald H. Preston. It then complements this by a similar journey through the writings of American contributors: Washington Gladden, Walter Rauschenbusch, Reinhold Niebuhr, John Bennett and J. Philip Wogaman.

The second part (Part II: Liberation Theology) begins with an extended argument by Ulrich Duchrow, followed by a major example of the work of Gustavo Gutiérrez. Although Duchrow is not a liberation theologian from Latin America, he was greatly influenced by his ministry there. As a result he has developed a radical critique of the market economy from within its German heartland. Working in close collaboration with the liberationist tendencies of the World Council of Churches, he has built up a theological case for a radical alternative to capitalism that complements the work of liberation theology.

The third and final part (Part III: Christian Conservatism) draws from the early nineteenth-century history of this tradition, as Christian political economy, through the work of John Bird Sumner. This is followed by a contribution from Brian Griffiths, head of Mrs Thatcher's Policy Unit in the 1980s. The important part played by Christians in the rise of neoconservatism in the United States, is reflected in the writing of Michael Novak.

The contributors span the histories of social Christianity, liberation theology, and Christian conservatism. They come from a cross-section of the great Christian denominations, including Anglican, Baptist, Congregational, Evangelical, Lutheran, Methodist, and Roman Catholic.

The contributions deal mainly with the *substantive* issues of urban-industrial society, with particular reference to the economy and industry as they affect social and political affairs. Social Christianity, liberation theology, and Christian conservatism have always recognized that political economy issues lie at the heart of the changes that have transformed the world. The central role of economics and the market economy in current affairs confirms that historical judgement. The contributors' work on important issues such as international politics has been omitted because of space limitations, but also because of the need to concentrate on matters of political economy.

The contributors have also recognized the importance of theological *method* in the development of Christian social thought. *What* is said about society is regarded as integrally connected to *how* that judgement is formed. Particular attention is therefore paid to methodology in a number of the contributions, including those of William Temple, Ronald H. Preston, John Bennett, Gustavo Gutiérrez, and Brian Griffiths. The importance of both aspects of Christian social thought, and their interrelationship, cannot be overemphasized to all who wish likewise to contribute effectively to contemporary social affairs.

The selection of *individual* contributions to Christian social thought reveals an obvious omission – namely, the contribution of official church statements. These have been so significant and substantial that justice could only be done to them through a Reader devoted to that end alone. However, that being said, it is important to recognize that the intimate relationship between social Christianity and the official pronouncements of denominational and ecumenical bodies is reflected in the choice of contributors to this Reader. For example, in England, William Temple influenced the Conference on Politics, Economics and Citizenship (COPEC 1924), the Oxford Conference (1937) and the Malvern Conference (1941). R. H. Tawney played an important part in the Fifth Committee and its report *Christianity and Industrial Problems* (1919), in COPEC (1924), the International Missionary Conference in Jerusalem (1928) and the Oxford Conference (1937). Ronald Preston edited the papers following the Geneva World Council of Churches Conference (1966), and was a prominent member of various Church of England working parties producing such significant reports as *Winters of Discontent* (1981), *Not Just for the Poor* (1986), and *Changing Britain* (1987). In the United States, Washington Gladden influenced both Congregational reports and, with Walter Rauschenbusch, the immensely influential *Social Creed* of the Federal Council of Churches (1908 and 1912). John Bennett played a prominent role in the Oxford Conference (1937), and the World Council of Churches Assemblies at Amsterdam (1948), Evanston (1954), and New Delhi (1961). He was also an important editing contributor to the 1966 Geneva Conference, and to the Federal Council of Churches study of economic life (1949).[6] Reinhold Niebuhr contributed important papers and speeches to both the Oxford and Amsterdam Conferences, and J. P. Wogaman chaired the United Methodist Task Force on the Nestlé controversy. The same intimate relationship exists in liberation theology, for example between Gustavo Gutiérrez and the foundational conferences for the development of liberationism at Medellín (1968) and Puebla (1979).

With regard to the contributions themselves, it is important to note the following points:
• I have chosen to rely on a few extended arguments, rather than on a greater number of shorter pieces. It is important to capture the integrity of an argument, even though this has sometimes required judicious editing to control the length of the passage. For example, Temple's arguments for policy guidelines, which relate so closely to the formation of the Welfare State, must be seen to emerge out of his arguments explaining *why* the Churches should interfere in society, and the principles on which that interference should be based. Similarly, it is important to encounter a comprehensive argument from Maurice, Rauschenbusch, Bennett, Duchrow, Gutiérrez and Griffiths, despite the cost of some editing. Brief excerpts do not treat

seriously the nature and significance of such contributions and contributors.

● References in the texts, with several exceptions, have been omitted to avoid an interruption of the argument, and to simplify the presentation of texts.

● The contributors, and their contributions, are introduced by a brief comment locating them in the context of their life and times, and drawing out their significance for today's context.

Notes

1. 'We will avoid yielding to a tendency found in some academic settings: the tendency to regard liberation theology as the radical, political wing of European progressive theology. Such a view of liberation theology is clearly a caricature for anyone with a good knowledge of this subject.' G. Gutiérrez, *A Theology of Liberation* (SCM Press, 1988 edition), p. xxix.
2. For a definition, and further elaboration, of the market economy, see J. Atherton, *Christianity and the Market* (SPCK 1992), Chapters 2 and 3.
3. A group, which met in Vancouver in 1990, and in Berlin in 1992, has made such representations to the W. C. C. See its: 'A Statement to the World Council of Churches on the Future of Ecumenical Social Thought'. Members included Dr John Habgood, Ronald Preston, Dr Roger Shinn, Dr Charles West, and Dr Paul Abrecht (Secretary).
4. The implications of interaction for theological method and Christian life are explored in Atherton, Chapter 9.
5. R. H. Tawney, *The Attack and Other Papers* (George Allen & Unwin 1953), p. 135.
6. See J. Bennett, ed., *Christian Social Ethics in a Changing World* (New York: Association Press 1966), and J. Bennett (co-author), *Christian Values and Economic Life* (New York: Harper & Row 1954).

Introduction:
Christian Social Ethics in Context

If we cross Blackstone Edge ... we enter upon that classic soil on which English manufacture has achieved its master-work and from which all labour movements emanate, namely, South Lancashire with its central city Manchester (Frederick Engels).[1]

When young Frederick Engels came to England in 1842, and looked down from the Pennine hills, he saw before him one of the great seats of the Industrial Revolution, the conurbation of greater Manchester. At its heart were the two cities of Manchester and Salford, surrounded by large industrial towns. Produced by the prodigious force of manufacturing industry, based on steam power, mechanization and 'the division of labour',[2] it combined with the equally revolutionary influence of urban life to tear old rural communities apart and create dramatically new forms of human habitation. Factories and tenements together produced the degrading and oppressive conditions so vividly described by Engels. Some of these were adjacent to the Cathedral,[3] in which this book has been written, and next to the Chetham's Library, where Engels did some of his own research. It was against such productive systems and their consequences, that Engels, with Marx, directed their devastating arguments.

Yet they were not isolated in their criticism. For, as Engels observed, the Manchester conurbation was also the home of the

10

countermovement to capitalist industry and urbanization. Consumer co-operatives originated in Rochdale and flourished in the area; the first Trade Union Congress was to meet in Manchester in 1868, and the Liberal and Labour parties were to gain strong roots there. No wonder R. H. Tawney was to describe all these changes as 'a phenomenon differing, not merely in degree, but in kind, from the social order preceding it.'[4]

Engels and the countermovement were not alone in their stance against these disturbing innovations. Manchester was important too, because of its influence on the development of a critical Christian response to these seminal changes. The first Christian socialists reserved their greatest scorn for 'the Manchester men', the school of radical *laissez-faire* capitalism, and F. D. Maurice accordingly lectured there on the co-operative alternative.[5] R. H. Tawney lived and worked in the conurbation, learning more from his mill-worker students than from his elitist education at Rugby School and Oxford University.[6] William Temple was Bishop of Manchester during the formative years of the Conference on Politics, Economics and Citizenship (COPEC), and the general strike of 1926. Finally, Ronald Preston has spent most of his working life in Manchester, developing the most adequate Christian comment on today's social order in England.

The story of Manchester's place in the processes of industrialization and urbanization illustrates the general significance of the social context for the development of modern Christian social thought. It began with Maurice in mid-nineteenth-century England, and continues in the late twentieth century with Gutiérrez in Peru. Yet acknowledging the general principle should never divert attention from the equally important recognition that such contexts are always specific to a time, place and history. That is why Manchester is as good a place as any to begin a narrative of Christian challenges to modern contexts. For the account of social Christianity is essentially about the Christian response to particular urban-industrial societies. It is, of necessity, an evolving narrative because such societies are an evolving reality. They soon emerged in other nations and continents, particularly in the United States, and more recently in Latin America, Asia and Africa.

11

The story of social Christianity, however, is focused on developments in England and the United States. The heartland of the modern market economy is still located, to a significant extent, in Western Europe and North America, even though the centre of gravity of economic growth is being shared increasingly with South East Asia.[7] Major contributions to social Christianity are therefore still emerging from the English and American contexts.

It is a story, too, that represents a complex of contributions from individuals, organizations and Churches. And, because its development needs to be located in the wider context of modern Christian social thought, any adequate consideration involves the recognition of liberation theology and Christian conservatism. In very different ways, both present strong challenges to social Christianity, and so assist in its elaboration.

To tell the account of social Christianity's encounter with such changing contexts is obviously a daunting task.[8] However, locating the following texts in that story confirms the recognition of key stages in the development of social Christianity. These, in turn, are related to major changes in the social context.

Social Christianity in England: the story of Christian socialism

> Let us not try to sever, for they are inseparable, those principles which affect the problems of earth from those which affect the Kingdom of Heaven. All unrighteous government whatever, all that sets itself against the order and freedom of man, is hostile to Christ's government, is rebellion against Him, in whatsoever name and by whatsoever instruments it is administered (Frederick D. Maurice).[9]

Rarely can the start of a great movement be traced to a particular day and place. Yet it can be with regard to the origins of Christian socialism. On 10 April 1848, in F. D. Maurice's house in Queens Square, London, Maurice, Charles Kingsley and John Ludlow met to plan a Christian response to the political events of that particular day. Hours earlier, the great demonstration of the Chartists had marched to present a petition to Parliament for radical political reform. By the next morning, the three churchmen had produced a placard addressed to the 'Workmen of England.' It sought to assure the workers that 'almost all men who [have] hands and hearts' know their great wrongs, and to challenge them and society by declaring: 'Who would dare refuse you freedom? For the Almighty God, and Jesus Christ, the poor Man, who died for poor men, will bring it about for you ...'[10] So began a great Christian movement. And, for the next six years, they carried on meeting, generating an influence far beyond their size and times.

Symptomatic of this origin and continuing stimulus was the group's description of themselves as Christian socialists. It symbolized a bold commitment to the growing army of urban and rural poor, and to the early attempts to formulate organizations and theories for their defence and support. Conversely, it also represented an equally courageous and provocative challenge to the conservative orthodoxies of the establishments of Church and society. The title itself emerged when Maurice was discussing with Ludlow a new series of tracts for working people:

> I see it clearly. We must not beat about the bush. What right have we to address the English people? We must have something special to tell them, or we ought not to speak. 'Tracts on Christian Socialism' is, it seems to me, the only title which will define our object, and will commit us at once to the conflict we must engage in sooner or later with the unsocial Christians and the unchristian Socialists.[11]

Of course, such a declaration reveals that the origins of Christian socialism were related to a much wider context than a particular date and place. Behind these events lay a series of revolutions that struck Europe in 1848, particularly France. Associated with them was a series of economic, social and political upheavals in England which provoked the failed Chartist demonstration in London. It was one of the great achievements of the first Christian socialists to read the signs of those times in the light of the gospel, to take the context seriously as an act of Christian discipleship.

The story was remarkable, too, because these early pioneers developed a more comprehensive Christian response to a modern context which included characteristics that have recurred throughout the history of social Christianity. The consistency of rejoinder, over one and a half centuries and two continents, and across major denominations and the ecumenical movement, suggests the cohesiveness of the tradition of social Christianity. It is a confirmation, too, of the adequacy of much of its reading of Christian belief and its implications for modern societies. Since these early characteristics do resonate across the stages of English Christian socialism and the American social gospel, it is worth recounting them in a little more detail:

1. Like F. D. Maurice, early Christian socialism was rooted in fundamental beliefs about God and his relationship to humanity: 'The truth is that every man is in Christ; the condemnation of every man is, that he will not own the truth.'[12] Consequently, all humankind constituted the living material of the spiritual and universal Kingdom of Christ. It resulted in a powerful sympathy and enthusiasm for humanity. From this basic belief flowed all the other characteristics of Christian socialism.

2. For example, because the world was part of the Kingdom's agenda, reading and interpreting the signs of the times in the light of that agenda became a primary Christian duty. Addressing the context became a fundamental part of the elaboration of Christian belief. It meant considering 'the questions which are most occupying our countrymen at the present moment, such as the Extension of the Suffrage; the relation of the Capitalist to the Labourer; what a Government can or cannot do, to find work or pay for the poor.'[13]

3. Since all were in Christ, whether they acknowledged it or not, the task was to address the context in the light of that belief, to work with the signs of the Kingdom. If that meant collaborating with socialists, trade unionists, Chartists and co-operators, so be it. Unlike Ludlow, Maurice was of the following opinion: 'I don't ask these people whether they acknowledge the bond of

union which I acknowledge. It does not change the fact, whether they do or not. There is a fellowship between me and them' rooted in the heavenly Father.[14]

4. As an integral part of the Christian response to the signs of the times, his collaborative endeavour also included an active contribution to practical initiatives reflecting these beliefs. The early Christian socialists were therefore involved in a variety of innovatory programmes including working-class adult education (the Working Men's College, 1854), and producer co-operatives. The latter were regarded as 'the practical application of Christianity to the purposes of trade and industry.'[15] (See Texts 1 and 2.) Pamphlets, books, sermons, addresses and novels were also produced by them, and have continued to play an important part in all the stages of social Christianity.

5. Such beliefs and commitments challenged the heart of the dominant economic system and ideology of *laissez-faire* capitalism. In particular, its reliance on competition was regarded as a blatant contradiction of God's purposes for human relationships. For Maurice, 'Competition is put forth as the law of the universe. That is a lie. The time is come for us to declare that it is a lie by word and deed.'[16]

6. Christian socialism also challenged the prevailing theological and ecclesiastical orthodoxies (the two establishments of Church and state were intimately connected). Its broad Christian humanitarianism was related to a belief in Christ as immanent in the world, and in eternal life as relationship with him. It therefore stood in stark contrast to the otherworldliness of evangelical beliefs, with their emphasis on the individual, eternal punishment, and a penal view of the cross. The attack on the age of atonement by a theology of the incarnation exercised a remarkable liberating effect on contemporaries. Years later, Stewart Headlam testified to such an emancipation: 'You, ladies and gentlemen, probably do not know what it is to have been delivered ... from the belief that a large proportion of the human race are doomed to endless misery. You are free–born mainly through Maurice's work and courage.'[17] And courage it was, because it cost Maurice his Chair at King's College, London, in 1853.

7. The small group that met throughout those years reflected the importance of spirituality for Christian social involvement.

Based on worship every Sunday, followed by Bible study each Monday evening, it constituted what Christensen has called 'a small brotherhood.'[18]

The first stage of Christian socialism finished as sharply as it began, in 1854. Yet so great was its influence that it provided a stimulus and continuity across 'the gap' of twenty years, before the next stage began: 'Without the breakthrough of the 1850s the struggles of the 1880s would have been incomparably harder.'[19] Running from the 1870s to the 1890s, this second stage faced a context marred by deep economic recession (the concept of 'unemployment' was first used in the 1870s).[20] It was a period of industrial and urban strife, and the rise of such socialist organizations as the Social Democratic Federation, the Fabian Society, and the Independent Labour Party. All took place in a context of great intellectual change: scientific (evolutionary theory), philosophical (idealism with its recognition of the personality, community, citizenship and state), and historical (affecting economic theory and history, and biblical studies).

Out of such a context and as a response to it, the development of social Christianity both continued the achievements of the first stage, and added significantly to them.

For example, with regard to the latter, the period witnessed the growth of social Christianity as radical Christian socialism and as more moderate Christian social reform. It was a development reflected in the contributions of individuals, organizations, theology, and church relations.

The emergence of organized radical Christian socialism owed much to the achievements of Stewart Headlam and his Guild of St Matthew (1877–1909). His radicalism and eccentricity ensured his rejection by the Church of England hierarchy, but inspired many who became leaders of social Christianity in the future. The characteristics of this radicalism included the following:

1. The creative development of sacramental socialism based on a combination of Maurician theology and Tractarian churchmanship. This stimulated the interpretation of the immanence of God through contemporary realities. Accordingly, baptism became the means of entry into the greatest democratic and egalitarian society in the world, and 'the mass was the weekly

16

meeting of a society of rebels against a Mammon-worshipping world order'.[21] So the secular was used to interpret Christianity, rather than a version of socialism chosen to fit it. The development of incarnational theology was continuing apace. From Maurice's belief that all people were in Christ, and the consequence of making no distinction between sacred and secular, Headlam sought to seek the illumination of God's purposes through such secular means as socialism and the London County Council's education policies.

2. Two secular organizations were of particular importance for radical Christian socialism. Headlam's membership of the newly founded Fabian Society involved him in the development of socialism as collectivism and a strong interventionist state. His support for Henry George and the Single Tax movement, although proving to be idiosyncratic, was initially a radical option for social change representing, as it did, a major 'hold upon radical social thinking in England' and in the United States.[22] Yet the problem with this, as with all such mono-causal interpretations of complex social and economic contexts, was its tendency to be quickly regarded as a panacea for all social problems. It soon became the key to open all doors. 'By easy transitions, he [Headlam] connected prostitution and drunkenness with the absence of a tax on land values.'[23] The temptations associated with the choice of a medium to express Christian social convictions have continued to bedevil social Christianity, including liberation theology, to the present day.[24]

The formation of the Church Socialist League in 1906 continued the commitment to political socialism, and to the use of secular media, like Guild Socialism, to achieve radical change.

3. The relationship between radical Christian socialism and the official Church has always been – at best – uneasy. For Headlam and his colleagues, the Church was expected to live the life of brotherhood as an agent of enabling society as a whole to express the same. As the 'shock-troops' of sacramental socialism,[25] their task was to capture the Church and society for such an aim. Headlam was clear it would involve the disestablishment of the Church of England.

The development of social Christianity as social reform was an acknowledgement of the significance of gradual evolutionary reform. The strong reaction against *laissez-faire* capitalism as competition and individualism was still a formative influence, but the emphasis was increasingly on working *within* the existing system; it was essentially an exercise in its modification rather than transformation. In pursuing such goals and methods, the clarification of Christian social reform took place in relation to supportive changes in the wider context. The year 1889, like 1848, was a year of marvels, an *annus mirabilis*. The disruptions of the great dock strike apart, it witnessed the publication of two influential 'evolutionary' books. The first, *The Fabian Essays*, reflected the belief 'that Socialism was but the next step in the development of society',[26] a step that would be achieved by gradualist methods. The second, *Lux Mundi*, likewise sought to achieve the same relationship 'to modern intellectual problems' for 'the Catholic faith'.[27] In particular, it tried to relate traditional Christian beliefs to advances in science, philosophy and biblical criticism. For the editor, Charles Gore, it resulted in a liberal Catholicism comparable to the progressive orthodoxy emerging in the United States. It expressed a powerful Christian engagement with the contemporary context. Because it was focused on the incarnation, and was one of the fruits of 'the Holy Party',[28] it is perhaps not surprising that out of this same context there arose in 1889 an organization, the Christian Social Union, to promote the consequences of the incarnation for society, using gradualist methods. Its major characteristics included the following:

1. Based on incarnational theology, the Christian Social Union sought 'to claim for the Christian law the ultimate authority to rule social practice', and 'to study in common how to apply the moral truths and principles of Christianity to the social and economic difficulties of the present time.'[29]
2. Its understanding of socialism as organic humanity and co-operation was essentially a reaction against *laissez-faire* capitalism as individualism and competition.[30] It had little understanding of or sympathy for the rise of economic or political socialism. (See Text 3.) Of course, many regarded such rhetoric as a great weakness: Conrad Noel, later a leader of radical Christian socialism, described how the CSU 'glories in

18

its indefiniteness, and seems to consider it a crime to arrive at any particular economic conclusion . . .'[31] However, many argued for the value of an evolutionary and progressive approach to social change. It certainly related more closely to other trends in the contemporary context, and enabled its members to play an active role in a variety of social reform programmes. These varied from mediating in industrial disputes,[32] promoting white lists (purchasing only from shops and firms that paid reasonable wages), and opposing the sweated trade. The latter led to effective pressure for the Trade Boards Act of 1909.

3. The CSU regarded the Church, like society, as being open to change. Because of its progressive orthodoxy and reformist tactics it was able to attract church leaders into its membership, and in turn to permeate official church bodies. If the Guild of St Matthew was shock troops, the CSU was 'an army of occupation',[33] 'an informal committee of the English Church upon social questions'.[34] As Christian social reformism, it represented a stance that still dominates official church statements on social affairs. Unfortunately, its Anglicanism typified the denominationalism that pervaded English social Christianity until well into the twentieth century. Until then, denominations had their own Christian socialist organizations:[35] 'Their activities, even as socialists, were far from ecumenical in spirit.'[36] This tendency was replicated in the branch of the CSU, founded in the United States in 1891. However, the cumulative effect of all these varied initiatives of social Christianity was that by 1900, 'the Christian socialist critique was lodging itself effectively enough in the mind of the Church'.[37] Compared with 1850, it was a remarkable change, and symbolized the achievement of Maurice's concern to socialize the Church.

The third stage of Christian socialism stretches from the end of the First World War to the end of the Second World War. It was a period dominated by the great economic depression and by international crises marking the rise of fascism and Stalinism. Inextricably related to these changes were dramatic theological developments on the European continent and in the United States. These came to affect, in substantial ways, the content and methodology of English social Christianity, but particularly the tradition of Christian social reform, and

especially through the work of William Temple.[38] Its characteristics included the following:

1. Theologically, it continued to be dominated by Anglicanism
and incarnational theology. However, the influence of the neoorthodoxy of Karl Barth and Emil Brunner, and the theological
realism of Reinhold Niebuhr and John Bennett, gradually
replaced the optimism of early Christian socialism with a more
realistic understanding of power, sin, and the associated importance of justice.

2. Predating these influences, and stimulated by the discussions
at COPEC, Temple began to develop a way of relating Christian
beliefs to complex social issues. It sought to avoid the problems
of earlier social Christianity, with its tendency to assume
biblical principles could be applied directly to social problems.

3. Temple's *Christianity and Social Order* (1942) reflected the
convergence of theological understandings and method in a
series of moral guidelines for the proposed reconstruction of
Britain after the Second World War. (See Text 4.) Along with
his personal programme for political action, they influenced
deeply the emergence of the Welfare State in Britain.

4. As the principal strand in social Christianity, social
reformism was manifested in the development of social service
agencies within the main denominations. It also came to dominate official church statements on social affairs, and to exercise a
formative influence on the early stages of the ecumenical movement, through COPEC (1924) and the Oxford Conference
(1937). Indeed, these two consultations symbolized the changing nature of English social Christianity; the former was the
'climax of a phase of social idealism', the latter 'the initiation of
a new phase of Christian realism'.[39]

Although never as influential as social reformism, radical
Christian socialism did continue to exercise a gadfly effect on
social Christianity, particularly through the work of R. H.
Tawney (see Text 5) and various organizations like the League
of the Kingdom of God (1924), the Christian Sociology summer
schools (1926), and the Christendom Group. Both individuals
and organizations used movements like Guild Socialism and
Social Credit to develop a Christian alternative to capitalism. It
was a methodology that also continued to assume the existence

of Christian insights which could be applied to the social order. Complementing these interpretations was a more sectarian view of the Church, based on a distinctively Christian way of life.

The fourth and final stage needs to be set in the context of the postwar growth of the Welfare State and social market economy, and the cold war between the two competing ideologies of capitalism and communism. After the tragic and untimely death of William Temple in 1944, social Christianity made little progress in England for over two decades. Biblical theology, the reform of canon law, the promotion of local church worship and community, and the increasing moral absorption with international, military and personal issues, diverted attention from matters of political economy. The late 1960s and 1970s, however, witnessed a decisive change of climate as Keynesian economics and the corporate state ran into the major problems of high unemployment and inflation, and public finance.

The arrival of neoconservatism in government in 1979, under the leadership of Margaret Thatcher, challenged this postwar consensus of welfarism and Keynesianism. In addition, Thatcherism provoked the Churches into a sharper defence and elaboration of the social reformist interpretation of modern trends. The virtual absence of any effective indigenous radical Christian socialism has ensured that official church opinion on social affairs in denominational and ecumenical bodies has continued to be dominated by Christian social reformism. The 1980s reports *Faith in the City* (Anglican), *Mission Alongside the Poor* (Methodist), and *Just Sharing* (Church of Scotland) exemplify this consistency and control.

Fortunately, the renewed interest in social Christianity coincided with Ronald Preston's long-awaited major contributions to Christian social thought. Nurtured on a combination of Temple and Tawney, and Reinhold Niebuhr and John Bennett, and well-versed in ecumenical social ethics, he exemplified the maturing of English social Christianity. The quality of his Christian comment on complex economic and social issues, and his refined theological method, lie at the centre of that achievement (see Texts 6 and 7). With regard to his social comment on the contemporary context, this is characterized by discerning balanced judgements advocating a mixed welfare-state economy avoiding the grave deficiencies of *laissez-faire* capitalism and state socialism. Methodologically, he has argued in strong terms against moving directly from the Bible or natural law. Instead he advocates the use of a more indirect way of promoting a reciprocal relationship between Christian insights and empirical trends. His development of middle axioms symbolizes this commitment.

Social Christianity in the United States: the story of the social gospel and beyond

> It is the duty of the minister of the Gospel to preach on every side of political life. I do not say that he *may*; I say that he *must*. That man is not a shepherd of his flock who fails to teach that flock how to apply moral truth to every phase of ordinary practical duty (Henry Ward Beecher).[40]

It was in the generation after F. D. Maurice, and in the decades after the Civil War, that social Christianity began to emerge in the United States. As a result of that war, many Protestants gained the confidence to attack the new problems presented by industrialization. It was Beecher, again, who cried: 'Now that God has smitten slavery unto death, he has opened the way for the redemption and sanctification of our whole social system.'[41]

The challenges of a new economic and social order were immense. Almost overnight 'the industrial revolution converted a peaceful agricultural country ... into an urban nation of bustling factories.'[42] The complementary forces of industrialization and urbanization created a new context differing from its predecessor in qualitative as well as quantitative ways.

Facing such change, the Churches, particularly Protestant ones, slowly began to acknowledge the need to respond to the challenge. Equally, they soon recognized that to do so effectively would involve radical changes in church life and witness.

Social Christianity as the social gospel was the product of these awakenings. Given the universal characteristics of industrial and urban processes, it was not surprising that there were many similarities between the American and English experiences, including in the nature of the Christian responses to modernization processes. The relationship was cemented by American recognition of earlier English achievements. This took the form of using the social theology of F. D. Maurice, Charles Kingsley, Wilfrid Richmond, Sir John Seeley, and B. F. Westcott, and organizations like the Christian Social Union (American branch, 1891). It was a trend confirmed by the close connections with England built up by Washington Gladden, Walter Rauschenbusch, Reinhold Niebuhr and, more recently, J. Philip Wogaman.

Such creative convergences, however, cannot divert attention from the essential character of the social gospel as an 'indigenous, typically American movement'. Along with the theological realism of Niebuhr and Bennett, it provided the United States' unique contribution 'to the great ongoing stream of Christianity'.[43] It is a story that falls easily into four main stages.

Despite foretastes of the social gospel from the 1830s to the 1860s, its substantive origins lay in the 1870s. Only then had the major impact of urbanization begun to transform American society. By 1890, the effects were comprehensive and alarming. In the decade after 1880, the population of Chicago increased by more than 100 per cent, with all the associated problems of poverty, unemployment, bad housing, vice, and political corruption. Yet, for the growing number of Christians sensitive to such change, the heart of 'the violent birth of a new world'[44] lay in the processes of industrialization in general, and industrial conflict in particular. The explosion of wealth creation (national wealth increased from 16 to 78 billion dollars between 1860 and 1890) was accompanied by growing and vast inequalities of income and wealth. For the great majority of workers, real wages were never above the bare subsistence level between 1870 and 1880. When such oppression was accompanied by the institutionalized violence of companies and police, the result was an explosion of great industrial conflict, on the railways in 1877 and 1886, and finally in the steel industry, in 1892–4. It represented a stark challenge to the prevailing belief that all life, including industry, was part of a 'divinely-regulated and unchangeable social order'.[45] It suggested that one of the most influential areas of modern life lay outside Christian law and influence.

Meeting the challenge was the calling of a small pioneering band of Protestant pastors, experiencing at first hand the industrial conflicts in their towns and cities, and in their congregations. The result was the reformulation of Christianity to engage this unchristianized area of life; Shailer Mathews, one of the later leaders of the social gospel, described it as 'the application of the teaching of Jesus and the total message of the Christian salvation to society, the economic life, and social institutions . . . as well as to individuals'.[46] Their work, epitomized by people like Washington Gladden (see Text 8) and Shailer Mathews, was characteristic of so much of the emerging importance of social Christianity. It arose out of a combination of pastoral work, preaching, practical involvement, theology and spirituality.

Reformulating Christianity to engage such a context came to involve a twofold approach. On the one hand, it required the rejection of much that characterized Protestant theology, intimately related as it was to *laissez-faire* capitalism. Conventional orthodoxy was unable to do the task, because it was dominated by an otherworldly pietism, biblical fundamentalism and a profound individualism; its Calvinism centred on a transcendent God and a judicial, mechanistic view of the atonement. For Moody, one of its great exponents, it meant: 'Separate yourself from all your kind, make of the world a solitude, depopulate the globe, and think of yourself as the only living soul upon which the attention of Heaven and Hell is fixed tonight.'[47]

On the other hand, the reformulation of Christianity involved bringing together two major experiences.

First, it meant coming to terms with the liberal theology developed by people like Horace Bushnell. This involved an emphasis on God's immanence, on God at work through the world. For Gladden, the fundamental affirmation was that 'God is in his world';[48] there arose a recognition of the Fatherhood of God, and its consequence for human living as 'the brotherhood of man'; it necessitated a profoundly solidaristic view of the human. It involved, too, the acceptance of Jesus as a person in the light of faith, but also through the use of reason as biblical criticism. The social teachings of Jesus therefore began to occupy a prominent place in social Christianity, along with the view of the atonement as an example of love rather than legal transaction. It was the combination of these understandings of immanence, and christology that generated a remarkable enthusiasm for humanity, and a view of citizenship doing 'as much good as possible to every other member';[49] it led to the belief in an achievable Kingdom. It was all productive of that progressive orthodoxy that has remained a recurring and central feature of American social Christianity.

Secondly, the reformulation involved taking the world seriously as God's arena. This required the major recognition of, and contribution to, the rise of sociology as a major medium for interpreting the contemporary context. Yet despite the intimate relationship between social Christianity and sociology,[50] through people like Richard Ely and Graham Taylor, and through organizations like the American Economic Association (1885), the social gospel was 'a parallel rather than a derivative movement'.[51] The use of secular means for interpreting and responding to the context also included a deep involvement with evolutionary thought-forms, and some reliance upon the early 'socialistic' tools provided by Henry George and his Single Tax movement.

The result of the coalition of theology and social analysis was a variety of responses to industrial change:

1. At the heart of the social gospel lay a deep hostility to *laissez-faire* capitalism, and particularly a rejection of unrestricted competition as 'profoundly untrue'[52] because it so contradicted the Golden Rule of love for human relationships.

2. It encouraged the advocacy of stewardship by employers and employees alike, but also more practically, it resulted in the recognition of labour unions, the support of mediation and arbitration in industrial disputes, and the recommendation of profit-sharing and co-operation in industry.

3. Although initially promoted by a small number of pioneers, by the end of this stage and century social Christianity had begun to make substantial inroads into the Churches. Vigorous church organizations like CAIL (Church Association for the Advancement of the Interests of Labor, 1887), and its educational complement in the American branch of the CSU,[53]

and the recognition of liberal theology and social Christianity by theological seminaries like Andover, Harvard and Chicago, were important ways in which this influence spread through the Churches. By 1894 Congregationalists were commenting on the impact of the social gospel on official church conferences and statements: 'Never perhaps, were the themes of discussion so nearly alike in church assemblies of all denominations as now.'[54]

The second stage ran from the 1890s to the end of the First World War. It witnessed the early maturing of industrial and urban life, with all the ambiguities associated with such a growth. For poverty, unemployment, vice, corruption and conflict were still rife, and the great corporations, accountable to none except their owners, increasingly dominated the context. Yet, at the same time, the growth of reform movements and the pervasive influence of beliefs in evolution and progress, gave American life a strong sense of realizable hope. 'There was a superabundance of zeal, a sufficiency of good causes, unusual moral idealism, excessive confidence in mass movements, and leaders with rare gifts of popular appeal. The people were ready to cry "God wills it" and set out for world peace, prohibition, the Progressive party, the "New Freedom" or "A World for Christ in this Generation".'[55]

It was out of this context and experience that American Protestantism produced one of its greatest leaders, and 'the most brilliant and generally satisfying exponent' of the social gospel.[56] For Rauschenbusch's experience reflected the ambiguities of the age (see Texts 9 and 10). Ministering on the edge of the notorious Hell's Kitchen in New York in the early 1890s, he had soon realized that traditional evangelical orthodoxy could not engage effectively the awful conditions he encountered – the endless procession of men 'out of work, out of clothes, out of shoes, and out of hope'.[57] Yet it was precisely in this context that he rediscovered the Kingdom of God as the means for encompassing all these realities. He began to realize that the Christian task was to Christianize the whole social order.

In 1907 Rauschenbusch's *Christianity and the Social Crisis* was published and was immediately acknowledged as capturing the mood of the Church and nation for religiously based protest and reform. Along with his other books, his contribution represented the great variety of individuals and organizations who typified the maturity of the social gospel. Out of all this effort, four features characterized its contribution to social Christianity:

1. Rauschenbusch exemplified the development of the social gospel into a more radical Christian socialist tradition, even though the gospel continued to be dominated by the social reformist tradition. His rejection of capitalism was therefore much more comprehensive and structural, using class analysis, and a condemnation of industry and the great corporations as 'the last entrenchment of autocracy'.[58] In its place, he promoted a Christianized social order, by extending democracy from family, Church, education and politics into the economic arena. This was to be accompanied by other socialist strategies, including selective public ownership. His *Christianizing the Social Order* (1912) therefore represented 'a frankly socialist critique of capitalism'.[59] Indeed many regarded it as a too secular book because they had failed to come to terms with the theological implications of God being at work in and through the world. For Rauschenbusch, its supposedly temporal arguments were profoundly religious because: 'Its sole concern is for the Kingdom of God and the salvation of men', and 'the Kingdom of God includes the economic life; for it means the progressive transformation of all human affairs by the thought and spirit of Christ'.[60]

Despite Rauschenbusch's dominant position, it should not be assumed that he was alone in his radicalization of the social gospel. Rather, he was representative of a strand in social Christianity that included people like William D. P. Bliss, and George D. Herron. The latter sought to 'reconstruct society' according to Christian ethics, by endorsing 'political socialism for religious reasons'.[61] It also included organizations such as the Christian Socialist Fellowship (1906).

2. Rauschenbusch was convinced that radical social Christianity had to be based on a strong articulation of faith. His *A Theology for the Social Gospel* (1917) sought to provide 'a systematic theology large enough to match the Social Gospel and vital enough to back it'.[62] Only an understanding of the

Kingdom of God could achieve these objectives, elaborated as 'humanity organized according to the will of God . . . [as] a social order that will best guarantee the highest development of personality, in accordance with Christ's revelation of the divine worth of human life'.[63] In this way, the social teachings of Jesus were also affirmed, but more emphasis was placed on the inevitability of progress, since 'Evolution has prepared us for understanding the idea of a Reign of God toward which all creation is moving'.[64] Although this optimism was qualified by a strong sense of social sin, the cumulative effect of all these insights was to produce the belief that it was possible to change man morally and therefore to make a moral society. It was a belief that came to characterize the social gospel, and against which theological realism was to react so strongly.

3. Undergirding all involvements was a powerful spirituality, epitomized by the Brotherhood of the Kingdom. Emerging in the late 1880s out of the friendship of three young Baptist ministers, Schmidt, Williams and Rauschenbusch, it began to meet for a summer retreat in 1893, and continued until 1915. Into its intimacy were brought the world's problems for prayer, discussion and action. Yet an organized spirituality was only the most focused feature of a widespread commitment to prayer, worship, and dedicated living.

4. By the end of this stage, the official Churches had been captured by the social gospel. Most major denominations had social service agencies or commissions (Episcopalians and Congregationalists in 1901, the Presbyterians in 1903, and Methodists in 1907). Just as important, the arrival of the ecumenical movement in 1908, when thirty denominations formed the Federal Council of Churches, owed much to the social gospel and in turn greatly influenced and propagated its views. Indeed, the same leaders of the social gospel in the denominations also occupied leadership positions in the ecumenical movement (for example, the Congregationalists Gladden, Strong, and Taylor, the Northern Baptists Rauschenbusch and Mathews, the Methodist Henry Ward, and the Presbyterian Charles Stelzle). Similar connections were to reappear in the later history of social Christianity in the United States, through the work of Bennett and Niebuhr. The Federal Council of Churches, through its Social Creed, simply represented these developments and the

message of the social gospel in an unusually clear and influential way.[65] As one commentator has observed, the social gospel was 'no longer a prophetic and occasional note. . . . The social gospel has become orthodox.'[66]

The third stage of the story runs from the 1920s to the early 1940s. It represents the important progression of social Christianity through the radical challenge of theological realism to the social gospel. Again, it was a development related intimately to a dramatically changing social context focused around the economy and international politics. The former took the form of the great depression and the near-collapse of free-market economies and economics. The latter moved from the devastations of the First World War to the rise of fascism and Stalinism, and the eventual outbreak of the Second World War. Economic and political events combined to undermine the optimism and progressivism of the social gospel. The emergence of theological realism was a response to both context and deficiencies in liberal social Christianity. It produced a decisive change in the message and method of social Christianity which has affected irretrievably American and English social Christianity up to the present day:

1. Theological realism emerged as a devastating criticism of the ethos and theology of the social gospel inherited from the first decades of this century. No longer able to tolerate the growing mismatch between the ideals and aspirations of the social gospel, and the actual context, John Bennett answered his question 'Whither liberalism?' by declaring that 'The most important fact about American theology is the disintegration of liberalism.'[67] Complemented by Niebuhr's more seminal criticism, the two elaborated the decisive rejection of the social gospel's central belief in the possibility of changing people in order to change society to the Kingdom on earth. Instead, they recognized that finitude and sin so affected classes, races and nations that Christian love was not attainable in the social arena. The self-interest of groups was a matter of power, and so the appropriate moral response needed to be based on justice not love. By 1940, realism over group behaviour was extended to realism about the nature and destiny of man (see Text 11). Theological realism had arrived. The Jesus ethic, so powerful in

29

the social gospel, had now become an impossible possibility. The theological revolution was completed.

2. Theological realism, like the social gospel before it, moved through criticism to the reconstruction of theology. The name itself was suggested by Walter Horton[68] in response to Bennett's article 'After Liberalism – What?' He concentrated on the need for a tough-minded realism over society, politics, history and man. Not long before, a Theological Discussion Group (including Richard and Reinhold Niebuhr, Paul Tillich and John Bennett) had begun to provide a regular forum for the development of such a theology. The processes of war, ideology, class egoism and depression, not the social gospel faith in man, provided the context. It was these realities that were then read in the light of the great Christian symbols. They were seen to illuminate the dramas of the context as the creative tension between love and justice, the sinful and creative inclinations of man, and the personal and the social. In turn, this stimulated a revision of the symbols. Theological realism was to be a dialectical relationship between realities and faith which challenged all theological and political idealism, and all unrealistic idealists and cynical realists. It allowed a theological interpretation of events which spoke increasingly to people bound up in them, and provided a common basis for action to an audience wider than the Church.

3. The development of Christian interpretations of the environment of the 1930s was not about the changing content of Christian comment alone. Its realism had to discover more accurate ways of relating realities to an understanding of Christian faith and symbols. Moving directly from the social principles of Jesus' teaching to the detailed reorganization of economics or politics was no longer feasible. The impossibility of imposing ideals on intractable politics and economics ruled that out. In addition, biblical scholarship and technical autonomies also suggested the need to find ways of morally mediating between the two arenas. The development of middle axioms by John Bennett provided such a tool for Christian social ethics (see Text 13).

4. The construction of the New Deal in the 1930s eventually provided a political and economic framework more in tune with the insights of theological realism. As a response to the eco-

nomic crisis it resulted in 'a dramatically reformed capitalism'.[69] By rejecting the extremes of *laissez-faire* capitalism and state socialism, it prefigured the emergence of mixed economies in the West. Many saw it as the culmination of the Federal Council of Churches' Social Creed. Indeed, in a speech in 1932, the author of the New Deal, Franklin Roosevelt, did announce that he was 'as radical as the Federal Council'.[70] Yet in other ways, it was more in tune with the emerging mood of theological realism. Its pragmatism meant that it was not a social gospel fusion of the Word and politics (see Text 12). Yet its realism was not a justification for reactionary conservatism. The leaders of theological realism did not support that interpretation, despite recent neoconservative claims to the contrary. Bennett and Niebuhr were members of the Fellowship of Socialist Christians in the 1930s, and Niebuhr was to affirm at the end of his life that 'a realistic conception of human nature should be made the servant of an ethic of progressive justice and should not be made into a bastion of conservatism, particularly a conservatism which defends unjust privileges'.[71]

5. For theological realism, the Churches were not, as with the social gospel, places where people developed the highest ideals. Rather, they were places where the transcendent God was encountered, for 'Every society lives under, not toward, the Kingdom of God.'[72] It was the combination of realism and justice, served by a Church itself under judgement but clear about its function in society, that ensured that Niebuhr and Bennett began to exert a major influence over the international ecumenical movement. Their promotion of middle axioms, and of moral judgements that held opposing tendencies in a creative tension, was well-suited to the kind of denominational statements on social affairs beginning to emerge in the postwar period. Both national and international church comment increasingly acknowledged the wisdom of Niebuhr's dialectical skills and their implications for religion and politics: 'In my opinion adequate spiritual guidance can come only through a more radical political orientation and more conservative religious convictions than are comprehended in the culture of our era.'[73]

The fourth stage runs from the 1960s to the 1980s. It

represents, essentially, a consolidation of the earlier achievements of the social gospel and theological realism as neoliberalism. Since it is still evolving, its 'unfinished' character means that it lacks the distinctive thrusts associated with the earlier stages. It poses, more sharply than in England, the challenges facing social Christianity. The changing context corroborates the ambivalent character of a bridge period. For example, the prolongation of the cold war between communism and capitalism confirmed social Christianity's option for a mixed economy model of the social market and political democracy. The major study conducted by the Federal Council of Churches in 1949, and its report *Christian Values and Economic Life* (1954), illustrate this commitment. Yet it was always an over-qualified support, influenced by the early history of social Christianity and its rejection of undue competition, profit and self-interest. That ambivalence was exacerbated by the debates over racism, feminism, Vietnam and poverty in the 1960s and 1970s. Although related to political economy matters, these issues diverted attention from the need to develop a public theology able to take a democratic market economy seriously, even though with discernment. The collapse of the command economy alternative to the market economy has therefore tended to strand the official Churches in the no-man's-land of a liberal protest too distanced from the processes of advanced economies. Despite its achievements, the inheritance of social Christianity has not left the Churches sufficiently equipped to engage this emerging context, for the following reasons:

1. Moral judgements on political economy matters may now be insufficiently served by the tradition of balancing the social gospel (as Christianizing the social order) and theological realism (as rejecting such a possibility). It can still provide an invaluable theological comment on more subordinate socioeconomic issues. Yet its work on the broader political framework must be more in question, because it is too associated with establishing a balanced position between *laissez-faire* capitalism and command economies. The context now is essentially one in which one end of the traditional spectrum, the command economy, has disappeared in modern societies. This may call in question the content of many of its other judgements.

2. The tradition of making discerning moral judgements in what Wogaman describes as the dominant mainstream liberal tradition[74] sits increasingly uneasily within its problematic understanding of the wider framework described above (see Text 14). The method in Christian social ethics of mediating between general principles and particular policies is still invaluable for dealing with second-order questions. Yet it may well be increasingly ill-suited to deal with the first-order issues of the end of economic socialism and the triumph of the market economy.

3. The problems relating to the content and method of the comment by social Christianity on the contemporary context have major implications for the Churches. For over eighty years, the Churches have been dominated by this tradition. To raise serious questions about its appropriateness for engaging our context obviously increases the problems of the Churches in developing an adequate public theology. These are exacerbated by the international ecumenical movement, which is now dominated by liberationist theologies, and by the major denominational bodies within the United States being challenged by the liberationist perspectives of black and feminist theology, with their positive involvement in the debate over democratic socialism.[75] Of course it can be argued that all these tendencies continue the reformist and radical traditions of social Christianity. Yet their cumulative effect may well have increased the inability of the Churches to develop a public theology able to come to terms with the democratic social market economy as the least harmful way known to us of operating advanced economies. The great tradition of criticizing capitalism, particularly in relation to a socialist alternative, has been marginalized by developments in our context in the last three or four years. The Churches' historic choice of social Christianity may now have to be made even more clearly between the social reform of the existing dominant system and the pursuit of new radical alternatives to it. Whether the Churches can make such a choice successfully will depend on the ability of social Christianity to read our context *at least* as successfully as its earlier exponents. It may well depend on developing a way of recognizing the primacy of the market economy without losing touch with the challenges to it. The

following accounts of other Christian perspectives on our context may well assist in this task.

Locating social Christianity in context is significantly about the story of a Christian tradition addressing greatly changing social contexts. In the course of that encounter, social Christianity was influenced by that changing context and, in turn, contributed to it. Yet there are other complementary relationships within this story that can be clarified if set in a context of wider Christian responses to the social context.

These additional complementary relationships, or indeed tensions, within social Christianity include the relationship between social Christianity as social reform and as radical Christian socialism. On the one hand, it has been a tension relating to the *content* of Christian responses to the market economy, as serious amendment or virtual rejection. On the other hand, it has related to the theological *method* for developing such responses, as moving directly from biblical understandings to policy proposals, or as mediating between them.

Locating these tensions in social Christianity within the wider context of Christian responses to modern contexts means coming to terms with liberation theology and Christian conservatism. The former reflects the rejection of the market economy for a Christian socialist alternative. Yet it does so in a radically new way through the praxis of standing with, and viewing life or theology from, the underside of history. Its power in the Third World, and connections with black and feminist movements in the First World, mean that it could offer a decisive way forward to a social Christianity in the West confused by increasing ambiguities.

The latter, Christian conservatism, reflects an essentially positive theological argument with the market economy. It includes a methodology that provides a discerning but ideological support for the free market but also a recognition of the relative autonomy of modern economics. It therefore provides social Christianity with ways of taking seriously the democratic market economy. How to relate these two traditions may well become the next stage of social Christianity in the West. My *Christianity and the Market: Christian Social Thought for our Times* tries to explore this possibility.[76]

34

Liberation theology: the radical challenge to social Christianity

> When I discovered that poverty was something to be fought
> against, that poverty was structural, that poor people were a
> class and could organize, it became crystal clear that in order
> to save the poor, one had to move into political action
> (Gustavo Gutiérrez).[77]

Taking the contemporary context seriously has been a formative
feature of social Christianity throughout its history. It should
not disturb its current exponents that to do so in Latin America
has generated a very different response from the Western
tradition of social Christianity. For Latin America endures
massive intractable poverty, with two-thirds of the people
hungry, most land and business in the hands of small wealthy
elites, and governments ruling through the use of institutionalized violence, often of a most ferocious kind. Unlike the West,
too, it is a continent that has not yet grown out of a history of
conquest, colonialism and neocolonialism. Indeed, it is one of
liberation theology's most powerful claims that the West is
bound inextricably in the destructive persistence of Latin
American dependency on external finance and military power.
The sad failure of the development programmes of the 1950s is
attributed to this alliance of multinational corporations, international finance, and national security states underpinned by
American military might.

Given the experience of social Christianity, to take such a
context seriously requires the development of a theology appropriate to its principal characteristics. It could suggest a theology
that stands against such universal endemic poverty and oppression, therefore arguing for revolution not reform, for socialism
not liberalization. It would then suggest a theology in deep
conflict not simply with free market capitalism and its alliance
with conservative theological orthodoxies. It would also stand
in sharp opposition to Western progressive theology and its
relationship to the Western project of democracy and the
market economy. For both are seen as integral to the oppression
that subjects Latin America to such degradation. It would
therefore suggest a theology free from such involvements, a

'decolonialized theological project' to reflect the 'realities of indigenous Latin American experience.'[78] And that is precisely what has emerged as a 'powerful new development in twentieth century Christianity'.[79] Indeed, its impact has been even more remarkable, because in twenty years it has come to dominate the World Council of Churches, in alliance with equivalent movements in Asia and Africa, and women and black people in the developed world.

The origins of liberation theology can be traced back to the 1960s, to the initiatives of individuals and Churches. Both represented an 'ethical indignation at the poverty and marginalization of the great masses of our continent'.[80] If Maurice was the founder of Christian socialism in London in 1848, then it can be claimed with equal justification that Gustavo Gutiérrez was the founder of liberation theology, developing the concept at the Chimbote Conference in Peru in 1968 (see Text 16). The thesis was subsequently elaborated into the founding book of liberation theology, *A Theology of Liberation*, in 1971. Complementing such individual effort was the formative influence of the Roman Catholic Church, the dominant ecclesiastical body in Latin America. For it was the second conference of the Latin American episcopate at Medellín, in 1968, which produced the other founding documents of liberation theology. It is important to note that Gutiérrez was a consultant at Medellín.

From such beginnings, liberation theology quickly spread to other denominations, church conferences, and individuals. Naming but a few of the latter is a roll call of some of the most innovative and courageous modern theologians of our times – Hugo Assmann, Clodovis and Leonardo Boff, Enrique Dussel, José Miranda, Juan Luis Segundo, Jon Sobrino, and José Miguez Bonino. Yet the distinctive response to the context of oppression has led also to the development of equivalent responses in, and to, other oppressed situations in Asia and Africa, and as black and feminist theologies. It has had only a limited response in the West (see Text 15). In the mid-1970s organizations were created to link them together (the Theology in the Americas conference at Detroit in 1975, and the Ecumenical Association of Third World Theologians – EATWOT – in 1976).

The main characteristics of Latin American liberation theology reflect this paradigmatic shift in theology, and yet also resonate with much in social Christianity:

1. The most distinctive feature of liberation theology relates to its theological method; it clarifies its similarities to, and differences from, social Christianity. Essentially, liberation theology is 'a practical, theological discourse on the faith of the poor'.[81] Because it seeks primarily to address the dominant features of the Latin American context, it inevitably involves taking the poor seriously as 'the reality of human existence in Latin America'.[82] It determines the *place* where theology must be done. It is therefore not primarily academic discourse, and will not 'sound nice, and it will not smell good'.[83] It is essentially a collaborative effort with the poor, and not the entrepreneurial work of individualist theologians.

To so begin with the poor is required by the demands of the situation and the gospel. It is about entering into their struggles both against the forces that oppress them, and for a more fulfilled human existence. It is about using socio-analytical methods, including Marxism and dependency theory, to explain the nature and causes of their predicament. It is about theology starting from 'the praxis of liberation'.[84]

Only after fully entering into such solidarity does the task become a reflection on that praxis, through the Bible and its Christian symbols. There, the central theme of liberation becomes dominant, reflecting three levels of understanding: as the socio-political liberation of the oppressed, as anthropology through a qualitatively different society, and as theology through liberation from sin as the root of oppression and the obstacle to human community.

After the illumination of praxis through Christian symbols (including the illumination of those symbols through praxis), the results of that process then influence the praxis of the Church, as practical and pastoral initiatives. This, in turn, affects the context. And so the circle begins once again, from the basis of Christian involvement in the praxis of the struggles of the poor.

In other words, for liberation theology, the *first act* is praxis (presupposing faith); the reflection on praxis as interpreting the Bible through the eyes of the oppressed is essentially the *second act*. Both are concerned with discerning God's activity among the poor, and therefore working for radical structural change.

2. To reduce liberation theology to the innovatory importance of its methodology as reflection on praxis, is to do a grave disservice to the breadth and variety of its creativity. For example, as a result of its orthopraxis, it also seeks to rework in radical ways the great Christian symbols through the eyes of the poor. It has focused particularly on christology and ecclesiology. So Leonardo Boff's pathfinding *Jesus Christ Liberator* (1972) presented the first christological synthesis of the new liberationist perspective. In doing so, he emphasized anthropology over ecclesiology (focusing on human beings not the Church), utopia over the factual (the Kingdom of God being anticipated in history), the critical over the dogmatic, the social over the personal, and orthopraxis over orthodoxy.[85]

3. Both theology as reflection on praxis, and the complementary reinterpretation of Christian symbols, represent a decisive rejection of modernity including traditional Western theology. For the progressive theology of the West, including political theology and social Christianity, is seen as reflecting a Western context. In the post-enlightenment age, its subject is 'Can modern man believe?' In the Latin American context the subject is quite different because it has to be the oppressed poor. Therefore, on further examination it quickly becomes apparent that the difference between the two theologies relates to much more than a difference of contexts. For liberation theology is also challenging the Christian legitimacy of the West's engagement with its context. It does so by uncovering the power and injustice of Western theology, with its focus on the bourgeois non-believer when over two-thirds of the world live in dire poverty and political oppression. The claim of liberation theology to a universal authority but complements its argument for a world revolution against the West and the market economy.

4. Given the commitment to the poor in Latin America, and their relationship with the Roman Catholic Church, it is not surprising that liberation theology is associated with a new awareness of the Church. For the leading exponent of liberation theology, 'The ecclesial objective of liberationism is no longer to be the church of the poor, but to become the poor church.' It becomes a matter not whether the Church will take sides in the

class struggle, but whether it will change sides.[86] In important ways, that is precisely what has been happening in the official church, and in the growth of base communities. For the Medellín and Puebla conferences established a 'preferential option for the poor' as official church teaching. And the rapid growth of base communities reflected the growing need for a grassroots Church in and of the poor; it suggested the need for new ways of being the Church, as a community of brotherhood faith and life, standing against oppression and for new life. Not surprisingly, these developments have led to growing tension between the official Church and the Church as base communities. This is evidenced most profoundly in Leonardo Boff's *Church: Charism and Power* (1981) and *Ecclesiogenesis: The Base Communities Reinvent the Church* (1986), where he argues against the hierarchical Church and for the pneumatological Church.

5. For exponents of liberation theology like Gutiérrez, 'theology is of necessity, both spirituality and rational knowledge'.[87] There can be no dualism of mysticism and commitment. Rather, the Christian life is a spirituality of change, intensely corporate, reflecting the collective endeavour of liberation theology. For spirituality is both an essential part of praxis, theological reflection, and pastoral practice. It is contemplation in and through action. To Gutiérrez 'our method is our spirituality'.[88]

Christian conservatism: the challenge of market economics to social Christianity

> Wherever markets are allowed to work, the result is an increase in prosperity and jobs. The remarkable contrast in economic performance between Asia-on-the-Pacific and Latin America over recent decades can be traced to the superior wisdom of faith in the market over faith in the state (Brian Griffiths).[89]

Christian conservatism is as notable as social Christianity for its continuing influence on faith and society. Although both are connected to the appearance of industrialization, Christian conservatism predates social Christianity by fifty years exactly,

Introduction

and represents an essentially positive response to modern market economics. In 1798 Parson Malthus, as Marx rudely called him,[90] published his seminal *An Essay on the Principle of Population as it Affects the Future Improvement of Society.* So began a creative link between Christianity and the emergence of modern economics and the market system. A decade before Christian socialism began, this tradition of Christian political economy no longer flourished. Yet the recent resurgence of neoconservatism in the West, and its intimate relationship with Christianity, illustrate the persistence and power of an important strand in Christian social thought and practice.

In its origins and most recent stage, Christian conservatism has continued to recognize the connection between faith and modern economics and the market economy, in a fundamentally positive yet never indiscriminate way. Acknowledging the disruptive effects of economic change, it has always paid serious attention to the 'condition of society' question in general, and its particular effects on the vulnerable.

Since the story of Christian conservatism is a response to modern contexts, it can best be told by beginning with recent events. For a generation after the Second World War, Western governments, using Keynesian economic policies, played a central role in generating a period of staggering economic growth. However, the West then entered a period of major economic turbulence, typified by both high unemployment and inflation, and by the pressure of public finance in the development of welfare state–new deal societies. In most Western nations, the response was the growth or reappearance of neoconservative thought and practice. Although the governments of Thatcher and Reagan personified these developments, their influence was much wider, affecting Western Europe, Canada, Australasia and south-east Asia. The amazing collapse of command economies in 1989–90 especially highlighted the resurgence of the free market. It was typified, in the West, by a recommitment to private ownership, a reduced role for the state, competition and innovation in a free market, political democracy and the contribution of voluntary bodies or intermediate associations, personal responsibility, and an unequivocal opposition to socialism.

What was more remarkable, given the dominating influence of social Christianity on the Churches, was the powerful relationship between the resurgence of neoconservatism and Christianity, particularly in the United States and Britain. In the former, Christian conservatism has occupied the highest political positions for over a decade, through the presidencies of Reagan and Bush, along with many of their leading advisers. It was strongly undergirded by the work of theologians like Richard Neuhaus (see Text 18), Ernest Lefever, Robert Benne, Peter Berger, and Michael Novak (see Text 19). Their contribution benefited greatly from such think-tanks as the Institute for Religion and Democracy (itself partly funded by the American Enterprise Institute), and the Religion and Public Life Institute.

In Britain, the relationship between neoconservatism and Christianity followed a similar pattern. Led by prime minister Thatcher and some of her senior ministers, there was also a particularly strong influence exercised by think-tanks such as the Institute of Economic Affairs and the Social Affairs Unit. Both were led by committed Christians (Lord Ralph Harris and the Reverend Dr Digby Anderson). Theologians like E. R. Norman were also influential, but the central role was played by Brian Griffiths as a lay theologian and head of Margaret Thatcher's Policy Unit (see Text 18).

In the United States and Britain, Christian conservatism was represented by Christians from all the great denominations, but never by the official Churches. The influence of the moral majority in the United States was unique to that country, illustrating the nebulous yet substantial connection between conservative evangelicalism and Christian conservatism.

What characterizes Christian conservatism most is its reasoned commitment to the free market, democracy, a reduced state, moral values, the rejection of socialism, and a restricted understanding of the market's limitations:

1. Christian conservatism has a fundamental faith in the free market economy based on two theological convictions. On the one hand, it points to the biblical insights into the stewardship of scarce resources, and the resulting emphasis on wealth

creation and work. On the other hand, powerfully aware of the role of original sin in the world, it accepts the need for checks and balances, the separation of politics and economics, and the rejection of utopias. The two convictions combine to produce a positive theological support for the free market as the least harmful way of operating modern societies.

2. It has an equal commitment to political democracy, for very similar theological reasons. The beliefs in human dignity and sin ensure that democracy sustains the possibility of humane government in a necessarily unsatisfying world. It is in this sense that Michael Novak makes use of theological realism but on behalf of Christian conservatism rather than social Christianity.[91] Just as important is the powerful identification with those voluntary bodies or intermediate associations that stand in between the state and the individual. Underwriting such organizations, certainly for Novak, is the principle of subsidiarity.[92]

3. It is committed to curtailing the power of the state and politics in modern society. Since 1945 the enormous growth of the modern state in social market economies is regarded as 'detrimental to liberty and the efficient functioning of the market'.[93] Yet Christian conservatism, unlike early *laissez-faire* capitalism, does not advocate a minimalist state, but rather one involved in the promotion of justice, and the defence of the vulnerable (including through a minimum income).

4. It places a very high estimate on religious values in resourcing democracy and the market. Consequently it rejects the Enlightenment's exclusion of religion from the public arena, and is concerned deeply over the erosion of 'accumulated moral capital'.[94] The reform of capitalism is therefore linked with spiritual renewal. In Novak's case, this extends to values wider than Christian ones.

5. Its strong support for the free market is associated with an equally decisive rejection of socialism and communism. Both are regarded as forms of idolatry, and 'incompatible with a Christian understanding of humanity and historical destiny'.[95] Christian conservatism is deeply disturbed over the official Churches' refusal to continue to underwrite the West as the standard-bearer of democracy and the market. As Neuhaus comments, 'much of the leadership of mainline Protestantism

cannot contribute to the moral legitimation and definition of the American experiment because, when all is said and done, it no longer believes in that experiment'.[96] These remarks apply equally to the Roman Catholic Church, and to the British situation.

6. It has some understanding of the free market's limitations, but only within an overall framework of acceptance. For example, with regard to Third World poverty, while recognizing it as a dominant international problem, it refuses to attribute the principal causes of this disaster to the market economy. Instead it regards Third World economies, their governments' policies, and cultural context, as the major cause of poverty.

Christian conservatism gains a new importance for Christian social thought in a world facing the collapse of command economies and the increasing domination of market economies. By taking seriously the market as modern economics and economic system, and particularly for theological reasons, it stands as a correction to the selective assertions of social Christianity and liberation theology. Understanding the nature of this correction is not simply a matter of contemporary enquiry. It is also the business of historical interpretation.

The early history of Christian conservatism, as with social Christianity, begins in England in the late eighteenth century, although it reached the United States within a generation. So in the latter, by 1825, the Reverend John McVickar was asserting that 'science and religion eventually teach the same lesson, is a necessary consequence of the unity of truth, but it is seldom that this union is so satisfactorily displayed as in the researches of Political Economy'.[97] It was that relationship between economics and religion that Christian political economy (as the tradition became known in England) was to explore so creatively. It arose as a clear response, therefore, to the growth of urban-industrial society and the intimate linkage with the discovery of modern economics, beginning with the seminal work of Adam Smith's *Wealth of Nations* in 1776. Accompanying these innovations was growing social distress. It was the skill of the Christian political economists to explore the links between these two realities of the new economics and the dichotomy between wealth and poverty. Beginning with

Malthus, in 1798, and his recognition of scarcity as the basic economic problem, later exponents like John Bird Sumner 'compared the poverty of many in more prosperous societies with the poverty of the majority in others'[98] and observed that the former operated on free-market principles (see Text 17). Despite the problems of such societies, he sought to demonstrate that 'political economy also reveals that the genuine evil associated with the inevitable outcome is remediable'.[99] Copleston, and then Whateley, also saw the significance of economics for Christianity, because they acknowledged its increasingly central role in modern life, and the need 'to clarify the relationship between economics and Christianity'.[100] Whateley did the latter by understanding the difference between economics as the study of means, and the study of ends informed by moral and theological principles.

It is these early 'discoveries' that need to be introduced into the interpretation of Christian conservatism. They form an important contribution to Christian social thought in its engagement with the modern market economy. They can be summarized as the significance of economics, the autonomy of the secular, and values.

With regard to economics, the early Christian economists helped to develop the understanding of scarcity as the fundamental economic problem, and a central ongoing principle of social science. Linked to the Christian symbols of finitude and sin, it was to result in the definition of modern economics as 'the study of rational choice in the face of scarcity'.[101]

Closely connected to this basic insight was the recognition of the relative autonomy of economic and political thought in the formation of Christian social comment. 'By distinguishing between religious and scientific knowledge, and the positive and normative strands in economics, it enables Christian social thought to develop an appropriate contribution to economic policy.'[102] It acts as a constant warning against Christian tendencies to impose ideals, however deeply held, on economic realities.

Finally, the Christian political economists, through the powerful evangelical movement of the early nineteenth century, contributed to those values or 'habits of the heart'[103] that were so important for the effective functioning of the market. So often,

44

Introduction

moral exhortation could and did underpin extreme *laissez-faire* beliefs. Yet such grave aberrations should not be confused with the more significant promotion of public probity, frugality, professionalism, creativity, personal responsibility, and personal rectitude. These are the stuff of any adequate modern society. It was such virtues that ranked high, and still do, in the tradition of Christian conservatism.

Notes

1. F. Engels, *The Condition of the Working Class in England* (Panther Books 1969 edition, Introduction by E. Hobsbawm), p. 75.
2. ibid., p. 75.
3. ibid., pp. 81–5.
4. R. H. Tawney, Foreword to M. Weber, *The Protestant Ethic and the Spirit of Capitalism* (George Allen & Unwin 1970 edition), p. 4.
5. E. R. Norman, *The Victorian Christian Socialists* (Cambridge University Press 1987), p. 19.
6. R. H. Tawney, *The Radical Tradition* (Penguin Books 1966 edition), p. 82.
7. For these developments, see J. Atherton, *Christianity and the Market: Christian Social Thought for our Times* (SPCK 1992), pp. 30–3.
8. For detailed treatments of these histories consult the Bibliography.
9. F. D. Maurice, quoted in M. B. Reckitt, *Maurice to Temple: A Century of the Social Movement in the Church of England* (Faber 1947), p. 20.
10. The full text of the placard can be found in S. Evans, *The Social Hope of the Christian Church* (Hodder & Stoughton 1965), pp. 152–3.
11. F. Maurice, *The Life of Frederick Denison Maurice*, (Macmillan 1883), vol.2, pp. 34–5.
12. ibid., (second edition 1884), vol.1, p. 155.
13. F. D. Maurice, Prospectus for the first issue of *Politics for the People* (London: J. W. Parker 1848), p. 1, quoted in T. Christensen, *Origin and History of Christian Socialism, 1848–54* (Universitetforlaget Aarhus 1962), pp. 74–5.
14. F. D. Maurice, 'A Clergyman's Answer', *Tracts on Christian Socialism*, no.8, p. 17, quoted in Christensen, p. 203.
15. Christensen, p. 147.
16. Maurice, *The Life of Frederick Denison Maurice*, vol.2, p. 32.
17. F. G. Bettany, *Stewart Headlam: A Biography* (John Murray 1926), p. 20.
18. Christensen, p. 91.
19. P. d'A. Jones, *The Christian Socialist Revival 1877–1914: Religion,*

45

Introduction

Class and Social Conscience in Late-Victorian England (Princeton University Press 1968), p. 26.

20. Reckitt, Chapter 5.
21. Adderley on Headlam, in Reckitt, p. 135.
22. Norman, p. 115.
23. D. O. Wagner, *The Church of England and Social Reform Since 1854* (Columbia University Press 1930), p. 193.
24. The choice of Marxist thought is but the contemporary manifestation of a recurring problem – affecting Guild Socialism in the early twentieth century, and Major Douglas's Social Credit schemes in the interwar years.
25. d'A. Jones, p. 164.
26. E. Pease, *The History of the Fabian Society* (London 1913), quoted in N. and J. Mackenzie, *The First Fabians* (Weidenfeld & Nicolson 1977), p. 111.
27. d'A. Jones, p. 171.
28. The subtitle of *Lux Mundi* was 'A series of studies on the Religion of the Incarnation'. The Holy Party began to meet in 1875, and included Illingworth, Scott Holland, and Gore. It continued to have a summer working retreat until 1915.
29. d'A. Jones, p. 177.
30. See B. F. Westcott, first President of the CSU, and his paper to the Church Congress, Hull, 1890 (The Guild of St Matthew 1890), p. 4 (Text 3).
31. C. Noel, *Socialism in Church History*, p. 257, quoted in d'A. Jones, p. 166.
32. Bishop Westcott's mediation in the miners' strike of 1892 is perhaps the best example.
33. d'A. Jones, p. 164.
34. d'A. Jones, p. 185, quoting P. Dearmer, *Beginnings of the CSU* (Commonwealth Press 1912).
35. For example, the great Baptist leader, John Clifford, and the Christian Socialist League (1894–8). Other denominations paralleled the Anglican CSU – the Friends Social Union of 1904 illustrates this tendency.
36. d'A. Jones, p. 5.
37. Norman, p. 185.
38. He was successively Bishop of Manchester, Archbishop of York, and then Archbishop of Canterbury in this period.
39. Reckitt, p. 172.
40. Henry Ward Beecher, 1852, quoted in H. F. May, *Protestant Churches and Industrial America* (New York: Harper and Bros. 1949), p. 40.
41. C. H. Hopkins, *The Rise of the Social Gospel in American Protestantism, 1865–1915* (New Haven: Yale University Press 1940, 1967 edition), p. 9.
42. ibid., p. 79.
43. ibid., p. 3.

Introduction

44. ibid., p. 11.
45. May, p. 264.
46. Hopkins, p. 3.
47. May, p. 83.
48. Hopkins, p. 123.
49. ibid., p. 23.
50. By 1900, the US Library of Congress used 'Christian Sociology' as a cataloguing category because of the wealth of material.
51. May, p. 147.
52. Washington Gladden, in Hopkins, p. 26.
53. May, p. 185; d'A. Jones, p. 190–3.
54. R. T. Handy, ed., *The Social Gospel in America, 1870–1920: Gladden, Ely, Rauschenbusch* (New York: Oxford University Press 1966), p. 11.
55. Gaius Glenn Atkins, 1932, in Handy, p. 3.
56. Reinhold Niebuhr, in Handy, p. 253.
57. Hopkins, p. 216.
58. ibid., p. 222.
59. ibid., p. 219.
60. Handy, p. 338.
61. Hopkins, p. 233.
62. ibid., p. 220.
63. ibid., p. 230.
64. ibid., p. 127.
65. The Social Creed begins: 'The problems of modern industry can be interpreted and solved only by the teachings of the New Testament and Jesus Christ is the final authority in the social as well as in the individual life.' See A. D. Ward, *The Social Creed of the Methodist Church: A Living Document* (Nashville: Abingdon Press 1961), p. 317.
66. Hopkins, p. 201.
67. Handy, p. 15.
68. D. B. Meyer, *The Protestant Search for Political Realism 1919–1941* (University of California Press 1960), pp. 240–1.
69. ibid., p. 322.
70. ibid., p. 314.
71. R. Niebuhr, *Man's Nature and His Communities* (Bles 1966), p. 16.
72. Meyer, p. 413.
73. ibid., p. 262.
74. For the mainstream liberal tradition, see Atherton, Chapter 6. The concept is developed in J. P. Wogaman, *Christian Perspectives on Politics* (SCM Press 1988), Chapter 6.
75. G. J. Dorrien, *Reconstructing the Common Good: Theology and the Social Order* (New York: Orbis Books 1990), Chapter 7. See J. H. Cone, *The Black Church and Marxism: What do they have to say to each other?* (New York: Institute for Democratic Socialism 1980); R. Radford Ruether, *Sexism and God-Talk: Toward a Feminist Theology* (Boston: Beacon Press 1983).

47

Introduction

76. See note 7 above.
77. Quoted in 'Statement by José Miguez Bonino', in S. Torres and J. Eagleson, eds, *Theology in the Americas* (New York: Orbis Books 1976), p. 278.
78. Dorrien, p. 103.
79. D. Ford, ed., *The Modern Theologians: An Introduction to Christian Theology in the Twentieth Century Volume II* (Basil Blackwell 1989), p. 171.
80. Leonardo Boff in R. Gibellini, *The Liberation Theology Debate* (SCM Press 1987), p. 4.
81. R. S. Chopp, 'Latin American Liberation Theology', in Ford, p. 176.
82. ibid., p. 177.
83. G. Gutiérrez, *The Power of the Poor in History* (New York: Orbis Books 1983), pp. 22,91.
84. Hugo Assmann in Gibellini, p. 4.
85. L. Boff, *Jesus Christ Liberator* (New York: Orbis Books and SPCK 1978), pp. 43–6.
86. Dorrien, pp. 124–5.
87. G. Gutiérrez, *A Theology of Liberation* (SCM Press 1988 edition), p. 5.
88. Gustavo Gutiérrez, in V. Fabella and S. Torres, eds, *Irruption of the Third World: Challenge to Theology* (New York: Orbis Books 1983), p. 225.
89. B. Griffiths, 'The Conservative Quadrilateral', in M. Alison and D. L. Edwards, eds, *Christianity and Conservatism: Are Christianity and Conservatism Compatible?* (Hodder & Stoughton 1990), p. 232.
90. A.M.C. Waterman, *Revolution, Economics and Religion: Christian Political Economy 1798–1833* (Cambridge University Press 1991), p. 223.
91. Wogaman, p. 5, quoting *Christianity and Democracy* (Washington DC: Institute on Religion and Democracy 1981). Novak confirms Niebuhr's support for democracy in M. Novak, *The Spirit of Democratic Capitalism* (New York: American Enterprise Institute/ Simon & Schuster 1982), Chapter 19.
92. 'It is a fundamental principle of social philosophy ... that one should not withdraw from individuals and commit to the community what they can accomplish by their own enterprise and industry.' (Pius XI, *Quadragesimo Anno* 1931.)
93. Atherton, p. 88.
94. R. Mouw, 'The Evangelical Protestant Perspectives on American Economic Life', quoting I. Kristol, *Three Cheers for Capitalism* (New York: Basic Books 1978), pp. 65–7, in C. R. Strain, ed., *Prophetic Visions and Economic Realities: Protestants, Jews and Catholics Confront the Bishops' Letter on the Economy* (Eerdmans 1989), p. 33.
95. Wogaman, p. 80.

48

96. Wogaman, p. 82.
97. J. McVickar, *Outlines of Political Economy* (New York 1825), p. 69. Quoted in May, p. 14.
98. Atherton, p. 104. For a more detailed discussion of the Christian political economists, and of scarcity, see Atherton, pp. 99–108, and pp. 50–2.
99. Waterman, p. 170.
100. Atherton, pp. 104–5.
101. Waterman referring to Samuelson, the great American economist, p. 259.
102. Atherton, p. 108.
103. R. N. Bellah et al., eds, *Habits of the Heart* (New York: Harper & Row 1986).

Social Christianity

*Christian Socialism
in England*

c h a p t e r   o n e

Frederick D. Maurice
1805–72

Introduction

Maurice was born into a Unitarian family in Lowestoft in 1805, his father being the local minister. He was educated at Cambridge University, but left without a degree because he was a Nonconformist. He then had a brief career in publishing. Having become an Anglican in 1831, he was able to go to Oxford University and obtain a degree. After ordination in 1834, he became chaplain at Guy's Hospital and Lincoln's Inn, and Professor of Theology at King's College, London. He was dismissed from the latter post in 1853 because of his liberal views on eternal punishment. It was in this period, 1848–54, that he led the Christian socialist group, with its involvement in populist publishing, producer co-operatives, and adult working-class education. He became Professor of Casuistry and Moral Philosophy at Cambridge University in 1866, and died in 1872.

First and foremost, Maurice was a theologian; his social teaching and practical involvements in society were a consequence of his beliefs. His published output was enormous, ranging from major theological studies, lectures and sermons, to polemical pamphlets. His greatest book, *The Kingdom of Christ* (1838), set out what became his major convictions and concerns for the rest of his life. They included the theological insights that drove him into Christian socialism in response to the political revolutions and economic disruptions of 1848. They have been a stimulus to generations of socially concerned Christians, despite his time-bound preferences and prejudices (he rejected Lord Goderich's proposed pamphlet, *Duty of the Age,* because it argued for democracy, and he shared the common belief in social ranks).

Texts 1 and 2 illustrate how Maurice's basic theological convictions influenced his involvement in the producer co-operative movement, and his rejection of the *laissez-faire* system of competition. They form one pamphlet: two sides of the same coin of Christian involvement in society. The first was a lecture delivered in December 1850 at the Christian Socialist's Office for Promoting Working Men's Associations. It is an argument for co-operatives, in which the theological convictions are mainly implicit. The second was a sermon preached in the following month, January 1851. He chose the local Anglican church nearest to the Office, in order to develop the explicit theological insights that influenced the preceding lecture. The letter to the local parson explaining this rationale introduces the pamphlet and Text 1.

The case for co-operatives in Text 1 is summarized very concisely by an appended letter to the press from Charles Kingsley. Kingsley's presence illustrates the importance of Maurice's references to the 'sweated trades' of the clothing industry. Kingsley elaborated these views in his pamphlet *Cheap Clothes and Nasty* (1850) and his novel *Alton Locke* (1850). Christian concern over the working conditions in this industry have continued to the present day. Soon after writing this letter, Kingsley was banned from preaching in London by the Bishop, because of a controversial sermon deeply critical of the existing social order.

Text 2 elaborates the Christian beliefs about co-operation as a way of educating the local church. It begins by emphasizing the challenge of idolatry, particularly as mammon-worship of the prevailing economic system. It has been a constant theme of social Christianity, particularly of the more radical contributors like Tawney and Rauschenbusch, and of liberation theology. The obverse of such idolatry is the recognition of Christ as the deliverer from bondage. This emancipation is reflected in the life of fellowship and co-operation as lived in industry as well as in the Church. For the law of Christ, as the constitution of humankind, covers all life.

———————

Text 1: Reasons for Co-operation

Letter to the Reverend G. S. Drew, Incumbent of St John's Church, St Pancras

MY DEAR MR. DREW,

The following Lecture was delivered at a house within your district; the Sermon was preached in your Church. I believe there is a connexion between them which might justify me in publishing them together at any time. I have a particular motive for doing so at this time. The writer of an article in the last Edinburgh Review has imputed to the promoters of Working Men's Associations opinions which they not only do not hold, but which they have always strenuously opposed. It seemed desirable that a short statement of their objects and convictions, which was made before the article appeared, should be put forth, not as an answer to it, but in order that those who assail us hereafter may proceed upon real – not fictitious – data. One of the Reviewer's charges, however, especially concerns those of us who are clergymen. It is more than insinuated that we encourage working men to hope for emancipation from a change of circumstances, not from a change of character and conduct. If we hold that doctrine we have abandoned our position as ministers of the Gospel; [. . .] Now we think that the work of trying to reform trade is one to which we are especially called by our Ordination vows. Why we think so, the Sermon which I addressed, a fortnight ago, to the young men of your congregation, though it contains no allusion to Associations or Co-operative Stores, will sufficiently explain. It may show you, and perhaps some of my other brethren in the ministry, why we so earnestly desire you as our fellow-labourers.

I venture to claim you in that character, though you have not committed yourself to any of our plans, and possibly do not approve them. For you have given abundant proofs that you believe a clergyman is not less a clergyman when he is attending to the outward occupations of his parishioners, and trying to bring those occupations under the government of Christian principles, than when he is preaching. At all events, you will allow me to present you with this little Tract, as a token of my desire to be reckoned

Your friend and brother,
F. D. MAURICE

Reasons for co-operation

You will have seen the words 'Co-operative Stores', and 'Office for Working-men's Associations' inscribed in large letters upon this house. I cannot suppose that these words are new to any of you. You have probably connected them with certain theories concerning the organization of labour, which you have heard of as prevailing in France, which perhaps you have read of in French books. Certain practical experiments have grown out of these theories, which are commonly associated in Englishmen's minds with the revolution of 1848, and are supposed to denote its peculiar character. [. . .]

Hereafter, I hope you may hear lectures in this place from persons who are competent to tell you something about the French systems, how far they agree with each other, how far they contradict each other, what there is to be learnt from each of them, what there is to be avoided in each. [. . .]

But the only reason that I can give why I should put myself forward on this occasion is, that I know nothing of the French systems, very little indeed of the French Associations. That negative qualification is certainly not one of which I can boast; it has, however, these advantages. I am compelled to confine myself to the most elementary questions; details and refinements, such as a person conversant with the subject would like to hear of I must not venture upon. Such an outline sketch as I can give, is the one which befits the state of our Associations, for they are quite in their infancy; the varieties and complications of system have at present nothing to do with them. On that account they bring the principle on which we are trying to act more simply before you; it will be seen just as it is in a building of the rudest construction without a single ornament. Moreover my ignorance compels me to look at the question altogether from an English point of view; it is the condition of the English working man in the present day, not love for any learned scheme of co-operation which has forced us to take part in this practical experiment. The principle commends itself to us not as a new one, but as one of the oldest in the history of the world. If we have learned it anywhere but in the Bible, it is from our English History and English Constitution. If we value it for any lower object than that of carrying out what seems to us the only law of fellowship among Christian men, it is as a means of averting an English revolution.

Much has been said of late against the extravagant sympathy which is shown for prisoners. I do not altogether join in these complaints though I see great excuse for them. It is a good thing that ladies and gentlemen should recognise a human being into whatever depth of degradation and crime he has sunk; though it is a very evil thing that they should recognise him only when he has been proclaimed an outcast from society – not while he is still regarded as a part of it. [. . .] The prison is a definite place, the inmates of which may always be found – but who knows where those are who may be on the way to it, who may be struggling night and day not to enter it? A lady or gentleman going to visit a prisoner at Pentonville or Newgate may stop at half-a-dozen shops on the way. The articles which are asked for are exposed on the counter, or are brought immediately, or will be procured at a short notice. There may be a momentary feeling of pity for those who have to pass ten or twelve hours in the wearisome employment of serving customers, perhaps a wish that something might be done for their improvement. But into whose mind is the thought likely to come, that there are certain human beings who produced the articles which seem to have entered that shop by magic and to come the moment they are called for? I am sure a person may be very benevolent, may have a great general sympathy with his fellow-creatures and a very particular sympathy with those whose misery he actually beholds, and yet may, day after day, go from one tradesman in Regent-street, or Oxford-street, to another, without even entertaining the thought that human hands have actually been concerned in the making of the goods which he buys, and that very bitter human tears may have been shed over them in the process. The kind-hearted district-visitor knows of course more. He enters the hovel, sees something of those who inhabit it, does something for their relief. He is told that wages are very low, or work slack in the branch of business which the person visited is engaged in. He knows, that where wages are low or work slack, the rent is probably in arrear, that most of the furniture, and many of the clothes are in pawn, – that there is a score at the baker's and tallow-chandler's shop. He knows that if there is bread enough to eat, this state of things is fatal to the moral condition, and will be fatal to the physical condition of the family. He sees, perhaps, that the family less and less deserves the name; that there is more and more strife and dislike among the members of it, – that each is in the way of the other, – that it is crowded into the same room with four or five other families sinking downwards into the same ruin. A clergyman or district-visitor sees all this, and begins to despair of the condition of his own particular neighbourhood, and of the land generally. But he feels that he really knows almost nothing of the people he comes in contact with – the greater part of their life is wholly out of his reach. He cannot raise their wages; he questions whether, if they were raised, they would not be spent in drinking, – he questions whether the money he has bestowed may not be doing more harm than good. Is it wonderful that he should find paupers or prisoners over whom the law has an actual control, whose condition may be brought under some definite rules, a more hopeful class than those who are only preparing for the one condition or the other? [. . .]

When evils of various and apparently opposite kinds have reached a head, it is a comfort that we are commonly able to trace the connexion between them. We owe to the writer of the Letters 'on Labour and the Poor,' in the *Morning Chronicle*, the full and clear discovery that a system which is undermining the honesty of the seller, which is promoting and promoted by the dishonesty of the consumer, is also a main cause of the demoralization and misery of the producer. I consider the demonstration of this fact, coming from a perfectly impartial witness who is entirely indifferent to theories, and who has made himself

acquainted with all the trades in the metropolis, a more important contribution to the cause of humanity, than even the graphic
stories of misery which those letters contain. They may be
attributed in part to the skill of the artist. But the evidence that
the rivalry of the cheap shops has led to the formation of a
system which abstracts from the producer all but a starvation
price for his labour, and bestows it upon slop-sellers and
middlemen, a system which makes a man's own wife and
children his most dangerous rivals, – the destroyers of the fruits
of his industry, – this evidence could not be regarded by any one
as something merely to be read and deplored. It must provoke
the inquiry, 'how may we strike at the root of this poison tree?
For if it is allowed to grow till it perishes by its own rottenness,
the whole country may perish with it.'

Accordingly it was this demonstration which led many who
had as little sympathy with the notions of French or English
Socialists as any of you can have, to ask whether the protest
which they have borne against Competition, is so monstrous
and anarchical as some have said that it is. Looking merely at the
condition of England, merely at facts, and leaving all doctrines,
socialist or anti-socialist out of the question, there seemed to
them strong proof that competition itself was introducing a
most monstrous and anarchical condition of things. They heard
of a war between Capital and Labour, and of the great sin of
those who were fomenting it and carrying it on. They perceived
the heinousness of the sin; they were determined, with God's
help, not to be guilty of it. But they felt that they were guilty of
it, if they looked on indifferently at the social evils which the
Morning Chronicle letters disclosed. It was clear that the war
had begun, and was becoming a war of extermination. Whether
the mere money force, or the physical force of numbers prevailed in it, the result must be equally terrible. But if such a
crisis was to be averted, in what way? This was not a question
which we had to decide. The working-men of England were
beginning to discover how little they had gained by experiments
of physical force, how far more they had suffered by such
experiments than those whom they had tried to put down. They
had made another discovery. They had resorted to combinations for various purposes. They had combined to strike for
wages, and had sometimes gained what they sought. Was it not

just as possible to combine for the purpose of doing work, as for the purpose of ceasing to work? Might they not help each other instead of destroying each other?

I do not say that the thoughts of those who began to reflect in this way on their own position, were friendly to the capitalist. I do not think they were. But I have no doubt that they were more friendly than the thoughts of those who were working under slop-sellers, and who saw no escape from that dominion. When they felt that it was possible to do something for themselves, they cared much less to do something against others. I cannot tell how it is in France; things may be quite different there. [. . .] But even there, I conceive, if the government knew how to avail itself of the impulse to co-operation among the trades of Paris, it might be the best of all safety-valves for the desire of self-government, the greatest security against popular outbreaks. Be that as it may, there is nothing more certain than that the corresponding impulse in England, encountering no rude and foolish opposition from the civil authorities, has done more to check the tendency to Red Republicanism among our people, than all other influences together. I repeat it, however; though I am convinced that this inclination was indirectly favourable to property because directly favourable to order, I will not pretend that it was positively charitable to the owners of property. I do not see how it could be, unless these owners proved that they were disposed and anxious to put an end to that utter disorder which the working-men felt that the system of trade was bringing into all their social relations. Let it be once seen that property is connected with order in the true honest sense of the word, that it does not merely seek to preserve itself, but to preserve the physical and moral well-being of the whole land; then there will be a real and solid hope of a reconciliation. I conceive that a demand of this kind the working classes had a full right to make, when they had first shown an earnestness to do something for themselves and to reform themselves. I conceive that the owners of property have the most direct interest in meeting this demand, because the present system of trade is not more destructive to the morality of the lower classes than of the higher.

It was this conviction which led the promoters of Associations to begin work on a very small scale last winter. They felt they could do next to nothing in the way of advancing capital. But they might set an example which others would follow in due time. If they could start a single association of men, who should work for their own profits and not for that of some slop-seller; if they could place this Association under the control of some person acquainted with the business, and possessing the confidence of the workers; if they could exact from the members of it the repayment, with interest, out of their profits of all that had been advanced for the purpose of enabling them to begin, that the sum which they no longer needed might be turned to a like use for some other set of workmen; a little immediate good might be done, and an impression might be left upon the minds of many besides those who were directly helped, that capital could benefit those who had regarded it as an enemy. No doubt immeasurably larger sums are advanced every day, and often by persons ill able to afford them, for the benefit of their poorer brethren. But ten times as much money given in this way does not produce one-tenth of the effect upon working-men, since it is laid out in behalf of some object which we have devised for them, and not for one in which they are interested themselves. According to the most recognised of all maxims, those afford the greatest help, who help men to help themselves. It may be a far less sacrifice to lend money than to give it; but if it is a greater recognition of poor men as men, and not merely as poor, it must do them more good; ultimately, I should think, ourselves. If they could be urged to work as friends and brothers with each other, they would be more likely to feel as friends and brothers to the members of all classes, than while each regarded the man professing his craft as a rival and a foe, and all remembered who had been the instruments in awakening this feeling.

With these views an Association of Tailors was commenced, which met with more success than we had any right to expect. Others were formed, of shoemakers, bakers, printers, and builders. A central board was formed of representatives from these Associations, which meets in this room every Monday, to deliberate upon their state, and upon the admission of any new Associations which may desire to be connected with them. A code of laws was framed for the guidance of the different Associations. The promoters formed themselves into a council, for the purpose of raising funds, of diffusing a knowledge of their principles and their acts,* and of offering suggestions respecting the course of a movement which had begun long before they took part in it. They meet here every Thursday evening. They have established monthly conferences among the working-men, where all questions respecting Associations, as well as their own manner of conducting them, are very freely discussed.

You will easily see that this organization is imperfect, and in a manner extemporaneous. We thought it un-English to begin with a large scheme. We judged it best to make a particular experiment, which, with all our different blunders, will be a lesson to us hereafter, and a still more valuable one to our successors. But though our doings have been at present on so small a scale, I dare not escape from any censure upon that pretext. I dare not pretend that though they are insignificant in themselves, they are not very wrong and mischievous if they proceed on a wrong principle. For it is certain, as I have said already, that the impulse to such Associations is exceedingly strong throughout England, and especially in those districts of it – I mean in the North – where there is most of practical strength and intelligence. – Though it was not in our power to check them, we were at least bound not to encourage them if they are pursuing some wicked or visionary end, or are taking some wicked or visionary means of bringing about an indifferent or a good end. We ought to have considered well before we advanced a step in such a course, and we should be ready now to explain ourselves frankly, and to answer any objections which may be raised in one quarter or another.

The great objection, that we are setting labour at war with capital I have considered already. I have stated how powerful a motive it was with us to begin, that we thought we might at least be opening a negotiation, and suggesting the preliminaries of a peace between labour and capital. It is as grave a charge, that we are destroying the relation of Master and Servant – a relation which forms a distinct part of the order of the world, and that in

---

* *A weekly Newspaper, entitled 'The Christian Socialist' (price 1d.) has been established by some of the promoters, [. . .] Its main object is to show that the connexion which its name expresses between the principles of Co-operation and the principle of the Gospel is a real and vital one.*

doing so we are preparing the way for the destruction of other still more sacred relations.

I answer in this case as I did before. The relation of master and servant is destroyed, or is in the most rapid course of destruction, by the present system of trade. I do not say that there are not noble masters and faithful servants in the shops of London; – I am sure there are; I believe that I could name some of them; – but they are so because they are rebels against that doctrine which is becoming the current and popular one, and which will soon treat every other as heretical. That doctrine makes it impossible for the master to look upon his servant except as one who is wanting wages which he is not disposed to give, or the servant upon the master, except as one who is offering wages upon which he cannot exist. Call this a relation, if you please; it is a relation of mutual suspicion and hostility, a relation in which obedience is impossible, because government (in any worthy sense of the word) is equally impossible. I boldly claim this merit for our Associations, that they are helping to make this relation a reality and not a fiction. I do not mean merely because the manager is one of the working-men, sharing their profits, having the same interest with them. That is true; but he is not the less a governor; he is not less obliged, by his position, to be a strict governor. We tell our associates so; we tell our managers so. And though there will be in these Associations all the usual restiveness against authority on the one side, and all the usual mistakes of over-indulgence and over-severity on the other; though these difficulties are greatly increased by the habits which men bring with them from the competitive shops, where they learn to hate their employers and to rebel against them as often as they can with safety, as well as by the notions which they had formed respecting the nature of Freedom, and of Rule, before they had any true experience of either, yet our very short trial has shown us that our Association-shops are schools, and very practical schools for learning obedience and government; in other words, for showing how a human relation may be substituted for the mere animal connexion between Driver and Slave.

The discipline of the ordinary shop deals with all misbehaviour on the part of the workmen which interferes with the success of the trade, with the fulfilment of engagements to the customers. Our discipline must have a further object. The sobriety of the men, their behaviour to each other, whatever concerns the economy of a household, must be seen after by our managers. You will not, surely, teach men to exhibit or require less order in their houses by accustoming them to this order in the shop. That I think is a sufficient answer to the charge of the effect we are likely to produce on the relations of the family, properly so called. I do not care to repeat what the facts I have referred to, have said already, in most awful language, that *we* are not the disturbers of family life; that the subversion of it is one of the horrible effects of our present social system; that unless that system is speedily reformed, an accursed and hateful communism of practice, and not of theory, will assuredly establish itself, if it has not established itself already amongst us.

But competition, I shall be told, is a great law of nature; in fighting against it we are warring with nature. Most competitive masters, I presume, acknowledge in terms at least, that Rest is a great 'Law of Nature', and that it is necessary for their workmen at certain seasons to sleep. [...] Allowing the advocate for competition to profit by the immense concession I have made to him; allowing him to say that Society could as little exist without competition as our bodies could perform their func- tions without sleep; I must yet affirm that men only work when they are *not* sleeping, and that they only produce any of the great fruits of work when they are *not* striving against each other, but are helping each other. And I shall say to the competitive master just what he said so reasonably to his servant. We find that this competition, whether it is natural or no, does not, under its present conditions, suffer us to work or to live. We find that as we must keep ourselves awake, if we have a job to finish, though our nature ever so much induces us to sleep, as we must keep ourselves awake in extreme cold when the impulse to sleep is still stronger, because death is the consequence of indulging it: so we must, in some way or other, overcome this power of competition – which we acknowledge to be very mighty in itself, and which you are strengthening by every kind of stimulus – because otherwise work will be done ill, or not done at all, and men's bodies and souls will perish as they are perishing.

But our principle is said to be a new one. The old reverence for property is opposed to it; the whole history of trade proves it to be monstrous; modern political economy demonstrates the futility of it. Let us take these charges in order.

What ground is laid for the old reverence of landed property in our own feudal institutions? They deny property to exist absolutely in any individual holder of it. The sovereign, as the head of the nation, is the real owner of the land. Each man has it by a tenure of service. But even the sovereign is not regarded as the ultimate proprietor. The tithes paid for the land are a witness that God is looked upon as the real Lord of the soil. This is our doctrine – we hold property not to be absolute, but dependent; necessarily, inevitably dependent upon certain services. We do not say that we can depose the holders of it if they do not acknowledge the obligations of it; but we say that there is One who can, and will, and that it is quite needful for them to remember this truth, and to reflect upon it.

But the feudal system, we shall be told, is broken up. As a system it certainly is broken up to a great extent. The selfishness of proprietors broke it up. Their opposition to the alienation of land showed that they counted it as their own. They forgot the principle upon which they held it; the principle remained, but their grasping disposition was punished.

And what new power was raised up to counteract theirs? The trading guilds and corporations of the towns; co-operative bodies, founded upon the idea of brotherhood, which had first been established in the monasteries; carrying out this idea even into the most minute details. To these, Trade owed its origin; by these it grew and flourished; it sprang, not from competition, but from fellow-work.

But the guilds and corporations have been found oppressive; they have been shaken to the centre. Certainly they have. They became exclusive bodies, full of narrowness, meanness, rivalry. Their principle remained; their selfishness was punished. The political economists asserted the freedom of trade, protested against the bondage which these bodies, once so useful, had been able to establish. Their principle was good, for it declared that a class had been excluded from the benefits of trade and commerce, which had a right to share in them. Unfortunately, in pleading the cause of emancipation, they used the word 'competition'. They spoke of men's right to compete with each other; an undoubted right – like the right of a man to cut his own throat, which must, except in certain cases, be conceded to an Englishman, but which he may find it inconvenient, on many accounts, to use. Gradually the lower class of writers – those who merely copied the phrases and names which represented the thoughts of greater men – began to boast of political economy, as if it meant little more than the defence of competition. But this miserable notion of a great science has been more and more repudiated by all the eminent teachers of it. To buy in the cheapest market and sell in the dearest is with them a mere vulgar maxim, not a principle at all. And the most comprehensive and logical of all the writers on the subject is the one who not only does not repudiate Co-operation as contemptible, but has uttered some very memorable words in commendation of it.

I apprehend, then, that we are not opposed to the old English doctrine of property, but are asserting it; that we are not contradicting the whole history of trade, but are illustrating it; that we are not setting at nought the principles of political economy, but are vindicating them from a mean and dishonourable perversion of them. And I conceive it is no slight evidence in confirmation of our principle, that it reconciles three great truths which have been set in violent opposition to each other, and that it suggests a hope that the protectionist landowners, the intrepid supporters of old English feudal notions, the mercantile class – the representatives of the old trading doctrine – and our political economists who are often regarded as the enemies of both, may find in the promotion of Associations a common object for which they may work together.

And yet I believe it is an older principle than that of the feudal aristocracy, or that of the middle age companies, or that of the free-traders, for which we are contending. I believe that men were taught, long before any of these came into existence, that they were meant to live and work together, and how they might live and work together. The doctrine that men should call nothing their own was proclaimed by Galilaean fishermen before it was adopted into the English Constitution, or gave an impulse to the thoughts of modern Frenchmen. It worked from the first as a truth and a power, not as a dead rule. It worked in that way all through the corruptions, superstitions, and violence, of the Middle Ages. It is working in that way in England at the present time. Everywhere there are attempts to do great works of mercy, which are based upon the doctrine that men are brothers, and that they can act as if they were, because there is an influence strong enough to overpower the tendencies to rivalry and division which exist among them. I think that these efforts want something to make them thoroughly practical, to make them harmonious with the practical habits of our countrymen. It may be thought that they are not national, – that they are derived from a source whence we do not like to derive anything.

The plan I have set before you tonight is founded upon the same eternal grounds as theirs. It looks for help and success only from the same strength. But it recognises wants which they do not take account of. It affirms God's kingdom to be on earth as well as in heaven.

The following letter [from the Reverend Charles Kingsley], which appeared in the *Morning Chronicle* of Tuesday, (28 January, is closely connected with the subject of the foregoing Lecture.

SIR, – In your notice of the first article in the last *Edinburgh Review*, you hinted an opinion that the writer of it had not been perfectly just to the 'English Socialists', who are therein denounced. I should not think of asking for any of your space to expose the different misrepresentations in that article, in as far as they bear on the great questions of labour and capital, but as the writer has attributed certain opinions to Professor Maurice and to me which we have always disclaimed, and never more distinctly and pointedly than in the publications from which the charge is deduced, I may, perhaps, ask your permission to contradict a few of the statements which are most directly at variance with fact. I am the more anxious to do so in your journal, because we both feel great gratitude to you for the light which you have thrown on the condition of the labouring poor.

First, then, the reviewer has founded on a single passage in a tract of mine, in which I attack the notions of those economists who maintain competition to be the great law of the universe, and who persist in trying to solve, by the canons of their own science, moral and anthropological problems utterly foreign to its sphere, the assertion that it is our practice and rule to revile political economy. This charge is not only not true, but the direct reverse of the truth. In letters addressed to working-men, whose prejudices against political economists are very strong, I have expressed my conviction of the necessity of diligently studying all that they have written, arguing that no social movement can prosper which violates any of those economic laws which they have discovered, and that we cannot hope to arrive at any clearer light on social points, if we do not avail ourselves of that which we possess already. In my 'Alton Locke' I have referred more than once, with the most heartfelt admiration, to Mr John Mill's great work; especially, if my memory serves me right, to the very chapter which the reviewer quotes for the purpose of demolishing our supposed conclusions. Professor Maurice has never, for the last twenty years, as far as either he or his friends are aware, spoken a word in disparagement of political economy, or of any who have contributed to the elucidation of its principles; and on a very recent occasion, when he delivered a lecture on the motives which led us to promote the establishment of working-men's associations, he pointed out the gross injustice of identifying political economy with the idolatry of competition. Mr Herman Merivale, formerly professor of political economy in the University of Oxford, attended that lecture, and may be quoted, if need be, as a witness for the truth of this assertion.

Secondly. – The reviewer says that we wish to call ourselves 'Communists'. If he had read a single one of the tracts upon which alone any knowledge of our principles can be founded, he would have seen that instead of choosing the name we have carefully avoided it – not only because its associations are offensive, but because it expresses exactly what we are not, and what, as he is [sic] shown in a passage of Proudhon, which he somewhat naively quotes, we cannot be. If his quoting that passage means anything it must mean this – that we, as Socialists, believe the sanctity of family life to be the germ of all society, as indeed we do; and that this leads necessarily to a firm respect for monarchy, as indeed it does in our case; but that Communism, because it begins by denying family life, is alone consistent with that modern 'coalition in which each is retained by the law of self-interest', of which he proclaims himself the

68

champion – with which assertion also we most fully agree. For we have asserted, and now assert again, that a most horrible and hateful form of Communism exists already in this country; that it is proved to exist, not only by your articles, but by the evidence of factory commissioners and Government statistics; that we attribute the growth of this Communism to the present system; that there is no object which we seek so earnestly as the restoration of that domestic life which threatens to become extinct among English labourers. When, then, the reviewer, acquitting us (in terms) of aiming at the more atrocious results which are connected with the word Communism, evidently wishes that they should be associated with our names and acts in the minds of his readers, we answer by boldly charging on him that which he only insinuates against us – by asserting, on the authority of his own quotation from the 'sagacious' Proudhon, that *his* doctrines, and not *ours*, are the ones which lead to the destruction of property, monarchy, and family life.

Thirdly. – He says that we 'deny that slow improvements of gradual ameliorations will meet the wants of society.' Professor Maurice distinctly said, in the only tract of his which the reviewer has noticed, that we look to nothing else; that we have no faith in great schemes, and only invite individuals to take part in the humblest and most cautious efforts on the very smallest scale.

Fourthly. – He says that we wish to *introduce* 'the antagonistic and regenerative principle of association into society', in order that we might '*remodel*' it. On the contrary, we have said repeatedly, that the co-operative principle is the principle of society *already*; that all great achievements have been the fruit of it. Professor Maurice told a meeting of working-men in Manchester, three weeks ago, that they owed their machines, their manufactures, their city itself to co-operation – that it is not a new principle, but the oldest of all.

Fifthly. – The reviewer charges us with appealing to feelings and rejecting science. I apprehend the very words 'organization of labour' are an answer to the complaint. Our science, or the science of Socialists generally, may be very bad, but any one who has ever read a line of any Socialist's knows that his temptation is to set too much, not too little, store by science. The exposure of evils which exist we call statements of facts. If the reviewer chooses to call them 'sentiments', he is welcome to do so. He is the innovator in the use of language, not we. We have protested again and again – 'Alton Locke' is full of protests – against the sentimentalism of bestowing all help upon the outcasts of society, and next to none upon its actual working members, a sentimentalism rendered inevitable by the present system, which for that reason especially we abominate. [...]

Lastly. – He insinuates that we would 'induce the working-men to rely on external aid for objects which must be achieved by themselves, if they are achieved at all, and to seek their emancipation in a change of circumstances or social arrangements rather than in a change of character and conduct.' I affirm this charge to be utterly unfounded. Professor Maurice has written more than one tract for the purpose of combating directly the latter error; and the whole moral of 'Alton Locke', from beginning to end, is directed against the former one. Nay, the whole autobiography of one of the characters is devoted to exposing the fallacy of 'Coningsbyism', or the system which would make the poor, feudal dependents [*sic*] on the exertions and bounty of the rich. The working-men at least can testify that our great aim throughout has been to show them that they 'must achieve all great ends for themselves, and not rely upon external aid' – that 'they can hope for no change of circumstances and social arrangements except by a change of character and conduct.' Instead of wishing the labourer to depend more upon his employer, our complaint has been that he already depends on him too much; and the only great change in the relation of rich and poor which we wish to see carried out, is one which, as Mr. John Mill has perfectly expressed it, 'shall enable the labourer to hire the capital which he requires, instead of, as at present, the capitalist hiring the labourer.' [...]

I am, sir,
Your obedient servant,
CHARLES KINGSLEY, jun.

Eversley Rectory, Jan.24, 1851.

Text 2: Christianity against Mammon

No man can serve two masters: for either he will hate the one, and love the other; or else he will hold to the one, and despise the other. Ye cannot serve God and Mammon
(Matthew VI.24).

The Old Testament is full of sentences against idolatry. It professes to be the history of a people whom the unseen God chose out of all the nations of the earth to know Him and worship Him; and whom He commanded first and chiefly not to bow down to anything in heaven above, or in the earth beneath, or in the waters under the earth. It tells us how this people clung to their idols, how they set up one visible God after another, how they became degraded and divided by their superstitions, how their neighbours enslaved them, because they had lost the secret of freedom, how God made use of their sufferings as instruments of their education, how He strove to make them understand that He was their Lord, and Judge, and Deliverer. [. . .]

When we pass from the Old to the New Testament, there seems to be a great change. In the Gospels we are reading about the same Jewish nation which we read of in the Kings and Chronicles and the Prophets. But we hear nothing of idols. It is clear that the Jews in the time of our Lord were not worshipping the likenesses of anything in heaven or in the earth, as their fathers had done. Ever since the Babylonian captivity, they had been free from that sin. [. . .]

We might be inclined to say, then, that God's education had done its work; that the great evil of which the prophets complained, and to which they referred all the other evils of the land, was cured. No doubt God's discipline had done much for the Jews. [. . .] And there were *some* who had entered into the very meaning of the words which God spoke by his prophets, who trusted the living and righteous God with their hearts, who desired to know Him better, who looked to Him to reveal himself more perfectly to them, who kept themselves from every false way, who cared for all Israelites, whether they were rich or poor, because they regarded them all as children of God's covenant, and therefore as brothers. These men had in very deed been delivered from idolatry, from the sin itself, from the inside as well as the outside of it. But we should commit a very great mistake, and misunderstand the New Testament altogether, if we believed that this was the case with the Jews generally.

You remember in what tremendous language our Lord speaks of the Scribes and Pharisees and Lawyers, at Jerusalem. [. . .] He declares that a judgement was coming upon that generation, which would be more fearful than any which had come upon previous generations, which would involve nothing less than the destruction of the city and of the nation. Now the Pharisees and Scribes and Lawyers were the very men who condemned idolatry most, and who had the greatest horror of any association with Gentiles. [. . .] How could they be filling up the measure of those forefathers, who bowed down before Baal and Ashtoreth, who were continually charged with forgetting the law and covenant of their God? [. . .]

My brethren, it was precisely the *same* sin that Isaiah and Jeremiah had denounced in the days of Ahaz and Jehoiakim, which our Lord denounced in the days of Herod and Pontius Pilate. It was the same evil in a worse and more deadly form, though stripped of its outward signs, though looking fair and respectable without. These later Jews had got the very poison of idolatry into their veins. They were penetrated with it through and through. They were worshipping the very demon whom the earlier idolaters had split up into a number of shapes; they gave him the more entire homage of their hearts; they were moulding their whole lives after his image. Nearly all that they did, and thought, and spoke, was done in obedience to his commands. They had not need to set up separate altars to him. They could worship him while they seemed to be kneeling in the temple to God. They could worship him in their families; they could worship him in the market-place. They could make the most secret and the most open acts of their lives acts of devotion to him.

What was the name of this demon? Our Lord gives him his name in the passage I have just read to you. He calls him MAMMON. The name was familiar to the Jews. They knew that Mammon meant the Money-God, and they knew, probably, that those in different lands who worshipped a god of money, whether by this title or by any other, applied to him because they hoped that he would make them rich, that he would enable them to find out hoards of gold which other people could not find, or to compass some end which would give them an advantage over their fellow-men, and help them to rise by their fall. They knew as much as this about the idol of which our Lord spoke. [. . .]

But if there was such a curse upon the land of Judea, and if rich men, poor men, religious men, were all in danger of falling under it, what was the deliverance? The whole of our Lord's Sermon on the Mount, from which my text is taken, is nothing else than an announcement of this deliverance: every parable that He spoke, every act of mercy and healing that He did, – His whole life upon earth, was an announcement of it. If you read over the fifth, sixth, and seventh chapters of this gospel, you will see how continually these words recur – 'your Father'. You will see that the whole charm and energy of the discourse is in them. Christ did not come saying, 'It is very humiliating, to be serving this money-god. It lowers you in the scale of creatures; it hinders you from being really men.' All this is true, and all this had been said again and again. But what good had come of it? Are men able to shake off a yoke because they are told it is a shame to wear it? Generally the effort to do so rivets the chains more tightly. Here it certainly would. [. . .] Our Lord went straight to the root. He said boldly, to poor men and rich men, to young and old, to Pharisees and Publicans, 'Mammon is not the God: I come to tell you who is. I tell you He is a Father. I tell you that He created this universe - that every tree and flower upon it is His; and that He clothes the lilies of the field, and orders the flight of every sparrow. And He cares for you more than for them. He did not make you to be His creatures merely as He made them. He made you to be His children, and now He claims you as His children. He has sent me forth for this very end – that I may redeem you out of bondage to the world; [. . .]

I come to say that the God who made you is one whom you may trust in, absolutely and altogether; one to whom you may give up the care of your bodies, and souls, and spirits, of the past, and present, and future; one who cares for your nation and your families – for each individual of you; one who is not a tyrant, but a deliverer, who has taken your fathers and you into covenant with Him, that you may be blessings to all the families of the earth, that you may testify to them what He is, and what He has done for them, and what He is doing for them. It will be for you, my disciples, poor fishermen as you are, to go forth with this message of peace and reconciliation to all the kindreds and tribes of the earth; it will be for you to tell them that God is about to make a better covenant with them than that which He made with you; that in His only begotten Son He is adopting them as His sons and daughters, owning them as members of the same family, and sealing them with His Spirit of love, that they may be His children indeed, verily and indeed brothers to each other.'

All our Lord's gospel, from first to last, has this ground, and no other. It begins with the proclamation of the absolute and eternal love of God; it goes on to declare that the Son of His Love, the only begotten of the Father, with whom He is well pleased, the brightness of His glory, the express image of His person, has taken our nature, has become a man, has entered into the sorrows, poverty, death of a man. It affirms that in Him God has reconciled the world to Himself, not imputing their trespasses unto them. It claims men as God's redeemed children in Christ, and assures them of His spirit, to go with them through the world as their life-giver, strengthener, comforter; to unite them to the Father, to unite them to each other; to shed abroad in their hearts God's forgiveness; to make them forgive; to endue them with a new, divine, eternal life. This is the doctrine which the apostles preached to men of every race and nation. And it was this doctrine our Lord told his disciples when they were only just beginning to receive His lessons, and to be fitted for their work, which just so far as they believed it and acted upon it, must set them in perpetual hostility with Mammon. [. . .]

Dear brethren, I have been speaking of Judea, and of those who dwelt in it; and yet you see how, almost without knowing it, or being able to help it, I have used the present tense, and seem as if I were speaking of England and Englishmen, in this year, 1851. And am I *not* speaking of them, and to them? Is not every word which I have said applicable to you and to me? Is not this struggle going on in each of our hearts? Have we not to say, every one of us, whether God or Mammon is our master? Do you think we can serve both, any more than the Pharisees and the disciples could?

I am sure that this is the question for us. We are asked, sometimes, why we bring forward this book, which was written 1800 years ago, some of it 4000 years ago, to people living in this civilized age of ours. This is my answer. Whenever these words were spoken, they tell us, all of us, the secret of our lives – what causes the strife and contradiction in them – how they may be set right. Talk to me about civilization as much as you like – I am as thankful for it as you can be. But it has not settled this controversy – it has not put down this money-god – this selfish spirit. If we believed some people, we should suppose that it had set up new altars to him – that it had invested him with a glory which he never had before. I do not say that: I believe that, in one form or other, all men, in all times, have been tempted by him, and have had to fight with him. But I believe that, as the world grows older, and the complications of society multiply, the fight becomes more terrible – that it becomes one of life and death, for our bodies, souls, and spirits – for each man, and for the whole human family. I believe, also, that all idolatries in our day, as in the days of our Lord's incarnation, are gathering themselves into this one idolatry; that money is becoming the god to which all are urged to bow the knee. That is my reason for choosing this subject tonight. I do not mean that young men are not exposed to a thousand different temptations. I know that a multitude of voices are beckoning them to surrender their souls and bodies to the lusts of the flesh. I am sure that the pulpit is a proper place for warning them of that danger, and that a minister of Christ has no business to omit specific exhortations on any topic whatever respecting which his hearers need teaching, through morbid delicacy, or a taste for generalities. But brethren, so long as the Mammon spirit is listened to, and obeyed, so long it will be utterly in vain to tell men, young or old, that they are not meant to be the slaves of their lowest appetites, and that the fairest part of God's creation is not made to minister to those appetites. The worth of the human being is so lowered by this worship – it is so impossible to hinder those who practise it, from believing that self is the supreme object to which every other *must* yield, that we are held to be absurd, if we call upon any one to rule the passions which God has given him,

75

unless we can persuade him that on the whole, restraint will answer better to him than indulgence. And since I am certain that such a motive with young men is utterly feeble, and often leads to as much evil as it cures, I say we must lay the axe to the root of the tree. We must strike at that mother-vice of our land, which infects the most decorous and respectable, as well as the most reckless; which sometimes puts on the shape of the most open profligacy; sometimes hides itself under the fairest names; which is setting class against class – man against man – which must destroy our national existence, if there is not some power adequate to destroy it.

Young men of England! I tell you there is a power and only one, which can deliver you, and me – any of us, from this fearful temptation, which can enable us to say to this Evil Spirit – we will not worship thee or the golden image which thou hast set up. When I speak of an evil Spirit I mean what I say. It is old language, but I know no other, and shall use no other. I feel it is an actual tempter who is speaking to the heart and spirit within me; one of whom my eyes tell me nothing, but who I am sure is setting before me actual bribes, inspiring me with actual false-hoods, inviting me to actual destruction. And when I speak of his calling upon us to worship him as a god, I mean what I say. It is not in any person's power to say, I will confess no God. He who fancies he is confessing none, is, in fact, setting some creature – it may be his money, it may be himself - on the throne of God. But it is possible for us to say whom we will worship. And if we have strength to say, we will acknowledge that God who has claimed us as His children, to be our God; we will submit to Him; then we shall be able to break the chain of Mammon from off our own necks; we shall be able to help our brethren, in shaking it from theirs. It is to this work I call you tonight. The Carthaginian general, we are told, led his son, when he was but nine years old, to the altar of his country, and bade him swear upon it eternal hatred and hostility to Rome. That son became a man, and he fulfilled the pledge of his boyhood. Long before you had reached the age at which Hamilcar devoted his child, the parents of most of you bound you to implacable war with Mammon. The minister took each of you in his arms, and said, 'I sign thee with the sign of the

Cross, in token that hereafter thou shalt not be ashamed to confess the faith of Christ crucified, and to fight manfully under his banner against sin, the world, and the devil.' In other words, he said, that One who sacrificed Himself was your Redeemer and King – the Redeemer and King of mankind – that you could not serve any other without making yourselves at once rebels and slaves. Do you believe that? Do you mean to act as if that were true? Then you must fight, night and day, against that other power which claims to rule you and the world. You must deny that self-seeking is your law and the law of human society. You must treat it as that which is aiming at the destruction of you and of human society. And remember, you cannot disclaim it in the Church, and acknowledge it in the shop or the counting-house. You cannot have one master here and another there. You must hate God and love Mammon, or hold to God and despise Mammon in one place, and in all places; our whole life must be, and we shall more and more find that it is, the service of the Reconciler or of the Divider. The half century upon which you are entering, young men of England! will teach you that the gospel must be either thrown away by Englishmen altogether, as a tale of other days, or recognised as the law of all their public and private life, of their inner selves, of their outward transactions. See that you consider that alternative solemnly and earnestly. Bring it before your minds continually; remember, that in every act you do you are pledging yourselves to one principle or the other. Ask for us, your teachers, that this thought may be always present to our minds, that we may reflect how dreadful our case will be, if we should be found at last the servants of him whom we are sent into the world to resist; ask that we may be delivered from every false way; that we may be made real, effectual witnesses for the God of Righteousness. But whether we are or not, whether we are working with God, which is the highest blessing that can be granted to any, or with Mammon, which is the most terrible curse, the Truth will prevail, and the Spirit of Lies will be cast out. Whatever is built upon Christ as its foundation will stand, though the winds and floods should beat vehemently against it; whatever is built upon Mammon as its foundation, however seemly and stately it may look, will fall, and great will be the fall of it.

Source: Frederick D. Maurice, *Reasons for Co-operation: A Lecture Delivered at the Office for Promoting Working Men's Associations* (11 December 1850); *God and Mammon: A Sermon to Young Men* (19 January 1851), (John W. Parker 1851).

chapter two

Brooke Foss Westcott
1825–1901

Introduction

Westcott was born into a moderately wealthy family in Birmingham in 1825. While at the King Edward VI School, he came under the formative influence of its headmaster, James Prince Lee, later the first Bishop of Manchester. Ordained from Cambridge University in 1851, Westcott became a master at Harrow School, where he began his theological writings. In 1870 he became the Professor of Divinity at Cambridge, building up a major tradition of biblical scholarship including through his less conservative pupils: Hort, Lightfoot and Benson. As a leading member of the Holy Party, his concern to appropriate modern intellectual discoveries for the development of theology was complemented by his commitment to the Christian Social Union as its first president. The correlation of liberal theology and more radical political idealism was becoming an important characteristic of social Christianity. In 1890 he became Bishop of Durham, continuing his theological work and social involvement. The latter included successfully mediating in the miners' strike of 1892. Westcott died in 1901.

The combination of scholar, mystic, moral concern, and ability to move others, made Westcott into a formidable influence in church life. It meant he was able to play the leading role in transforming Christian socialism into the Christian social reform of the official Churches. He made radicalism respectable in the church establishment. As a great popularizer of Christian socialism, he brought together two important theological and secular trends. Because of his Maurician views, his incarnational theology meant that he discerned eternal realities in the material. Collaborating with these signs of the

Kingdom drove him to social action. That way of interpreting, and being involved in, society was confirmed by his strong belief in evolutionary processes. It gave him a solidaristic organic understanding of humanity, and an equally fervent opposition to an individualistic and mechanistic view of relationships. That is why he advocated socialism and rejected *laissez-faire* political economy. It encouraged his optimistic belief that to change individuals, as employers or workers, would progress the development of the Kingdom on earth. It would replace class divisions.

Text 3 illustrates these understandings and commitments. It was given, as a paper, to a meeting of the Church Congress in Hull in 1890. In this, it illustrates both the importance of official church organizations and conferences, and the way the Christian social reform movement was beginning to capture them (the addresses were published as pamphlets and widely circulated).

The paper itself reflects Westcott's deeply moral interpretation of life in general, and socialism in particular; it also popularizes the more substantial arguments of his *Social Aspects of Christianity* (1887). In the tract, Westcott rejects the way of precise political and economic definitions of socialism with their propensity to harmful sectarian divisions. In doing so, of course, he avoids certain political realities. Many therefore rejected the style and argument, so typical of the CSU, because of its moral vacuity and dilatory reformism. However, it is worth noting that Conservative opinion was enraged by the address. It also illustrates the considerable influence of ethical socialism in British radical politics. The commitment to socialism as a way of life, and therefore more than a matter of political and economic arrangements, continued to play a major part in the thinking of radical Christian socialists such as R. H. Tawney, as well as in the Christian social reform tradition.Interestingly, with the collapse of most command economies, as economic socialism, in 1989–90, it is this strand of ethical socialism as democratic social reform, which has survived more effectively in the West.

Text 3: Socialism as Christian Social Reform

It is not my intention to discuss in this paper any of the representative types of Socialism – the paternal Socialism of Owen, or the State Socialism of Bismarck, the international Socialism of Marx, or the Christian Socialism of Maurice, or the evolutionary Socialism of the *Fabian Essays*. I wish rather to consider the essential idea which gave, or still gives, vitality and force to these different systems, to indicate the circumstances which invest the idea with paramount importance at the present time, and especially to commend it to the careful study of the younger clergy.

The term Socialism has been discredited by its connection with many extravagant and revolutionary schemes, but it is a term which needs to be claimed for nobler uses. It has no necessary affinity with any forms of violence, or confiscation, or class selfishness, or financial arrangement. I shall therefore venture to employ it apart from its historical associations as describing a theory of life, and not only a theory of economics. In this sense Socialism is the opposite of Individualism, and it is by contrast with Individualism that the true character of Socialism can best be discerned. Individualism and Socialism correspond with opposite views of humanity. Individualism regards humanity as made up of disconnected or warring atoms; Socialism regards it as an organic whole, a vital unity formed by the combination of contributory members mutually interdependent.

It follows that Socialism differs from Individualism both in method and in aim. The method of Socialism is co-operation, the method of Individualism is competition. The one regards man as working with man for a common end, the other regards man as working against man for private gain. The aim of Socialism is the fulfilment of service, the aim of Individualism is the attainment of some personal advantage, riches, or place, or fame. Socialism seeks such an organisation of life as shall secure for every one the most complete development of his powers; Individualism seeks primarily the satisfaction of the particular wants of each one in the hope that the pursuit of private interest will in the end secure public welfare.

If men were perfect, with desires and powers harmoniously balanced, both lines of action would lead to the same end. As it is, however, experience shows that limitations must be placed upon the self-assertion of the single man. The growing sense of dependence as life becomes more and more complex necessarily increases the feeling of personal obligation which constrains us each to look to the circumstances of others. At the same time in the intercourse of a fuller life we learn that our character is impoverished in proportion as we are isolated, and we learn also that evil or wrong in one part of society makes itself felt throughout the whole.

But if we admit the central idea of Socialism, that the goal of human endeavour is the common well-being of all alike, sought through conditions which provide for the fullest culture of each man, as opposed to the special development of a race, or a class, by the sacrifice of others in slavery or serfdom or necessary subjection, it does not follow that the end can be reached only in one way. The powers of men are different, and equal development does not involve equality. Experience will direct and confirm reform, for life is manifold. But a common end will hallow individuality for more effective service. The single man will not be sacrificed to the society. He will be enabled to bring to it the offering of his disciplined powers and so to realise his freedom.

Socialism, as I have defined it, is not, I repeat, committed to any one line of action, but every one who accepts its central thought will recognise certain objects for immediate effort. He will seek to secure that labour shall be acknowledged in its proper dignity as the test of manhood, and that its reward shall be measured, not by the necessities of the indigent, but by its actual value as contributing to the wealth of the community. He will strive to place masses of men who have no reserve of means in a position of stability and to quicken them by generous ideas. He will be bold to proclaim that the evils of luxury and penury cannot be met by palliatives. He will claim that all should confess in action that every power, every endowment, every possession, is not of private use, but a trust to be administered in the name of the Father for their fellow-men.

Such a view of the social destiny of the individual, with all he has, is brought home to us at the present time by the conception which we have gained of the evolution, or rather of the providential ordering of life. There have been, from very early times, dreams of ideal states fashioned by great thinkers who felt how far the world in which they lived fell short of the society for which man was made. They looked within for the laws of their imaginary commonwealths. We have at length a surer guide for our hopes in the records of the past. Studying the course which history has taken, we can forecast the future, for the broad outline of human discipline is clear. In the Old World the ruling thought was the dignity of a race or of a class, to which all beside, in a greater or less degree, were made to minister. In the New World, ushered in by the Advent, the ruling thought has been the dignity of man as man, of men as men, and however imperfectly the great truth revealed in the Incarnation has been grasped and embodied, still it has in some sense been brought home to the West little by little through many lessons.

At first in the middle ages the society was dominant, ordered in a hierarchy of classes: then at the Reformation the individual claimed independence, and the voice of authority was followed by the voice of reason. Now, when the complexity of life baffles purely rational analysis, theoretical freedom has been found to degenerate into anarchy; and we catch sight of a fuller harmony in which the offices of the society and of the citizen, of tradition and conscience, shall be reconciled. Functions which were once combined have been sharply separated as a step towards a more complete union. For here also the law of a higher life has been fulfilled, and the parts of the body have been differentiated, so that their dependence one upon another may be seen in its beneficent operation. In order to deal rightly with these new conditions we must fix our attention on facts and not on words. The permanence of technical terms often tends to mislead. The modern conceptions of capital and trade, for example, or rather isolated facts which foreshadowed them, usury and buying to sell again, were repugnant to mediaeval religious feeling; but now that the range of production and distribution has been indefinitely extended we have to face problems which mediaeval experience could not anticipate and cannot help us to solve. Even in the last century, capitalist, producer, and consumer were not unfrequently united. If each of these three classes has now been sharply distinguished and hitherto kept apart by conflicting material interests, it is, if we may trust the teachings of the past, that they may in due time be brought together again in a full, free, and chosen fellowship. The relations which exist between them at present are modern and transitional. Wage-labour, though it appears to be an inevitable step in the evolution of society, is as little fitted to represent finally or adequately the connection of man with man in the production of wealth as at earlier times slavery or serfdom.

Our position then is one of expectancy and preparation, but we can see the direction of the social movement. We wait for the next stage in the growth of the State when in full and generous co-operation each citizen shall offer the fulness of his own life that he may rejoice in the fulness of the life of the body.

Such an issue may appear to be visionary. It is, I believe, far nearer than we suppose. It is at least the natural outcome of what has gone before. Society has been organised effectively without regard to the individual. The individual has been developed in his independence. It remains to show how the richest variety of individual differences can be made to fulfil the noblest ideal of the State, when fellow-labourers seek in the whole the revelation of the true meaning of their separate offerings. And nothing has impressed me more during my years of work than the rapidity and power with which the thoughts of dependence and solidarity and brotherhood, of our debt to the past and our responsibility for the future, have spread among our countrymen.

Men have grown familiar with the principle of combination for limited objects. Such unions are a discipline for a larger fellowship. There is, indeed, enough to sadden us in the selfishness which too often degrades rich and poor alike, but self-respect has grown widely among those who are poor in material wealth. The consciousness of a high calling has quick-ened to self-denial and a noble activity many who are oppressed with the burden of great possessions. There is on all sides an increasingly glad recognition of duties answering to opportuni-ties; and if education has created or deepened the desire for reasonable leisure, it has opened springs of enjoyment which riches cannot make more healthy or more satisfying.

At the same time our public wealth is quickly accumulating. Buildings, galleries, gardens, bring home to every Englishman that he has an inheritance in the grandeur of his country; and the English family still guards in honour the fundamental types of human communion and fatherhood and brotherhood, which are a sufficient foundation for a kingdom of God. All things, indeed, once more are ready, and a clear call is given to us to prove our faith.

Here, then, lies the duty of the Christian teacher. The thoughts of a true Socialism – the thoughts that men are 'one man' in Christ, sons of God and brethren, suffering and rejoicing together, that each touches all and all touch each with an inevitable influence, that as we live by others we can find no rest till we live for others, are fundamental thoughts of the Law and the Prophets, of the Gospels and the Epistles which he is empowered and bound to make effective under the conditions of modern life.

The result is that reflection and experience have at length made them intelligible. To interpret and embody them in a practical form is the office of believers now. They must show that Christianity, which has dealt hitherto with the individual, deals also with the State, with classes, with social conditions, and not only with personal character. In the endeavour to fulfil this duty the past will help them by analogy, but not by example. New questions cannot be settled by tradition. There is an order in the accomplishment of the Divine counsel. Even great evils are not met and conquered at once.

Discerning our own work, we shall not condemn or blame our fathers that they did not anticipate it. They did more or less perfectly the work that was prepared for them to do. We are required not to repeat their service, but, enriched and strengthened by what they have won, to bring the doctrine of the Incarnation to bear upon the dealings of man with man and of nation with nation. As we strive to do this we shall come to understand the force of the loftiest truths of theology. We shall find that that which is transcendental is, indeed, practical as a motive, and an inspiration. We alone, I do not scruple to affirm it, we alone, who believe that 'The Word became flesh' can keep hope fresh in the face of the sorrows of the world, for we alone know that evil is intrusive and remediable; we alone know that the victory over the world has been won, and that we have to gather with patience the fruits of the victory. Violence can destroy, but it cannot construct. Love destroys the evil when it replaces the evil by the good.

But while we affirm the absolute supremacy of the spiritual and the universal sovereignty of Christ reigning from the Cross, we remember that our work must be done under the conditions of earth, and that it is here on the sordid field of selfish conflicts that we must prepare the kingdom of God. At the same time we recognise that the social problem of to-day, the relations of capital and labour, belongs especially to Englishmen, who by their national character have ruled the development of modern industry. As Englishmen have set the problem, so on Englishmen lies the responsibility of solving it. And the position of the English clergy gives them peculiar opportunities for moderating with wise faith discussions which will open the way for the solution. The clergy of the National Church are not a close and isolated caste: they are drawn from every class: they are trained in sympathy with every variety of thought and culture: they are in habitual contact with all forms of experience: they are lifted above the influence of party by the greatness of their work: they are enabled to labour for a distant end by the greatness of the Faith which they proclaim.

I ask then – I ask myself not without sorrowful perplexity – whether we have, in view of the teaching of present facts, considered what God's counsel for men in creation and redemption is? Whether the state of things in our towns and in our villages either answers or tends to answer the Divine idea? Whether the present distribution of wealth is not perilous alike to those who have and to those who want? Whether we have not accepted the laws of the material order as the laws of nature? Whether we have pondered over the moral significance of the poor, and whether we have reflected on the wider application of that principle which it is the glory of medicine to have guarded, that every discovery affecting men's well-being is the property of the race, and not of the finder?

I do not enter now on any questions of detail. I desire simply to direct attention to questions which go to the very heart of the Gospel; and I beg the younger clergy, with whatever strength of persuasion I can command, to think over these things; to discuss them with one another reverently and patiently; to seek to understand and not to silence their adversaries; to win for themselves the truth which gives to error what permanence it has; to remember that bold and sweeping statements come more commonly from doubt or ignorance than from just conviction. But I beg them not to improvise hasty judgements. The personal value of an opinion depends for the most part upon the pains which have been spent in forming it. Zeal, enthusiasm, devotion are not enough to guide us in the perplexity of conduct; we need above all things knowledge as the basis of action. We have not yet mastered the elements of the problems of society. Theories have been formed from the examination of groups of isolated phenomena; but life is complex. We must, indeed, see our end before we begin our work; but it may be that different ways will be found to lead to it, and as far as I can judge the social question of our day will finally receive not one answer, but many. But in one respect all the answers will agree; all will be religious.

Meanwhile, our office as Christian teachers is to proclaim the ideal of the Gospel and to form opinion. And if we do this, if we confess that our mission is to hasten a kingdom of God on earth, and if we ourselves move resolutely forward as the Spirit guides us, I believe that we shall find through the common offices of our daily intercourse that peace which springs out of the consciousness of common sacrifice made for one end, and that assurance of strength which comes through new victories of faith.

We cannot doubt that God is calling us in this age, through the characteristic teachings of science and of history, to seek a new social application of the Gospel. We cannot doubt, therefore, that it is through our obedience to the call that we shall realise its Divine power. The proof of Christianity which is prepared by God, as I believe, for our times, is a Christian society filled with one spirit in two forms – righteousness and love.

Source: Brooke Foss Westcott, *Socialism* (The Guild of St Matthew, London, 1890).

William Temple
1881-1944

Introduction

Temple was born into 'the purple' in 1881, his father being Bishop of Exeter, and later Archbishop of Canterbury. Educated accordingly at Rugby and Oxford, he began there a lifelong friendship with R. H. Tawney. Ordained in 1908, Temple progressed from headmaster of Repton School, rector of a London church, organizer of the Life and Liberty movement, canon of Westminster Abbey, to Bishop of Manchester in 1921. It was there that his pastoral skills and talent for leadership began to make a national impact. His subsequent moves to Archbishop of York (1929) and then Canterbury (1942) built on these foundations. Complementing his ecclesiastical career was a variety of involvements in social affairs. They ranged from President of the Workers' Educational Association (1908) and attempted mediation in the General Strike (1926), to a close relationship with Beveridge and the emergence of the Welfare State. By the time of Temple's premature death in 1944, he had become a national and international spokesman for the Christian and social conscience. This position was confirmed by his long involvement in, and leadership of, the ecumenical movement in Britain and the wider world (including the conferences at Birmingham (1924), Jerusalem (1928), Edinburgh and Oxford (1937), and the negotiations to set up the World Council of Churches). All these achievements were supported by his skills as theologian, philosopher, and communicator, and by the powerful impact of his spirituality.

It was out of his commanding presence in so many fields that Temple's great genius emerged for convincing people and society to take seriously the Christian faith, to recognize that it had so much to say to the world. Rooted in the tradition of Anglican incarnational theology and idealist philosophy, he was committed to the ultimate significance of the historical process, to a sacramental view of the world uniting spiritual and material in a divine reality. The influence of such beliefs inclined him to identify the latest secular movements with Christian ideals. However, the turbulent interwar period, and some contact with neoorthodoxy and theological realism, meant that he began to take more account of sin, power and justice by the end of the 1930s. Yet this was overridden by his continued recognition of the significance of natural morality.

Text 4 summarizes, very concisely, these social views and experiences. Published in 1942, it was written out of the depths of the war, and the early British hopes for the reconstruction of society on the achievement of peace. Like the Beveridge Report on the Welfare State (also in 1942), it became an instant bestseller, capturing the British mood for a fundamental change based on moral principles. Later regarded as one of the pillars of the Welfare State, it still stands as one of the most formative and classic tracts for the times produced by social Christianity.

Temple's skill was to show how such social change was required and illuminated by Christian belief. In the first part of the text, he argues that the Church's claim to interfere in society is not a new phenomenon, but is based on the Bible, the Fathers, medieval theology, the Reformation, and the re-emergence of social Christianity in the mid-nineteenth century. It is a reminder of the constant need to justify Christian social involvement to Church and society. In the second part, he shows *how* the Church can be involved in society, by developing Christian guidelines or principles derived from great Christian doctrines. It is the vocation of individual Christians to translate them into particular political and economic programmes. It is not the Church's responsibility. Technical skills and practical judgements are needed for this task, and on these, Christians, like anyone else, can and will differ. However, to illustrate how Christian principles could be developed into policy options, he elaborates his personal views in the appendix as 'A Suggested Programme'. Sadly, fifty years after the publication of *Christianity and Social Order*, its principles still stand in judgement on contemporary poverty and unemployment. They still urge the reconstruction of society.

————

Text 4: Why and How the Church Should Interfere in the Social Order

What right has the Church to interfere?

The claim of the Christian Church to make its voice heard in matters of politics and economics is very widely resented, even by those who are Christian in personal belief and in devotional practice. [. . .] When a group of Bishops attempted to bring Government, Coal-Owners and Miners together in a solution of the disastrous Coal Strike of 1926, Mr. Baldwin, then Prime Minister, asked how the Bishops would like it if he referred to the Iron and Steel Federation the revision of the Athanasian Creed; and this was acclaimed as a legitimate score.

Few people read much history. In an age when it is tacitly assumed that the Church is concerned with another world than this, and in this with nothing but individual conduct as bearing on prospects in that other world, hardly any one reads the history of the Church in its exercise of political influence. It is assumed that the Church exercises little influence and ought to exercise none; it is further assumed that this assumption is self-evident and has always been made by reasonable men. As a matter of fact it is entirely modern and extremely questionable. [. . .]

[. . .] history shows that the claim of the Church today to be heard in relation to political and economic problems is no new usurpation, but a re-assertion of a right once universally admitted and widely regarded. But it also shows that this right may be compromised by injudicious exercise, especially when the 'autonomy of technique' in the various departments of life is ignored. Religion [. . .] may declare the proper relation of the economic to other activities of men, but it cannot claim to know what will be the purely economic effect of particular proposals. It is, however, entitled to say that some economic gains ought not to be sought because of the injuries involved to interests higher than economic; and this principle of the subordination of the whole economic sphere is not yet generally accepted. We all recognize that in fact the exploitation of the poor, especially of workhouse children, in the early days of power-factories was an abomination not to be excused by any economic advantage thereby secured; but we fail to recognize that such an admission in a particular instance carries with it the principle that economics are properly subject to a non-economic criterion.

The approach to the problem in our own time is to be made along four distinct lines: (1) the claims of sympathy for those who suffer; (2) the educational influence of the social and economic system; (3) the challenge offered to our existing system in the name of justice; (4) the duty of conformity to the 'Natural Order' in which is to be found the purpose of God.

(1) The suffering caused by existing evils makes a claim upon our sympathy which the Christian heart and conscience cannot ignore. Before the outbreak of war there were three main causes of widespread suffering – bad housing, malnutrition, and unemployment. The varied forms of suffering which bad housing causes are easy to imagine in part, but few who have had no personal knowledge of it are able to imagine the whole – the crushing of a woman's pride in her home through ceaseless and vain struggle against dirt and squalor; the nervous fret; the lack of home comforts for the tired worker; the absence of any space for children to play. The bad conditions in slum quarters are not chiefly due to the people living there. When they are moved to new housing estates, more than half of them rise fully to the fresh opportunity, and three-quarters of them make a reasonable use of it. The toleration of bad housing is a wanton and callous cruelty.

Malnutrition is a direct result of poverty and ignorance. It produces enfeebled bodies, embittered minds and irritable spirits: thus it tells against good citizenship and good fellowship. Children are the most obvious sufferers, but those who have suffered in this way as children seldom come later to full strength or to physical and spiritual stability. It was found, when attempts were made to organise physical training classes for the unemployed, that most of these could not take advantage of the training offered; it made them too hungry.

Unemployment is the most hideous of our social evils, and has lately seemed to have become established in a peculiarly vicious form. We have long been acquainted with transitional, seasonal and cyclical unemployment – in which catalogue the adjectives represent a *crescendo* of evil; but now we have also to face long-term unemployment. [...]

The main points to notice are these:

(a) The worst evil of such unemployment, whether due to cyclical or to more permanent conditions, is its creating in the unemployed a sense that they have fallen out of the common life. However much their physical needs may be supplied (and before the war this supply was in many cases inadequate) the gravest part of the trouble remains; they are not wanted! That is the thing that has power to corrupt the soul of any man not already far advanced in saintliness. Because the man has no opportunity of service, he is turned upon himself and becomes, according to his temperament, a contented loafer or an embittered self-seeker. It has not been sufficiently appreciated that this moral isolation is the heaviest burden and most corrosive poison associated with unemployment: not bodily hunger but social futility. Consequently it is no remedy to pay the unemployed man as much as the employed; unless he has intellectual interests with which to occupy his leisure and is able to turn these into a means of service by study resulting in books or lectures, this will only make him content with idleness; and we have enough people suffering from that form of deadly sin (technically called Sloth) at the other end of the social scale. Nothing will touch the real need except to enable the man to do something which is needed by the community. For it is part of the principle of personality that we should live for one another.

(b) Much depends on the history and experience of the particular individuals concerned. A recent enquiry disclosed the disquieting fact that in a town where long-term unemployment was rife, the older men, who had formerly had experience of full employment, preferred to get back to work even at a wage less than their unemployment benefit, while the younger, who had never had regular employment, preferred to be idle 'on the dole' even if they could earn a larger weekly sum. This does not mean that they were happy in idleness; most of them were conscious of futility and frustration (though they would not use those words about it), and they were bitter against a world which had no use for them and made no room for them; but they had a strong distaste for the drudgery of regular work. They were degraded into a condition of universal dissatisfaction.

The only real cure for unemployment is employment – beginning from the time when school-education is complete and continuing, with no longer intervals than can be appreciated as holidays, till strength begins to fail. In other words we are challenged to find a social order which provides employment, steadily and generally, and our consciences should be restive till we succeed. Christian sympathy demands this.

(2) What has been said about unemployment has already carried us on to the second ground for the Church's concern in social questions - the educational influence of the social and economic system in which men live. [. . .] The social order at once expresses the sense of values active in the minds of citizens and tends to reproduce the same sense of values in each new generation. [. . .]

It is recognized on all hands that the economic system is an educative influence, for good or ill, of immense potency. Marshall, the prince of orthodox economists of the last generation, ranks it with the religion of a country as the most formative influence in the moulding of a people's character. If, so, then assuredly the Church must be concerned with it. For a primary concern of the Church is to develop in men a Christian character. When it finds by its side an educative influence so powerful it is bound to ask whether that influence is one tending to develop Christian character, and if the answer is partly or wholly negative the Church must do its utmost to secure a change in the economic system so that it may find in that system an ally and not an enemy. How far this is the situation in our country today we shall consider later. At present it is enough to say that the Church cannot, without betraying its own trust, omit criticism of the economic order, or fail to urge such action as may be prompted by that criticism.

(3) The existing system is challenged on moral grounds. It is not merely that some who 'have not' are jealous of some who 'have'. The charge against our social system is one of injustice. The banner so familiar in earlier unemployed or socialist processions – 'Damn your charity; we want justice' – vividly exposes the

situation as it was seen by its critics. If the present order is taken for granted or assumed to be sacrosanct, charity from the more or less fortunate would seem virtuous and commendable; to those for whom the order itself is suspect or worse, such charity is blood-money. Why should some be in the position to dispense and others to need that kind of charity?

An infidel could ignore that challenge, for apart from faith in God there is really nothing to be said for the notion of human equality. Men do not seem to be equal in any respect, if we judge by available evidence. But if all are children of one Father, then all are equal heirs of a status in comparison with which the apparent differences of quality and capacity are unimportant; in the deepest and most important of all – their relationship to God – all are equal. Why should some of God's children have full opportunity to develop their capacities in freely-chosen occupations, while others are confined to a stunted form of existence, enslaved to types of labour which represent no personal choice but the sole opportunity offered? The Christian cannot ignore a challenge in the name of justice. He must either refuse it or, accepting it, devote himself to removal of the stigma. The moral quality of the accusation brought against the economic and social order involves the Church in 'interference' on pain of betraying the trust committed to it.

(4) For the commission given to the Church is that it carry out the purpose of God. This is what is meant by the description of it as 'the Body of Christ'. It is to be the instrument or organ of His will, as His fleshly Body was in the days of His earthly ministry. That Body has many functions to fulfil, and one of them is suffering. The members of the Church do not, or should not, belong to it for what they can get in this world or in any other world; they – we – should belong to it in order to take our share in the great work, the fulfilment of God's purpose in the world and beyond it.

We know in outline what that is. God could make, and did make, multitudes of things which always obey His law for them – suns and planets, molecules and atoms, all that is studied in the 'natural sciences'. But He also made men and women, with hearts and wills that cannot be coerced but can respond freely, in order that they might be a fellowship of love answering the love with which He made them. But they used their freedom for self-seeking; so He came Himself to share our life and our death, in order that He might show that love which prompted the activity of creation in a form intelligible to men and women, the form of a human life. Thereby He gathered together a fellowship of those who respond to that appeal, to be at once the nucleus of the universal fellowship of love and the chief means to its establishment. [. . .]

If we belong to the Church with such a purpose and hope as this, we are obliged to ask concerning every field of human activity what is the purpose of God for it. If we find this purpose it will be the true and proper nature of that activity, and the relation of the various activities to one another in the divine purpose will be the 'Natural Order' of those activities. To bring them into that Order, if they have in fact departed from it, must be one part of the task of the Church as the Body of Christ. If what has true value as a means to an end beyond itself is in fact being sought as an end in itself, the Church must rebuke this dislocation of the structure of life and if possible point out the way of recovery. It is bound to 'interfere' because it is by vocation the agent of God's purpose, outside the scope of which no human interest or activity can fall.

How should the Church interfere?
Christian social principles

The method of the Church's impact upon society at large should be twofold. The Church must announce Christian principles and point out where the existing social order at any time is in conflict with them. It must then pass on to Christian citizens, acting in their civic capacity, the task of re-shaping the existing order in closer conformity to the principles. For at this point technical knowledge may be required and judgements of practical expediency are always required. If a bridge is to be built, the Church may remind the engineer that it is his obligation to provide a really safe bridge; but it is not entitled to tell him whether, in fact, his design meets this requirement; a particular theologian may also be a competent engineer, and, if he is, his judgement on this point is entitled to attention; but this is altogether because he is a competent engineer and his theological equipment has nothing whatever to do with it. In just the same way the Church may tell the politician what ends the social order should promote; but it must leave to the politician the devising of the precise means to those ends.

This is a point of first-rate importance, and is frequently misunderstood. If Christianity is true at all it is a truth of universal application; all things should be done in the Christian spirit and in accordance with Christian principles. 'Then', say some, 'produce your Christian solution of unemployment.' But there neither is nor could be such a thing. Christian faith does not by itself enable its adherent to foresee how a vast multitude of people, each one partly selfish and partly generous, and an intricate economic mechanism, will in fact be affected by a particular economic or political innovation – 'social credit', for example. 'In that case,' says the reformer – or, quite equally, the upholder of the status quo – 'keep off the turf. By your own confession you are out of place here.' But this time the Church must say 'No; I cannot tell you what is the remedy; but I can tell you that a society of which unemployment (in peace time) is a chronic feature is a diseased society, and that if you are not doing all you can to find and administer the remedy, you are guilty before God.' Sometimes the Church can go further than this and point to features in the social structure itself which are bound to be sources of social evil because they contradict the principles of the Gospel.

So the Church is likely to be attacked from both sides if it does its duty. It will be told that it has become 'political' when in fact it has been careful only to state principles and point to breaches of them; and it will be told by advocates of particular policies that it is futile because it does not support these. If it is faithful to its commission it will ignore both sets of complaints, and continue so far as it can to influence all citizens and permeate all parties. [. . .]

[*Temple then discusses two kinds of principles.*]

A: Primary principles

The primary principle of Christian Ethics and Christian Politics must be respect for every person simply as a person. If each man and woman is a child of God, whom God loves and for whom Christ died, then there is in each a worth absolutely independent of all usefulness to society. The person is primary, not the society; the State exists for the citizen, not the citizen for the State. [. . .]

[*From this primary principle, others are derived.*]

B: Derivative principles

1. Freedom The first aim of social progress must be to give the fullest possible scope for the exercise of all powers and qualities which are distinctly personal; and of these the most fundamental is deliberate choice.

Consequently society must be so arranged as to give to every citizen the maximum opportunity for making deliberate choices and the best possible training for the use of that opportunity. In other words, one of our first considerations will be the widest possible extension of personal responsibility; it is the responsible exercise of deliberate choice which most fully expresses personality and best deserves the great name of freedom.

Freedom is the goal of politics. To establish and secure true freedom is the primary object of all right political action. For it is in and through his freedom that a man makes fully real his personality – the quality of one made in the image of God.

Freedom is a great word, and like other great words is often superficially understood. It has been said that to those who have enough of this world's goods the claim to freedom means 'Leave us alone', while to those who have not enough it means 'Give us a chance'. This important difference of interpretation rests on a single understanding of freedom as absence of compulsion or restraint. But if that is all the word means, freedom and futility are likely to be so frequently combined as to seem inseparable. For nothing is so futile as the unhampered satisfaction of sporadic impulses; that is the sort of existence which leads through boredom to suicide. Freedom so far as it is a treasure must be freedom *for* something as well as freedom *from* something. It must be the actual ability to form and carry out a purpose. This implies discipline – at first external discipline to check the wayward impulses before there is a real purpose in life to control them, and afterwards a self-discipline directed to the fulfilment of the purpose of life when formed. Freedom, in short, is self-control, self-determination, self-direction. To train citizens in the capacity for freedom and to give them scope for free action is the supreme end of all true politics.

But man is a self-centred creature. He can be trusted to abuse his freedom. Even so far as he wins self-control, he will control himself in his own interest; not entirely; he is not merely bad; but he is not altogether good, and any fraction of self-centredness will involve the consequence that his purpose conflicts to some extent with that of his neighbour. So there must be the restraint of law, as long as men have any selfishness left in them. Law exists to preserve and extend real freedom. First, it exists to prevent the selfishness of A from destroying the freedom of B. If I am left untouched when I knock my neighbours on the head, their freedom to go about their duties and their pleasures may be greatly diminished. But the law which restrains any occasional homicidal impulse that I may have, by threatening penalties sufficiently disagreeable to make the indulgence of it seem to be not good enough, also protects my purpose of good fellowship against being violated by that same impulse. In such a case the restraint of the law increases the true freedom of all concerned. [. . .]

2. Social Fellowship No man is fitted for an isolated life; every one has needs which he cannot supply for himself; but he needs not only what his neighbours contribute to the equipment of his life but their actual selves as the complement of his own. Man is naturally and incurably social.

Recent political theories have given ostensible emphasis to this truth and have then, as a rule, gone far to ignore it. Certainly our social organization largely ignores it. For this social nature of man is fundamental to his being. [. . .] By our mutual influence we actually constitute one another as what we are. This mutual influence finds its first field of activity in the family; it finds other fields later in school, college, Trade Union, professional association, city, county, nation, Church.

Now actual liberty is the freedom which men enjoy in these various social units. But most political theories confine attention to the individual and the State as organ of the national community; they tend to ignore the intermediate groupings. But that makes any understanding of actual liberty impossible; for it exists for the most part in and through those intermediate groups – the family, the Church or congregation, the guild, the Trade Union, the school, the university, the Mutual Improvement Society. (Only in the nineteenth century could English people devise such a title as the last or consent to belong to a society so named; but the thing which that name quite accurately describes is very common and very beneficial.)

It is the common failing of revolutionary politics to ignore or attempt to destroy these lesser associations. They are nearly always the product of historical growth and do not quite fit any theoretical pattern. So the revolutionary, who is of necessity a theorist, is impatient of them. It was largely for this reason that the great French Revolution, which took as its watchword Liberty, Equality and Fraternity, degenerated into a struggle between Liberty and Equality wherein Fraternity was smothered and Liberty was judicially murdered. For the isolated citizen cannot effectively be free over against the State except at the cost of anarchy. [. . .]

In any case the Christian conception of men as members in the family of God forbids the notion that Freedom may be used for self-interest. It is justified only when it expressed itself through fellowship; and a free society must be so organized as to make this effectual; in other words it must be rich in sectional groupings or fellowships within the harmony of the whole.

It is impossible to lay excessive emphasis on this point. Pope Leo XIII gave great prominence to it in the Encyclical *Rerum Novarum*; its prominence there was pointed out with strong approval by Pope Pius XI in *Quadragesimo Anno*; and the profound importance of it has lately been pointed out again by the distinguished French thinker, Jacques Maritain. In his recent book, *Scholasticism and Politics*, he draws a valuable distinction between Personality and Individuality; of course every person is an individual, but his individuality is what marks him off from others; it is a principle of division; whereas personality is social, and only in his social relationships can a man be a person. Indeed, for the completeness of personality, there is needed the relationship to both God and neighbours. The richer his personal relationships, the more fully personal he will be.

This point has great political importance; for these relationships exist in the whole network of communities, associations and fellowships. It is in these that the real wealth of human life consists. If then it is the function of the State to promote human well-being, it must foster these many groupings of its citizens. [. . .]

A democracy which is to be Christian must be a democracy of persons, not only of individuals. It must not only tolerate but encourage minor communities as at once the expression and the arena of personal freedom; and its structure must be such as to serve this end. That is the partial justification of Fascism which has made its triumphs possible. It sins far more deeply against true freedom than it supports it; yet in the materialist and mechanical quality of the democratic movement from Rousseau to Karl Marx and his communist disciples, it had real justification for reacting against them.

It is impossible to say how much we owe in our own country to the schooling in democratic habits provided, first by the old Trade Guilds, then, when the fellowship of trade had been broken up by the release of individualist acquisitiveness, by the Trade Unions, and ever since the seventeenth century by the dissenting congregations. Many of our most effective Labour leaders learned their art of public speech as local preachers; and the self-government of the local Chapel has been a fruitful school of democratic procedure. Our 'Left Wing' has by no means always maintained this close association of democratic principle with conscientious worship of God! But the historical root is there. And the British tradition of freedom has probably more of the element which consists of the claim to obey God rather than men and less of the element of mere self-assertiveness than has the democratic tradition in most other countries. The element of self-assertiveness is morally bad and politically disastrous; a freedom based upon it is only an opportunity for selfishness and will decline through anarchy to disruption of the State; the claim to obey God rather than men is a source both of moral strength, for it inspires devotion to duty, and of political stability, for such freedom may only be used in the service of the whole fellowship.

3. Service The combination of Freedom and Fellowship as principles of social life issues in the obligation of Service. No one doubts this in so far as it concerns the individual. Whatever our practice may be, we all give lip-service to this principle.

Its application to the individual is pretty clear. It affects him in two main ways – as regards work and leisure. In England we have depended a great deal on voluntary service given in leisure hours. We want a great deal more of it; and we have a right to expect more than we get from the Christian Churches. Yet it is certain that a very large proportion of the day-to-day drudgery of social service is done by Christian men and women in the inspiration of their Christian faith. We want more of them; but the greater part of what is done at all is done by Christian folk.

What is less often recognized in practice is the obligation to make of the occupation, by which a man or woman earns a living, a sphere of service. This may be done in two ways. Some young people have the opportunity to choose the kind of work by which they will earn their living. To make that choice on selfish grounds is probably the greatest single sin that any young person can commit, for it is the deliberate withdrawal from allegiance to God of the greatest part of time and strength. This does not mean that no attention is to be paid to inclinations. Inclination is often a true guide to vocation; for we like doing what we can do well, and we shall give our best service by giving scope to our own aptitudes and talents. But a young man who is led by his inclination to take up teaching or business or whatever it may be, must none the less make his choice because in that field he can give his own best service. This will enormously affect the spirit in which he does his work and his dealings with the other people engaged in it or with whom it brings him into contact. Let no one say that this has no application to modern business; there are many men engaged in business to-day, and leaders of industry on the largest scale, who entered on their work in this spirit of service and have maintained that spirit in the conduct of their business.

But there are many for whom there seems to be little choice; life offers one opening and no more; or they have to take what the Labour Exchange can suggest. For them it is harder to find in daily work a true vocation; but it is not impossible. Circumstances as well as inclination may be the channel through which God's call comes to a man. And His call is sometimes to self-sacrifice as well as to self-fulfilment. (No doubt self-sacrifice is in the end the truest self-fulfilment, as Christianity alone of religions or ethical systems teaches. And this explains how it may happen that the God of love calls men to self-sacrifice.) It is possible to accept the one job available, however distasteful and dreary, as God's call to me; and then I shall enter on it in the spirit of service.

Of course, this does not justify an order of society which offers to many men only such forms of livelihood as require a miracle of grace to appear as forms of true vocation. But we must recognize that the source of my vocation is in God and not in me. It is His call to me. And when it is said that we need to create or restore a sense of vocation in relation to all the activities of men, it does not mean chiefly that every individual should be able to find there his self-expression or self-fulfilment otherwise than by self-sacrifice. But it does mean, first that he should do his work, interesting or dreary, 'as unto the Lord', and secondly that the alternatives presented be such as shall not make this insuperably difficult apart from a true miracle of grace.

It is not only individuals who must, if Christianity is the truth, guide their policy or career by the principle of service; all groupings of men must do the same. The rule here should be that we use our wider loyalties to check the narrower. A man is a member of his family, of his nation, and of mankind. It is very seldom that anyone can render a service directly to mankind as a whole. We serve mankind by serving those parts of it with which we are closely connected. And our narrower loyalties are likely to be more intense than the wider, and therefore call out more devotion and more strenuous effort. But we can and should check these keener, narrower loyalties by recognizing the prior claim of the wider. So a man rightly does his best for the welfare of his own family, but must never serve his family in ways that injure the nation. A man rightly does his best for his country, but must never serve his country in ways that injure mankind.

Of course, this apparent collision of claims will not arise so far as he accepts in its completeness the Christian standard of values; for in that scale of values service itself, even at cost of real sacrifice, is highest. But no man can in fact apply this exacting code, and it is of the utmost importance that we recognize this inability and the reasons for it.

A man cannot regulate his service of his family and of his country by the Christian scale of values in its purity, first because he does not effectively accept it for himself, and secondly because his family and country do not accept it. [. . .]

We see then why a man cannot without more ado take as his

guide for the treatment of his fellows the Christian standard that service to the point of self-sacrifice is our truest welfare. Let him live by that as far as he can; and let him invite others to join him in that enterprise; but let him not force that standard on his fellows, and least of all on those dependent on him. They will always have the opportunity to act on it if they are so minded.

The general rule in such matters must be very general indeed, and gives little help beyond an indication of the direction in which we must move. A man must chiefly serve his own most immediate community, accepting as the standard of its welfare that which its members are ready to accept (though trying, it may be, to lead them nearer to a fully Christian view), but always checking this narrower service by the wider claims, so that in serving the smaller community he never injures the larger.

But as a member of each small group – with a voice in determining its conduct and policy – e.g. as a Christian Trade Unionist or Managing Director, or as the Governor of a School – he will do all he can to secure that his own group accepts for itself the principle of service and sets its course in the way that will benefit not only its own members in their own self-interest, but also the larger community in which this group is a part.

Freedom, Fellowship, Service – these are the three principles of a Christian social order, derived from the still more fundamental Christian postulates that Man is a child of God and is destined for a life of eternal fellowship with Him.

The task before us
So far we have been occupied with general considerations, trying to ascertain what are the principles that should guide us in handling the social and economic problems of our time. Those problems were urgent enough before the war; the war has vastly increased their urgency. When it is over, the interest on the National Debt will be a heavy burden and a serious drain on our resources, and there will be the need to reconstruct the devastated areas of many towns with all the adjustment of rights, vested interests and social welfare which any planning must involve. The structure of life as we knew it before the war has already been profoundly modified. How far do we want to restore it if we can? In which respects is it desirable that it should be changed in its inner principle? [. . .]

Let us test this by some of the principles by which the Christian tradition would lead us to direct human life.

(1) *The Family as the Primary Social Unit* – If this principle is admitted some results immediately follow. A community committed to this principle would see that there were houses available for all citizens, within their means, in which a family could be brought up in health and happiness, in the unity of family life and in the decency and dignity proper to human beings who are the children of God. But the supply of houses, as of other commodities, was until very lately left to private enterprise, and the *entrepreneur* carried out his functions not with a primary regard to the needs of the people but with a view to the profit which he could make. He is not to be blamed for this; there is nothing wrong about profits as such, and the private builder or firm cannot carry on at all unless there results a profit to supply a livelihood. But the result has been horrible overcrowding and all the horror of slums. It is not the builders who are to blame; it is the public. We ought to have felt a responsibility in the matter, and most of us felt none. Now at any rate we must secure a public opinion which we lay it upon Government as a primary obligation to see that the housing necessary to healthy family life is available for all citizens. Great strides were taken before the war broke out; but the goal is not yet reached.

Family life involves some leisure which the members of the family may spend together. In these days hours of work are seldom excessive, unless the occupation is so monotonous that for this reason the period spent in it should be reduced. But it seldom appears as though the unity of the family were one of the considerations kept in mind in the planning of a 'shift' system; it cannot be claimed that in this matter it should be decisive, but it ought not to be forgotten as it would seem very often to be in industry to-day.

There must be some periods of greater and fuller opportunity for united family enjoyment than leisure on working-days can give, or even that Sunday which can be so precious in the life of any family. Holidays have a great part of their meaning and value in the fact that they give this fuller opportunity; but it will be less than it should be if there is anxiety about the money. Either wages should be high enough to enable a man to put by what he will need for full and free enjoyment with his wife and children during the holiday, or payment must be continued throughout. The latter is the right principle, for a holiday ought not to be regarded as a time away from industry but as a time of recuperation for better service, so that industry itself is interested to promote it; holidays with pay should be a universally accepted principle.

Real extravagance is always wrong. But to splash about a little on holiday is thoroughly right. It is not only permissible; it is a duty.

But even though payment is continued through holidays, it must be sufficient at other times to ensure the possibility of a good upbringing for the children. Here there is a real difficulty. The care of his children is a man's natural responsibility. Yet it is difficult to say that every man, even though unmarried, should be paid at a rate needed by another man who has six children. The economic case for Family Allowances seems unanswerable. Of course they must be paid by the State, not by the industry – for if the industry has to meet this charge it will tend to employ unmarried or childless men.

At present there is urgent need to attend to this matter, for many children are under-nourished. But that theme connects with our next principle as well as with the family.

(2) *The Sanctity of Personality* – Our established order of life recognizes the sanctity of Personality in many ways. We have freedom of thought and speech in England, at least in the sense of absence of legal restrictions upon them, such as has seldom been achieved in any nation. We have freedom within the law and equality before the law – except so far as the cost of litigation may interfere with this equality. But in one great department of life the principle receives scanty recognition. When the new industry began, about a century and a half ago, the pioneers showed little respect for the personality of those who earned their living by working in factories and mills. They were often called 'hands'; and a hand is by nature a 'living tool', which is the classical definition of a slave. The worst horrors of the early factories have been abolished, but the wage earners are not yet fully recognized as persons. For the supreme mark of a person is that he orders his life by his own deliberate choice; and the 'workers' usually have no voice in the control of the industry whose requirements determine so large a part of their lives. How such a voice is to be

found for them, and when, are questions for the expert to answer; but industry will not be free from the charge of neglecting this principle until in some form labour shares at least equally with capital in the control of industry.

But our regard for this principle must carry us further back than this. The foundation of personal life is the body and its powers. Respect for the sacredness of Personality in all citizens will lead us to demand that no child shall be condemned to grow to maturity with faculties stunted by malnutrition or by lack of opportunities for full development. We have made great progress in these matters, but there is need for very much more. Sir John Orr declared a few years ago that 'the diet of nearly one half of the population is deficient for health'. And if children suffer from malnutrition, so do adolescents from lack of appropriate outdoor exercise for the development of their physique. The loss from these two causes is not only physical; an under-nourished and under-developed body is likely to house an irritable, querulous and defensive soul. We have begun to attend to these two matters; but we had long neglected them, and now our attention to them is no more than languid. [. . .]

(3) *The Principle of Fellowship* – Our discussion of the former principle has already led us up to fellowship, which is at once an inherent need of human nature and the means through which the best things possible to men are realized. [. . .]

How far does the ordering of social life as we know it express and inculcate this principle of Fellowship?

To a great extent it does. As compared with some other countries or with our own at other times, we find in the British people a magnificent unity. In many parts of the countryside, especially where the old families have kept their estates and live among the people, there is often a genuine social fellowship and a real personal equality on the basis of an accepted differentiation of function. For example, I treasure the memory of the elderly farmer on the Garrowby estate who, meeting Lord Halifax for the first time after he had become Foreign Secretary, patted him on the arm and said: 'Ye've made a good start; keep it oop.' And in the industrial world, especially in family firms, there is sometimes a real and admirable fellowship of employer and employed. I remember, for example, the Works Committee of an engineering firm in Manchester at which an operative said: 'Well, if there's no particular business today, Mr. Chairman, I've got a question to ask: "What about this 'ere Predestination?"' To which the Chairman replied: 'I should like notice of that question, and I'll ask the Bishop' – which explains how I came into it.

Yet allowing for all this, the breaches in our fellowship are pretty serious. Our snobbery as a nation is, I suppose, without parallel; it is worst in suburbia; but it is bad in most parts of society and at every level; and our educational methods tend to intensify it. In the world of industry as a whole, despite admirable exceptions, the division between Labour, Management and Capital is very wide and deep. At this point, however, we should take note of a new factor in the situation which is full of hope. 'Management' is fast becoming a profession, with its own standards and its own objectives. Its primary interest is not dividends for the shareholders, but efficiency of service. Profits are for it not so much a source of income – for Managers receive a fixed salary which is part of the cost of production – but an index of efficiency. The sympathy of Managers is usually with Labour, though the terms of their appointment tend to class them with Capital. Some adjustment at this point might have very great results.

The existing system has many triumphs to its credit; it has raised the standard of life for the common people to a level never reached before. The life of the 'working people' is for the most part neither impoverished, nor over-burdensome, nor lacking in interest. But it suffers from one great lack, from one common evil, and from one terrible menace. The great lack is the absence of any voice in the control or direction of the concern to which most of the waking hours of the day are given. Till this can be remedied there will be one most important respect in which the working class is shut out from a vitally important expression of personality. Men have fought and died for a voice in making the laws which they are to obey; that is the essence of political liberty. But the government of the firm for which he works affects a man's life more closely than the Government of his State; yet in it he has no part except so far as he may threaten to hold up the process by withdrawing his labour and that of his fellow-workers in a strike. In many businesses nowadays the workers are often consulted, especially about regulations affecting hours and conditions of work. So far, so good; but this is done as a favour and not as a matter of secured right. The cause of freedom will not be established till political freedom is fulfilled in economic freedom.

Moreover, until this is done, the breach in the fellowship – of which the class-war is the ultimate expression – must remain. It is important to remember that the class-war was not first proclaimed as a crusade by Marx and Engels; it was first announced as a fact by Adam Smith. Nothing can securely end it except the acquisition by Labour of a share in the control of industry. Capital gets its dividends: Labour gets its wages; there is no reason why Capital should also get control and Labour have no share in it, except that hitherto Capital had education and Labour had not; but that defect in the equipment of Labour is well on the way to being remedied.

A great evil afflicting many in modern industry is that the work required of them is so monotonous and engages so few human faculties that it is hard for a man to find in it any real vocation. It is true that there is often some misunderstanding here. People sometimes speak as if finding a vocation in one's work were the same thing as finding in it self-expression or self-fulfilment: but God's calling or vocation for us may very well be to self-sacrifice; and for a perfect saint it might be possible to perform the most wearisome and monotonous task 'as unto God' because it was his contribution to human welfare. But to ask any ordinary man so to regard monotonous drudgery occupying the whole of a working day is sheer mockery. He cannot so regard it; and if so, the conditions of his work are making it impossible for him to worship in any full sense. For worship is the offer of our whole being and life – therefore very prominently our work – to God; and no one but an already perfect saint could sincerely offer that sort of work to God.

When Moses observed the conditions in which Israelites were working in Egypt he did not say: 'Your surroundings are drab and your work dreary; you shall have a specially beautiful Church to lift your thoughts above these mundane cares to heaven'; he said: 'We can't worship God here; we must get away from it.'

The worst evil afflicting the working-class in England is insecurity; they live under the terrible menace of unemployment. And in our own time a new and horrible evil has appeared – long-term unemployment on a considerable scale. Unemployment is a corrosive poison. It saps both physical and moral strength. The worst effect of it, especially now that the community takes some care of its unemployed members, is not the physical want, but the moral disaster of not being wanted. This brings most misery to the mature man who has been in regular work for many years and relies on it as the framework of his life; but it does most harm to the young man who never forms habits of regular work at all.

Now it is no part of the duty of a Christian as such to draw plans of a reformed society. But it is part of his duty to know and proclaim Christian principles, to denounce as evil what contravenes them, and to insist that these evils should be remedied. Further, it is his duty to judge how far particular evils are symptoms of a disease deeper than themselves, and if that seems to be so to ask how far the whole existing order is contrary to the Natural Order.

It seems clear that such evils as we have mentioned cannot be due to mere lack of goodwill. For there is an abundance of goodwill. Some deeper cause must be sought. So we are led to ask how far it is true that our existing order corresponds to the Natural Order. How far, for example, is it true that the primary concern of those who control production is so to direct it that all engaged in it find in their activity a truly human life, and that the needs of the public are met? How often are these questions discussed at Boards of Directors? Is it not evident that the primary concern is for profits out of which dividends may be paid to shareholders? Of course there must be profits; without them the industry must close down, workers fall into unemployment and shareholders lose their capital. Also, of course, it is only through supplying the needs of consumers that the producers can make those necessary profits. But the consumer ought not to come in only or chiefly as a means to the interest of the producer; his interest ought to be paramount. For in the Natural Order consumption is the end of production.

As I write it is frequently reported that so soon as the price of a commodity is fixed by the Ministry of Food, it disappears from the market. Why?

To many it appears evident that we have allowed the making of profits, which is necessary as a means to the continuance of the industry, to get into the first place which properly belongs to the supply of human needs – the true end of industry. We have inverted the 'natural order'. Instead of finance existing to facilitate production and production existing to supply needs, the supply of needs is made the means to profitable production; and production itself is controlled as much as it is facilitated by finance.

If that is true, it is the duty of Christians to become aware of it and to demand a remedy. It cannot be said that it is their duty as Christians to know what the remedy is, for this involves many technical matters. But they are entitled to call upon the Government to set before itself the following objectives and pursue them as steadily and rapidly as opportunity permits:

1. Every child should find itself a member of a family housed with decency and dignity, so that it may grow up as a member of that basic community in a happy fellowship unspoilt by under-feeding or overcrowding, by dirty and drab surroundings or by mechanical monotony of environment.

2. Every child should have the opportunity of an education till years of maturity, so planned as to allow for his peculiar aptitudes and make possible their full development. This education should throughout be inspired by faith in God and find its focus in worship.

3. Every citizen should be secure in possession of such income as will enable him to maintain a home and bring up children in such conditions as are described in paragraph 1 above.

4. Every citizen should have a voice in the conduct of the business or industry which is carried on by means of his labour, and the satisfaction of knowing that his labour is directed to the well-being of the community.

5. Every citizen should have sufficient daily leisure, with two days of rest in seven, and, if an employee, an annual holiday with pay, to enable him to enjoy a full personal life with such interests and activities as his tasks and talents may direct.

6. Every citizen should have assured liberty in the forms of freedom of worship, of speech, of assembly, and of association for special purposes.

As a background to these six points we need to insist on the principle laid down by the four religious leaders in their Foundations of Peace (*The Times*, December 21st, 1940): 'The resources of the earth should be used as God's gifts to the whole human race, and used with due consideration for the needs of the present and future generations.'

Utopian? Only in the sense that we cannot have it all tomorrow. But we can set ourselves steadily to advance towards that six-fold objective. It can all be summed up in a phrase: *the aim of a Christian social order is the fullest possible development of individual personality in the widest and deepest possible fellowship.*

This book is about Christianity and the Social order, not about Evangelism. But I should give a false impression of my own convictions if I did not here add that there is no hope of establishing a more Christian social order except through the labour and sacrifice of those in whom the Spirit of Christ is active, and that the first necessity for progress is more and better Christians taking full responsibility as citizens for the political, social and economic system under which they and their fellows live.

Appendix: a suggested programme

Temple believed that 'every Christian ought to endorse what I have said so far', although some would argue over the details. He then developed his policies for implementing his 'six-fold aim'. It was only fair 'to ask the proclaimer of principles if he has any proposals for bringing life into conformity to them'. Others would have quite different suggestions, because economic and political means were the responsibility not of the Church but of individual Christians and citizens. Their task was to embody Christian principles in *a* Christian social programme. Such *a* programme could never be imposed on other Christians, nor could it 'be substituted for the truths of the Gospel as the mark of the real Christian'.

Source: William Temple, *Christianity and Social Order* (Penguin Books 1942). The text is taken from the 1976 edition, SPCK and Shepheard-Walwyn, pp. 29–98.

c h a p t e r   f o u r

R. H. Tawney
1880–1962

Introduction

Born into the family of a senior civil servant in India, Tawney's education followed the same path as his friend, William Temple – Rugby and Oxford. Moving to one of the great university settlements in the East End of London, Toynbee Hall, he was soon immersed in some of the key social issues of his times, including education, the labour movement, and poverty. As one of the first tutor organizers of the Workers' Education Association, he always professed that he was educated by the workers in his classes, rather than at Rugby and Oxford. Serving as a sergeant in the First World War, Tawney was badly wounded at the Somme in 1916. He resumed his career as a lecturer, and then professor, of economic history at the London School of Economics (1921–49). It was there that he established an international reputation in the economic history of Britain in the sixteenth and seventeenth centuries. One of his greatest books, *Religion and the Rise of Capitalism* (1926), reflected this concern.

Yet reviewers rightly recognized that Tawney's purpose was much wider than the historical; it was aimed at respiritualizing society. His contributions therefore spread beyond studying the early relationship between capitalism and Calvinism. They included education, as President of the Workers' Education Association (1928–43) and member of important government committees on education; the labour movement, as a principal adviser to, and philosopher of, the Labour Party and trade unions; and the Churches, as an influential contributor to official church thinking on social affairs through the Fifth

R. H. Tawney

Committee (1918), and conferences at Birmingham (1924), Jerusalem (1928), and Oxford (1937). He was married to Jeannette, the sister of William Beveridge. Although Tawney died in 1962, he has continued to influence the moral concerns of the labour movement.

Linking all these involvements was an unequivocally moral view of life. As a young undergraduate, Tawney was provoked by the Master of Balliol's question as to why there was so much poverty amidst so much wealth, and then devoted the rest of his long life to pursuing the answer. It soon meant advocating a radical challenge to the existing capitalist order, and developing a socialist alternative. Involving, as they did, politics, economics and education, he realized that what was called for was a total way of life. It was essentially a religious matter, because, influenced by Charles Gore and the tradition of social Christianity, he recognized Christianity as, first and foremost, a way of life. Theological reflection was always subordinate to this end. The primary task was to reject the heresy of capitalism and to reconstruct a socialist society on basic Christian principles. He therefore stood firmly in the tradition of radical Christian socialism.

Text 5, the final chapter from *The Acquisitive Society* (1921), is one of the great tracts for the times. Its insights are those of a bridge-building type. For it stands between the church reports, *Christianity and Industrial Problems* (1919) and COPEC's *Industry and Property* (1924), both of which closely follow its views, and reflect Tawney's formative influence on official church statements. Its original title as a Fabian pamphlet, *The Sickness of an Acquisitive Society*, particularly captures the mood of the twofold argument. In the first stage, Tawney recognizes that the problems of industrial conflict and poor productivity were essentially symptoms of an underlying malaise, the fundamental moral disorder of industrial capitalism. By promoting the acquisition of wealth and property as the end of society, unhindered by moral or other restraints, capitalism had produced the fetish-worship of industrialism. The task therefore was to replace the acquisitive with a functional society in which social purpose would determine function according to agreed moral principles.

In the second stage of his argument, Tawney elaborates the

113

religious character of his social philosophy, making explicit the beliefs that were normally quite implicit. For if the way to industrial and social health was to encourage a community of wills capable of common ends, then that was a profoundly moral and religious task. It was a proper role for the Christian Church. Yet it was equally clear that the contemporary Church was incapable of performing such a function, and needed to be reformed. For, on the one hand, the last two centuries had seen the disappearance of a Christian social ethics able to stand in judgement on social affairs. On the other hand, the Church had ceased to exercise any social discipline on its members with regard to their economic activities. Both problems called for the reformulation of Christian principles to guide the conduct of industry and of Christians. The first has continued to influence Christian thought, ignoring the contribution of the Christian political economists, and resulting in imbalanced judgements on modern economics. The second has had less influence on the official Churches, but continues as the radical Christian support for a more sectarian view of the Church (the smaller but purer stance).

Text 5: Moreover, One Thing Is Necessary: The Christian Rejection of the Acquisitive Society

So the organization of society on the basis of functions, instead of on that of rights, implies three things. It means, first, that proprietary rights shall be maintained when they are accompanied by the performance of service and abolished when they are not. It means, second, that the producers shall stand in a direct relation to the community for whom production is carried on, so that their responsibility to it may be obvious and unmistakable, not lost, as at present, through their immediate subordination to shareholders whose interest is not service but gain. It means, in the third place, that the obligation for the maintenance of the service shall rest upon the professional organizations of those who perform it, and that, subject to the supervision and criticism of the consumer, those organizations shall exercise so much voice in the government of industry as may be needed to secure that the obligation is discharged.

It is obvious, indeed, that no change of system or machinery can avert those causes of social *malaise* which consist in the egotism, greed, or quarrelsomeness of human nature. What it can do is to create an environment in which those are not the qualities which are encouraged. It cannot secure that men live up to their principles. What it can do is to establish their social order upon principles to which, if they please, they can live up and not live down. It cannot control their actions. It can offer them an end on which to fix their minds. And, as their minds are, so in the long run and with exceptions, their practical activity will be.

The first condition of the right organization of industry is, then, the intellectual conversion which, in their distrust of principles, Englishmen are disposed to place last or to omit altogether. It is that emphasis should be transferred from the opportunities which it offers, to the social functions which it performs; that those concerned should be clear as to its end and should judge it by reference to that end, not by incidental consequences which are foreign to it, however brilliant or alluring those consequences may be. What gives its meaning to any activity which is not purely automatic is its purpose. It is because the purpose of industry, which is the conquest of nature for the service of man, is neither adequately expressed in its organization nor present to the minds of those engaged in it, because it is not regarded as a function but as an opportunity for personal gain or advancement or display, that the economic life of modern societies is in a perpetual state of morbid irritation. If the conditions which produce that unnatural tension are to be removed, it can only be effected by the growth of a habit of mind which will approach questions of economic organization from the standpoint of the purpose which it exists to serve, and which will apply to it something of the spirit expressed by Bacon when he said that the work of men ought to be carried on 'for the glory of God and the relief of men's estate'.

Sentimental idealism? But consider the alternative. The alternative is war; and continuous war must, sooner or later, mean something like the destruction of civilization. The havoc which the assertion of the right to unlimited economic expansion has made of the world of States needs no emphasis. Those who have lived from 1914 to 1921 will not ask why mankind has not progressed more swiftly; they will be inclined to wonder that it has progressed at all. For every century or oftener it has torn itself to pieces, usually, since 1648, because it supposed prosperity was to be achieved by the destruction of an economic rival; and, as these words are written, the victors in the war for freedom, in defiance of their engagements and amid general applause from the classes who will suffer most from the heroics of their rulers, are continuing the process of ruining themselves in order to enjoy the satisfaction of more completely ruining the vanquished. The test of the objects of a war is the peace which follows it. Millions of human beings endured for four years the extremes of misery for ends which they believed to be but little tainted with the meaner kinds of self-interest. But the historian of the future will consider, not what they thought, but what their statesmen did. He will read the Treaty of Versailles; and he will be merciful if, in its provisions with regard to coal and shipping and enemy property and colonies and indemnities, he does not find written large the *Macht-Politik* of the Acquisitive Society, the natural, if undesired, consequence of which is war.

There are, however, various degrees both of war and of peace, and it is an illusion to suppose that domestic tranquillity is either the necessary, or the probable, alternative, to military collisions abroad. What is more probable, unless mankind succeeds in basing its social organization upon some moral principles which command general acceptance, is an embittered struggle of classes, interests, and groups. The principle upon which our society professed to be based for nearly a hundred years after 1789 – the principle of free competition – has clearly spent its force. In the last few years Great Britain – not to mention America and Germany – has plunged, as far as certain great industries are concerned, into an era of something like monopoly with the same light-hearted recklessness as a century ago it flung itself into an era of individualism. No one who reads the Reports of the Committee on Trusts appointed by the Ministry of Reconstruction and of the Committees set up under the Profiteering Act upon soap, or sewing cotton, or oil, or half-a-dozen other products, can retain the illusion that the consumer is protected by the rivalry of competing producers. The choice before him, to an increasing extent, is not between competition and monopoly, but between a monopoly which is irresponsible and private and a monopoly which is responsible and public. No one who observes how industrial agreements between workers and employers are actually reached can fail to see that they are settled by a trial of strength between two compactly organized armies, who are restrained from collision only by fear of its possible consequences. Fear is a powerful, but a capricious, motive, and it will not always restrain them. When prudence is overborne by rashness, or when the hope of gain outweighs the apprehension of loss, there will be a collision. No man can say where it will end. No man can even say with confidence that it will produce a more tolerable social order. It is idle to urge that any alternative is preferable to government by the greedy materialists who rule mankind at present, for greed and materialism are not the monopoly of a class. If those who have the will to make a better society have not at present the power, it is conceivable that when they have the power, they too, like their predecessors, may not have the will.

So, in the long run, it is the principles which men accept as the basis of their good organization which matter. And the principle which we have tried to put forward is that industry and property and economic activity should be treated as functions, and should be tested, at every point, by their relation to a social purpose. Viewed from that angle, issues which are insoluble when treated on the basis of rights may be found more susceptible of reasonable treatment. For a purpose is, in the first place, a principle of limitation. It determines the end for which, and therefore the limits within which, an activity is to be carried on. It divides what is worth doing from what is not, and settles the scale upon which what is worth doing ought to be done. It is, in the second place, a principle of unity, because it supplies a common end to which efforts can be directed, and submits interests, which would otherwise conflict, to the judgement of an over-ruling object. It is, in the third place, a principle of apportionment or distribution. It assigns to the different parties of groups engaged in a common undertaking the place which they are to occupy in carrying it out. Thus it establishes order, not upon chance or power, but upon a principle, and bases remuneration not upon what men can with good fortune snatch for themselves, nor upon what, if unlucky, they can be induced to accept, but upon what is appropriate to their function, no more and no less, so that those who perform no function receive no payment, and those who contribute to the common end receive honourable payment for honourable service.

Such a political philosophy implies that society is not an economic mechanism, but a community of wills which are often discordant, but which are capable of being inspired by devotion to common ends. It is, therefore, a religious one, and, if it is true, the proper bodies to propagate it are the Christian Churches. During the last two centuries Europe, and particularly industrial Europe, has seen the development of a society in which what is called personal religion continues to be taught as the rule of individual conduct, but in which the very conception of religion as the inspiration and standard of social life and corporate effort has been forgotten. The phenomenon is a curious one. To suggest that an individual is not a Christian may be libellous. To preach in public that Christianity is absurd is legally blasphemy. To state that the social ethics of the New Testament are obligatory upon men in the business affairs which occupy nine-tenths of their thought, or on the industrial organization which gives our society its character, is to preach revolution. To suggest that they apply to the relations of States may be held to be sedition. Such a creed does not find it difficult to obey the injunction: 'Render unto Caesar the things that are Caesar's and unto God the things that are God's.' To their first hearers the words must have come with a note of gentle irony, for to the reader of the New Testament the things which are Caesar's appear to be singularly few. The modern world is not seriously inconvenienced by rendering to God the things which are God's. They are not numerous, nor are they of the kind which it misses.

The phenomenon is not the less singular because its historical explanation is comparatively easy. When the Church of England was turned into the moral police of the State, it lost the independence which might have enabled it to maintain the peculiar and distinctive Christian standard of social conduct – a standard which must always appear paradoxical and extravagant to the mass of mankind and especially to the powerful and rich, and which only an effort of mind and will perpetually renewed, perpetually sustained and emphasized by the support of a corporate society, can preserve in the face of their natural scepticism. Deprived of its own vitality, it had allowed its officers to become by the eighteenth century the servile clients of a half-pagan aristocracy, to whose contemptuous indulgence they looked for preferment. It ceased to speak its mind and as a natural consequence, it ceased to have a mind to speak. As an organization for common worship it survived. As an organ of collective thought and of a common will it became negligible.

Had the Nonconformist societies taken up the testimony which the Church of England had dropped, the Christian tradition of social ethics might have continued to find an organ of expression. Among individual Puritans, as the teaching of Baxter, or the life of Woolman, shows, it did, indeed, survive. But the very circumstances of their origin disposed the Nonconformist Churches to lay only a light emphasis on the social aspects of Christianity. They had grown up as the revolt of the spirit against an overgrown formalism, an artificial and insincere unity. They drew their support largely from the earnest and sober piety of the trading and commercial classes. Individualist in their faith, they were individualist in their interpretation of social morality. Insisting that the essence of religion was the contact of the individual soul with its Maker, they regarded the social order and its consequences, not as the instrument through which grace is mediated, or as steps in the painful progress by which the soul climbs to a fuller vision, but as something external, alien, and irrelevant – something, at best, indifferent to personal salvation, and, at worst, the sphere of the letter which killeth and of the reliance on works which ensnares the spirit into the slumber of death.

In a society thus long obtuse to one whole aspect of the Christian Faith, it was natural that the restraints imposed on social conduct by mere tradition, personal kindliness, the inertia of use and wont should snap like green withies before the intoxicating revelation of riches which burst on the early nineteenth century. It was the more natural because the creed which rushed into the vacuum was itself a kind of religion, a persuasive, self-confident, and militant Gospel proclaiming the absolute value of economic success. The personal piety of the

Nonconformist could stem that creed as little as the stiff conservatism of the Churchman. Indeed, with a few individual exceptions, they did not try to stem it, for they had lost the spiritual independence needed to appraise its true moral significance. So they accepted without misgiving the sharp separation of the sphere of Christianity from that of economic expediency, which was its main assumption, and affirmed that religion was a thing of the spirit, which was degraded if it were externalized.

'In the days when Oliver, master of the Schools at Cologne, preached the Crusade against the Saracens,' a certain rich miller, who was also a usurer, heard, as he lay in bed, an unwonted rumbling in his mill. He opened the door, and saw two coal-black horses, and by their side an ill-favoured man as black as they. It was the devil. The fiend forced him to mount, and rode with him to hell, where, amid the torments of others who had been unscrupulous in the pursuit of gain, he saw 'a burning fiery chair, wherein could be no rest, but torture and interminable pain,' and was told, 'Now shalt thou return to thy house and thou shalt have thy reward in this chair.' The miller died unconfessed, and the priest who, in return for a bribe, buried him in consecrated ground, was suspended from his office.

The fancies of an age which saw in economic motives the most insidious temptation to the disregard of moral principles may serve to emphasize, by the extravagance of the contrast, the perils of one in which the economic motive is regarded as needing no higher credential. The idea that conduct which is commercially successful may be morally wicked is as unfamiliar to the modern world as the idea that a type of social organization which is economically efficient may be inconsistent with principles of right. A dock company which employs several thousand casual labourers for three days a week, or an employers' association, which uses its powerful organization to oppose an extension of education, in order that its members may continue to secure cheap child labour, or a trade union which sacrifices the public to its own professional interests, or a retail firm which pays wages incompatible with a self-respecting life, may be regarded as incompetent in its organization or as deficient in the finer shades of public spirit. But neither they, nor the community which may profit by their conduct, are regarded as guilty of sin, even by those whom professional exigencies have compelled to retain that unfashionable word in their vocabulary.

The abdication by the Christian Churches of one whole department of life, that of social and political conduct, as the sphere of the powers of this world and of them alone, is one of the capital revolutions through which the human spirit has passed. The medieval church, with all its extravagances and abuses, had asserted the whole compass of human interests to be the province of religion. The disposition to idealise it in the interests of some contemporary ecclesiastical or social propaganda is properly regarded with suspicion. But, though the practice of its officers was often odious, it cannot be denied that the essence of its moral teaching had been the attempts to uphold a rule of right, by which all aspects of human conduct were to be judged, and which was not merely to be preached as an ideal, but to be enforced as a practical obligation upon members of the Christian community. It had claimed, however grossly the claim might be degraded by political intrigues and ambitions, to judge the actions of rulers by a standard superior to political expediency. It had tried to impart some moral significance to the ferocity of the warrior by enlisting him in the service of God. It had even sought, with a self-confidence which was noble, if perhaps over-sanguine, to bring the contracts of business and the transactions of economic life within the scope of a body of Christian casuistry.

The Churches of the nineteenth century had no strong assurance of the reality of any spiritual order invisible to the eye of sense, which was to be upheld, however much it might be derided, however violent the contrast which it offered to the social order created by men. Individuals among their officers and members spoke and acted as men who had; but they were rarely followed, and sometimes repudiated. Possessing no absolute standards of their own, the Churches were at the mercy of those who did possess them. They relieved the wounded, and comforted the dying, but they dared not enter the battle. For men will fight only for a cause in which they believe, and what the Churches lacked was not personal virtue, or public spirit, or practical wisdom, but something more simple and more indispensable, something which the Children of Light are supposed to impart to the children of this world, but which they could not impart, because they did not possess it – faith in their own creed and in their vocation to make it prevail. So they tended to make religion the ornament of leisure, instead of the banner of a Crusade. They became too often the home of a 'fugitive and cloistered virtue, unexercised and unbreathed, that never sallies out and seeks her adversary, but slinks out of the race, where that immortal garland is to be run for, not without dust and heat.' They acquiesced, in short, in the popular assumption that the acquisition of riches was the main end of man, and confined themselves to preaching such personal virtues as did not conflict with its achievement.

The world has now sufficient experience to judge the truth of the doctrine – the Gospel according to the Churches of Laodicea – which affirms that the power of religion in the individual soul is nicely proportioned to its powerlessness in society. Whether the life of the spirit is made easier for the individual by surrendering his social environment to a ruthless economic egotism is a question which each man must answer for himself. In the sphere of social morality the effect of that philosophy is not dubious. The rejection of the social ethics of Christianity was only gradually felt, because they were the school in which individuals continued to be educated long after other standards had taken their place as the criteria for judging institutions, policy, the conduct of business, the organization of industry and public affairs. Its fruits, though they matured slowly, are now being gathered. In our own day the horrors which sixty years ago were thought to be exorcized by the advance of civilization have one by one rolled back, the rule of the sword and of the assassin hired by governments, as in Ireland, a hardly-veiled slavery, as in East Africa, a contempt for international law by the great Powers which would have filled an earlier generation with amazement, and in England the prostitution of humanity and personal honour and the decencies of public life to the pursuit of money.

These things have occurred before, in ages which were nominally Christian. What is distinctive of our own is less its occasional relapses or aberrations, than its assumption that the habitual conduct and organization of society is a matter to which religion is merely irrelevant. That attempt to conduct human affairs in the light of no end other than the temporary appetites of individuals has as its natural consequences oppression, the unreasoning and morbid pursuit of pecuniary gain of which the proper name is the sin of avarice, and civil war. In so far as Christianity is taken seriously, it destroys alike the arbitrary power of the few and the slavery of many, since it maintains a standard by which both are condemned – a standard which men did not create and which is independent of their convenience or desires. By affirming that all men are the children of God, it insists that the rights of all men are equal. By affirming that men are men and nothing more, it is a warning that those rights are conditional and derivative – a commission of service, not a property. To such a faith nothing is common or unclean, and in a Christian society social institutions, economic activity, industrial organization cease to be either indifferent or merely means for the satisfaction of human appetites. They are judged, not merely by their convenience, but by standards of right and wrong. They become stages in the progress of mankind to perfection, and derive a certain sacramental significance from the spiritual end to which, if only as a kind of squalid scaffolding, they are ultimately related.

Hence the opinion, so frequently expressed, that the religion of a society makes no practical difference to the conduct of its affairs is not only contrary to experience, but of its very nature superficial. The creed of indifferentism, detached from the social order which is the greatest and most massive expression of the scale of values that is the working faith of a society, may make no difference, except to damn more completely those who profess it. But then, so tepid and self-regarding a creed is not a religion. Christianity cannot allow its sphere to be determined by the convenience of politicians or by the conventional ethics of the world of business. The whole world of human interests was assigned to it as its province. 'The law of divinity is to lead the lowest through the intermediate to the highest things.' In discharging its commission, therefore, a Christian Church will constantly enter the departments of politics and of economic relations, because it is only a bad modern convention which allows men to forget that these things, as much as personal conduct, are the sphere of the spirit and the expression of character. It will insist that membership in it involves obedience to a certain rule of life and the renunciation of the prizes offered by economic mastery.

A rule of life, a discipline, a standard and habit of conduct in the social relations which make up the texture of life for the mass of mankind – the establishment of these among its own members, and their maintenance by the corporate conscience of the Christian society, is among the most vital tasks of any Church which takes its religion seriously. It is idle for it to expound the Christian Faith to those who do not accept it, unless at the same time it is the guardian of the way of life involved in that Faith among those who nominally do. Either a Church is a society, or it is nothing. But, if a society is to exist, it must possess a corporate mind and will. And if the Church, which is a Christian Society, is to exist, its mind and will must be set upon that type of conduct which is specifically Christian. Hence the acceptance by its members of a rule of life is involved in the very essence of the Church. They will normally fail, of course, to live up to it. But when it ceases altogether to attract them, when they think it, not the truest wisdom, but impracticable folly, when they believe that the acceptance of Christianity is compatible with any rule of life whatsoever or with no rule of life at all, they have ceased, in so far as their own choice can affect the matter to be members of the 'Church militant here on earth'. When all its members – were that conceivable – have made such a choice, that Church has ceased to exist.

The demand that a Church should possess and exercise powers of moral discipline is not, therefore, the expression of that absurd, if innocent, pose, a romantic and undiscriminating Medievalism. Such powers are a necessary element in the life of a Church, because they are a necessary element in the life of any society whatsoever. It is arguable that a Church ought not to exist; it is not arguable that, when it exists, it should lack the powers which are indispensable to any genuine vitality. It ought to be the greatest of societies, since it is concerned with the greatest and most enduring interests of mankind. But, if it has not the authority to discipline its own members, which is possessed by the humblest secular association, from an athletic club to a trade union, it is not a society at all. The recovery and exercise of that authority is thus among the most important of the practical reforms in its own organization at which a Church, if it does not already possess it, can aim, since, without it, it cannot, properly speaking, be said fully to exist.

If a Church reasserts and applies its moral authority, if it insists that, while no man is compelled to belong to it, membership involves duties as well as privileges, if it informs its members that they have assumed obligations which preclude them from practising certain common kinds of economic conduct and from aiming at certain types of success which are ordinarily esteemed, two consequences are likely to follow. It can hardly, in the first place, continue to be established. It will probably, in the second place, lose the nominal support of a considerable number of those who regard themselves as its adherents. Such a decline in membership will, however, be a blessing, not a misfortune. The tradition of universal allegiance which the Church – to speak without distinction of denominations – has inherited from an age in which the word 'Christendom' had some meaning, is a source, not of strength, but of weakness. It is a weakness, because, in the circumstances of the twentieth century, it is fundamentally, if unconsciously, insincere. The position of the Church to-day is not that of the Middle Ages. It resembles more nearly that of the Church in the Roman Empire before the conversion of Constantine. Christians are a sect, and a small sect, in a Pagan Society. But they can be a sincere sect. If they are sincere, they will not abuse the Pagans, as sometimes in the past they were inclined to do; for a good Pagan is an admirable person. But he is not a Christian, for his hopes and fears, his preferences and dislikes, his standards of success and failure, are different from those of Christians. The Church will not pretend that he is, or endeavour to make its own Faith acceptable to him by diluting the distinctive ethical attributes of Christianity till they become inoffensive, at the cost of becoming trivial.

'He hath put down the mighty from their seat, and hath exalted the humble and meek.' A society which is fortunate enough to possess so revolutionary a basis, a society whose Founder was executed as the enemy of law and order, need not seek to soften the materialism of principalities and powers with mild doses of piety administered in an apologetic whisper. It will teach as one having authority, and will have sufficient confidence in its Faith

to believe that it requires neither artificial protection nor judicious under-statement in order that such truth as there is in it may prevail. It will appeal to mankind, not because its standards are identical with those of the world, but because they are profoundly different. It will win its converts, not because membership involves no change in their manner of life, but because it involves a change so complete as to be ineffaceable. It will expect its adherents to face economic ruin for the sake of their principles with the same alacrity as, not so long ago, it was faced by the workman who sought to establish trade unionism among his fellows. It will define, with the aid of those of its members who are engaged in different trades and occupations, the lines of conduct and organization which approach most nearly to being the practical application of Christian ethics in the various branches of economic life, and, having defined them, will censure those of its members who depart from them without good reason. It will rebuke the open and notorious sin of the man who oppresses his fellows for the sake of gain as freely as that of the drunkard or adulterer. It will voice frankly the judgement of the Christian conscience on the acts of the State, even when to do so is an offence to nine-tenths of its fellow-citizens. Like Missionary Churches in Africa to-day, it will have as its aim, not merely to convert the individual, but to make a new kind, and a Christian kind of civilization.

Such a religion is likely to be highly inconvenient to all parties and persons who desire to dwell at ease in Zion. But it will not, at any rate, be a matter of indifference. The marks of its influence will not be comfort, but revolt and persecution. It will bring not peace, but a sword. Yet its end is peace. It is to harmonize the discords of human society, by relating its activities to the spiritual purpose from which they derive their significance.

> *Brother, the virtue of our heavenly love,*
> *tempers our will and makes us want no more*
> *than what we have – we thirst for this alone.*
>
> *If we desired to be higher up,*
> *then our desires would not be in accord*
> *with His will Who assigns us to this sphere.*

R. H. Tawney

*Indeed, the essence of this blessed state
is to dwell here within His holy will,
so that there is no will but one with His;*

*Then it was clear to me that every where
of Heaven is Paradise, though there the light
of Grace Supreme does not shine equally.*

[*Penguin Classics translation of Dante's* Divine Comedy; *Tawney
used the original Italian version.*]

The famous lines in which Piccarda explains to Dante the order
of Paradise are a description of a complex and multiform society
which is united by overmastering devotion to a common end. By
that end all stations are assigned and all activities are valued.
The parts derive their quality from their place in the system,
and are so permeated by the unity which they express that they
themselves are glad to be forgotten, as the ribs of an arch carry
the eye from the floor from which they spring to the vault in
which they meet and interlace.

Such a combination of unity and diversity is possible only to a
society which subordinates its activities to the principle of
purpose. For what that principle offers is not merely a standard
for determining the relations of different classes and groups of
producers, but a scale of moral values. Above all, it assigns to
economic activity itself its proper place as the servant, not the
master, of society. The burden of our civilization is not merely,
as many suppose, that the product of industry is ill-distributed,
or its conduct tyrannical, or its operation interrupted by embittered disagreements. It is that industry itself has come to hold a
position of exclusive predominance among human interests,
which no single interest, and least of all the provision of the
material means of existence, is fit to occupy. Like a hypochon-
driac who is so absorbed in the processes of his own digestion
that he goes to his grave before he has begun to live, industrialized communities neglect the very objects for which it is worth
while to acquire riches in their feverish preoccupation with the
means by which riches can be acquired.

That obsession by economic issues is as local and transitory as
it is repulsive and disturbing. To future generations it will

127

appear as pitiable as the obsession of the seventeenth century by religious quarrels appears to-day; indeed, it is less rational, since the object with which it is concerned is less important. And it is a poison which inflames every wound and turns every trivial scratch into a malignant ulcer. Society will not solve the particular problems of industry which afflict it until that poison is expelled, and it has learned to see industry itself in the right perspective. If it is to do that, it must rearrange its scale of values. It must regard economic interests as one element in life, not as the whole of life. It must persuade its members to renounce the opportunity of gains which accrue without any corresponding service, because the struggle for them keeps the whole community in a fever. It must so organize its industry that the instrumental character of economic activity is emphasized by its subordination to the social purpose for which it is carried on.

Source: R. H. Tawney, *The Acquisitive Society* (Bell 1921), Chapter 6: 'Porro Unum Necessarium . . .'

chapter five

Ronald H. Preston
1913–

Introduction

Preston's education and early work experience equipped him to become the leading British Christian social ethicist. His interpretation of advanced modern societies arose out of this ability to bring together secular analysis and Christian beliefs. After studying economics at the London School of Economics, where he came under Tawney's influence, he linked this skill with Christian thought in an organized way through his work for the Student Christian Movement (SCM), initially as Industrial Secretary, and later as Study Secretary (1935–8, 1943–8). In between the two, he studied theology at Oxford, and was ordained in the Church of England, serving a curacy in Sheffield. His work for the SCM brought him into close contact with such leading exponents of social Christianity and theological realism as William Temple, Joe Oldham, Reinhold Niebuhr, John Bennett, and Paul Abrecht.

From 1949 onwards, Preston's ability to produce discerning judgements on complex contemporary affairs was developed through his academic career. As lecturer in Christian ethics at Manchester University (1949–70), he was also Canon Theologian at Manchester Cathedral (1957–71) before he became Professor of Social and Pastoral Theology (1970–80). Preston's writings have focused on the key contemporary subjects of industrial conflict, economics and politics, and social policy, all complemented by his work on theological method. Ordination in the Church of England, and work for the SCM, illustrate the formative influence of the Church on his theology. His deep loyalty to it has acted as a constant source of nourishment, and a vehicle for his judgements and method. His most important ecumenical contribution was to the World Council of Churches' Conference at Geneva in 1966; he has also exercised a formative influence on Church of England statements on social affairs.

Preston stands firmly in the developing tradition of social Christianity, as both recipient and contributor. He has achieved this position by combining the Maurician criticism of the assumptions behind the social order, and the theological realism of Niebuhr and Bennett. The result has been a continual flow of wise comment on the affairs of contemporary societies, particularly in the West. His long life, through greatly changing contexts, has spanned the great conflicts between capitalism and communism, and the emergence of social market capitalism into its present dominant position. Learning from a careful appraisal of the strengths and limitations of free market capitalism and command economies, he has recognized the important contribution to human living of the mixed economies of social democracy and democratic socialism. Combining, as they do, a strong social framework, with economic processes subordinated to the political, he has always acknowledged the dangers of absolutizing either. The balanced nature of his moral judgements are reflected in his theological method. This serves to relate Christian insights to complex social affairs, by avoiding idealistic generalities and detailed policies. The emerging middle ground allows him to suggest directions for a particular society at a particular time in history. His strong commitment to eschatology means that he never invests such guidelines with absolute authority.

Texts 6 and 7 illustrate these aspects of the content and method of Preston's judgements. Text 6 weaves together three pieces to produce a sustained comment on modern economies. The first and third are taken from *Religion and the Persistence of Capitalism* (1979), and the second from *Church and Society in the Late Twentieth Century* (1983). Interestingly, the former book includes the F. D. Maurice lectures, and the latter, the Scott Holland lectures, commemorating two great leaders of early Christian socialism. The argument begins with a brief discussion of his theological method and the basic economic problem. It then examines the two opposing ideal types of economic system, the free market and command economies, before commenting on their actual performance. His comment on the problem of reconciling seemingly irreconcilable claims in modern democracies is all the more illuminating given the triumph of democracy and the market economy in the post-1989 era (rightly recognized in his *Religion and the Ambiguities of Capitalism*, 1991).

Text 7, on middle axioms, expounds his interpretation of a theological method particularly suited to the development of church statements on complex social issues. Their appearance at the Oxford conference partly accounts for their prominent role in Preston's and Bennett's methodology. Preston elaborates them further in his *Church and Society in the Late Twentieth Century*.

Text 6: Ambiguities in Capitalism and Socialism Today

Theological method and the economic problem

When a moral theologian lectures on a theme like 'Ambiguities in Capitalism and Socialism Today', the question is bound to arise, What is the status of his remarks? He obviously cannot derive them solely from Biblical Studies, or Church History, or Systematic Theology, or any of the classical theological disciplines. His theological studies provide him with a basic stance or orientation by which he interprets the heights and depths of human life. Indeed everyone has a basic orientation, explicit or implicit, through which he interprets the basic 'facts' of life. Mine is the Judaeo-Christian one. However, in examining contemporary economic systems he needs also not only the competence which ought to be possessed by anyone who seeks to be well informed on public affairs, he must also draw upon a certain expertise in the social sciences which he may not personally possess. How then can he escape the charge of amateurishness and presumption?

These questions indicate a genuine dilemma. Once it is clear that we cannot proceed directly from the Christian tradition, whether the Bible or Natural Law or Systematic Theology, to conclusions in the spheres of various specialist studies, in this case economics, industry and politics, there is no escape from coming to grips with the empirical data in those fields and mastering the various intellectual disciplines needed to cope with them, the moral theologian cannot do so on the basis of his discipline alone. Ideally this is a co-operative enterprise, an interdisciplinary one. More and more this activity is seen to be necessary. Sometimes when group activity is not immediately possible he can produce the material by himself, but in fact drawing upon the experience of other individuals and groups, together with any special competence he may happen to possess. In this case I am following the latter process. The analysis that I am about to make draws upon a mixture of theological resources and empirical studies. It is a personal assessment which draws on the work of many others and many group studies. Moral theologians do not lay down a law from above, they try to clarify issues from within, in association with those of relevant experience of them, whether experts or lay folk. Therefore my diagnosis, whilst it asks for serious attention, also asks that those who disagree with it should advance other reasoned considerations where they consider mine erroneous or incomplete.

There is an inescapably hazardous element in all such enterprises. However well buttressed interdisciplinary work may be, however well the necessary expertise is drawn upon, we find in every discipline that within the broad lines of the subject there are different schools of thought, and that the experts differ. It is often said that where you find three economists there will be four opinions. It was partly because of this that the Christians we were considering in the last lecture thought they were entitled to ignore the subject altogether and invent their own, or adopt the thought of 'cranks', not realizing that there is a core of the subject which underlies the different schools of thought and to which a proper autonomy has to be allowed. The matter is yet more difficult in that now and again those whom the established authorities have considered cranks have later been proved right after all. There is no escape from careful discrimination, and no guarantee that a moral theologian by himself, or a group with which he works and on which he draws, may not make errors of diagnosis. We can be alert to the dangers, and devise methods of trying to reduce them (and here the study of issues of Christian social ethics in the Ecumenical Movement has pointed the way), but it is impossible to be sure that they have been overcome. In any case there remain irremovable uncertainties about present trends and future situations in studying social processes of which one is a part as one studies, and which do not stay still whilst one is studying them. That is why there are no simple 'Christian' solutions to ethical problems, but a general Christian orientation to them and, after empirical investigations, a range of considerations and options to be borne in mind (though there may well be certain courses of action which practically speaking can be ruled out).

In interdisciplinary work the moral theologian has his own part to play. One is to be alert to open or unavowed doctrinal and moral presuppositions in what appears to be, as presented, 'scientific' in the sense of value-free. There has been a tendency for theologians to move from ignoring the proper autonomy of other disciplines to becoming uncritical of them. This has sometimes happened in the field of pastoral counselling with respect to various schools of psychology, and it is characteristic of the Liberation Theologians of Latin America with respect to Marxism. But to pursue these themes would take me too far afield, and after these preliminary cautions I turn to the specific theme of this lecture.

I begin with the basic economic problem which every society has to solve and which is the subject matter of economics, that is, how to allocate scarce resources which can enter into the economic system and which have alternative uses. There are far more things that human beings would like to do with the resources that are available to them than they are able to do, and a selection must be made. To an economist the real cost of something is the alternatives which might have been undertaken if those which have in fact been chosen had not been chosen. It is a study of this problem which makes economics autonomous, to use the term frequently used in a pejorative sense by R. H. Tawney and others. Some economists are more ambitious and try to apply economic analysis to every aspect of life. Professor

Gary Becker, for instance, in *The Economic Approach to Human Behaviour* applies economic techniques to the question of marriage, and decides that marriage will occur if the expected benefits exceed the costs in the sense of opportunities forgone. I leave this hazardous enterprise aside as hardly relevant to our concerns, and return to the basic economic problem of any society, the need to maximize scarce resources.

Within this problem are subsidiary problems, such as how to register demands for goods and services, how to see that the production of them matches the demand for them, how to decide the distribution of rewards for producing them, and how to allocate resources between present consumption and future consumption. The only strictly economic value is the avoidance of waste. If resources are scarce it seems to the economist a pity to waste them by using them less efficiently than they might be used. But an economist will always add that this consideration is 'other things being equal'. He must admit that it is only one value among others, and that there may be many reasons why one would not wish to maximize resources in particular instances. Nevertheless the economist thinks it is as well to be aware of the cost of alternatives foregone if one does not maximize them, and not cover up the cost by camouflage. To take an example, the National Coal Board has since the war reduced the mining force from three quarters of one million to one quarter without undue social hardship. We have all paid more for our coal in order that this should happen than otherwise we would have done, but most people would agree that it was an economic waste well spent.

The two classical economic systems to solve society's basic economic problems are that of the free or market economy and that of the command or planned economy. The first is commonly called capitalism, the second socialism. [. . .]

Source: R. H. Preston, *Religion and the Persistence of Capitalism* (SCM Press 1979), pp. 22–5.

Fundamental economic problems of market and command economies

The opposite of the ideal free market demand economy is the ideal centrally planned command one. Before considering that let us consider some of the problems the demand economy gives rise to and some it does not solve, after paying tribute to the efficiency of a market system in maximizing human productivity in using relatively scarce resources.

There are a number of collective demands with which it cannot deal. Defence is an obvious example. There are many more. It was health considerations which did most to undermine the pure theory of *laissez-faire* in the nineteenth century. It was impossible to deal with cholera on a liberal individualist basis, for it was no respecter of persons and was liable to spread from the poor to the rich. The demand economy also has great difficulty in dealing with what are called externalities, or the deleterious consequences of economic actions by one producer which affect others for the worse and which are not reflected (unless the market is deliberately interfered with by state policy) in the price level. Pollution is an obvious example. This is also no respecter of national boundaries. Prevailing wind currents bear our acid rain in the direction of Scandinavia and North Germany. The free market, moreover, has difficulties in seeing far enough ahead. Even if the future is discounted at the rate of about 10% per annum, it only means taking about fifteen years ahead into market considerations. Yet many projects need a longer perspective than that. Nuclear energy, and especially dealing with radio-active nuclear waste, is an obvious example. Difficult as it is to forecast more than a limited time ahead, most of us would think that we have a responsibility to future generations, at least as far as our grandchildren, to the extent that we can plausibly foresee the likely consequences of our actions.

Then, again, the free market system has not proceeded in a smooth way, but in a series of booms and slumps, which in the last century was almost a ten-year cycle. This means that, for example, in a slump men and women are threatened by unemployment and poverty in a way vital to their well-being through processes over which they have no control and circumstances which they could not avoid. Since 1918 we have not had a ten-year cycle, but a particularly vicious slump in 1929 and another one now. It is certainly arguable that government actions made the 1929 one worse and are making this one worse. But that does not mean that in principle there could not be better and less short-sighted government actions; nor that it can be right to subject people's lives to the vagaries of the trade cycle without remedial action. Indeed government actions are inevitable. If any country decided to adopt a totally free market policy it would come up against the fact that, whatever they say, every country subsidizes some of its industries and finds ways of protecting its home market. American actions, for instance, are different from President Reagan's theories. The problem is how to minimize the perpetuation of the inefficient which these interferences usually entail.

Most people are aware of the inequalities of wealth and income which result from the free market system. Rights of inheritance tend to make this cumulative, and the system then works on the principle of 'to him that has shall be given', in a way of which the gospels were not thinking. Those who have wealth have a great pull on the market because they can bid for more luxuries than the poor can for necessities, as well as commanding the best attention in the basics of living – food, clothes, houses – and in personal services in education and medicine. Also the possession of capital tends to lead to the accumulation of more in a cumulative way, in spite of a number of stories of families which have gone from rags to riches and back to rags in three generations. Incomes have become more equal in this country, but we have not done much more with respect to the inequalities of wealth than re-distribute that of the top 1% among the top 5%. How far this is considered a defect depends on a value judgement. My judgement is that men and women who are wise will think rather of their resemblances to their fellow human beings than of their differences from them, and this will give an egalitarian direction to their judgements about the direction of the distribution of goods and services. It is not, however, the only consideration. There is a lot to be said for another remark of J. M. Keynes. 'The political problem of mankind is to combine three things: economic efficiency, social justice, and individual liberty.' If that is so, egalitarian tendencies still have their force and, I may add, are entirely consistent with the Judaeo-Christian affirmation that the most important thing about each person is that he or she is made in the image of God.

With wealth goes power; power to command economic resources, including those which influence opinions. This in turn relates to property rights. Without going into detail in the matter it is worth noting that the classical Christian defence of private property, that of St Thomas Aquinas, presupposes the widest possible distribution of it, so that each person or family has so to speak a space round itself to express personal qualities. This is quite different from the distribution of wealth and property in Western industrial societies.

These inadequacies of the free market are not the flaws alleged by the Christian socialist critique, which I think were mistaken. Christian socialists thought there was something unchristian in competition itself, not distinguishing the falsity of thinking of it as the key to man's relation with man from the innocuous and indeed useful place it can have in human relationships. With their talk of production for use and not for profit they did not distinguish the usefulness of profit as a criterion for solving many problems of the allocation of economic resources from crude theories of private property. Lastly they talked about the motive of service to such an extent as not to consider the place of self-interest (and with it family interest) in human life. Christians read in the New Testament Jesus' summary of the Jewish Torah, 'You shall love your neighbour as yourself', yet have often found difficulty in thinking this through. There have been many discussions of the matter, but the essence of them is that without a proper self-affirmation it is not possible to relate adequately to others, or even to have a proper self to lose when it is necessary. Of course life is not all the time lived at the highest levels of either self-affirmation or self-sacrifice, and entire societies cannot operate economic and political structures which presuppose those levels of affirmation, though they should not exclude them. I have often quoted the sentence of William Temple, 'The art of government in fact is the art of so ordering life that self-interest prompts what justice demands.' A good case can be made for maintaining that there is not a great deal of difference between the actions which would result from an enlightened pursuit of self-interest and those which would result from an other-regarding attitude. But the exclusive pursuit of self-interest tends not to be enlightened; most self-interest is too crude and needs refining, and other-regarding motives, which tend to be weaker, need fostering.

Moral and religious agencies in society have a major part to play here. Governments should devise institutions which help and do not hinder this process, and in particular find ways of harnessing self-interest to the most constructive uses. The free market is one such institution in its due place.

Advocates of this place often do their case a disservice by their political naiveté. They will not trust people as voters in economic matters, because they are so aware of the corruption of judgement by interests; they will trust them only as consumers. That is why they favour the automatic processes of the free market with its impersonal decisions. There are some reasons to support this position which will be mentioned in the next chapter, but they are far from decisive. It is clear that human beings when they are able to influence governments will not allow their vital interests to be settled by impersonal and automatic processes. Whatever their official ideologies, trade unions, professional associations functioning as trade unions, and management, all react in the same way. They want decisions which will have major economic consequences for them made in the *political* realm. That is why the verbal commitment to the more automatic processes of monetarism which we have seen in the last few years in Britain and the USA has been only imperfectly matched by deeds, and why a monetarist policy has been only partially followed.

The theory, however, is a strange return to the situation of 1929. Then monetarist policies were one element in intensifying the depression. After that we had a long period of Keynesian management of the economy which led to an unprecedented period of economic growth, until it began to be checked by the OPEC-inspired oil price rise of 1973. The difficult political choices which this made necessary were fudged by Western governments, abetted by management and unions, so that we have seen a return to pre-Keynesian monetarism by the two administrations of Britain and the USA. We hear once more that because of the uncertainties of life it is best if governments do little, for if they have an active policy they will be sure to make a mess of it. There is even talk in the USA of a return to the Gold Standard in order to remove discretion over monetary matters from government hands. It does not need a Christian to point out that there was no golden age of the Gold Standard.

Ronald H. Preston

The pursuit of automatic economic decisions to this extent is the pursuit of a chimera. There is no escape from political decisions on economic problems. The free market itself is not a divine or 'natural' institution; it is a human device designed for particular human purposes and needing a well-thought-out framework of political and economic institutions surrounding it.

On the other hand the command economies have run into difficulties. They operate detailed planning by rationing of materials and capital, and control of wages. The complexities of deciding everything by central planning are cumbersome in the extreme. There are said to be twelve million identifiably different products in the USSR needing between two and a half and three and a half million planned indicators at the centre. Hence the vast centralized bureaucracy. It is true that the development of computers has made the holding together of masses of simultaneously changing variables much easier, but it does nothing to solve the problem of innovation, which is a weak point of command economies because technical progress de-stabilizes the Plan. (By contrast demand economies are troubled by industrial espionage.) Also computers depend on the basic data which are fed into them, and if these have no rational basis there can be no rational outcome.

Moreover there are many other weak points. Because there is always a seller's market, shortages (as distinct from relative scarcity) are endemic; quality is hard to achieve, except where there is a naturally homogeneous product like electricity, or where the central government is the direct customer as in armaments. Agriculture is handled badly because of the hetero-geneous nature of the resources such as the varying quality of land and uncertain weather. There is a perpetual tendency to over-invest and neglect routine maintenance. Above all there is the problem of pricing. If prices are kept low because price rises are unpopular the result is that the privileged bureaucracy get the product, a black market and bribery develop, and a kind of barter system may spring up which even draconian police activity cannot suppress. No wonder that Nove says 'There is a long agenda awaiting socialist economists. They cannot even begin to face the real problems unless they openly reject the utopian elements of the Marxist tradition.'

It is not only that Marx's picture of what amounts to an economic paradise where there are no economic problems because relative scarcity has been overcome, gives no guidance for running a socialist economy, but that his analysis of value in a capitalist society as distinct from the 'real' value of a product is faulty. His labour theory of value which is based upon the 'socially necessary labour time' involved in the production of a good or service has given rise to an immense debate, into which it is not possible to enter now. However the result has been that almost all discussions of economic issues in the socialist command economies have felt constrained to work within this framework, and have complicated the efforts to move away from the stifling centralized bureaucracy. In practice the attempts to do so have had varied success. The Polish economy has been badly mishandled. An attempt was made to increase both investment and consumption at the same time, especially when Gierek succeeded Gomulko. The necessity of raising prices was not faced, and only heavy borrowing from the 'West' averted complete disaster. It does not appear that the various strains in Solidarity have faced this issue. Yugoslavia has experimented with a more decentralized system of Workers' Councils. It is hampered by the age-old rivalries of the six republics and two autonomous provinces which constitute the country, and where regionalism compounds the difficulty of arriving at rational economic decisions. The experiment is revealing some of the problems of workers' democracy. They are not the co-owners nor share-holders and their influence tends towards inflation and poor investment decisions because they want to keep things as they are; that is to say to keep their jobs if results are bad and to keep others from being added to the work force if they are good. They tend to show a lack of concern for the enterprise considered as a whole in relation to the economy as a whole and, indeed, it is not easy to see what either their real interests or the general interest is, as I have already mentioned. All complex economies face this problem.

Hungary seems the most successful of the command economies. From 1968 there has been a New Economic Model which has confined central planning to key sectors, such as energy and transport. Almost alone among command economies Hungary has successfully achieved price rises to dampen excessive demand, and successfully handled the agricultural sector. There is no worker self-management. Recently one of Hungary's leading economists, Tibor Liska, has advocated a form of entrepreneurial socialism which would involve insecurity of *tenure*, though not of *income*, in every entrepreneurial or managerial job. Anyone would be free to bid to take over the resources if he thought he could do better with them, but he would have to guarantee his income to the previous entrepreneur, and pay the state the rent it charges for the use of them. Every citizen would have a basic personal inheritance; he could draw on this for entrepreneurial activity if he wished, or not. Obviously this system cannot apply to large units. It has already been implemented to a slight extent, but it remains to be seen how far the central authorities will tolerate it or will be fearful that it will undermine their power.

From 1949–57 China followed the economic model of the USSR. Then came the Great Leap Forward from 1958, and relative economic chaos. The Cultural Revolution from 1966 was not much better. Now there seems to be an emphasis on agricultural production, and more attention to consumer goods, but whether there is any breakthrough in Chinese economics in dealing with the basic economic problems remains to be seen. In all this there is little help from Marx as an economist. More is to be obtained from Marx as a sociologist, with his analysis of the alienation of the labourer in capitalist society, and the inhumanity of treating human beings as merely a factor of production in the sense in which land and capital are; because relationship is essentially a characteristic of human beings.

For the rest, in this very brief reflection, which is all that is possible, on the command economies there is the very important point to note, that the concentration of political and economic power in the same hands has sinister possibilities. It has proved extremely hard in these socialist command economies to arrive at checks on the abuse of power. So much is this the case that many socialists, having become disillusioned with centralized Marxist states, elaborate theories of a decentralized, minimal state verging on almost spontaneous local participatory decision making, which has no relation to the problems of advanced post-industrial societies. There is talk of rule by 'the people', as if it is a unified group within which there are no conflicts of interest. Moreover the problem of harmonizing them in a roughly acceptable fashion is complicated by the sheer difficulty for different groups of knowing what their real interests are, because of the number and scale of inter-related factors. [...]

Source: R. H. Preston, *Church and Society in the Late Twentieth Century* (SCM Press 1983), pp. 45–52.

The practice of market and command economies

However we do not live under either a simple free economy or a simple command economy. In the West we veer between a social democracy where the emphasis is rather more on the political process of participatory democracy, and democratic socialism where the emphasis is rather more on the public control of economic activities. The situation is changing all the time. For instance the state is taking over in many countries not just basic monopolies but companies operating against others in the market economy as well. [...] Are these half-way houses, if we may so call them, workable? They are certainly limited by the extent to which a purely national economy has limits set upon it by international economic factors; even the strongest economy, that of the United States, is not free from external constraints. But whether the mixed economies are workable is more a political than an economic problem.

The problem is that of reconciling group conflicts and group expectations. Certainly the efficiency which the economist wishes for is necessary to avoid waste but, to quote the words of Tawney, 'To convert efficiency from an instrument into a primary object is to destroy efficiency itself.' The reason is that if you destroy co-operation you insult self-respect. The problem is that we all gain by creativity, and creativity means change, and we also all have a vested interest in job security and stability, which militates against change. The problem of a participatory democracy as far as economics is concerned is that the government is bound to have more responsibility, because of the inadequacies of a purely automatic system, for reasons that we have already discussed, but now it also has to secure the broad agreement of the entire population, not least the organized body of workers who, until recently, could very largely be ignored. This requires an informed political and industrial electorate which can see beyond the end of its political and economic nose. It requires a sense of the common good and a sense of fairness. It requires the qualities of prudence and proportion which are traditionally emphasized in Christian ethics. And it requires governments who lead, who are prepared to implement unpopular policies where necessary, and at the same time are sensitive to those who have less power in either industrial or political weighting.

The easiest line for them is to by-pass the problems of injustice by economic growth, but when international factors do not permit the buying off of competing claims, the next easiest policy is to resort to inflation, which makes matters worse. The lucky and the unscrupulous in the use of power are the ones who benefit at a time of inflation. Yet governments cannot easily deflate because of the danger of creating an unacceptable level of unemployment. At the moment we are doing this at the expense very largely of teenagers who are less powerful politically than other sections of the community. We all want stable prices and full employment and most of us want free collective bargaining. The three are incompatible. How to achieve the right mix between the three calls for the highest art of government. There is no reason to suppose, however, that it is inherently impossible to achieve, and therefore no reason to suppose that either social democracy or democratic socialism is necessarily unworkable. In particular there is no inherent reason why elements of a command economy in the shape of planning cannot be mixed with elements of a market economy to make the market a better instrument for maximizing public benefit. Doubtless it will be rough and ready, like all political and economic processes. The main problem is to secure consistent policies rather than patchy ones. This requires political wisdom from both government and electorate, and this in turn requires moral wisdom. But this is what politics is about. What is clear is that both types of social democracy present very considerable challenges to the maturity of their constituencies.

However there is the further problem. An individualistic and hedonist outlook is not a sufficient basis for any society. This was ignored by classical capitalism, and its *laissez-faire* view is its most serious and fundamental defect. Classical socialism realized this, but overlooked inherent conflicts of interest which have to be brought into tolerable harmony in any society. This is a political problem with economic aspects. To achieve this harmony, self-interest has to be harnessed to social ends, and in this process the automatic devices of the market have a part to play, but subordinate to firm political and social controls. Moreover self-interest has to be balanced by a much firmer commitment to the common good; no 'divine hand' will automatically bring it about.

Both the market and the command economies present difficulties whether as ideal types or as they have worked out in practice. We are likely to live under some form of mixed economy which has to cope with the problems indicated in this lecture. Christians will hope to be a source of disinterested good will which the economic order certainly needs, but they also hope to shed some light, by the processes of reflection to which I referred at the beginning of this lecture, on how we can move towards a just and and sustainable society [. . .]

Source: Ronald H. Preston, *Religion and the Persistence of Capitalism* (SCM Press 1979), pp. 38–41.

Text 7: Middle Axioms in Christian Social Ethics

An underlying issue in the increasing concern for Christian social ethics is how far and with what justification the Christian faith can provide guidance about detailed and specific decisions as distinct from giving a fundamental insight into human life and destiny. We get a pretty clear picture from the New Testament of the qualities of a Christian life, for instance St Paul's list of the fruit of the Spirit in Galatians 5, but how do they bear on specific ethical problems, and in particular on the collective affairs of men? Further, in what way can guidance or instruction be given in these matters by church bodies of an official or semi-official character?

After the Geneva Conference of the World Council of Churches on 'Church and Society' in 1966, Paul Ramsey of Princeton University wrote a criticism of it, *Who Speaks for the Church?* in which he raised very sharply the two-fold question

Ronald H. Preston

'Who Speaks?' and 'How do they speak?' At a much less sophisticated level, however, there remains a good deal of unease, sometimes expressed in such a phrase as 'politics and religion don't mix', or more specifically 'I don't like to hear politics from the pulpit'. Yet Christians can see that such a simple dichotomy will not do, for it plays straight into the hands of totalitarian governments who will tolerate a church so long as it confines itself to an individualistic and other-worldly piety leaving the powers that be to deal with the world. Nevertheless a sense of unease remains that the basic truths of the Christian faith and detailed politics are not on the same level, and that the distinction between them should be kept clear.

On the other hand there is also a widespread feeling that the church ought to have something to say on current issues in debate, whether it be the sale of arms to South Africa or the character of TV programmes. The problem is how whatever organ of the church which does say something can avoid harmless generalities on the one side, or the endorsing of very particular and often highly disputable policies on the other. They are disputable because they involve a whole series of judgements about the facts of an issue, and the possible consequences of different lines of action, about which there are inescapable uncertainties (if only because we cannot foresee with certainty), and therefore more than one possible opinion.

Both characteristics are frequently found in church statements. The more common is a desire to speak significantly but to take refuge in statements of such generality as to be vacuous. At one time I made a collection of examples. Here are two. One of them urges men 'to promote increasing co-operation between individuals and groups in all phases of economic life'. The other says, 'the real needs and just demands of nations should be benevolently examined'. It is hardly possible to disagree with them because they do no more than commend good will. They are against sin. Sometimes they can appear to be specific and yet remain vacuous; an example is a resolution on Vietnam of the 1966 Geneva Conference which said that hostilities and military action should be stopped and the conditions created for a peaceful settlement. The same conference was in danger of passing a detailed resolution on the Rhodesian rebellion against Britain which was based on misinformation. Having been

145

baulked on this, and yet being determined to say something, it evaded a problem by passing an unrealistic motion that the whole matter be handed over to the United Nations. Yet another way is to pass a resolution which is ambiguous and which protagonists of opposing views then interpret in different ways.

A method of avoiding these courses was adumbrated in the preliminary volume issued to all those attending the Oxford Conference on 'Church Community and State' in 1937, which is rightly considered a landmark in the recovery of an adequate method in Christian social ethics. The book, *The Church and its Function in Society*, was by W. A. Visser 't Hooft and J. H. Oldham. Among other things it discusses the need to arrive at some middle ground between general statements and detailed policies. On page 210 it refers to what it calls 'middle axioms'. It describes them as 'an attempt to define the directions in which, in a particular state of society, Christian faith must express itself. They are not binding for all time, but are provisional definitions of the type of behaviour of Christians in a given period and given circumstances.' The idea was taken up by William Temple in his Introduction to the Malvern Conference volume 1941, and by the war-time Church of Scotland Report on 'The Interpretation of God's Will in our Time'. It is discussed by John Bennett in *Christian Ethics and Social Policy* (1946: the title of the British edition was *Christian Social Action*). And there is an interesting footnote by Reinhold Niebuhr in an essay in the Amsterdam volume, *The Church and the Disorder of Society* issued after the first General Assembly of the World Council of Churches in 1948, where he says, 'The Oxford Conference sought to find a middle ground between a Christian view which offered no general directives to the Christian with regard to social and political institutions, and the view which tried to identify the mind of Christ too simply with specific economic social and political programmes. For the ecumenical movement, in the opinion of many, this middle ground is still the proper basis of approach.'

John Bennett gives several illustrations of middle axioms. Two in the economic field are (i) the government has the responsibility of maintaining full employment; (ii) private centres of economic power should not be stronger than the government. The point now is not whether these are agreed, relevant or meaningful, but merely that they are illustrations of suggested Christian policies which are neither simply general, nor detailed, but halfway between; in short, in the middle.

I am not aware of any discussions of them since 1948, but that does not mean that they have faded out. Quite a lot of work done by the Board for Social Responsibility of the Church Assembly (now the General Synod), the Methodist Christian Citizenship Department, the British Council of Churches and the World Council of Churches has in fact been in this middle region. It does not matter whether the name is used or not. It is, however, worthwhile to look explicitly at the idea of middle axioms, their nature and authority, in the cause of greater coherence in Christian social ethics, and not least because there are other and less satisfactory ways of bridging the gap between the fundamentals of the faith and the immediate situation. We will look briefly at these at the end.

Middle axioms are arrived at by bringing alongside one another the total Christian understanding of life and an analysis of an empirical situation. The Christian understanding of life involves all the elements of an articulated theology which have arisen in the church out of reflection on the witness to Christ in the Bible. It includes a picture of the proper way of life, personal and social, which follows from the Christian faith. On this all Christians will broadly agree, though doubtless there will be different theological emphases. The Christian way of life is so far-reaching that it transcends any particular embodiment either in personal life or social structures. When we look at an empirical situation our job is to establish the facts and the underlying trends, and to ask where the Christian understanding of life is particularly being disregarded. A middle axiom is formed to indicate the general direction in which action should be taken to improve the situation. Here we enter upon a debatable area. Our factual enquiry is open to all the hazards of trying to ascertain facts. (The Christian has no privileged position over any other citizen in this task; he has to do his home-work like anyone else.) On the other hand the Christian brings a distinctive understanding of life which may lead him to see facts differently and weigh them differently from others, because significant facts are always seen in a wider context.

Sometimes he may not see them differently. Christians and humanists, for instance, often share an outlook in common to a considerable extent. But not always. Some of the recent disagreements on abortion law clearly arise out of a different understanding of facts between some Christians and some humanists. With middle axioms we are at a halfway stage between what is clear Christian judgement and what is an opinion subject to empirical hazards and checks. To get to a detailed policy recommendation would be to go much further towards the latter.

If middle axioms can be arrived at, how authoritative are they? They cannot be 'of faith' because they involve an element of empirical judgement on a specific situation. On the other hand they can only be arrived at if they represent a good cross-section of relevant opinion. Thus they do carry high informal authority. Within one country if a representative group arrives at a consensus it carries more weight than if only one confessional tradition does. If a consensus is reached within the World Council of Churches, crossing national and confessional boundaries on a world scale, that is more impressive. Should the Roman Catholic Church and the WCC achieve a consensus that is the most weighty of all. All the more significant, therefore, for Christians is the similarity between so much of the Geneva Conference of 1966 and the Pastoral Constitutions of the Second Vatican Council, *Gaudium et Spes*, and the joint work on 'Society, Development and Peace' which has sprung from it. Perhaps we can say that middle axioms shift the burden of proof. The onus is on those who disagree to make out a good case for their disagreement rather than the other way round.

How detailed can they be? It is impossible to say precisely, except that they do not go as far as policy formulation. This is not to say that church bodies should never be specific and detailed, but the occasions will be rare; what Paul Ramsey calls 'before the gates of Auschwitz'. For the most part church bodies as such should hesitate to rush in with a detailed policy on each controversy as it occurs. It is better to try to disentangle the issues, indicate the areas of judgement and the range of possible actions (perhaps excluding one or more as impermissible), and looking out for inconvenient aspects of the problem which the government or the community or both is inclined to gloss over.

In this way the church can then help Christians in the first instance, and often the community at large, to make informed judgements. But we are concerned here with the degree of particularity of middle axioms. All one can say is that the more detailed they are, the more dated they are likely to be by the time they have got over to the Christian public, let alone the general public. For they need to be under constant revision as circumstances change. Moreover the means used to correct an unfavourable judgement on the *status quo* will sooner or later lead to a new situation and consequences which in turn will need correction by a new middle axiom.

Of course no one – not even the theologian – can stop at the level of middle axioms. As citizens we have to support detailed policies in the direction they indicate. Here many differences between Christians will arise. Two equally sincere Christians in agreement about a middle axiom may disagree as to how it is best implemented by particular policies, perhaps because of different estimates of the probable consequences of them. There is an irreducible uncertainty in life which is reflected in Christian ethics. It is chiefly for this reason that political parties and trade unions with the name 'Christian' in their title are best avoided. We can be glad that we do not have them in this country.

Some may think all this rather disappointing and something of a damp squib. But middle axioms do have many advantages. I can think of eight.

1. They are a help to the individual Christian in making his own decisions, as citizen and perhaps in his job.

2. They are a link between different confessions. For the most part there does not seem much point in the different churches 'going it alone' in this enterprise.

3. They are a link between Christians and non-Christians in facing a common problem. The expertise of non-Christians can often and usefully be brought into the discussions out of which they arise.

4. They give the Christian community something to say relevant to the concerns of the general public.

5. They are useful in breaking down the clerical–lay division in the church. They cannot be arrived at by clergy or by theologians alone. Relevant lay experience is absolutely essential.

6. They can help to create a bad conscience where people are complacent, whether in the church or the community at large. It is no accident that they arise out of a negative judgement on the *status quo*. For instance in so far as equality is a concept having relevance (among others like justice, freedom, order) to a Christian understanding of a humane society – and it certainly has some place though it is extraordinarily difficult to define exactly what we mean by it – we understand it and its implications better by seeing where it is being markedly infringed than by approaching it directly.

7. They help the church to take some purchase over events, and not lag far behind with an irrelevant message. We cannot be too grateful for the work of the ecumenical movement in social ethics which has enabled the churches to be up to date, in the sense of knowing what is happening, for the first time since the Industrial Revolution accelerated the speed of social change.

8. They help the church to avoid either the pietism which takes no interest in this world, or the perfectionism which can only deal in absolutes and therefore never has a relevant word to those who have to do the best possible in tangled situations, and in structures of life in which God has placed us alongside others of all faiths with whom we have to work, and which cannot presuppose a shared Christian faith as a basis for their working.

In view of all this one would hope to see continuous efforts made by the churches to get together different groups of people with different confessional, occupational and, where appropriate, national backgrounds, to keep abreast of the different areas of life. As we have seen, this is being done to some extent, but there is a lot of scope for more. In the professions, for instance, only teaching is well catered for; medicine and social work much less so, industry and commerce only sporadically. Further the churches are not good at feeding the work they have sponsored into their own life. The attention paid by the church in this country to the very important Geneva Conference of 1966 has been minimal. And few Anglicans know of the excellent work done in recent years by groups convened by their own Board for Social Responsibility. There is abundant material here for sermons and church groups of all kinds.

In conclusion the significance of middle axioms can be seen by a brief reference to three other ways of arriving at church

Ronald H. Preston

pronouncements, none of them satisfactory. One is to make a detailed pronouncement on the basis of an *a priori* deduction from an alleged maxim of Natural Law. This has been characteristic of much Roman Catholic and some Anglican social teaching. The papal encyclical *Humanae Vitae* is a recent instance. Here the Pope arrived at a detailed conclusion that various forms of contraception are 'unnatural' on an *a priori* basis. (This is the root of the encyclical though, because the conclusion lacks the self-evidence that in theory it ought to have, he brings in church authority to back up his verdict of 'unnatural' and he further adds logically irrelevant and in fact weak empirical arguments.) The question of Natural Law is a vast and complex one. All we say here is that this way of using what is a necessary concept is growingly discredited, not least in Roman Catholic moral theology itself. One can dare to be an optimist and hope that there will be no successors to *Humanae Vitae*.

Another position is that of an extreme Lutheran interpretation of the doctrine of the two kingdoms. On this view the kingdom of God's left hand (the orders of society) is so sharply separated from the kingdom of his right hand (the church) that it can get no guidance from the Christian faith. This extreme autonomy is viewed with growing disfavour in Lutheran circles. Hitler was a great shock to it. Lutherans are now engaged in expressing the two kingdoms doctrine in a way which allows for a Christian light to be thrown on the structures of society, as Roman Catholics are beginning to stress a view of Natural Law which allows for empirical data.

A third position, which springs more from a Calvinist background, is to want to go direct from the Bible to a specific conclusion on a contemporary issue. There has been a good deal of this in WCC documents, especially in the now-faded era of 'biblical theology'. Karl Barth was an unfortunate influence in this respect. Because Jesus Christ is the light of the world there must be no secret diplomacy. Because Jesus Christ has risen from the dead, Hitler must be resisted. Such a procedure never escapes from the arbitrary; and there is always the possibility of other Christians making the same incomprehensible leap from a particular text to a different conclusion. The latest example of this approach are the Christians who claim to be able to move

151

directly from a Christian perspective to say what God is doing in the world. Apparently he is always creating revolutions and never conserving. To thank him for 'creation, preservation and all the blessings of this life' is outmoded. This approach springs from a desire to have too unambiguous a Christian word for empirical situations. It is fond of quoting the Old Testament prophets and forgets that in a Christian dispensation there are *two* kingdoms, whereas in the old dispensation there was only one. Israel was both state and church.

By comparison the method of middle axioms is sounder. It is critical of the *status quo*, but it keeps contingent political and social judgements in their proper and necessary but secondary place. It requires Christian social action and will not sanction a private pietism, but it differentiates between God's cause and our causes. It takes the religious overtones out of politics whilst insisting that it is a necessary area of Christian obedience. The fact that we have a long way to go before the Christian community has grasped this and followed it is a reason for taking the method of the middle axiom approach seriously.

[*The following is from the Introduction to* Explorations in Theology 9, *p.viii – commenting, in retrospect, on the above chapter on middle axioms.*]

[. . .] The subject of the third paper, middle axioms, is one on which little has been written, and I have been asked on several occasions for copies of it. It needs expansion, partly to meet three criticisms. The first is that the method is élitist as compared with grass-roots participation. The previous paper deals implicitly, but only partially with this point. To answer it fully would require a treatment of both political and liberation theology, which I have in a form needing revision, and which I hope to publish in due course. The second criticism is that the method cannot work because ideological differences in modern society so influence thought as to make agreement on middle axioms impossible. This possibility has always been allowed for; that both because of ideological and other differences agreement at this middle level cannot be arrived at. But those who thought about middle axioms were well aware of ideologies, and of the study of the sociology of knowledge which alerts us to them. I myself have been familiar with these considerations since my undergraduate days. Those who think that humanity is so shut up in separate ideological groups that no common understanding is possible between them are in effect adopting a Marxist view in a particularly sharp and allegedly 'scientific' form which they need to justify. I do not think it can be justified on 'scientific' grounds; and there is of course a vast amount in the Christian tradition which would deny it, the Natural Law tradition in *any* form. Lutheran civic righteousness and Calvinist common grace among others. However, this is too large a subject to pursue further in this introduction. The third criticism is that it presupposes too static a view of Christian doctrine from which one starts, whereas there is a reciprocal relation between our understanding of the Christian faith we have received and our understanding of the world in the midst of which we are seeking to understand what we have received. Too static an impression of Christian doctrine may have been given by some exponents of the method of middle axioms, perhaps I have done so, but it is not essential to the position; and Reinhold Niebuhr, to quote one who approved of it, is certainly not open to this criticism.

Source: Ronald H. Preston, *Explorations in Theology 9* (SCM Press 1981), Chapter 3.

Social Christianity

*The Social Gospel
and Beyond:
The United States*

c h a p t e r   s i x

Washington Gladden
1836–1918

Introduction

Gladden's life spanned the transformation of the United States from the anti-slavery movement, civil war, and the opening of the frontiers, to the emergence of the great cities and industries. Brought up on a farm, he was educated at Williams College and worked as a teacher and journalist before undertaking the pastorates of two great Congregational churches, the North Church, Springfield, Massachusetts (1875–82), and the First Church, Columbus, Ohio (1882–1918). Epitomizing the transition from Calvinism to liberal theology and the social gospel, he rose to become one of the foremost leaders of American Protestantism, and of his denomination. From 1904–7 he was the Moderator of American Congregationalism, and was a major influence on the Federal Council of Churches. As a prolific author (over forty books and numerous articles) and preacher around the country, he played a principal role in the spread of liberal theology and social Christianity in the churches and society. Through his deep commitment to civic betterment (including as a Councilman from 1900–2, and a strong relationship with Theodore Roosevelt), he was also a national figure in the movement for political reform.

Gladden was pre-eminently a pastor and preacher who welded into a powerful movement the emerging forces of liberal theology and social Christianity. By adjusting Christian faith to the modern intellectual developments of sociology, evolution and biblical criticism, he was able to make it relevant to the dramatic changes of industrialization and urbanization. Centred on the immanence of God and the application of Christian principles to the whole of life, there emerged a large view of theology, pervaded by a real optimism in human ability to gradually realize the Kingdom of God on earth. Inseparable from these theological beliefs was a commitment to apply them to society. The key Christian task was to address the economic question in general and the industrial conflicts in particular. It was not to pursue the speculative theological arguments of the Andover Theological Seminary. For Gladden, social Christianity was essentially Christian social reform as a journey from the Christian stewardship of individuals to the gradual changing of the economic and political system (the latter to include government involvement in factory inspection, the regulation of working conditions, limited public ownership, and compulsory arbitration).

Text 8 is taken from one of the great founding publications of the social gospel. It emerged out of the context of a Springfield that was experiencing strong industrial and urban growth, but also economic depression, unemployment, and savage industrial conflicts. Arriving in 1875, Gladden immediately saw the need to engage this turbulent context as the primary theological task. The means he chose was a series of Sunday evening addresses to the jobless, employers and employees, in which he illustrated the application of the gospel to current economic and social problems. The results were published as *Working People and their Employers* in 1876, and widely disseminated as the first shoots of social Christianity. Beginning with an analysis of the industrial conflict between employers and workers, he traced its origins firmly to the wages system in a competitive *laissez-faire* economy. The solution was for individual employers and workers to apply the Golden Rule to their situations. Yet Gladden's real hope lay in the replacement of the wages system with a co-operative system through industrial partnerships. Thirty years later, he expressed his disquiet with this book, mainly because it was too hard on the labour unions. Despite this, it represents the remarkable, courageous innovation of a clergyman addressing the great industrial question of the times. His acceptance of the moral legitimacy of labour unions and their resort to strikes against the oppressive feudal force of the large industrial empires marks the book out as 'one of the first mileposts set by American social Christianity'.

Text 8: The War between Labor and Capital

History shows us three different systems by which capital and labor have been brought together, – the system of slavery, the wages system, and the system of co-operation.

In the first of these there is no conflict between capital and labor, because the capitalist owns the laborer. On the one side is force, on the other side submission. Labor and capital are indeed identified, because the laborer is part of the property of the capitalist which is engaged in production. There is no dispute about wages; the word is never heard.

This system of slavery is recognized and regulated in the legislation of the Bible, just as polygamy and blood vengeance are recognized and regulated. The laws of Moses do not sanction either of these evils: they only set bounds to them, and secure their administration on certain principles of justice and humanity which will in due time put an end to them. And when these principles begin to root themselves in the convictions of the people, prophets arise announcing the higher law of perfect righteousness, of which the Levitical legislation was only the precursor; and bidding the people, in the name of the Lord, to undo the heavy burdens, and to let the oppressed go free.

Under such a moral regimen, slavery could not thrive. And when Christ appeared, declaring that the law and the prophets were all summed up in the rule which bids us do to others as we would have others do to us, the doom of the system was sealed. There is no express legislation against it in the New Testament; but there is no great need of express legislation against wearing fur overcoats in July. What Christianity did was to create a moral atmosphere in which slavery could not exist.

Men have always been quoting the Bible on the side of

slavery; but, while pettifogging theologians have been searching its pages for texts with which to prop their system, the spirit of the book has been steadily undermining the system.

There are those who still choose to represent Christianity as the ally of despotism. A newspaper published in this Common-wealth made, not long ago, the sweeping assertion, that 'free-dom and Christianity are fundamentally and irreconcilably antagonistic; and that whoever strikes a blow for the one strikes a blow against the other.' In contradiction to this statement, we may quote the whole of history. Go back to the dark ages, to the period when the Church was most corrupt and faithless, and you will find that even then it always was the champion of the oppressed. Mr. Fitzjames Stephen, one of the most brilliant of living English writers, – himself a barrister and a student of ancient law, though a sceptic as regards revealed religion, – bears this testimony to what Christianity has done for liberty:–

> 'The glory of the mediaeval Church is the resistance which it offered to tyranny of every kind. The typical bishop of those times is always upholding a righteous cause against kings and emperors, or exhorting masters to let their slaves go free, or giving sanctuary to harassed fugitives. . . . What is true of the bishops is true in a still more eminent degree of the religious orders.'

Read Guizot's History of Civilization in Europe for abundant confirmation of these statements. The power of the keys which the Church put into the hands of the priest was used in behalf of the enslaved, in unlocking their shackles and in lightening their burdens. The destruction of the feudal system in Europe, and the abolition of serfdom, was, in considerable part, the work of the Christian Church.

I have dwelt upon this fact of history, because I wish to make it plain to working-men that the religion of Christ is not hostile to their interests; that it has indeed done more for the mitigation of their hardships, and the enlargement of their privileges, than any other power on earth. The suspicion with which the laboring classes, especially in Europe, have been taught by some of their leaders to regard Christianity, may be excusable in view of the corrupt and perverted nature of the Christianity by which they are surrounded; but it would surely be impossible, if they had any clear notion of what the religion of Christ is, and of what it has done for them.

If, then, this system in which history brings together the capitalist and the laborer, the system of bondage, be largely a thing of the past; if the workman has now, in many lands, been emancipated, – this result is due, in great part, to the prevalence of the Christian religion.

The second of these systems is that in which, throughout the civilized world, we now find capital and labor, in which they freely exchange services. The workman gives his work in exchange for the employer's money. There is a contract between them, by which the rate of remuneration is fixed. The fundamental principle of this wages system is competition, that is, conflict. If all men were benevolent, if the Golden Rule were the rule of all exchanges, of course this need not be; but unfortunately, the business of the world is for the most part organized on a basis of self-interest; and thus, by the wages system, the interest of the employer and the interest of the laborer come directly into collision. The laborer wants to get all he can for his labor, the employer wants to give for it no more than he must; and between the two there is an unceasing struggle for advantage and mastery. How sharp and fierce this struggle is, let the history of England and America for the last twenty-five years bear record.

Thus the second stage in the progress of labor is a stage of conflict. Slavery first, then war. All the kingdoms of the world's industry are now in a state of war. Sometimes the strife is suppressed, and there is apparent peace; sometimes the warfare is only one of words or of unfriendly combinations: but very often, as lately in the Pennsylvania coal-fields, the parties come to blows. Violence is constantly resorted to when the contest waxes hot. Either between the employers and the laborers there is a direct issue of force, or else part of the laborers take the side of the employers, and are attacked as traitors to the army of labor. But even when the arbitrament of brickbats and bludgeons is not appealed to, there is none the less a state of war. Capital will assert and maintain its claims, so will labor; and neither will yield to the other more than it is compelled to do. Labor and capital work together in production. They must work together. Capital is worth nothing without labor; labor

161

cannot subsist without capital. The contest arises in dividing the profits of this joint production. Over these profits there is a perpetual quarrel. It is generally believed, among working-men, that the capitalist gets the lion's share of them; it is commonly asserted nowadays by capitalists, that business cannot be done without a loss on account of the high rate of wages. I do not pretend to know which side is right: I only see the quarrel going on, and wish that it might in some way be stopped. Can it be stopped? That is the question.

I have read what the political economists have to say about this matter, and I confess that it does not help me very much. There is much learned talk about the wages fund; and no little dispute among the professors as to what this wages fund is, and whether the laborers are paid out of it or out of the product. Indeed, it would seem that the warfare of which the wages system is the occasion is not confined to the factories, but extends to the universities as well. They tell us that a certain part of the profits of production is set aside by the capitalists to pay future laborers, and that the price of wages depends upon the relation of this wages fund to the number of laborers, and can depend on nothing else; that when the wages fund is large, and the laborers are few, the wages will be high because each man's share will be larger; that, on the other hand, when the wages fund is small and the laborers are many, the wages must be low because each man's share will be small. Accordingly, they tell us, the whole question is one of supply and demand: the rate of wages is determined by fixed economical laws; the will of the employer cannot alter it; no combinations of workmen can affect it; it is just as vain to undertake to control it by legislation or by organization as it would be to control the winds or the tides in that way.

Well, that may be true, and probably is true if men are not moral beings; if the doctrines of materialism or of high Calvinism are true, and if the actions of men are determined by forces outside of themselves. But we shall venture to assume for a little while longer that the wills of men are free; that their choices have something to do with their destinies; and that by the presentation to them of truth, by an appeal to their reason and their moral sense, their conduct may be influenced. The questions of social science or of political economy are in part moral questions; and my business is to find out what are the moral considerations that enter into this problem, by which the strife between labor and capital may be tempered, and the good of both parties may be promoted.

In the first place, then, it would appear that what the economists call the wages fund – that portion of the capital which is devoted to the remuneration of labor – does depend somewhat on the will of the capitalist. It depends partly on his habits of living whether it shall be increased or diminished. If he is lavish in his personal expenditures, he will not of course have so large a wages fund as if he is economical. Here is an employer who during the year spends ten thousand dollars in the merest luxuries of life, – in feasting and in dressing, – in that which is consumed and cast aside with the using: must not his power to remunerate his workmen be reduced by that amount? Might he not, if he had chosen, have used this money in increasing the wages of his laborers?

'But that is all nonsense,' answers the capitalist. 'Business is business. Supply and demand, my dear parson! Supply and demand! Every man must pay the market price for labor, and any man is a fool who pays more.' No, my friend: you do yourself wrong. You are not wholly the victim of these economical laws: you resist them and rule them sometimes, in the interest of humanity. There is a poor man in your employ who has been partly disabled. In the market, he could get almost nothing for his labor. But you take pity on him and his household, and continue his wages at the rate you paid him when he was in health. That is not 'supply and demand' at all. Another law comes in here, a better law, – the law of love. You do bring it in, now and then, to alleviate the hardships that would result from the inflexible enforcement of those economical laws of which you speak. The question is, whether you might not bring it in a little oftener; whether, indeed, you might not incorporate it into all your dealings with your working-men; and instead of saying, 'Business is business,' say, 'Business is stewardship: business is the high calling of God, into which I am bound to put conscience and benevolence, as well as sagacity and enterprise.' This is just what Christian principle ought to effect on the side of capital, in the relation between capital and labor; just what it does effect in some degree: but if, on the present basis of production, there is to be any enduring peace between these now warring parties, there must be on the part of capitalists a good deal more of this intervention of Christian principle, to hold in check the cruel tendencies of the economic forces.

Not only on the side of the capitalist must this spirit of sweet reasonableness find expression: the workman must govern himself by the same law. If employers are sometimes heartless and extortionate, laborers are sometimes greedy and headstrong. I have known of more than one case in which workmen have demanded an increase of wages when the business was yielding no profits; when the balance every month was on the wrong side of the employer's books; when with the strictest economy in his personal expenditures, and the most careful attention to his affairs, he was growing poorer instead of richer every day. I have known other cases, in which workmen have resisted a reduction of wages, when that was the only condition on which the business could be carried on without disaster. As a mere matter of policy, this is suicidal. For workmen to exact a rate of pay that shall destroy the business by which they get their living, is simply to kill the goose that lays the golden egg every day, because she does not lay two every day. It is not, however, with the policy of the transaction that I am chiefly concerned, but with the rightfulness of it. Grave wrongs are often in this way inflicted upon employers: their business is paralyzed, their credit is impaired, their property is swept away; and, in the destruction of the enterprises which they are carrying on, their power to help and serve their fellowmen is crippled. For nothing is plainer than that a man who organizes and carries on any honest business, in which he gives employment and fair remuneration to laborers, ought to be considered a public benefactor. All depends, of course, upon the manner in which he manages his business. If it is managed in the spirit of Shylock, it may be an injury to the community; but if it is based upon principles of justice and fair play, it is a benefit to the community, and the destruction of it is a calamity and a wrong, not only to him, but also to the public. Any combination of laborers that undertakes to cripple or to kill an enterprise of this kind is engaged in a bad business.

'Is this meant, then, for a condemnation of strikes?' asks

Washington Gladden

somebody. Not necessarily. I have no doubt that such combinations of laborers are often unwise and unprofitable; that, as
a general thing, they result in more loss than gain to the laboring
classes; but it does not appear to me that they are always morally
wrong. This is a free country: if you do not choose to work for a
man unless he will pay you a certain rate of wages, no one can
compel you to do so; and if ten or twenty or two hundred of your
fellow-workmen are of the same mind, and prefer to be idle for a
season rather than to take less than the price demanded for their
services, they have a right to do it. But it seems to me that you
ought to consider whether by your combination you may not be
inflicting serious damage upon the whole community, and that
you ought to have some regard to the public good in what you
do. If the Christian law governs your conduct, you will think of
this. But if you can satisfy yourself that the public welfare will
take no serious detriment from your action, I do not know that it
can be shown to be morally wrong. You and your fellows may
find it for your advantage to take this course; and it is a lawful
means of securing your own advantage. On the other hand, it
may be for your disadvantage; you may be worse off in the end:
but that is your concern and the concern of those dependent on
you. So long as you pay your honest debts, and support your
families, no one else has a right to complain if you do take a
course which results in loss and damage to yourself.

Certain measures are, however, frequently resorted to at such
times that are morally wrong. You have a right to refuse to work
for less than a certain rate, and you have a right to *influence*
others to join with you in this refusal; but you have no right to
use force or intimidation to keep any man from working for less.
Nobody has any right to force you to work: you have no right to
compel anybody to be idle who is satisfied with less wages than
you demand. He may be a poor workman; but that is his
employer's concern, not yours. If you can persuade him to join
you, very good; but you have no right to lay a straw in his way if
he refuses to join you. We believe in free labor in this country,
do we not? And that belief implies that no laborer ought to be
enslaved or coerced by his employer or by his fellow-laborers.

If, now, workmen will endeavor to deal with their employers
and with one another without threatening or violence, in a spirit
of good-will and fair play; recognizing the important service

165

that is rendered them by the men who organize the various industries by which they get a living, and trying to render a fair equivalent in work for the wages they receive; they will do *their* part toward terminating this unhappy strife which has so long prevailed between labor and capital. It is a most melancholy quarrel: society is disturbed and unsettled by it, and the human brotherhood is rent into discordant and hostile factions. If the capitalist would measure his profits, and the working-man his wages, by the Golden Rule, there would be instant peace. And that is the only way to secure peace on the basis of the wages system. Political economy cannot secure it: its maxims breed more strife than they allay. Political economy only deals with natural forces; and the natural forces, even those which manifest themselves in society, often seem to be heartless and cruel. The law of nature would appear to be the survival of the strongest; and it is the workings of this law with which political economy has to do. Legislation cannot stop this strife. What, indeed, is law but an edict of force? Behind every law is the policeman's billy or the soldier's bayonet. It has no meaning, no efficacy, unless there is force behind it. And you cannot make peace with a sword between these contending interests. A gentler influence, a subtler but a mightier force, must take possession of the minds and hearts of the combatants on either side before the warfare will cease. If the spirit that dwelt in Christ be in you, – if you will learn to 'look not every man on his own things, but also on the things of others'; to love your neighbors as yourselves; to put yourselves in their places now and then, and judge their conduct and yours too from their point of view, – you will speedily come to terms in all your quarrels. And is it not about time for all of you, capitalists and laborers, in view of the wasting warfare that you have so long been waging, to lay to heart the injunction of Paul, 'If ye bite and devour one another, take heed that ye be not consumed one of another'?

I must own that I have not much hope, however, that the war to which the wages system gives occasion will ever cease until the system is abolished or greatly modified. Christian principle can do much to mitigate the strife, so far as it gains control of the lives of men; but it will be a good while before the masses of men, whether capitalists or laborers, are so fully governed by the Christian law that they will cease to struggle for the advantage and mastery. The wages system is better than slavery, because conflict is better than apathy; but there is something better than the wages system, and I hope that we some time shall reach it.

The subjugation of labor by capital is the first stage in the progress of industry; the second stage is the warfare between labor and capital; the third is the identification of labor and capital by some application of the principle of co-operation. This is what we are coming to by and by. The long struggle between these two conflicting interests promises to end by uniting them, and making the laborer his own capitalist.

I need not stop to describe this system to you: you are all familiar with the principles on which it rests. By combining their savings, the workmen employ themselves, and divide the profits of the business among themselves.

Not only will peace be promoted by such an organization of labor, but thrift and morality also. None but those who have a mind to save their earnings can become members of such an association. Business requires capital, and the capital must be provided from the savings of the workmen themselves. In furnishing a strong motive to economy, co-operation will do good. The miseries of the working people in this country are often due to extravagance and improvidence, rather than to insufficient incomes. Besides, it is always necessary in these associations to enforce rigid rules of moral conduct. Drunkards or idlers are immediately turned out. Sober and steady workers are not at all disposed to divide their profits with the lazy and dissolute.

We may hope, too, that co-operation will secure greater economy of material, and better work. The workmen working for themselves, and having a direct interest in the profits of their work, are likely to be careful about waste. This carefulness will be of advantage not only to them, but to everybody else. The world is enriched not only by the discovery of new wealth, but by the frugal use of that which is already in men's hands. All waste makes the world poorer.

For the same reason, because each man is working for himself, it is directly for his interest to make all his work as nearly perfect as he can; and that is a result at which the whole world ought to rejoice.

Such are some of the results which may be expected from the success of industrial co-operation. The expectation is not based upon theory, but upon accomplished facts. Already in France and in England the experiment has been tried with remarkable success. A year ago, Mr. Thomas Brassey, M.P., in an address before the Co-operative Congress, stated that there were in England and Wales 746 co-operative societies, with more than 300,000 members, the share capital amounting to nearly $14,000,000; and that during the previous year they had transacted a business amounting to nearly $57,000,000. The larger part of this business, however, was in the mercantile rather than in the manufacturing line. In England the system has worked better in distribution than in production; but there has been considerable success in both directions.

But some of you may ask why a system so excellent has not been universally adopted. There are two or three reasons. So far as this country is concerned, the wages of labor have hitherto been so large that working-men have been pretty well satisfied with their condition, and have not been driven to devise new ways of gaining a livelihood.

In the second place, working-men everywhere lack confidence in the honesty and fidelity of one another. They hesitate to risk their savings in such enterprises, for fear some faithless treasurer will default and run away with them. Very many of the co-operative stores in this country have come to grief in this way.

In the third place, in the members of such an organization, a certain trait is essential which I may find it difficult to describe in one word, and which is not so fully developed as it might be among our working-people, or among our people who do not work, for that matter. It is the trait that makes a man work well in harness. It is the spirit of concession, the spirit of subordination, the spirit that thinks less of personal power or gain or glory than of the common good. It is the spirit that we ought to find as the bond of union in all our churches, and *do* find sometimes, thank God! It is the virtue Paul inculcates when he bids the Romans, 'Be kindly affectioned one toward another with brotherly love, in honor preferring one another.' Where this spirit abounds, there is always unity and fruitfulness; where this spirit is not, there is confusion and all kinds of evil. And it is the absence of this spirit that hinders the success of many of our co-operative societies.

There is or was an Iron-Workers' Co-operative Association in Troy, N.Y., whose success at the beginning was quite remarkable. Last summer I wrote to a gentleman living there, to inquire how it was flourishing; and he replied that it seemed to be losing ground. Dissensions among the members were killing it. There had been frequent changes of managers, and it appeared that every man wanted to be boss.

More than one association of the kind has met its fate in this way. You cannot have co-operation till you can find men who can co-operate. How can you?

Add to these considerations, the fact that comparatively few among our working-men have the intelligence and sagacity requisite to organize and manage a large business, and you have a pretty clear explanation of the reasons why co-operation has not been more generally introduced. Before the production of the country can be carried on in this way, there must be a great improvement in the mental and moral qualities of working-people. But this improvement is steadily going on; our free schools and our open churches are offering to the children of our mechanics and operatives a culture in morality and intelligence that we may hope will qualify them after a while, to take their destinies into their own hands. The hour is not yet come, but it is sure to come; and the bell that strikes it will

'Ring out the feud of rich and poor.'

The transition from the wages system to the system of co-operation is likely to be made through the introduction of what are called industrial partnerships: by which the work-people in a manufacturing establishment are given an interest in the business; and, in addition to their wages, a stipulated portion of the profits is divided among them at the close of every year, in proportion to the amount of their earnings. It would seem that the times are fully ripe for the adoption of this principle. I have no doubt that many of our manufacturers would find it greatly to their advantage to introduce it; that it would result in securing steadier workmen and better work, and that it would put an end to strikes and all other forms of strife.

But, if I am right, working-men, as to the obstacles that hinder your entrance upon the better system, they are mainly such as arise out of your own defective conduct toward each other; they are such, too, as the Christian religion is calculated to remove. Indeed, is it not just because the Christian principle does not govern your lives, that you cannot co-operate? If the law of love ruled your treatment of each other, you would have no difficulty whatever in working together; in taking into your own hands all the grand industrial enterprises of the age, and carrying them forward with a vigor and a success that the world has never seen under the principle of competition.

For, let no one fail to see that co-operation is nothing more than the arrangement of the essential factors of industry according to the Christian rule, 'We being many are one body in Christ, and every one members one of another.' It is capital and labor adjusting themselves to the form of Christianity; and, like every other outward symbol, is a false deceitful show, a dead form, unless filled with the living spirit of Christianity itself.

Working-men, I ask you to ponder these things. There are those who seek to make you think that the Church of Christ is an enemy, or at best but a heartless stepmother, greedy to get your service, but careless of your welfare. I know that there are elements in the Church – corrupted fragments of the Church – against which such a charge as this might be truly brought; but it is not true of the Christian doctrine or the Christian system. The power that has stricken the shackles from the laborer, that has lightened his burdens, that has lifted him up to a happier and a nobler life, and that has put into his hands the key of a great future, is the power that came into the world when Christ was born.

Source: Washington Gladden, *Working People and their Employers* (1876; this edition: New York: Funk and Wagnalls, 1885), Chapter 2.

c h a p t e r   s e v e n

Walter Rauschenbusch
1861–1918

Introduction

Born into a German clerical family in Rochester, and educated at Rochester University and in Germany, Rauschenbusch's life has much in common with Reinhold Niebuhr's. One of his most formative experiences occurred in his eleven-year pastorate in New York City, on the edge of the notorious Hell's Kitchen (1886–97). There he underwent a second 'conversion', from a conservative orthodoxy of a pietist, other-worldly, individualist kind, to a liberal social Christianity able to engage the social realities of that great city. It was a process stimulated by his meeting with Henry George, who provided him with a radical social analysis, and by a trip to England and Germany in 1891. This brought him into contact with the co-operative movement, and with the theological liberalism of Ritschl and Harnack.

A greater influence on Rauschenbusch was the Brotherhood of the Kingdom. Founded in 1893, it formed, for a growing number of Christians, a powerhouse for promoting the Kingdom in Church and society. Through the discipline of prayer, Bible study and discussion, it soon became Rauschenbusch's intellectual and spiritual home. In 1897 he moved to Rochester Theological Seminary, becoming Professor of Church History in 1902. Like Niebuhr, his thinking was pervaded by a strong sense of history, and he always taught for a verdict. The publication of *Christianity and the Social Crisis* (1907) projected him into the national leadership of the social gospel movement. Followed by four more books, they confirmed his influence on the Baptist Church, but particularly on the Federal Council of Churches. The impact of the First World War was doubly traumatic, challenging his belief in progress and his German origins and loyalties. Like Temple, he died before his time.

Pre-eminently, Rauschenbusch was the great formulator and communicator of the social gospel. It was a position reinforced by his skills as mystic, prophet, and theologian, and his ability to capture the mood of Churches and nation through the overarching idea of the Kingdom of God. Early in his ministry in New York, he struggled to reconcile saving souls and applying Christianity to the social order. He did so by seeking to encounter the historical Jesus and his domination by the Kingdom of God. It was the Kingdom that became for Rauschenbusch the most essential dogma of Christianity, the social ideal of Christendom. As an all-embracing concept, it held together care for the poor, political and economic change, spirituality, sociological studies and biblical insights. It confirmed the possibility of evolutionary, progressive reform. Achieving such a social aim drew Rauschenbusch to socialism as a criticism of unchristian capitalism and as the moral basis for a more Christianized society. He therefore stood clearly in the radical strand of the social gospel. In so much of his progressive views, he was a child of his times, yet later criticism of the social gospel misinterpreted his understanding of sin, the realizing of the Kingdom on earth, and the role of conflict, power and class in the development of moral principles. In all these fields there were signs of the later perspectives of theological realism.

Text 9, from *Christianizing the Social Order* (1912), brings together three pieces into one argument. It defines the meaning of Christianizing society, then analyses why a capitalist economy is unchristian, and, finally, suggests how it can be Christianized. Originally given as lectures at Berkeley and Ohio, it represents Rauschenbusch's most developed argument for socialism and against capitalism. For over four hundred pages, it reads like a secular treatise on political economy. Yet he regarded it as profoundly religious, an account of the progressive transformation of all life by the Kingdom. As an encounter with his context, it reflected the high-water mark of American socialism. It was in 1912 that the socialist candidate, Eugene Debs, received 12 million votes in the presidential elections, and that the Social Creed finally emerged from the Federal Council of Churches.

Text 10 is taken from the preface and prayers of *For God and the People: Prayers of the Social Awakening* (1910). It reflected both the general concern of the Brotherhood of the Kingdom to complement *Christianity and the Social Crisis* with a spiritual dimension, and the particular experience of the Rochester branch. Expressing the spiritual depths of their social witness, it sought a prayerful basis in the new human and urban-industrial realities that were appropriate to them. In doing so, it challenged the belief that the social gospel was simply a political substitute for faith.

Text 9: Christianizing the Social Order

What do we mean by 'Christianizing' the social order?

We often hear the assertion that no one can tell whether Christianity would work, because Christianity has never been tried.

I deny it. Christianity has been tried, both in private and in social life, and the question is in order whether anything in the history of humanity has succeeded except Christianity.

It is true enough that there has never been a social order which was Christian from top to bottom. But large domains of our social life have come under the sway of Christ's law in their spirit and in their fundamental structure, and these are by common consent the source of our happiness and the objects of our pride, while those portions of the social order which are still unchristianized are the source of our misery and the cause of our shame. [. . .]

But first we shall have to define what we mean by 'Christianizing' the social order or any part of it. [. . .]

Christianizing the social order means bringing it into harmony with the ethical convictions which we identify with Christ. A fairly definite body of moral convictions has taken shape in modern humanity. They express our collective conscience, our working religion. The present social order denies and flouts many of these principles of our ethical life and compels us in practice to outrage our better self. We demand therefore that the moral sense of humanity shall be put in control and shall be allowed to reshape the institutions of social life.

We call this 'Christianizing' the social order because these moral principles find their highest expression in the teachings, the life, and the spirit of Jesus Christ. Their present power in Western civilization is in large part directly traceable to his influence over its history. To the great majority of our nation, both inside and outside of the churches, he has become the incarnate moral law and his name is synonymous with the ideal of human goodness. To us who regard him as the unique revelation of God, the unfolding of the divine life under human form, he is the ultimate standard of moral and spiritual life, the perfect expression of the will of God for humanity, the categorical imperative with a human heart. But very many who do not hold this belief in a formulated way or who feel compelled to deny it, including an increasing portion of our Jewish fellow-citizens, will still consent that in Jesus our race has reached one of its highest points, if not its crowning summit thus far, so that Jesus Christ is a prophecy of the future glory of humanity, the type of Man as he is to be. Christianizing means humanizing in the highest sense. I ask the consent of both classes to use his name for the undertaking which he initiated for us. To say that we want to moralize the social order would be both vague and powerless to most men. To say that we want to Christianize it is both concrete and compelling. Christ's spirit is the force that drives us. His mind is the square and plumb line that must guide us in our building.

The danger in using so high a word is that we shall be led to expect too much. Even a Christian social order cannot mean perfection. As long as men are flesh and blood the world can be neither sinless nor painless. [. . .]

But within the limitations of human nature I believe that the constitutional structure of the social order can be squared with the demands of Christian morality. At every new step of moral progress the clamor has gone up that fairness and decency were utopian fanaticism and would ruin society, but instead of making the social machinery unworkable, every step toward collective Christian ethics proved an immense relief to society.

An unchristian social order can be known by the fact that it makes good men do bad things. It tempts, defeats, drains, and degrades, and leaves men stunted, cowed, and shamed in their manhood. A Christian social order makes bad men do good things. It sets high aims, steadies the vagrant impulses of the weak, trains the powers of the young, and is felt by all as an

174

uplifting force which leaves them with the consciousness of a broader and nobler humanity as their years go on. [. . .]

[*Rauschenbusch then proceeds to analyse the economic order as capitalism, which he sees as the chief obstacle to Christianizing the social order.*]

The case of Christianity against capitalism

Let us sum up the case of Christianity against Capitalism.

We saw that the distinctive characteristic of the capitalistic system is that the industrial outfit of society is owned and controlled by a limited group, while the mass of the industrial workers is without ownership or power over the system within which they work. A small group of great wealth and power is set over against a large group of propertyless men. Given this line-up, the rest follows with the inevitableness of a process in physics or chemistry.

Wherever the capitalist class remains in unorganized and small units, they will struggle for the prizes held out by modern industry. Capitalism in its youth threw off the restraints upon competition created by the older social order, and a fierce, free fight followed. Wherever the competitive principle is still in operation, it intensifies natural emulation by the size of the stakes it offers, enables the greedy and cunning to set the pace for the rest, makes men immoral by fear, and puts the selfish impulses in control. The charge of Christianity against competitive capitalism is that it is unfraternal, the opposite of cooperation and team-work.

Capitalism gives the owners and managers of industry auto-cratic power over the workers. The dangers always inherent in the leadership of the strong are intensified by the fact that in capitalistic industry this power is unrestrained by democratic checks and fortified by almost absolute ownership of the means of production and life. Consequently the master class in large domains of industry have exacted excessive toil, and have paid wages that were neither a just return for the work done nor sufficient to support life normally. The working class is every-where in a state of unrest and embitterment. By great sacrifices it has tried to organize in order to strengthen its position against

175

these odds, but the master class has hampered or suppressed the organizations of labor. This line-up of two antagonistic classes is the historical continuation of the same line-up which we see in chattel slavery and feudal serfdom. In recent years the development of corporations has added a new difficulty by depersonalizing the master. The whole situation contradicts the spirit of American institutions. It is the last intrenchment of the despotic principle. It tempts the class in power to be satisfied with a semimorality in their treatment of the working class. It is not Christian.

The capitalist class serves society in the capacity of the middleman, and modern conditions make this function more important than ever before. But under the capitalistic organization this wholesome function is not under public control, and the relations created call out the selfish motives and leave the higher motives of human nature dormant. Under competition business readily drifts into the use of tricky methods, sells harmful or adulterated goods, and breaks down the moral self-restraint of the buyer. Under monopoly the middleman is able to practice extortion on the consumer. The kindly and friendly relations that abound in actual business life between the dealer and the consumer are due to the personal character of the parties and the ineradicable social nature of man, and are not created by the nature of business itself.

In all the operations of capitalistic industry and commerce the aim that controls and directs is not the purpose to supply human needs, but to make a profit for those who direct industry. This in itself is an irrational and unchristian adjustment of the social order, for it sets money up as the prime aim, and human life as something secondary, or as a means to secure money. The supremacy of Profit in Capitalism stamps it as a mammonistic organization with which Christianity can never be content. 'Profit' commonly contains considerable elements of just reward for able work; it may contain nothing but that; but where it is large and dissociated from hard work, it is traceable to some kind of monopoly privilege and power, – either the power to withhold part of the earnings of the workers by the control of the means of production, or the ability to throw part of the expenses of business on the community, or the power to overcharge the public. In so far as profit is derived from these sources, it is tribute collected by power from the helpless, a form of legalized graft, and a contradiction of Christian relations.

Thus our capitalistic commerce and industry lies alongside of the home, the school, the Church, and the democratized State as an unregenerate part of the social order, not based on freedom, love, and mutual service, as they are, but on autocracy, antagonism of interests, and exploitation. Such a verdict does not condemn the moral character of the men in business. On the contrary, it gives a remarkable value to every virtue they exhibit in business, for every act of honesty, justice, and kindness is a triumph over hostile conditions, a refusal of Christianity and humanity to be chilled by low temperature or scorched by the flame of high-pressure temptation. Our business life has been made endurable only by the high qualities of the men and women engaged in it. These personal qualities have been created by the home, the school, and the Church. The State has also made Business tolerable by pulling a few of the teeth and shortening the tether of greed. Thus moral forces generated outside of Capitalism have invaded its domain and supplied the moral qualities without which it would have collapsed. But capitalistic business in turn is invading the regenerate portions of the social order, paralyzing their activities, breaking down the respect for the higher values, desecrating the holy, and invading God's country. [. . .]

Devotion to the common good is one of the holy and divine forces in human society. Capitalism teaches us to set private interest before the common good. It follows profit, and not patriotism and public spirit. If war is necessary to create or protect profit, it will involve nations in war, but it plays a selfish part amid the sacrifices imposed by war. It organizes many of the ablest men into powerful interests which are at some points antagonistic to the interest of the community. It has corrupted our legislatures, our executive officers, and our courts, tampered with the organs of public opinion and instruction, spread a spirit of timidity among the citizens, and vindictively opposed the men who stood for the common good against the private interests.

When men of vigorous character and intellectual ability obey the laws of Capitalism, and strive for the prizes it holds out to them, they win power and great wealth, but they are placed in an essentially false relation to their fellow-men, the Christian virtues of their family stock are undermined, their natural powers of leadership are crippled, and the greater their success in amassing wealth under capitalistic methods, the greater is the tragedy of their lives from a Christian point of view.

These are the points in the Christian indictment of Capitalism. All these are summed up in this single challenge, that Capitalism has generated a spirit of its own which is antagonistic to the spirit of Christianity; a spirit of hardness and cruelty that neutralizes the Christian spirit of love; a spirit that sets material goods above spiritual possessions. To set Things above Men is the really dangerous practical materialism. To set Mammon before God is the only idolatry against which Jesus warned us.

As Capitalism has spread over the industrial nations, a smoke bank of materialism has ascended from it and shut the blue dome of heaven from the sight of men. All the spiritual forces of society have felt themselves in the grip of a new, invisible adversary with whom they had to wrestle, and whose touch made their heart like lead. [. . .]

When literature, art, education, the learned professions, and all other organized expressions of the spiritual life are being blanketed by the materialistic spirit generated in our business world, how can religion and the Church escape?

The churches are the socialized expression of the religious life of men. They awaken the religious instinct in the young of the race, teach them spiritual conceptions of life, put them into historical continuity with the holy men of the past, hand down the socialized treasures of religion, the Bible, the prayers, the hymns of the Church, and give the people an opportunity to connect their religious impulses with the service of men. Presumably the religious instinct would live on even if the churches perished, but in many it would starve by neglect or relapse into barbaric forms if deprived of the social shelter given by the Church. But without some light of religion in our lives our spiritual nature would vegetate in an arctic night, and many of us would fall a prey to vice, discouragement, and moral apathy. Even those who do not believe in the reality of what the churches teach will acknowledge that religion has been the most potent form of idealism among the great masses of men throughout history.

The churches have to make their appeal to the spiritual nature of men, which is but slenderly developed even in the best of us, compared with the powerful instincts of hunger, sex, and pleasure. They are always like engines pulling a train on an upgrade, and they feel it if the brakes are set in addition. In every industrialized community the churches have had a hard time of it. They are weakest where Capitalism is strongest. If this does not suggest a causal connection, our mind is duller than it might be. Of course the decline of the churches is due to a combination of causes. They have lost force through their own faults, through traditionalism, narrow ecclesiastical interests, and opposition to science and democracy. But to a large extent they are victims of the same influences which have crippled all the other noble forms of social life. Instead of chastising the churches, those who believe in the spiritual values of life might inquire sympathetically why the strongest and most ancient institution devoted to higher ends languishes wherever industrialism grows. We are not so rich in fraternal and spiritual institutions that we can afford to laugh while any of them die.

In *Christianity and the Social Crisis* I explained how the external interests of the churches are affected by the economic conditions about them. They are cramped for space by the rise of land values; straitened in their income by the poverty of the wage-earning classes; deprived of their volunteer workers by the exhausting toil of the week; endangered in the supply and spirit of their ministry; loaded down with the burden of caring for a mass of poverty; and compelled to work on human material that is morally debilitated. I have seen no contradiction of the line of thought presented there.

But beyond these external difficulties of the churches lies the spiritual antagonism between the genius of Christianity and the genius of capitalistic Business.

Religion declares the supreme value of life and personality, even the humblest; Business negatives that declaration of faith by setting up Profit as the supreme and engrossing object of thought and effort, and by sacrificing life to profit where necessary.

Christianity teaches the unity and solidarity of men; Capitalism reduces that teaching to a harmless expression of sentiment by splitting society into two antagonistic sections, unlike in their work, their income, their pleasures, and their point of view.

True Christianity wakens men to a sense of their worth, to love of freedom, and independence of action; Capitalism, based on the principle of autocracy, resents independence, suppresses the attempts of the working class to gain it, and deadens the awakening effect that goes out from Christianity.

The spirit of Christianity puts even men of unequal worth on a footing of equality by the knowledge of common sin and weakness, and by the faith in a common salvation; Capitalism creates an immense inequality between families, perpetuates it by property conditions, and makes it hard for high and low to have a realizing sense of the equality which their religion teaches.

Christianity puts the obligation of love on the holiest basis and exerts its efforts to create fraternal feeling among men, and to restore it where broken; Capitalism has created world-wide unrest, jealousy, resentment, and bitterness, which choke Christian love like weeds.

Jesus bids us strive first for the Reign of God and the justice of God, because on that spiritual basis all material wants too will be met; Capitalism urges us to strive first and last for our personal enrichment, and it formerly held out the hope that the selfishness of all would create the universal good.

Christianity makes the love of money the root of all evil, and demands the exclusion of the covetous and extortioners from the Christian fellowship; Capitalism cultivates the love of money for its own sake and gives its largest wealth to those who use monopoly for extortion.

Thus two spirits are wrestling for the mastery in modern life, the spirit of Christ and the spirit of Mammon. Each imposes its own law and sets up its own God. If the one is Christian, the other is antichristian. Many of the early Christians saw in the grasping, crushing hardness of Roman rule a spiritual force that was set against the dominion of Christ and that found a religious expression in the cult of the genius of the Emperor. The conflict between that brutal force and the heavenly power of salvation was portrayed in the Revelation of John under the image of the Beast and the Lamb. If any one thinks that conflict is being duplicated in our own day, he is not far out of the way.

Whoever declares that the law of Christ is impracticable in actual life, and has to be superseded in business by the laws of Capitalism, to that extent dethrones Christ and enthrones Mammon. When we try to keep both enthroned at the same time in different sections of our life, we do what Christ says cannot be done, and accept a double life as the normal morality for our nation and for many individuals in it. Ruskin says: 'I know no previous instance in history of a nation's establishing a systematic disobedience to the first principles of its professed religion.'

The most important advance in the knowledge of God that a modern man can make is to understand that the Father of Jesus Christ does not stand for the permanence of the capitalistic system.

The most searching intensification that a man can experience in his insight into sin and his consciousness of sin is to comprehend the sinfulness of our economic system and to realize his own responsibility for it.

The largest evangelistic and missionary task of the Church and of the individual Christian is to awaken the nation to a conviction of that sinfulness and to a desire for salvation from it.

The bravest act of faith and hope that a Christian can make is to believe and hope that such a salvation is possible and that the law of Jesus Christ will yet prevail in business.

The most comprehensive and intensive act of love in which we could share would be a collective action of the community to change the present organization of the economic life into a new order that would rest on the Christian principles of equal rights, democratic distribution of economic power, the supremacy of the common good, the law of mutual dependence and service, and the uninterrupted flow of good will throughout the human family.

[*Rauschenbusch then examines what Christianizing this economic order will mean.*]

Economic democracy

When Jesus, at the beginning of his public career, came to the synagogue of his home city of Nazareth, they handed him the roll of the prophet Isaiah, and he singled out these words to read:—

'The spirit of the Lord Jehovah is upon me,
Because Jehovah hath anointed me to proclaim glad tidings to the poor;
He hath sent me to bind up the broken-hearted,

To proclaim liberty to the captives
And the bursting of the prison to them that are bound;
To proclaim the year of Jehovah's favor,
And the day of vengeance of our God.'

When these words were first written, they had promised an exiled nation freedom and restoration of its national life. Jesus declared that he found the purpose of his own mission in fulfilling this prophecy, and thereby he adopted it as the pronunciamento and platform of Christianity. The words reverberate with freedom, and wherever the Gospel has retained even a breath of the spirit of Jesus in it, it has been a force making for freedom. If its official exponents have ever turned it into a chain of the mind, may God forgive them.

Christianity necessarily must be on the side of freedom if it is to fulfill its twofold purpose of creating strong and saved characters, and of establishing a redeemed and fraternal social life, for neither of the two is possible without freedom.

Freedom is the life breath of a Christianized personality. A servile class or nation lacks virility. Slaves and flunkies cringe, lie, and steal. Oppressed peoples resort to conspiracies and assassinations. Free people organize. The general judgment of past ages that woman was a clog to the higher aspirations of able men was really true in large part. As long as women were a subject class, they had the vices of a subject class. Men kept them ignorant and oppressed, and then were cursed by pulling with unequal yoke-mates. Freedom is to character what fresh air is to the blood. This is the truth in Nietzsche's contempt for the morals of servility.

Freedom is also the condition of a Christianized social order. Men can have no fraternal relations until they face one another with a sense of freedom and of equal humanity. Despotism is always haunted by dread, and fear is not a symptom of the prevalence of fraternity. In tracing the moral evolution of the Family, the School, the Church and the State, we saw that every social organization is on the road to redemption when it finds the path of freedom.

We are told that democracy has proved a failure. It has in so far as it was crippled and incomplete. Political democracy without economic democracy is an uncashed promissory note, a pot without the roast, a form without substance. But in so far as

182

democracy has become effective, it has quickened everything it has touched. The criminal law, for instance, has lost its bloody vindictiveness since the advent of democracy; men are now living who will see our penal institutions as agencies of human redemption and restoration. Democracy has even quickened the moral conscience of the upper classes. The most awful poverty has always existed before the eyes of the rich, yet they failed to see it till the lower classes became articulate through democracy. Is the cure of such blindness not a moral achievement?

Some forms of evil merely seem to multiply in a democracy because they get publicity there. Things that remain discreetly hidden in a despotism are dragged into the open by the impertinent curiosity of the plebs. What an aristocracy calls hereditary rights, a democracy calls scandalous graft. When Roman patricians or French seigneurs unloosed the anger of the common man, they could retire within the haughty class consciousness of a solid social group as into a bomb-proof shelter. In a democracy the extortionate rich must trust mainly to the thickness of their private skins.

Rightly considered, even the sins of democracy have some background of honor. Three of our presidents have been assassinated within fifty years. Few despotisms have such a record. But let the czars and sultans mingle with their people as our presidents do, and who will carry their insurance risks? A former czar is said to have asked the king of Prussia to lend him a Prussian officer to massage his imperial back, for he had no servant whom he could trust.

Other things being equal, a free State is always stronger, for it commands the devotion of the people. The boasted military efficiency of a despotism goes bankrupt when the trained armies are used up; a republic can stamp the ground and new armies will rise from the dust, as the history of Switzerland, Holland, the first French Republic, and the Boers testify. Switzerland has a citizen militia practicing marksmanship constantly with guns furnished by the government. Russia would not dare to arm and train its people; neither would Germany and Austria.

If the faults of our American democracy depress the mind of any one, let him consider this problem. When our Constitution was adopted, the suffrage was so restricted that only about

120,000 inhabitants out of 3,000,000 had a vote. During the colonial period a very large percentage of the immigrants arrived in a state of unfreedom; not only the black people imported from Africa and the Antilles, and the subjugated Indians, but about half of the white immigrants. Some were criminals sent by England; many thousands were children and young people kidnapped for the colonial trade; most of them were persons who had bought their passage by selling themselves for a term of years as 'indentured servants'; all these were sold at the wharf when a vessel arrived or hawked about the villages in chains. Given such beginnings, what would be the social condition of our country today if democracy had not meanwhile established manhood suffrage and prohibited slavery and peonage? Is democracy, then, a failure?

Whatever theorists may say, the verdict of the people is all one way. No nation wants less freedom than it has. The people always seek to remedy the faults of democracy by still more democracy. For five hundred years democracy has widened its concentric circles. The Renaissance of the fifteenth century began the democratizing of Education and the Intellect. The Reformation of the sixteenth century began the democratizing of the Church (which has taken more than three hundred years). The Revolution of the eighteenth century began the democratizing of the State and the political order. The Industrial Revolution of the nineteenth century began the democratizing of property. For let us not forget that Capitalism in its youth raised the battle cry of freedom. It was a revolutionary force bursting the rusty chains of feudal privilege and bringing property down where plain merit and ability could own it. It is true, the blessings of freedom and property were mainly confined to the merchants and manufacturers, and when Capitalism now raises its old watchwords of liberty, it is usually to defeat some movement for real liberty. The democratizing of property was only begun by Capitalism. A new form of aristocracy has been built up. To-day we have neither free competition for business men, nor free contracts for workingmen, nor free markets for the consumers. Capitalism set out as the opponent of privilege and the champion of freedom; it has ended by being the defender of privilege and the intrenchment of autocracy. The democratizing of property and industry must be resumed under new leadership.

The ideal of Capitalism – in so far as it has a moral ideal and is not frankly mammonistic – is the wise and benevolent employer, who can manage the affairs of the workingmen better than they can do it themselves, and whose plans for their welfare will be rewarded by their respect and gratitude. A great deal of good will, earnest thought, and faithful effort have gone into the realization of this ideal, and not without permanent results. The danger which dogs it is that it leaves the working class in a dependent attitude and fails to call out the qualities of independence and initiative. It is the ideal of paternalism, and it is very funny to hear men who put their trust in it cry down labor legislation and public ownership as 'paternalistic'. In point of fact, the benevolent-employer theory is as utopian as any scheme of socialism in its infancy. The weight of experience is against it. Only scattered individuals have had enough moral vigor to act on it. In the long run it is easier to educate the workers to govern themselves than to educate a set of superior persons to do the governing for them. Moreover, it is more lasting. The benevolent employer dies or sells out, and therewith the constitutional guarantees of his happy employees are swept away. In politics the drift is away from one-man power; in industry we shall have to move the same way.

The alternative for an aristocracy of superior persons is the democracy of labor. John Stuart Mill formulated the ideal of industrial democracy finely: 'The form of association which, if mankind continue to improve, must be expected in the end to predominate, is not that which can exist between a capitalist as chief, and workpeople without a voice in the management, but the association of the laborers themselves on terms of equality, collectively owning the capital with which they carry on their operations, and working under managers elected and removable by themselves.'

Two great movements are pushing toward the realization of this idea. The more radical of the two is Socialism. It stands in the midst of capitalistic society like a genuine republican party in a monarchical State, and seeks to lead the working class from 'the kingdom of compulsion into the republic of freedom'. The more conservative movement for industrial democracy is Trades-unionism. Just as a liberal party in a strong monarchy leaves the dynasty and its fundamental rights untouched, but demands parliamentary representation and the right to vote on the budget, so Trades-unionism recognizes the rights of the owner and employer under the present social order, but seeks constitutional guarantees and a Bill of Rights for the working class.

In the long view of history I think there is not a shadow of doubt that the powerful employers and associations of employers that have set themselves rigidly against both of these movements toward industrial democracy, have chosen the wrong side. They have aligned themselves with all the absolutist kings who resented the demand for a parliament or a douma as an interference with God-given rights, and yielded to compulsion as slowly and ungraciously as they could. The determination of great corporations to allow no labor organization to lift its head in their works is a present-day echo of the famous challenge of Louis XIV, 'L'État, c'est moi!' These employers speak of their 'private business' and resent the interference of outsiders in it; they use illustrations and maxims that might have been proper when a master mechanic employed three journeymen in his own home. Yet they command an industrial army of thousands; the bread and life of great industrial towns is dependent on their decisions; personal touch with their men is practically impossible. How can they call that a 'private' business? In all respects except legal property rights it is a public affair and the concern of all society. When one corporation combines the ownership of coal mines with the ownership of the railway that carries the coal, the business world protests against such a combination of powers as dangerous. But some corporations have twisted all the strands of a workingman's life into one rope in far different fashion. They have fixed his wages and given him no voice about them; they have provided the conditions under which he must work; they have housed him in drab-colored shanties in a fenced village in which the company owns every foot of the soil as landlord, even the roads; they have compelled him to run an account at the 'pluck' store of the company and to accept their prices and measures. If then the man proved troublesome, they can twitch the man's living, his home, his friendships, his whole existence from under him as the sheriff springs the death trap of a condemned man. Yet even such employers think there is no call for labor organizations. The belief in hell has waned at a time when we need it badly. Some think we shall be born again on this earth under conditions such as we have deserved. It would certainly be a righteous judgment of God if he placed us amid the conditions we have created and allowed us to test in our own body the after-effects of our life. How would a man feel if he knew that the little daughter that died in his arms twelve years ago was born as the child of one of his mill hands and is spinning his cotton at this moment?

If industrial democracy is coming, the workingmen as a class must be trained for the responsibility which the future will put upon them. In their own organizations and under their own leaders they must learn by practice that fairness and self-restraint without which democracy cannot work. If the labor organizations are suppressed and stunted, and if their energy is consumed in fighting their enemies instead of educating their members, the transition to the cooperative commonwealth will find them untrained, factious, and without tried leaders. Then we shall reap the results of the policy of suppression.

The errors of the Unions, their excesses, and their brutalities have been spread out for all to see. Their opponents and the newspapers have not allowed us to under-estimate the number of dynamite outrages. But after the worst is said – they have never inflicted as much wrong as they have suffered. They have never been as rotten as the political parties we have supported and cheered. Social workers and upper-class people who come into inside contact with the organizations of labor usually gain a deep respect for their moral soundness. As individuals the workingmen have all the faults of raw human nature, but their organizations act on higher and more humane principles than the corresponding organizations of the commercial class.

It is not enough to give the organizations of the workingmen legal toleration. The Law must facilitate and regulate the organization of the industrial workers. They must have legal recognition and honorable rights and duties as important groups within the social body. Subject always to the supreme interests of the whole community, every trade must have jurisdiction over the qualifications of its members; the workingmen must have the right to bargain collectively with their employers; and jointly with the latter they must constitute tribunals of conciliation and arbitration. If any group can organize cooperative production and dispense with an employer entirely, it is to the interest of the commonwealth that they shall have all facilities to try the experiment.

Some men see behind the slightest recognition of organized labor the specter of a 'labor trust', combining all the labor of a given industry and charging extortionate prices for their work. It is true that a legalized trade organization may become a nest of privilege, but at present that danger seems remote. Capitalistic monopolies unite the corporate powers bestowed by law with the rights secured by private property, and the real grip of their extortionate power lies in the latter. A monopoly of labor would at least not own the earth in addition, and any revolution which our children may have to start against the extortionate labor prices of the coal miners would be far more hopeful and easy than our revolution against the extortionate coal prices of the mining corporations.

The transition to industrial democracy will put every employer to a moral test, perhaps the severest of all. Is he willing to relinquish autocratic power and trust increasingly to superior moral and intellectual efficiency for the leadership he claims? If he heartily consents to that, he proves that he is an American indeed, and that Christianity is more than a fine emotion to him. Even if he is willing, he will encounter misunderstandings, suspicions, unreasoning waves of emotion, and malicious demagogism among those whom he is trying to meet halfway. If so, he will suffer vicariously for the sins of other employers, of foreign nations, and of past generations. This stunted life and these instinctive antagonisms are the results of generations of wrong, and it will take time to outgrow them. On the other hand, if he has sober expectations, he may find himself rewarded beyond all his hopes by the good will of his workmates. And whether he fares well or ill, the old despotic relation is played out. It is becoming intolerable to both sides. The finer spirits among the employing class are ready for a new deal. If they have to choose between the present industrial war and the possible troubles of industrial democracy, the latter may be a real relief.

Economic democracy means more than the right of the organized workers to control their own industry. It means also the control of the people over their own livelihood. It means the right and power to straighten out the line of communication that runs from the farm to the kitchen and the elimination of the middleman's profits that make food prices dear. It means the power to cut all monopoly prices out of business and to base prices solely on service rendered. Democracy means the absence of class rule; monopoly contains the essence of class rule. The power to charge a monopoly price shows that part of the taxing power of the government has gone astray into private hands, and that a privileged class is exercising the attributes of sovereignty over the rest. Therefore every lessening of monopoly profit is a step toward economic democracy. When we limit the price charged by common carriers so that they earn only a reasonable return on the capital actually invested; when we prohibit capitalization that has no actual investment behind it; when public ownership converts the lucrative stock of a corporation into the modest bonds of a city or state, we are moving away from economic aristocracy and modern feudalism.

Every genuine advance in economic democracy in history has involved a fight for political democracy. The larger economic and political movements are invariably two sides of the same thing. The possessing classes are also the governing classes. They have to control the government and make the laws in order to exercise their economic privileges in safety. Consequently if the people want to stop exploitation, they must get control of government. When the English democracy tried to tax unearned wealth for social purposes, a political crisis promptly arose. The Lords tried to block the Commons and had to be curbed. In our country the effort to curb the arrogant power of the monopolies and lessen their unearned profits has resulted in a political conflict all along the line. The smoke of masked batteries has risen from every political hilltop, showing how completely the enemy had occupied every strategical position. The movements for direct primaries, for commission government, for direct legislation, for the recall, and for the direct election of senators are the political counterpart of the struggle for economic democracy and emancipation. The political confusion and bitterness of the presidential campaign of 1912 get their significance and dignity only from the economic issues involved and the immense social forces struggling for the mastery of the country. The genuine leaders of these movements are not fighting for names and forms, but for realities, for our homes, our children, and our manhood.

In their struggle with economic aristocracy the people are

handicapped by their inveterate morality. The great Interests have had no mercy on the public; they have crippled the public good for private profit, resisted public control, hired the best lawyers to thwart the law, and tampered with the poorly paid servants of the people. On the other hand the people are more than fair. They fall in with the point of view that when graft has been enjoyed securely for some time it becomes a vested right. They are merciful toward those who have accommodated themselves to unearned wealth. A mature democracy, such as the Swiss, the English, and our own, is usually highly conservative. Democracy constantly balances conflicting interests, and so becomes a college of compromise. But when public opinion is convinced, it moves with the finality of a landslide. Democracies seem vacillating, but they stay put when they move.

Democracy has become a spiritual hope and a religious force. It stands for the sanitation of our moral relations, and for the development of the human soul in freedom and self-control. In some future social order democracy may possibly stand for the right to be unequal. In our present social order it necessarily stands for more equality between man and man.

Men are unequal in their capacities, and always will be, and this inherent inequality of talent will inevitably be registered in some inequality of possessions. But beneath the superficial inequalities of intellect lies the fundamental endowment of human personality, and in that we are all equal. Wherever we get close enough to our fellows to realize their humanity, we feel an imponderable spiritual reality compared with which all wealth-getting gifts are trivial. Our children may differ widely in physical perfection and intellectual ability, but the strong child and the crippled child are alike life of our life, and the same mysterious human soul gazes at us out of their inscrutable baby eyes. Outsiders may rate the gifts of a husband and his wife very unequally, but the gifted partner often knows that all his cleverness is like autumn leaves and that in human worth his quiet mate outranks him. In the family it is love which acts as the revealer of this profound human dignity and equality. In society at large the Christian religion has been incomparably the strongest force in asserting the essential equality of all souls before God.

Democracy aids in Christianizing the social order by giving political and economic expression to this fundamental Christian conviction of the worth of man. We do not want absolute equality; we do want approximate equality. We can at least refrain from perpetuating and increasing the handicap of the feebler by such enormous inequalities of property as we now have. To assert that they really correspond to the actual differences in intellectual ability is idle talk, and it becomes more absurd with every year as we see the great fortunes grow. They are an institutionalized denial of the fundamental truths of our religion, and Democracy is the archangel whom God has sent to set his blazing foot on these icebergs of human pride and melt them down.

Men say that equality would hold ability down under a dead weight of mediocrity. If ability can be held down it is not very able. If the time ever comes when the strong are oppressed, I shall gladly join a crusade for their emancipation. Meantime I judge with the old German composer Zeller: 'A genius can do anything. A genius will shampoo a pig and curl its bristles.' Disciplined intellect will ask no odds except of the Almighty.

Source: Walter Rauschenbusch, *Christianizing the Social Order* (New York: Macmillan 1912), pp. 123–7, 311–23, 352–64.

Text 10: Prayers of the Social Awakening

Preface

The new social purpose, which has laid its masterful grasp on modern life and thought, is enlarging and transforming our whole conception of the meaning of Christianity. The Bible and all past history speak a new and living language. The life of men about us stands out with an open-air colour and vividness which it never had in the dusky solemnity of the older theological views about humanity. All the older tasks of church life have taken on a new significance, and vastly larger tasks are emerging as from the mists of a new morning.

Many ideas that used to seem fundamental and satisfying seem strangely narrow and trivial in this greater world of God. Some of the old religious appeals have utterly lost their power over us. But there are others, unknown to our fathers, which kindle religious passions of wonderful intensity and purity. The wrongs and sufferings of the people and the vision of a righteous and brotherly social life awaken an almost painful compassion and longing, and these feelings are more essentially Christian than most of the fears and desires of religion in the past. Social Christianity is adding to the variety of religious experience, and is creating a new type of Christian man who bears a striking family likeness to Jesus of Galilee.

These new religious emotions ought to find conscious and social expression. But the Church, which has brought down so rich an equipment from the past for the culture of individual religion, is poverty-stricken in face of this new need. The ordinary church hymnal rarely contains more than two or three hymns in which the triumphant chords of the social hope are struck. Our liturgies and devotional manuals offer very little that is fit to enrich and purify the social thoughts and feelings.

Even men who have absorbed the social ideals are apt to move within the traditional round in public prayer. The language of prayer always clings to the antique for the sake of dignity, and plain reference to modern facts and contrivances jars the ear. So we are inclined to follow the broad avenues beaten by the feet of many generations when we approach God. We need to blaze new paths to God for the feet of modern men.

I offer this little book as an attempt in that direction. So far as I know, it is the first of its kind, and it is likely to meet the sort of objections which every pioneering venture in religion has to encounter. I realize keenly the limitations which are inevitable when one mind is to furnish a vehicle for the most intimate spiritual thoughts of others. But whenever a great movement stirs the deeper passions of men, a common soul is born, and all who feel the throb of the new age have such unity of thought and aim and feeling, that the utterance of one man may in a measure be the voice of all. A number of the prayers in this collection were published month by month in the American Magazine. The response to them showed that there is a great craving for a religious expression of the new social feeling.

If the moral demands of our higher social thought could find adequate expression in prayer, it would have a profound influence on the social movement. Many good men have given up the habit of praying, partly through philosophical doubt, partly because they feel that it is useless or even harmful to their spiritual nature. Prayer in the past, like the hiss of escaping steam, has often dissipated moral energy. But prayer before battle is another thing. That has been the greatest breeder of revolutionary heroism in history. All our bravest desires stiffen into fighting temper when they are affirmed before God.

Public prayer, too, may carry farther than we know. When men are in the presence of God, the best that is in them has a breathing-space. Then, if ever, we feel the vanity and shamefulness of much that society calls proper and necessary. If we had more prayer in common on the sins of modern society, there would be more social repentance and less angry resistance to the demands of justice and mercy.

And if the effect of our prayers goes beyond our own personality; if there is a centre of the spiritual universe in whom our spirits join and have their being; and if the mysterious call of our souls somehow reaches and moves God, so that our longings come back from Him in a wave of divine assent which assures their ultimate fulfilment – then it may mean more than any man knows to set Christendom praying on our social problems. [. . .]

A prayer for working men

O God, Thou mightiest worker of the universe, source of all strength and author of all unity, we pray Thee for our brothers, the industrial workers of the nation. As their work binds them together in common toil and danger, may their hearts be knit together in a strong sense of their common interests and destiny. Help them to realize that the injury of one is the concern of all, and that the welfare of all must be the aim of every one. If any of them is tempted to sell the birthright of his class for a mess of pottage for himself, give him a wider outlook and a nobler sympathy with his fellows. Teach them to keep step in a steady onward march, and in their own way to fulfil the law of Christ by bearing the common burdens.

Grant the organizations of labour quiet patience and prudence in all disputes, and fairness to see the other side. Save them from malice and bitterness. Save them from the headlong folly which ruins a fair cause, and give them wisdom resolutely to put aside the two-edged sword of violence that turns on those who seize it. Raise up for them still more leaders of able mind and large heart, and give them grace to follow the wiser counsel.

When they strive for leisure and health and a better wage, do Thou grant their cause success, but teach them not to waste their gain on fleeting passions, but to use it in building fairer homes and a nobler manhood. Grant all classes of our nation a larger comprehension for the aspirations of labour and for the courage and worth of these our brothers, that we may cheer them in their struggles and understand them even in their sins. And may the upward climb of Labour, its defeats and its victories, in the further reaches bless all classes of our nation, and build up for the republic of the future a great body of workers, strong of limb, clear of mind, fair in temper, glad to labour, conscious of their worth, and striving together for the final brotherhood of all men.

A prayer for men in business

We plead with Thee, O God, for our brothers who are pressed by the cares and beset by the temptations of business life. We acknowledge before Thee our common guilt for the hardness and deceitfulness of industry and trade which lead us all into temptation and cause even the righteous to slip and fall. As long as man is set against man in a struggle for wealth, help the men in business to make their contest, as far as may be, a test of excellence, by which even the defeated may be spurred to better work. If any man is pitted against those who have forgotten fairness and honesty, help him to put his trust resolutely in the profitableness of sincerity and uprightness, and, if need be, to accept loss rather than follow on crooked paths.

Establish in unshaken fidelity all who hold in trust the savings of others. Since the wealth and welfare of our nation are controlled by our business men, cause them to realize that they serve not themselves alone, but hold high public functions, and do Thou save them from betraying the interests of the many for their own enrichment, lest a new tyranny grow up in a land that is dedicated to freedom. Grant them far-sighted patriotism to subordinate their profits to the public weal, and a steadfast determination to transform the disorder of the present into the nobler and freer harmony of the future. May Thy Spirit, O God, which is ceaselessly pleading within us, prevail at last to bring our business life under Christ's law of service, so that all who share in the processes of factory and trade may grow up into that high consciousness of a divine calling which blesses those who are the free servants of God and the people and who consciously devote their strength to the common good.

A prayer for the co-operative commonwealth

O God, we praise Thee for the dream of the golden city of peace and righteousness which has ever haunted the prophets of humanity, and we rejoice with joy unspeakable that at last the people have conquered the freedom and knowledge and power which may avail to turn into reality the vision that so long has beckoned in vain.

Speed now the day when the plains and the hills and the wealth thereof shall be the people's own, and Thy freemen shall not live as tenants of men on the earth which Thou hast given to all; when no babe shall be born without its equal birthright in the riches and knowledge wrought out by the labour of the ages; and when the mighty engines of industry shall throb with a gladder music because the men who ply these great tools shall be their owners and masters.

Bring to an end, O Lord, the inhumanity of the present, in which all men are ridden by the pale fear of want while the nation of which they are citizens sits throned amid the wealth of their making; when the manhood in some is cowed by helplessness, while the soul of others is surfeited and sick with power which no frail son of the dust should wield.

O God, save us, for our nation is at strife with its own soul and is sinning against the light which Thou aforetime hast kindled in it. Thou hast called our people to freedom, but we are withholding from men their share in the common heritage without which freedom becomes a hollow name. Thy Christ has kindled in us the passion for brotherhood, but the social life we have built denies and slays brotherhood.

We pray Thee to revive in us the hardy spirit of our forefathers that we may establish and complete their work, building on the basis of their democracy the firm edifice of a co-operative commonwealth, in which both government and industry shall be of the people, by the people, and for the people. May we, who now live, see the oncoming of the great day of God, when all men shall stand side by side in equal worth and real freedom, all toiling and all reaping, masters of nature but brothers of men, exultant in the tide of the common life, and jubilant in the adoration of Thee, the source of their blessings and the Father of all.

Source: Walter Rauschenbusch, *Prayers of the Social Awakening* (SCM Press 1927), pp. 7–11, 57–8, 62–4, 127–9. First published as *For God and the People: Prayers of the Social Awakening* (Boston 1910).

Reinhold Niebuhr
1892–1971

Introduction

Born in Missouri, Niebuhr was brought up in the German Evangelical Church by his father, a local pastor. Educated at the Eden Theological Seminary and Yale School of Religion, he served his major pastorate at the Bethel Evangelical Church in Detroit (1915–28). It was in this turbulent city that he moved from the moral homilies of liberal Protestantism to the Christian realism that dominated the rest of his life. Here the great conflicts of a modern society provoked his reconstruction of social Christianity. Henry Ford and the Ku Klux Klan were opposed, and the labor movement, the Mayor's Inter-Racial Committee, and the Churches' Industrial Relations Commission were supported. Out of these experiences began to emerge his contribution to Church and society through constant public speaking and publishing across the nation. Moving into academic life in 1928 at Union Theological Seminary, New York, he made this, and Christian social ethics, his home until 1960.

By the 1940s and 1950s, Niebuhr had reached the height of his national and international career as theologian of public life. Yet his ability to reflect on events continued to be nourished by his involvement in political life. Supporting the Socialist Party in the 1930s, including running for Congress in 1932, he moved to the left of the Democratic Party, leading such pressure groups as Americans for Democratic Action. As a major influence on public opinion, he became a member of the Council on Foreign Relations and consultant to the US State Department. The Churches, too, regarded him as an adviser on social affairs. He played an important part in the Federal Council of Churches, and the World Council of Churches (particularly at the Oxford and Amsterdam Conferences). All this tireless output was influential far beyond the Churches. Diplomats like George Kennan, political scientists like Hans Morgenthau, and historians like Arthur Schlesinger Jnr, all bear the marks of Niebuhr's creative mind. Despite suffering a stroke in 1952, he continued to teach and write until his death in 1971.

A prolific author and preacher, with a deep spirituality, Niebuhr was one of the great apologists of Christian social thought. His work covered the varied field of politics, history and theology. All reflected his passionate concern to relate the transcendent principle of love to the changing contingent realities of political life. It was an intellectual journey into Christian realism, profoundly dynamic, changing over time in response to events. Beginning as a socio-ethical criticism of politics in the 1920s and early 1930s, it concentrated on the rejection of all utopias, whether liberalism or communism. By the end of the 1930s, Niebuhr had moved the focus of his attention from the dialectical relationship between man and society to the greater conflict within man himself, his nature and destiny. It was a theological development paralleled by his movement from a socialist criticism of Western societies to a critical realism. It was a journey in which events were addressed and interpreted through Christian symbols, whose formulation was also affected by the process. Consequently, throughout his reflections on society, the languages of Zion and the secular are juxtaposed. Out of that creative interaction emerged his ability to read the signs of the times to his times. It has produced a social Christianity in which social gospel and theological realism are held in creative conflict.

Text 11 is the final chapter of *Moral Man and Immoral Society* (1932). The book asserts the premise that the morality of groups, whether as nations or classes, is concerned with justice rather than the love of personal morality. As a result, it is a profoundly polemical book, confronting secular and religious liberalism with the reality of power in social relations, and rejecting communism for its equally religious illusions. Not surprisingly, the *New York Times* heralded it with the title *Doctrine of Christ and Marx Linked*, recognizing the secular realities through which Niebuhr developed his religious convictions. Despite the furore, it is arguably his most important book.

It certainly launched him as public theologian and creator of American Christian realism.

Text 12, on Christian pragmatism, was written towards the end of his career in 1957, and is more concisely argued than his *Christian Realism and Political Problems* (1953). It represents the development of his understanding of man and society from Text 11, into the theological stance of Christian pragmatism. Accordingly, he recognizes its impact on the Churches, and on an ecumenical movement still influenced by Western thought. It also represents his movement from socialism to critical realism, from Marx's insights to Burke's. Yet its realism should not be confused with Christian conservatism, or with the underwriting of the status quo. Its recognition of biblical insights into history, finitude and sin gives some support to the realism of conservatism. Yet its commitment to love and justice mean that it is also conservatism's consistent critic.

Text 11: The Conflict Between Individual and Social Morality

A realistic analysis of the problems of human society reveals a constant and seemingly irreconcilable conflict between the needs of society and the imperatives of a sensitive conscience. This conflict, which could be most briefly defined as the conflict between ethics and politics, is made inevitable by the double focus of the moral life. One focus is in the inner life of the individual, and the other in the necessities of man's social life. From the perspective of society the highest moral ideal is justice. From the perspective of the individual the highest ideal is unselfishness. Society must strive for justice even if it is forced to use means, such as self-assertion, resistance, coercion and perhaps resentment, which cannot gain the moral sanction of the most sensitive moral spirit. The individual must strive to realize his life by losing and finding himself in something greater than himself.

These two moral perspectives are not mutually exclusive and the contradiction between them is not absolute. But neither are they easily harmonized. Efforts to harmonize them were analysed in the previous chapter [of *Moral Man and Immoral Society*]. It was revealed that the highest moral insights and achievements of the individual conscience are both relevant and necessary to the life of society. The most perfect justice cannot be established if the moral imagination of the individual does not seek to comprehend the needs and interests of his fellows. Nor can any non-rational instrument of justice be used without great peril to society, if it is not brought under the control of moral goodwill. Any justice which is only justice soon degenerates into something less than justice. It must be saved by something which is more than justice. The realistic wisdom of the statesman is reduced to foolishness if it is not under the influence of the foolishness of the moral seer. The latter's idealism results in political futility and sometimes in moral confusion, if it is not brought into commerce and communication with the realities of man's collective life. This necessity and possibility of fusing moral and political insights does not, however, completely eliminate certain irreconcilable elements in the two types of morality, internal and external, individual and social. These elements make for constant confusion but they also add to the richness of human life. We may best bring our study of ethics and politics to a close by giving them some further consideration.

From the internal perspective the most moral act is one which is actuated by disinterested motives. The external observer may find good in selfishness. He may value it as natural to the constitution of human nature and as necessary to society. But from the viewpoint of the author of an action, unselfishness must remain the criterion of the highest morality. For only the agent of an action knows to what degree self-seeking corrupts his socially approved actions. Society, on the other hand, makes justice rather than unselfishness its highest moral ideal. Its aim must be to seek equality of opportunity for all life. If this equality and justice cannot be achieved without the assertion of interest against interest, and without restraint upon the self-assertion of those who infringe upon the rights of their neighbors, then society is compelled to sanction self-assertion and restraint. It may even, as we have seen, be forced to sanction social conflict and violence.

200

Historically the internal perspective has usually been cultivated by religion. For religion proceeds from profound introspection and naturally makes good motives the criteria of good conduct. It may define good motives either in terms of love or of duty, but the emphasis is upon the inner springs of action. Rationalized forms of religion usually choose duty rather than love as the expression of highest virtue (as in Kantian and Stoic morality), because it seems more virtuous to them to bring all impulse under the dominion of reason than to give any impulses, even altruistic ones, moral pre-eminence. The social viewpoint stands in sharpest contrast to religious morality when it views the behavior of collective rather than individual man, and when it deals with the necessities of political life. Political morality, in other words, is in the most uncompromising antithesis to religious morality.

Rational morality usually holds an intermediary position between the two. Sometimes it tries to do justice to the inner moral necessities of the human spirit rather than to the needs of society. If it emphasizes the former it may develop an ethic of duty rather than the religious ethic of disinterestedness. But usually rationalism in morals tends to some kind of utilitarianism. It views human conduct from the social perspective and finds its ultimate standards in some general good and total social harmony. From that viewpoint it gives moral sanction to egoistic as well as to altruistic impulses, justifying them because they are natural to human nature and necessary to society. It asks only that egoism be reasonably expressed. Upon that subject Aristotle said the final as well as the first authoritative word. Reason, according to his theory, establishes control over all the impulses, egoistic and altruistic, and justifies them both if excesses are avoided and the golden mean is observed.

The social justification for self-assertion is given a typical expression by the Earl of Shaftesbury, who believed that the highest morality represented a harmony between 'self-affections' and 'natural affections'. 'If', said Shaftesbury, 'a creature be self-neglectful and insensible to danger, or if he want such a degree of passion of any kind, as is useful to preserve, sustain and defend himself, this must certainly be esteemed vicious in regard of the end and design of nature.'

It is interesting that a rational morality which gives egoism equality of moral standing with altruism, provided both are reasonably expressed and observe the 'law of measure', should again and again find difficulty in coming to terms with the natural moral preference which all unreflective moral thought gives to altruism. Thus Bishop Butler begins his moral theorizing by making conscience the balancing force between 'self-love' and 'benevolence'. But gradually conscience gives such a preference to benevolence that it becomes practically identified with it. Butler is therefore forced to draw in reason (originally identified with conscience) as a force higher than conscience to establish harmony between self-love and conscience.

The utilitarian attempt to harmonize the inner and outer perspectives of morality is inevitable and, within limits, possible. It avoids the excesses, absurdities and perils into which both religious and political morality may fall. By placing a larger measure of moral approval upon egoistic impulses than does religious morality and by disapproving coercion, conflict and violence more unqualifiedly than politically oriented morality, it manages to resolve the conflict between them. But it is not as realistic as either. It easily assumes a premature identity between self-interest and social interest and establishes a spurious harmony between egoism and altruism. With Bishop Butler most utilitarian rationalists in morals believe 'that though benevolence and self-love are different ... yet they are so perfectly coincident that the greatest satisfaction to ourselves depends upon having benevolence in due degree, and that self-love is one chief security of our right behavior to society.' Rationalism in morals therefore insists on less inner restraint upon self-assertion than does religion, and believes less social restraint to be necessary than political realism demands.

The dangers of religion's inner restraint upon self-assertion, and of its effort to achieve complete disinterestedness, are that such a policy easily becomes morbid, and that it may make for injustice by encouraging and permitting undue self-assertion in others. Its value lies in its check upon egoistic impulses, always more powerful than altruistic ones. If the moral enterprise is begun with the complacent assumption that selfish and social impulses are nicely balanced and equally justified, even a minimum equilibrium between them becomes impossible.

The more the moral problem is shifted from the relations of

Reinhold Niebuhr

individuals to the relations of groups and collectives, the more
the preponderance of the egoistic impulses over the social ones
is established. It is therefore revealed that no inner checks are
powerful enough to bring them under complete control. Social
control must consequently be attempted; and it cannot be
established without social conflict. The moral perils attending
such a political strategy have been previously considered. They
are diametrically opposite to the perils of religious morality.
The latter tend to perpetuate injustice by discouraging self-
assertion against the inordinate claims of others. The former
justify not only self-assertion but the use of non-rational power
in reinforcing claims. They may therefore substitute new forms
of injustice for old ones and enthrone a new tyranny on the
throne of the old. A rational compromise between these two
types of restraint easily leads to a premature complacency
toward self-assertion. It is therefore better for society to suffer
the uneasy harmony between the two types of restraint than to
run the danger of inadequate checks upon egoistic impulses.
Tolstoi and Lenin both present perils to the life of society; but
they are probably no more dangerous than the compromises
with human selfishness effected by modern disciples of
Aristotle.

If we contemplate the conflict between religious and political
morality it may be well to recall that the religious ideal in its
purest form has nothing to do with the problem of social justice.
It makes disinterestedness an absolute ideal without reference
to social consequences. It justifies the ideal in terms of the
integrity and beauty of the human spirit. While religion may
involve itself in absurdities in the effort to achieve the ideal by
purely internal discipline, and while it may run the peril of
deleterious social consequences, it does do justice to inner needs
of the human spirit. The veneration in which a Tolstoi, a St.
Francis, a crucified Christ, and the saints of all the ages have
been held, proves that, in the inner sanctuary of their souls,
selfish men know that they ought not be selfish, and venerate
what they feel they ought to be and cannot be.

Pure religious idealism does not concern itself with the social
problem. It does not give itself to the illusion that material and
mundane advantages can be gained by the refusal to assert your
claims to them. It may believe, as Jesus did, that self-realization

203

is the inevitable consequence of self-abnegation. But this self-realization is not attained on the level of physical life or mundane advantages. It is achieved in spiritual terms, such as the martyr's immortality and the Saviour's exaltation in the hearts of his disciples. Jesus did not counsel his disciples to forgive seventy times seven in order that they might convert their enemies or make them more favorably disposed. He counselled it as an effort to approximate complete moral perfection, the perfection of God. He did not ask his followers to go the second mile in the hope that those who had impressed them into service would relent and give them freedom. He did not say that the enemy ought to be loved so that he would cease to be an enemy. He did not dwell upon the social consequences of these moral actions, because he viewed them from an inner and a transcendent perspective.

Nothing is clearer than that a pure religious idealism must issue in a policy of non-resistance which makes no claims to be socially efficacious. It submits to any demands, however unjust, and yields to any claims, however inordinate, rather than assert self-interest against another. 'You will meekly bear,' declared Epictetus, 'for you will say on every occasion "It seemed so to him".' This type of moral idealism leads either to asceticism, as in the case of Francis and other Catholic saints, or at least to the complete disavowal of any political responsibility, as in the case of Protestant sects practicing consistent non-resistance, as, for instance, the Anabaptists, Mennonites, Dunkers and Doukhobors. The Quakers assumed political responsibilities, but they were never consistent non-resisters. They disavowed violence but not resistance.

While social consequences are not considered in such a moral strategy, it would be short-sighted to deny that it may result in redemptive social consequences, at least within the area of individual and personal relationships. Forgiveness may not always prompt the wrongdoer to repentance; but yet it may. Loving the enemy may not soften the enemy's heart; but there are possibilities that it will. Refusal to assert your own interests against another may not shame him into unselfishness; but on occasion it has done so. Love and benevolence may not lead to complete mutuality; but it does have that tendency, particularly within the area of intimate relationships. Human life would, in fact, be intolerable if justice could be established in all relationships only by self-assertion and counter-assertion, or only by a shrewd calculation of claims and counter-claims. The fact is that love, disinterestedness and benevolence do have a strong social and utilitarian value, and the place they hold in the hierarchy of virtues is really established by that value, though religion may view them finally from an inner or transcendent perspective. 'The social virtues', declares David Hume, 'are never regarded without their beneficial tendencies nor viewed as barren and unfruitful. The happiness of mankind, the order of society, the harmony of families, the mutual support of friends, are always considered as a result of their gentle dominion over the breasts of men.' The utilitarian and social emphasis is a little too absolute in the words of Hume, but it is true within limits. Even the teachings of Jesus reveal a prudential strain in which the wholesome social consequences of generous attitudes are emphasized. 'With what measure you mete, it shall be measured to you again.' The paradox of the moral life consists in this: that the highest mutuality is achieved where mutual advantages are not consciously sought as the fruit of love. For love is purest where it desires no returns for itself; and it is most potent where it is purest. Complete mutuality, with its advantages to each party to the relationship, is therefore most perfectly realized where it is not intended, but love is poured out without seeking returns. That is how the madness of religious morality, with its trans-social ideal, becomes the wisdom which achieves wholesome social consequences. For the same reason a purely prudential morality must be satisfied with something less than the best.

Where human relations are intimate (and love is fully effective only in intimate and personal relations), the way of love may be the only way to justice. Where rights and interests are closely interwoven, it is impossible to engage in a shrewd and prudent calculation of comparative rights. Where lives are closely intertwined, happiness is destroyed if it is not shared. Justice by assertion and counter-assertion therefore becomes impossible. The friction involved in the process destroys mutual happiness. Justice by a careful calculation of competing rights is equally difficult, if not impossible. Interests and rights are too mutual to allow for their precise definition in individual terms. The very effort to do so is a proof of the destruction of the spirit of mutuality by which alone intimate relations may be adjusted. The spirit of mutuality can be maintained only by a passion which does not estimate the personal advantages which are derived from mutuality too carefully. Love must strive for something purer than justice if it would attain justice. Egoistic impulses are so much more powerful than altruistic ones that if the latter are not given stronger than ordinary support, the justice which even good men design is partial to those who design it.

This social validity of a moral ideal which transcends social considerations in its purest heights, is progressively weakened as it is applied to more and more intricate, indirect and collective human relations. It is not only unthinkable that a group should be able to attain a sufficiently consistent unselfish attitude toward other groups to give it a very potent redemptive power, but it is improbable that any competing group would have the imagination to appreciate the moral calibre of the achievement. Furthermore a high type of unselfishness, even if it brings ultimate rewards, demands immediate sacrifices. An individual may sacrifice his own interests, either without hope of reward or in the hope of an ultimate compensation. But how is an individual, who is responsible for the interests of his group, to justify the sacrifice of interests other than his own? 'It follows,' declares Hugh Cecil, 'that all that department of morality which requires an individual to sacrifice his interests to others, everything which falls under the heading of unselfishness, is inappropriate to the action of a state. No one has a right to be unselfish with other people's interests.'

This judgment is not sufficiently qualified. A wise statesman is hardly justified in insisting on the interests of his group when they are obviously in unjust relation to the total interests of the community of mankind. Nor is he wrong in sacrificing immediate advantages for the sake of higher mutual advantages. His unwillingness to do this is precisely what makes nations so imprudent in holding to immediate advantages and losing ultimate values of mutuality. Nevertheless it is obvious that fewer risks can be taken with community interests than with individual interests. The inability to take risks naturally results in a benevolence in which selfish advantages must be quite apparent, and in which therefore the moral and redemptive quality is lost.

Every effort to transfer a pure morality of disinterestedness to group relations has resulted in failure. The Negroes of America have practiced it quite consistently since the Civil War. They did not rise against their masters during the war and remained remarkably loyal to them. Their social attitudes since that time, until a very recent date, have been compounded of genuine religious virtues of forgiveness and forbearance, and a certain social inertia which was derived not from religious virtue but from racial weakness. Yet they did not soften the hearts of their oppressors by their social policy.

During the early triumphs of fascism in Italy the socialist leaders suddenly adopted pacifist principles. One of the socialist papers counselled the workers to meet the terror of fascism with the following strategy: '(1) Create a void around fascism. (2) Do not provoke; suffer any provocation with serenity. (3) To win, be better than your adversary. (4) Do not use the weapons of your enemy. Do not follow in his footsteps. (5) Remember that the blood of guerilla warfare falls upon those who shed it. (6) Remember that in a struggle between brothers those are victors who conquer themselves. (7) Be convinced that it is better to suffer wrong than to commit it. (8) Don't be impatient. Impatience is extremely egoistical; it is instinct; it is yielding to one's ego urge. (9) Do not forget that socialism wins the more when it suffers, because it was born in pain and lives on its hopes. (10) Listen to the mind and to the heart which advises you that the working people should be nearer to sacrifice than to vengeance.' A nobler decalogue of virtues could hardly have been prescribed. But the Italian socialists were annihilated by the fascists, their organizations destroyed, and the rights of the workers subordinated to a state which is governed by their enemies. The workers may live 'on their hopes', but there is no prospect of realizing their hopes under the present regime by practicing the pure moral principles which the socialistic journal advocated. Some of them are not incompatible with the use of coercion against their foes. But inasfar as they exclude coercive means they are ineffectual before the brutal will-to-power of fascism.

The effort to apply the doctrines of Tolstoi to the political situation of Russia had a very similar effect. Tolstoi and his disciples felt that the Russian peasants would have the best opportunity for victory over their oppressors if they did not become stained with the guilt of the same violence which the czarist regime used against them. The peasants were to return good for evil, and win their battles by non-resistance. Unlike the policies of Gandhi, the political programme of Tolstoi remained altogether unrealistic. No effort was made to relate the religious ideal of love to the political necessity of coercion. Its total effect was therefore socially and politically deleterious. It helped to destroy a rising protest against political and economic oppression and to confirm the Russian in his pessimistic passivity. The excesses of the terrorists seemed to give point to the Tolstoian opposition to violence and resistance. But the terrorists and the pacifists finally ended in the same futility. And their common futility seemed to justify the pessimism which saw no escape from the traditional injustices of the Russian political and economic system. The real fact was that both sprang from a romantic middle-class or aristocratic idealism, too individualistic in each instance to achieve political effectiveness. The terrorists were diseased idealists, so morbidly oppressed by the guilt of violence resting upon their class, that they imagined it possible to atone for that guilt by deliberately incurring guilt in championing the oppressed. Their ideas were ethical and, to a degree, religious, though they regarded themselves as irreligious. The political effectiveness of their violence was a secondary consideration. The Tolstoian pacifists attempted the solution of the social problem by diametrically opposite policies. But, in common with the terrorists, their attitudes sprang from the conscience of disquieted individuals. Neither of them understood the realities of political life because neither had an appreciation for the significant characteristics of collective behavior. The romantic terrorists failed to relate their isolated acts of terror to any consistent political plan. The pacifists, on the other hand, erroneously attributed political potency to pure non-resistance.

Whenever religious idealism brings forth its purest fruits and places the strongest check upon selfish desire it results in policies which, from the political perspective, are quite impossible. There is, in other words, no possibility of harmonizing the two strategists designed to bring the strongest inner and the

208

most effective social restraint upon egoistic impulse. It would therefore seem better to accept a frank dualism in morals than to attempt a harmony between the two methods which threatens the effectiveness of both. Such a dualism would have two aspects. It would make a distinction between the moral judgments applied to the self and to others; and it would distinguish between what we expect of individuals and of groups. The first distinction is obvious and is explicitly or implicitly accepted whenever the moral problem is taken seriously. To disapprove your own selfishness more severely than the egoism of others is a necessary discipline if the natural complacency toward the self and severity in the judgment of others is to be corrected. Such a course is, furthermore, demanded by the logic of the whole moral situation. One can view the actions of others only from an external perspective; and from that perspective the social justification of self-assertion becomes inevitable. Only the actions of the self can be viewed from the internal perspective; and from that viewpoint all egoism must be morally disapproved. If such disapproval should occasionally destroy self-assertion to such a degree as to invite the aggression of others, the instances will be insignificant in comparison with the number of cases in which the moral disapproval of egoism merely tends to reduce the inordinate self-assertion of the average man. Even in those few cases in which egoism is reduced by religious discipline to such proportions that it invites injustice in an immediate situation, it will have social usefulness in glorifying the moral principle and setting an example for future generations.

The distinction between individual and group morality is a sharper and more perplexing one. The moral obtuseness of human collectives makes a morality of pure disinterestedness impossible. There is not enough imagination in any social group to render it amenable to the influence of pure love. Nor is there a possibility of persuading any social group to make a venture in pure love, except, as in the case of the Russian peasants, the recently liberated Negroes and other similar groups, a morally dubious social inertia should be compounded with the ideal. The selfishness of human communities must be regarded as an inevitability. Where it is inordinate it can be checked only by competing assertions of interest; and these can be effective only if coercive methods are added to moral and rational persuasion.

Moral factors may qualify, but they will not eliminate, the resulting social contest and conflict. Moral goodwill may seek to relate the peculiar interests of the group to the ideal of a total and final harmony of all life. It may thereby qualify the self-assertion of the privileged, and support the interests of the disinherited, but it will never be so impartial as to persuade any group to subject its interests completely to an inclusive social ideal. The spirit of love may preserve a certain degree of appreciation for the common weaknesses and common aspirations which bind men together above the areas of social conflict. But again it cannot prevent the conflict. It may avail itself of instruments of restraint and coercion, through which a measure of trust in the moral capacities of an opponent may be expressed and the expansion rather than contraction of those capacities is encouraged. But it cannot hide the moral distrust expressed by the very use of the instruments of coercion. To some degree the conflict between the purest individual morality and an adequate political policy must therefore remain.

The needs of an adequate political strategy do not obviate the necessity of cultivating the strictest individual moral discipline and the most uncompromising idealism. Individuals, even when involved in their communities, will always have the opportunity of loyalty to the highest canons of personal morality. Sometimes, when their group is obviously bent upon evil, they may have to express their individual ideals by disassociating themselves from their group. Such a policy may easily lead to political irresponsibility, as in the case of the more extreme sects of non-resisters. But it may also be socially useful. Religiously inspired pacifists who protest against the violence of their state in the name of a sensitive individual conscience may never lame the will-to-power of a state as much as a class-conscious labor group. But if their numbers grew to large proportions, they might affect the policy of the government. It is possible, too, that their example may encourage similar non-conformity among individuals in the enemy nation and thus mitigate the impact of the conflict without weakening the comparative strength of their own community.

The ideals of a high individual morality are just as necessary when loyalty to the group is maintained and its general course in relation to other groups is approved. There are possibilities for individual unselfishness, even when the group is asserting its interests and rights against other communities. The interests of the individual are related to those of the group, and he may therefore seek advantages for himself when he seeks them for his group. But this indirect egoism is comparatively insignificant beside the possibilities of expressing or disciplining his egoism in relation to his group. If he is a leader in the group, it is necessary to restrain his ambitions. A leadership, free of self-seeking, improves the morale of the whole group. The leaders of disinherited groups, even when they are avowed economic determinists and scorn the language of personal idealism, are frequently actuated by high moral ideals. If they sought their own personal advantage they could gain it more easily by using their abilities to rise from their group to a more privileged one. The temptation to do this among the abler members of disinherited groups is precisely what has retarded the progress of their class or race.

The progress of the Negro race, for instance, is retarded by the inclination of many able and educated Negroes to strive for identification and assimilation with the more privileged white race and to minimize their relation to a subject race as much as possible. The American Labor Movement has failed to develop its full power for the same reason. Under the influence of American individualism, able labor men have been more ambitious to rise into the class of owners and their agents than to solidify the laboring class in its struggle for freedom. There is, furthermore, always the possibility that an intelligent member of a social group will begin his career in unselfish devotion to the interests of his community, only to be tempted by the personal prizes to be gained, either within the group or by shifting his loyalty to a more privileged group. The interests of individuals are, in other words, never exactly identical with those of their communities. The possibility and necessity of individual moral discipline is therefore never absent, no matter what importance the social struggle between various human communities achieves. Nor can any community achieve unity and harmony within its life, if the sentiments of goodwill and attitudes of mutuality are not cultivated. No political realism which emphasizes the inevitability and necessity of a social struggle, can absolve individuals of the obligation to check their own egoism, to comprehend the interests of others and thus to enlarge the areas of co-operation.

Whether the co-operative and moral aspects of human life, or the necessities of the social struggle, gain the largest significance, depends upon time and circumstance. There are periods of social stability, when the general equilibrium of social forces is taken for granted, and men give themselves to the task of making life more beautiful and tender within the limits of the established social system. The Middle Ages were such a period. While they took injustices for granted, such as would affront the conscience of our day, it cannot be denied that they elaborated amenities, urbanities and delicate refinements of life and art which must make our age seem, in comparison, like the recrudescence of barbarism.

Our age is, for good or ill, immersed in the social problem. A technological civilization makes stability impossible. It changes the circumstances of life too rapidly to incline any one to a reverent acceptance of an ancestral order. Its rapid developments and its almost daily changes in the physical circumstances of life destroy the physical symbols of stability and therefore make for restlessness, even if these movements were not in a direction which imperil the whole human enterprise. But the tendencies of an industrial era are in a definite direction. They tend to aggravate the injustices from which men have perennially suffered; and they tend to unite the whole of humanity in a system of economic interdependence. They make us more conscious of the relations of human communities to each other, than of the relations of individuals within their communities. They obsess us therefore with the brutal aspects of man's collective behavior. They, furthermore, cumulate the evil consequences of these brutalities so rapidly that we feel under a tremendous urgency to solve our social problem before it is too late. As a generation we are therefore bound to feel harassed as well as disillusioned.

In such a situation all the highest ideals and tenderest emotions which men have felt all through the ages, when they become fully conscious of their heritage and possible destiny as human beings, will seem from our perspective to be something of a luxury. They will be under a moral disadvantage, because they appear as a luxury which only those are able to indulge who are comfortable enough to be comparatively oblivious to the desperate character of our contemporary social situation. We live in an age in which personal moral idealism is easily accused of hypocrisy and frequently deserves it. It is an age in which honesty is possible only when it skirts the edges of cynicism. All this is rather tragic. For what the individual conscience feels when it lifts itself above the world of nature and the system of collective relationships in which the human spirit remains under the power of nature, is not a luxury but a necessity of the soul. Yet there is beauty in our tragedy. We are, at least, rid of some of our illusions. We can no longer buy the highest satisfactions of the individual life at the expense of social injustice. We cannot build our individual ladders to heaven and leave the total human enterprise unredeemed of its excesses and corruptions.

In the task of that redemption the most effective agents will be men who have substituted some new illusions for the abandoned ones. The most important of these illusions is that the collective life of mankind can achieve perfect justice. It is a very valuable illusion for the moment; for justice cannot be approximated if the hope of its perfect realization does not generate a sublime madness in the soul. Nothing but such madness will do battle with malignant power and 'spiritual wickedness in high places'. The illusion is dangerous because it encourages terrible fanaticisms. It must therefore be brought under the control of reason. One can only hope that reason will not destroy it before its work is done.

Source: Reinhold Niebuhr, *Moral Man and Immoral Society* (Charles Scribner's Sons 1932; first British edition, SCM Press 1963), Chapter 10.

Text 12: Christian Pragmatism: Theology and Political Thought in the Western World

The assertion is not too hazardous that the ecumenical movement has achieved more telling results in the field of Christian political and social ethics than in any other field of thought and life. These results may be briefly defined as the dissolution of traditional dogmas which Christian thinkers had inherited from the political right or the political left and a gradual elaboration of what Dr Visser 't Hooft has designated as 'Christian pragmatism'. 'Pragmatism' has been a *Schimpfwort* in Christian circles for some time. How then do we arrive at a 'Christian' pragmatism? One can answer that question very simply by the assertion that Christian pragmatism is merely the application of Christian freedom and a sense of responsibility to the complex issues of economics and politics, with the firm resolve that inherited dogmas and generalizations will not be accepted, no matter how revered or venerable, if they do not contribute to the establishment of justice in a given situation.

Consider for instance the state of Christian social thought at both the Stockholm and Oxford conferences. The first of these at Stockholm was still laboring under secular illusions, which we would now define as 'liberal'. One thinks for instance of the extravagant hopes which were placed in the League of Nations. At Oxford the atmosphere, in keeping with the mood of the time, when the second world war already cast its shadow before it, was more realistic. But it was still necessary to entertain ideas which were derived from the right and the left in politics and to ask whether or not they were 'Christian'.

We have now come to the fairly general conclusion that there is no 'Christian' economic or political system. But there is a Christian attitude toward all systems and schemes of justice. It consists on the one hand of a critical attitude toward the claims of all systems and schemes, expressed in the question whether they will contribute to justice in a concrete situation; and on the other hand a responsible attitude, which will not pretend to be God nor refuse to make a decision between political answers to a problem because each answer is discovered to contain a moral ambiguity in God's sight. We are men, not God; we are responsible for making choices between greater and lesser evils, even when our Christian faith, illuminating the human scene, makes it quite apparent that there is no pure good in history; and probably no pure evil either. The fate of civilizations may depend upon these choices between systems of which some are more, others less, just.

This Christian 'pragmatism' has dissolved the certainties of Christian Marxists and Christian conservatives. Perhaps it would be more modest to assert that it has profited by the refutation of claims and counterclaims in actual historical experience. It has been Christian only in the sense that it drew upon Christian insights which were long obscured in the minds of even the most pious, but which have been clarified by historical experience even as they have clarified that experience.

There were those, for instance, who were so outraged by the injustices of a 'capitalist' system that they were ready, though usually with some reservations, to embrace that part of the Marxist creed which promised a higher degree of justice through the socialization of property. Experience has proved that socialization does not remove economic power from the community. The nationalization of property may on the other hand merely cumulate both economic and political power in the hands of a single oligarchy. We know the baneful effects of this policy in the realities of contemporary communism. But even the more moderate and democratic socialism no longer offers the attraction to the Christian conscience which it once did. For it has become apparent that the measures which it may take to establish a minimum of justice in the community are in danger of destroying the freedom and spontaneity which its economic life requires. In the effort to correct unjust inequalities such measures may bind the community in a static equalitarianism. This will remind us that equality is the regulative principle of justice but that it is, like liberty and love, no simple possibility in any political community.

Other illusions of the left have been dispelled. Nationalism was once thought to be the product of capitalism and idealists embraced socialism for the sake of its alleged internationalism. Now the Socialist Parties are all tempted to espouse nationalistic interests partly because socialization means nationalization (a fact which throws many European socialists into opposition to such supranational institutions as the European Coal and Steel Community) and partly because socialists find the liberal Catholic parties espousing the cause of international co-operation. How strangely history dispels our illusions and punctures our pretensions!

It would, however, be quite wrong to espouse economic

conservatism because of this disillusionment of the left or with the left. Conservatism in America and in some parts of Europe means the anachronistic espousal of physiocratic theories, which promise justice through the emancipation of economic life from every kind of political and moral control. It rests on the illusion that there are 'laws of nature' in history, that there are 'pre-established' harmonies in nature, and therefore presumably in history, which is equated with nature.

These physiocratic theories lie at the foundation of what has become the 'philosophy' of the 'free enterprise' system on which the whole bourgeois world has consistently prided itself, and which did indeed emancipate economic enterprise from irrelevant political restraints and encourage productivity through economic incentives.

But naturally the basic theory was as heretical, from the Christian standpoint, as Marxism. The self-interest was not as harmless as the theory assumed; and the trusted 'pre-established harmonies' did not exist. Ironically enough, the static disharmonies of history, due to the disbalances of social power characteristic of an agrarian civilization, were transmuted into the dynamic disproportions of power of a commercial civilization at the precise moment when they were so confidently proclaimed.

The social consequences of this miscalculation were catastrophic in the early days of industrialism. The social distress among industrial workers was responsible for their defection from the hopes of the democratic world, and for a rebellion which ultimately led to their adoption of the Marxist creed, in its various versions.

The social history of the Western world could be summarized as the gradual refutation in experience of both dogmas, which inspired the political activities of both the middle classes and the workers. In the healthiest of the nations of Western civilization, each of the dogmas or presuppositions contributed something to the extension of both freedom and justice; and contributed the more certainly because neither political force was able to gain a clear victory over the other.

The political and social history of Great Britain is perhaps a classical symbol of the social history of the whole Western world. For in Britain (and possibly in the British Commonwealth of Nations), the dogmatic distance between the two contending parties consistently narrowed; and no party has been able to gain a secure dominance over the other. This is the historical expression of the paradoxical relation of freedom to equal justice, which makes it impossible to sacrifice either value to the other. Christians will recognize this history as one evidence of the providential workings of God in history, generating more wisdom than the proposals of the human agents in the social struggle, the wisdom of each being clouded by interest to such a degree that it cannot see the obvious facts. Thus the social history of the Western world has been the gradual attainment of wisdom and justice through the inconclusive contest between two social forces, informed by equally heretical dogmas and partially true presuppositions.

Christian thought must not pretend that what we have described as its growing pragmatism has not been influenced by this general history in Western thought and life. But we must also recognize that what has been wrought out has actually been a view of life and the establishment of justice in a community which could have been elaborated originally if we had had a clear biblical insight into the nature of history, the freedom of man, and the corruption of sin in that freedom, and had therefore realized that history cannot be equated with nature; nor can the political judgments which we make about our and each other's interests be equated with the judgments which a scientist makes about natural phenomena. In other words the process we have described has been the gradual extrication of our thought from the baneful effects of heresies about man and God which have infected it ever since the French Enlightenment.

It would be wrong however to suggest that our civilization gained nothing from this conflict of heresies, for they established precisely that contest of political and social forces which was the prerequisite of justice in our society. These developments were not anticipated in the traditional 'Christian' societies before the rise of these heresies. If we ask why they were not anticipated we will learn why it was necessary to challenge 'Christian conservatism' before either political or economic justice could be established. We are now speaking of 'Christian conservatism' in the traditional sense, and not in the sense which it has acquired in America and some continental countries. For, according to that connotation, this conservatism is only the religious sanctification of *laissez-faire* economics.

This older conservatism may be defined as the religious sanctification of established authority, which made it difficult to resist such authority and to correct the injustices which arose from permitting an unchallenged authority in the human community. We must humbly confess the limitations of this conservative approach to political problems, for they prove that Protestant Christianity is not as directly related to the rise of free societies as we would all like to believe. Ever since the Reformation this Christian conservatism has made the mistake of interpreting the Christian reverence for orders in society, providentially established beyond the contrivance of men, as the uncritical acceptance of a particular authority and a particular order. We must remember that it required a whole century for later Calvinism to add the proper discriminations to the thought of Calvin and Luther, so that it was possible for Christians both to accept the providentially established order of a nation, and to resist a particular government for its injustice.

Upon this distinction between the principle of order and a particular government, established by seventeenth-century Calvinism in Scotland, Holland, France and England, the health of our whole free world depends. It is important to establish this point, because it contains both the resources of the Christian faith in the political sphere and the limitations of a conventional interpretation of that faith. The resource is a proper reverence for providential order and justice, established beyond the resources of the human agents, and not to be lightly challenged. The limitation is an undue and uncritical respect for any particular authority and a consequent disinclination to challenge it. Secular idealists are therefore right in drawing attention to the contributions which rational discrimination made to the creation of contemporary democratic institutions. But they are wrong when they conceal the fact that the worship of 'reason' was as fruitful in generating modern tyrannies as the veneration of established authority was in preserving ancient tyrannies.

If we fully analyze the complex relation which exists between religious and rational factors in the establishment of justice, we must come to the conclusion that two elements are equally necessary for the solution of the problems of the human community. One is a proper reverence for factors and forces which are truly absolute; and the other is a discriminate attitude toward relative and ambiguous factors and forces. As Christians we insist that there be a proper reverence for the absolute factors, which might be enumerated as: (1) The authority of God beyond all human and historic authorities, enabling us to defy those authorities on occasion with a resolute 'We must obey God rather than men.' (2) The authority of the moral law embodied in the revelation in Christ, which is to be distinguished from any particular version of that law which may have evolved historically, including the different versions of 'natural law'. (3) The insistence upon the 'dignity' of the person which makes it illegitimate for any community to debase the individual into a mere instrument of social process and power and try to obscure the fact of his ultimate destiny, which transcends all historic realities. This acknowledgment of the 'dignity' of man must be accompanied in Christian thought by a recognition that this precious individual is also a sinner, that his lusts and ambitions are a danger to the community; and that his rational processes are tainted by the taint of his own interests. (4) Reverence for the 'orders' of authority and social harmony which have actually been established among us, beyond the wisdom of man and frequently by providential workings in which 'God hath made the wrath of man to praise him.'

Every one of these 'absolutes' is in danger of corruption; which is why we cannot speak so simply of Christian 'civic virtue'. Reverence for the will of God may degenerate into a too-simple identification of our interests with the divine will, a fact which may make conventional Christianity a source of confusion in the community. Reverence for the historical dignity of the person may degenerate into a 'bourgeois' individualism in which the individual is falsely exalted above the community and the cause of justice. The moral law may be falsely interpreted from the standpoint of the interests of any portion of the community, and more particularly of the pious section of the community. Reverence for the principle of order may degenerate into an undue respect for a particular order, a form of degeneration which Calvinism, and later Lutheranism,

219

overcame only at the price of bitter experience with tyranny. If we summarize these developments we must recognize that the same faith which prompted reverence for the absolutes, which transcend the relativities of history, may also confuse the picture of the human community in its political and economic perplexities by imparting religious sanction to one of the relative factors and removing it from the wholesome challenges which have been discovered to be necessary to prevent any power in the human community from becoming pretentious in its pride or vexatious in its power. In short we must face the fact that the Reformation did not draw sufficiently rigorous conclusions from its principle *Justus et Peccator simul*. For according to that principle the redeemed man could not be trusted to exercise power without sin. Therefore the checks upon his power were necessary, even if it was the power of government which was involved. It required a full century to gain the necessary discrimination for the distinction between the principle of order and the providentially established political order of a given nation, and a particular government, upon which close check must be placed and its power, in the words of Sam Rutherford, 'measured out ounce by ounce'.

To this failure in discriminate judgment in our Reformation heritage one must add all those indiscriminate judgments which result from deriving political judgment from analogies between historically contingent social norms, embodied in the canon, and the contingent circumstances of contemporary life. After all, the original error in regard to government was due not only to a failure to distinguish between the majesty of government and the majesty of a particular government; it was also due to an excessive emphasis upon St Paul's admonition in Romans 13, an admonition which obviously had the immediate purpose of arresting 'eschatological unrest' and which would, taken alone, disturb the scriptural 'consensus' upon the attitude toward government. For that consensus includes two motifs. The one is appreciation of government as divinely ordained, and established by forces greater than the conscious contrivance of men. The other is a critical attitude toward government as inclined to usurp the divine majesty by its pretensions of pride and the injustices of its power.

The power of relating scriptural insights to the flowing

stream of human events is a very important one to this day. We cannot deny that frequently scriptural insights are falsely related to highly contingent situations, in such a way as to bring confusion into our judgments. We children of the Reformation pride ourselves on freedom from the inflexible standards which Catholics draw from their conception of 'natural law'. But it must be confessed that an indiscriminate biblicism is as much a source of confusion as Catholic natural law theories.

In the history of the slow development of justice in the free societies of Western civilization, the secular section of our civilization claims that it provided exactly those discriminations which the religious elements found such difficulty in achieving. This is partly true but partly false. For modern secularism obscured its rational discrimination between constant and variable factors in the problems of the community by its worship of human 'reason' as a source of virtue. This worship, which had its rise in the eighteenth century, failed to take account of the sinful corruption of reason, which made the 'checks and balances' of justice as necessary in an 'enlightened' as in an ignorant community. The observer of history will note that all the illusions which lie at the foundation of modern Communist tyranny had their inception in the eighteenth century worship of 'reason' or 'nature'. These illusions were insensible of the unique character of human freedom, and consequently of human history. Above all, they obscured the fact that sinful self-assertion might rise from the same human capacities which were praised as 'rational'.

If the secular part of our culture derived grave errors from its worship of reason and nature, rather than the worship of God, it compounded those errors by its extreme voluntarism, which was blind to the workings of providence in history and thought that men could create both governments and communities by the 'social contract'. This mistake, of imagining that men are in complete control of their historical destiny, reveals itself today in the secular proposals for 'world government', which our secular idealists press upon us, and they are disappointed when we refuse to share their illusions.

But we would do well to note that even the errors of the social contract theorists served some purpose when they were brought into contact with truth, which removed their evil effects. Thus the principle of government 'by consent of the governed' is a legitimate political principle of democracy, drawn from the illegitimate illusions of social contract theorists. In this way error contributed to truth and served to counteract the error in the Christian truth. For it was true that God established order in human society beyond the contrivance of men; and it was an error to give particular governments an undue reverence and deny the citizen the political power involved in the right of suffrage.

The manner in which the errors and truths of Christians and secularists, of later Calvinists and sectarian Christians, of Catholics and Protestants, have been used for the attainment of justice in a technical age, is itself a remarkable display of providence as contrasted with the wisdom and the foolishness of men. For it is quite apparent that no single force, whether pious or impious, could have accomplished what has been done.

The political and economic sphere, as a realm of relative and contingent realities and of ambiguous moral choices, makes discriminate judgment so necessary, because it is always important to distinguish between the constant and the variable factors, and between the ultimate and the proximate moral norms. This fact has led to one type of Christian politics, which merely asserts the moral ambiguity of all political positions and exhibits its Christian transcendence by refusing to make a choice 'which the Pope or Mr. Truman could make just as well'. There is no particular wisdom in this kind of neutrality. It leads, in fact, to the political confusion before Nazism, which led to Nazism. Nor is it very helpful to introduce discriminations into the fields of judgment which are supposed to be uniquely Christian but which detract from consideration of the main problems of justice. The judgment, for instance, that Communism is preferable to Nazism because it is not morally nihilistic, or not militaristic, or that it does not intend to corrupt the Christian faith (its only purpose being to annihilate it), or that it is not anti-Semitic. All these judgments obscure the very significant fact that utopian illusions may be as fruitful of tyranny as moral cynicism. This fact is one of the most significant experiences of our day. Observers, whether theologians or rationalists, who obscure this fact do our generation a disservice.

Incidentally, it would be well for theologians and religious people generally to recognize that when they claim to make political judgments on hazardous issues from the standpoint of their faith, their knowledge of the Bible or their theology, they run exactly the same danger of seeking absolute sanction for their frail human judgments as our secular friends run when they claim 'scientific' or 'objective' validity for their judgments. Every judgment is hazardous and corrupted in the realm where we judge each other. Theologians are just as tempted to obscure that fact as 'social scientists'.

In the contest between the free world and Communism, for instance, we have all the perplexities which have confused the consciences and minds of men through the centuries. If we become obsessed with the distinction between our righteousness and the evil of Communism we may reduce the conflict to one between two forces which Professor Butterfield has defined as 'two organized systems of self-righteousness'. If on the other hand we insist that this struggle is merely one more illustration of the fact that all historic struggles are between sinful men, we run the danger of conniving with a vicious tyranny and playing traitor to the God of justice.

The sum of these considerations is that we have an obligation as Christians to establish and extend community and justice as far as lies within our power. We must obey the law of love under conditions and within limits which make no simple application possible. It is not possible because the sins of men, the persistence of individual and collective self-interest, force us to maintain order by coercion and may make resistance and war a necessity of justice. We assume our responsibilities in this community with many other citizens who do not share our faith. We assume them from the standpoint of a faith which discerns a mysterious divine sovereignty over the whole drama of human events, which ought not be surprised by any manifestations of evil history but is not prepared to yield to any evil for motives of self-love. We believe that this majestic God who created the world and sustains it by his providence is finally revealed in Christ our Lord. We are protected by this faith from many aberrations into which the 'children of this world' perennially fall: hope of gaining purely human mastery over the drama of history; hope that evil will gradually be eliminated from the human community by growing human goodness or by more adequate instruments of justice; trust in the power of human reason and blindness to the corruption of that reason.

These resources give us some treasures to contribute to the community in its struggle for justice. Among them are an understanding of the fragmentary character of all human virtue; the tentative character of all schemes of justice, since they are subject to the flow of history; the irrevocable character of the 'moral law' transcending all historical relativities; and the hazardous judgments which must be made to establish justice between the competing forces and interests. We can tolerate all these hazards, relativities and tentativities because we 'look for a city which has foundations whose builder and maker is God'.

But we must also accept in all humility the fact that this Christian faith is mediated to the community by sinful men and that our sins frequently obscure the wisdom of the Gospel and interfere with the course of God's grace to men. We must therefore also acknowledge that the community needs protection against our religious aberrations, against our tendency to fanatic intrusions into the tolerance which the community requires for its harmony, against our inclination to indiscriminate judgment.

In short, the health of any of our communities is best served if Christians try at one and the same time to bear witness to their faith, humbly accept treasures of wisdom which may be mediated to the community by those who do not share their faith, and welcome those policies of communal justice which are designed to correct the aberrations of men.

Source: Ronald H. Stone, ed., *Faith and Politics: A Commentary on Religious, Social and Political Thought in a Technological Age* (New York: George Braziller 1968). Originally published in the *Ecumenical Review*, 1957, and titled 'Theology and Political Thought in the Western World'.

c h a p t e r   n i n e

John C. Bennett
1902–

Introduction

Bennett was born in Ontario, and educated at Williams College, Oxford University, and Union Theological Seminary. Entering academic teaching at Union, he moved to Auburn Theological Seminary, then to the Pacific School of Religion, and spent the rest of his career back at Union (1943–70), including as dean, and Reinhold Niebuhr Professor of Social Ethics. In public life, he was vice-chairman of the New York State Liberal Party, and he exercised a significant influence on the Churches' social statements through his own United Church of Christ, but more especially in the ecumenical movement. A strong promoter of Protestant-Roman Catholic dialogue, he was also a major influence at Oxford, and subsequent World Council of Churches' conferences at Amsterdam, Evanston, New Delhi, Geneva, and Uppsala.

Bennett's long life moved through four stages, each reflecting a change of context, and each contributing to the development of his Christian social thought. Beginning with the social gospel, he could remember the great steel strike of 1919, and the Churches' involvement in it as the high-water mark of the Social Creed and gospel. Next, the depression of the 1930s, and the rise of Hitler and Stalin, witnessed his commitment to theological realism, supported by his membership of the Theological Discussion Group, with the two Niebuhrs and Tillich. Like Reinhold Niebuhr, the realism was combined with a radical criticism of capitalism, symbolized in their membership of the Fellowship of Socialist Christians. The rise of the New Deal, the success of Western mixed economies in the postwar period and a growing criticism of communism, diverted him from Christian socialism. His leadership role in the Federal Council of Churches' enquiry into economic life expressed this accommodation to welfare capitalism. Finally, in the 1960s and 1970s, the Vietnam War (he led a Christian opposition to it), and a growing awareness of Third World poverty and liberation theology, confirmed his need to reaffirm the Christian radical imperative.

Bennett's theological work brings together these experiences to become the clearest expression of the emerging nature of Christian social ethics in the West. Never a charismatic leader like Rauschenbusch or Niebuhr, he was none the less a major Christian leader and thinker. Essentially, his is the contribution of a bridge-builder. The content of his discerning judgements on foreign policy, politics and economic life illustrate this ability very clearly. Yet it is in the *character* of his Christian social ethics that we best see his ability to hold together in a corrective synthesis insights from the social gospel and Christian realism. The latter is revealed in his rejection of the illusions of optimists (as in the social gospel) and pessimists (as in many conservatives), his realistic view of man and the world (as hope and sin), and his recognition of the role of power in human affairs. His *Christian Realism* (1941) characterizes this strand in his thought. The other strand, the *Christian Radical Imperative* (1975), indicates his commitment to the criticism of Western society. Rooted in the social gospel and the Christian realism of the 1930s, it was expressed in his *Social Salvation* (1935), but persisted into today's context, chiefly through his sensitivity to the challenge of liberation theology. By taking account of its criticism of Western economic and political power, but more particularly of its appearance as black and feminist theology, he has sought to develop Western social Christianity by correcting its earlier prejudices. He has therefore developed social Christianity by taking substantive account of Christian realism, but also by listening to new radical Christian social movements.

Text 13 was originally given as lectures at the University of Virginia in 1945, with the title 'Christian Ethics and Public Life'. Forming a central part of Bennett's task of bringing Christian visions to bear on modern social realities, it therefore complements his substantive work on Christian realism and radical imperatives. It does this by developing a *theological method* for applying ethical criteria to public life in ways that take account of ethical limits. The latter include the constraints of sin, but equally of finitude, particularly as the need to respect technical autonomies in decision-making.

The argument is edited into three stages: the problem of moving from faith to public policies; four classic ways that Christians have done this (indicating the importance of typologies, and predating Richard Niebuhr's more famous *Christ and Culture* by five years); and finally, an elaboration of his own, fifth, strategy. In particular, like Preston, he uses middle axioms to show how faith can suggest social goals, which take creative account of ethical limits. This reflects the great influence on him of the Oxford conference and ecumenical social ethics.

Text 13: Christian Ethics and Social Policy

The distance between

[...] Why is it so difficult to find a straight line from Christian ethics to the concrete problems of society? In the case of all human problems it is difficult to live according to the Christian ideal. Personal relations are deeply infected by jealousy and hostility. [...] But there are factors in the social order which enormously intensify the problem. I shall mention some of them.

1. In public life there is a long unbroken history which provides opportunity for the accumulation of disorders, for the development of encrusted prejudices, vested interests that have the sanction of the fathers, vicious circles of fear, hatred and vindictiveness which the wisest contemporaries do not know how to overcome. [...] Who can see a clear way to overcome the consequences in American life of the sins of the slave trade? [...] In most contemporary social decisions we find ourselves forced to act at some point in a vicious circle that has a long history.

2. The decisions of public life involve large mixed communities in which only a minority, and often a very small minority, is guided by Christian standards. The Christian citizen must

always act in cooperation with citizens who do not even admit the authority of Christian ethics. [. . .] This difficulty is very great but it is well for us not to estimate the situation in terms of labels and avowed commitments. While there are profound conflicts in the world between Christians and those who reject even the ethical goals of Christianity, and while there are serious questions concerning the dependence of Christian ethics upon Christian faith, it remains true that in many nations, not least in our own, there is a general deposit of ethical purpose that has been influenced by Christianity. [. . .]

Moreover, so distorted and one-sided has been the grasp of Christians themselves upon their own faith that it is often true that men who reject their faith and who have no part in the Christian Church may stand for social objectives that are essentially just, but which perhaps a majority of Church members oppose. No degree of theological soundness and no religious training or experience can be depended on, of themselves, to overcome the limitations of perspective that are the result of one's position in society. Those who know from experience what it is to be unemployed or to be members of a minority race or to be in other ways the victims of society have insights which are essential for social wisdom.

3. The large-scale problems of society are greatly aggravated by the fact that we are constantly dealing with people with whom we have no direct personal relationship. Initimate personal relations have their own difficulties that are the result of the emotional development of the individual whose early life is largely a response to the attitudes of parents and others in the family. I do not say that these difficulties are in their way more or less serious than those that we encounter in dealing with people at a distance. It is enough to insist that there is a vast difference between the two kinds of difficulty and that the latter conditions our decisions in public life. The imagination of any one of us is so limited that it is impossible for us to grasp fully the experience of those whom we have never seen and who are in superficial ways quite different from ourselves. [. . .]

4. This limited imagination is often combined with conflicting interests, and when such is the case moral blindness is intensified. To see another group, which is difficult to understand anyway, through the distortions of group-interest is to see

many illusions. [...] Where the interest is justified, it has a constructive role. Anyone who is concerned about justice must ally himself with those movements which have as part of their dynamic the pressure of group interest in those who are at present victims of injustice. This is one valid element in the great emphasis upon the Labor Movement that has been characteristic of the Social Gospel in this country. But it is obvious that even justified group interest is not restrained within the limits set by a concern for justice. There is always a push for gains that exceed any just demands – partly as revenge for past wrongs, partly as defense against future misuse of power by opponents, partly as a natural expression of self-interest. [...]

5. The limitations of our imaginations and the distortions that arise from conflicting interests are further complicated by the extraordinary resources in the human spirit for cloaking self-interest with idealism. Often this is done sincerely. It is much easier to be deceived when there is a grain of truth in the way in which the ideals are used. Religion and patriotism are perhaps the most frequent sources of this confusion. [...]

6. A sixth factor which makes public life especially difficult from the moral point of view is that personal responsibility is in many ways diluted. The individual citizen has some responsibility for the policies of his nation but it is shared with so many others that it does not come home to him with full force. [...]

The problem of diluted responsibility is as serious in economic relations as in the policies of the nation. The directors of a corporation are responsible to the stockholders; and the chief interest of the stockholders as stockholders, not necessarily as human beings, is in dividends. The whole momentum of a corporation is on the side of increasing profits and all other interests – the welfare of the workers or of the community at large – are secondary. The stockholders themselves may be Christians – they may even be Churches – but they have only a marginal interest in anything but dividends, and since their holdings are usually divided among many corporations, they cannot follow intelligently in each case policies that have ethical importance. [...] This state of affairs makes moral choices very difficult. It blurs even the most important issues so far as the individual is concerned.

The six factors that we have discussed help us to see why the problems of social life are so difficult for the Christian. These considerations show why it is that often we must deal with a vast accumulation of evil, why our public choices are so often choices between only evil alternatives. Emil Brunner has laid bare the full bitterness of the problem in his statement that there are times when we are *obliged* to do evil. I shall quote a passage from *The Divine Imperative*, which is the greatest book on Christian Ethics written by any Protestant in our time:

> We never see the real meaning of 'original sin,' we never perceive the depth and universality of evil, or what evil means in the depths common to us all, until we are *obliged* to do something which, in itself, is evil; that is, we do not see this clearly until we are obliged to do something in our official capacity – for the sake of order, and therefore the sake of love – which, apart from our 'office' would be absolutely wrong. [. . .]

There is yet another set of complications which must be mentioned before we try to find our way to some solution of the problem. The factors which I have already mentioned are in some way related to the moral decisions of the Christian. They all involve some spiritual blindness or they refer to some objective situation which can be kept under moral judgment. The complications with which I shall now deal are morally neutral. In actual life they never come as neatly separated from moral choices as they do in this analysis, and yet it is important to recognize that they have this distinctive character. There are aspects of most social policies concerning which there is no distinctively Christian guidance. There are at least three such strands in most decisions about which we get no distinctively Christian guidance, if we analyze our situation carefully. First there are the technical issues which call for expert judgment. These involve matters of fact about which exact information is called for. They also involve reasoning within an area which calls for special training. Many questions of method are of this sort. The debate about specific methods of preventing unemployment or the debate concerning international monetary arrangements are illustrations of this kind of issue. Most often when we come to specific legislation we find that the difference between two proposed bills for dealing with a complicated social problem, such as health insurance or industrial relations, involves technical issues and that these bills are couched in a jargon with which we cannot deal adequately without special knowledge.

A second kind of issue is one that requires the prediction of how groups of men will behave if a particular policy is followed. This is both a political and a psychological question. Expert knowledge is called for but the experts may know very little that is conclusive. Indeed this kind of difficulty is far more perplexing than the technical issues. Through what political party should one work in America – through an existing party or through some new party? That is the kind of issue. Most of our decisions about foreign policy illustrate what I mean. [...] Nearly every hard problem of foreign policy that we face as a nation – how to prevent Germany from becoming the disease center of Europe, how to make stable the changes of attitude that have already appeared in Japan, how to prevent civil war in China, etc. – raises for us questions of this kind to which there is no clear Christian answer.

A third type of issue is the choice between two or more competing values when we know that both or all are important. The discussion concerning the line to be drawn between various forms of private initiative, or the freedom of the individual and over-all public planning of economic life, is of this kind. In the discussion of the dangers of totalitarianism, of the 'road to serfdom' there are involved both clear moral issues and also all of these neutral issues. We have to ask ourselves technical questions about any proposed step in the direction of social planning. We have to ask ourselves questions concerning the effect of such a step upon human behavior. Will it necessarily become the first stage in the development toward totalitarianism or will there be various brakes along the way? If this step is not taken what will happen? Usually that question is ignored by the opponents of all planning. We are here dealing quite obviously with competing values – with two sets of values, both of which have a valid claim upon us, the values of freedom and order, the values of personal responsibility and of social security, the values of freedom and justice – different kinds of freedom as well. Here we can argue endlessly and the issues do not yield themselves to sure Christian judgment. [...]

The difficulties with which we have been dealing have long been recognized in varying degrees, and in the light of one or more of them Christians have developed various strategies in relating Christian ethics to social policy. In the next chapter we shall examine several Christian social strategies.

Four Christian social strategies

(A) Catholic strategy

First, I shall consider some of the resources of Catholicism, especially Roman Catholicism, in helping Christians to deal with the perplexities which have been outlined. There are three resources that are distinctively Catholic.

There is, most obviously, the Catholic idea of the two levels of the Christian life, the level of the ordinary Christian citizen and the level of the monastic life with its detachment from the conflicts of the world. [. . .]

A second Catholic resource of an entirely different character is the assimilation of the ethics of natural law or rational morality into the authoritative teaching of the Church concerning public questions. This means in practice that Catholics – Roman Catholics and also in many cases Anglo-Catholics – have a whole system of social ethics which is regarded as Christian, and which helps them to relate the Christian social imperative to the most tangled problems of the world without in their judgment abandoning Christian ethics for a secular standard of morality. It is possible for Catholics to think in terms of Christian states and Christian societies whereas these conceptions can only be held by Protestants with great reservations. [. . .]

The resources of an ecclesiastically developed natural law become of special importance in the concrete case because the Church is able to relate its ethical teaching authoritatively to particular social choices. The Church is wise in making sparing use of the full authority which it claims on a world scale. But the enormous prestige of the hierarchy enables the Church to teach with effective though not absolute authority concerning many issues that arise in the social order. The practical effect of this is that the Church can often take moral responsibility for difficult john#

choices and thus relieve the individual conscience of a burden from which the Protestant knows no escape. This would be true of participation in war, for example, which has in most cases been fully approved by the Church without qualification.

These two Catholic instruments of interpretation – natural law and the authority of the Church – which can relate Christian ethics absolutely to the ambiguities of public life do not in practice work as effectively as my description of the theory would suggest. Certainly it is true that Catholics are better able than Protestants to say what the pattern of a Christian society should be. Also, it is true that the Church can take a strong line, negatively, in rejecting a major social alternative. This is true of Communism, for example, and for many reasons apart from the teaching about property. The exigencies of the Church as an institution may determine for the Catholic the attitude that he should take toward public questions. But, there are serious limitations to all of these factors. [. . .]

So, while there are habits of mind and also theoretical resources for dealing with questions of social policy which distinguish Catholicism from Protestantism, the thoughtful Catholic who is independent enough to be critical of the local or national hierarchy has few decisions made for him.

The Catholic emphasis upon natural law has much to commend it when we contrast it with the theology of Barth, which insists on an absolute chasm between the revealed will of God in the Bible and all forms of morality based upon reason or upon common experience. There is a moral order that we know something about apart from Christian faith, even though this knowledge is more likely to be distorted than the Catholic moralist admits. The Christian can make much use of the deposit of the moral wisdom of Plato, Aristotle and the Stoics which is already an important part of the Christian tradition. And he can learn from the moral experience of modern men with or without Christian faith who have seen more clearly and in more concrete terms than the ancients the claims of equal justice and of a universal human community.

The chief criticisms of the Catholic use of natural law is that it is thought of in too static and precise terms and that the application of it to specific circumstances, even when the Church speaks, is never so disinterestedly Christian as is claimed. Not sufficient place is given to the autonomy of technical issues with which every moral question is intertwined, and the degree of moral ambiguity in most Christian decisions concerning social policy is not recognized. The difficulties outlined in the last chapter create a greater problem for the Christian thinker than the Catholic can consistently admit. A Christian state or a Christian civilization even under the best Catholic auspices is more corrupted by the self-interest of the groups that control it, not least if they be priests, than is admitted. The root of the difficulty is that there are two areas of human experience where Catholic theology does not prepare the Catholic to find sin to be pervasive – the life of Reason and the Church – and so he is not sufficiently prepared to correct the aberrations of either. I do not claim that Protestants do this correcting well either but historic Protestant theology should leave them with less excuse.

These are my criticisms of this Catholic strategy when it works, but it should be said, as I have already suggested, that it does not always work and that differences of judgment in the Church may leave the Catholic almost as perplexed as the Protestant. He may have an added perplexity: what to do about a Church that claims such superior wisdom and sanctity and yet shows on all sides the weakness that comes when any human institution is exalted above criticism.

(B) The strategy of withdrawal

A second Christian strategy is the total or partial withdrawal of the individual Christian or a limited Christian group or sect from those aspects of public life which create special problems for the Christian conscience. The ascetic withdrawal associated with Catholic monasticism is made possible by the fact that the Church as an institution does not seek to withdraw from the world. It is linked with a frank acceptance of a double standard for the ordinary citizen or householder and for the religious ascetic who seeks to realize holiness on a level of heroic renunciation. The sectarian withdrawal characteristic of Protestantism has no place for such a double standard as an essential aspect of the Christian life, though sometimes in modern days of religious tolerance a kind of double standard is admitted in practice for those who share the convictions of the sect and those who do not but who are yet regarded by the members of the sect as Christians within the larger ecumenical fellowship. The Anabaptist protest against the participation of Christians as magistrates in public life is an important example of this Protestant withdrawal. The Quaker protest against war and all forms of participation in war is perhaps the best known contemporary example of this strategy. [. . .]

One of the most interesting contemporary examples of this Protestant strategy of partial withdrawal is the case of the Mennonites. Their theology is influenced by the main line Reformation doctrines concerning human nature and they are under no illusions concerning what can be expected of society as a whole or of the state. Their ideal is the development of a community that is as self-sufficient and thus as free from compromise with the world as possible. They are a rural people and find that a rural community is a better environment in which to escape the sin of the world than is urban civilization. They are pacifists but they do not expect the state to adopt their pacifist principles. [. . .]

I have enlarged on this strategy because it is more consistent than the Quaker policies and it illustrates so well the problems inherent in the attempt to relate Christian ethics to social policies. Its solution is based upon an essential pessimism concerning the world and – perhaps as a second best – the acceptance of the necessity of developing islands of Christian holiness in a sea that will always be the scene of violence and injustice. The most serious criticism is that it has nothing effective to say to the vast multitude that must flounder in that sea.

This Mennonite strategy seems to most of us who assume full responsibility for the political order to be dangerously complacent and legalistic. It promises holiness to a limited group at the cost of evasion of one's responsibilities as a member of the larger community. Such holiness is itself illusory, for there is real participation in the sins of the larger community that is overlooked. Christians who withdraw from the world are guilty of sins of omission that involve responsibility for evils not prevented. When these things are said, I believe that there may be situations in which the Mennonite strategy would be the best available for Christians though they should always strive for a better situation in which more possibilities are open. In a totalitarian society that has become involved in a succession of wars which have no positive meaning in them the Christian Church might be driven to some such strategy as a desperate expedient. Probably in such a case it would know only a martyred and underground existence. The Mennonite strategy so far has been the search for an environment of political freedom in which governments recognize the significance of conscience. The fact that such environments and such governments exist might seem to be a refutation of the Mennonite pessimism concerning the social order. The choice between that kind of society and one that is totalitarian and oppressive would seem to be one choice for the political order to which the Christian with Mennonite principles would be bound to make as direct a contribution as possible.

(C) The identification of Christianity with particular social programs

The third strategy is the identification of Christianity with particular social programs or institutions or movements. Those who follow this strategy fail to take seriously the kind of neutral issues which I have discussed – technical questions, problems involving the prediction of human behavior, and the weighing of two competing values when both have real claims upon us. It is these issues which make it difficult to have Christian solutions that include both goals and methods. Those who follow this strategy are usually unconvinced by the argument that most social policies which involve large mixed groups are morally ambiguous.

This strategy is at times the consequence of Roman Catholic assumptions and methods, though Roman Catholicism as a total religious system will preserve areas of transcendence that will not be permanently lost, no matter how much at a given time and in a particular country the Church may identify itself with a particular cause – perhaps a crusade against Communism, perhaps a corrupt Feudalism.

This third strategy is the constant temptation of liberal Protestantism. It is the line of least resistance among all optimistic and idealistic Christians, among all who become easily

236

convinced that their solution of a complex social problem is the only Christian solution. It may be sufficient to suggest familiar examples of this strategy in order to show how pervasive it is in the modern Church, not least in the American Church.

The identification of Christianity with pacifism as a political program is one example. [. . .]

It is a common temptation to identify Christian ethics with a particular program for economic reconstruction. There have been many Christian Socialist movements, for example, which have assumed such a relationship between Christianity and Socialism. These have varied a great deal in emphasis, some of them making absolute claims for Socialism as the only Christian position. There was a group in Britain that called itself 'The Christian Left', inspired largely by Professor John Macmurray, which, at least before the recent war, found a partial embodiment of its ideal for society in the Soviet Union. It was easier to believe in a necessary connection between Socialism and Christianity so long as the threat of totalitarianism was not taken seriously. It was easy to assume that Capitalism was the Devil, that collectivism *per se* was good and that if society overcame the evils of Capitalism, we could be confident that freedom would be added to justice and security, and that the major cause of imperialism and war would be destroyed.

In contrast to this simple identification of Christianity and Socialism there is a movement that is called the Fellowship of Socialist Christians which has worked out a view of the relationship between Christianity and Socialism that is circumspect and, as I believe, sound at these points. Its members are convinced that the Socialist criticisms of both individualistic and monopoly Capitalism are essentially correct and that it is their function as Christians to work for the social ownership and control of the chief centers of economic power. They do not claim that this is the only possible position for Christians to take because they recognize the morally neutral factors that enter into judgments on these questions. They stress the positive gains that have been made by the bourgeois democracies even though they reject the assumption that democratic freedom depends upon free enterprise for the business man. They are critical of the utopianism of most leftist movements and reject the idea that Socialism is a final panacea that will solve all human problems.

There are many other social programs with which at one time or another Christians have identified Christian ethics without any significant qualification, from national prohibition to the kind of political democracy that has been developed in America. The difficulties suggested in the previous chapter indicate some of the reasons for rejecting this strategy. But deeper than all of them is the recognition that Christianity transcends every social institution and every program that includes both goals and methods.

(D) The double standard for personal and public life

A fourth strategy that is clearly marked is the opposite of the third. It is based upon the assumption that Christian ethics are so distant from social policy that they are irrelevant to the problems of public life and that there must be two independent moral standards, one for personal relationships, for the Church or for the Kingdom of God understood in either an other-worldly or in a futuristic sense, the other for the state and the world of nations. This strategy may be rejected and yet it has great importance for thought because it always hovers over our decisions as a real possibility. It may be on the other side of the boundary of our own convictions and yet we may be tempted by this position, whether or not we realize it, if we do justice to the factors which make public life the difficult problem for Christian ethics that I have described. This strategy is consistently defended and followed under the influence of Lutheranism. It is alien to Catholicism, Calvinism and sectarian conceptions of the Christian life. It would be a mistake to call this position the Lutheran view because it would be rejected by many Lutherans. It is not characteristic of Scandinavian Lutheranism and it would be disowned by a considerable part of American Lutheranism. It is encouraged by assumptions which are characteristic of Lutheranism, by the sharp contrast between law and gospel, by the strong sense of the state as having primarily a negative function as a dyke against the consequences of sin, and by the tendency to accept the authority of the state in its own sphere as final. Theological pessimism about what is possible in public life combined with a rigorous view of the distinctiveness of the spheres of Church and state make this position seem plausible.

There have been accidental historical factors in the case of German Lutheranism which have accentuated the belief of the supremacy of the state and in the divine calling of the nation. Professor Paul Althaus, an influential German Lutheran theologian, during the recent war stated this position with great clarity. He wrote: 'Christianity has neither a political program, nor any inclination to control or censure the political life in the name of Jesus and the Gospels. No Christian law, no Christian standard, exists for the State or for Politics. The order of the Kingdom of God is on a different plane from that of the political order. The latter cannot conform to the former.' [. . .]

Since the end of the war in Europe we have learned that many of the leaders of Lutheranism in Germany have abandoned this ethical dualism and have come to recognize that it had some part in lowering the resistance of Germany to the moral poison of National Socialism. The Stuttgart Declaration of German Church leaders in October 1945 and the utterances of Martin Niemöller express profound repentance for what Niemöller calls 'a mountain of sins and crimes' that appear 'after the fog of lying propaganda has dispersed' and reveal, for the future, a new conception of Christian political responsibility.

This development illustrates the extent to which Christian thought can be influenced by political conditions. In Luther's time the great tyranny was the Church and he emphasized the place of the Christian prince as a protection against this tyranny. In our time the great tyranny has been the totalitarian state and anyone who would be faithful to Luther's spirit rather than to the letter of his teaching could hardly fail to sanction Christian resistance to so evil a power.

This fourth strategy is based upon a profound analysis of the difficulties in relating Christian ethics to social policy; but it is fatal to allow the standards by which the institutions of society are to be judged and the standards which the Christian acknowledges for his own life to fly apart. In the next chapter I shall show how they can be kept together.

The relevance of Christian ethics to social policy: a fifth strategy

We are now ready to frame the central question concerning the difference that Christian ethics should make in our choice of a social policy. It may seem to the reader that up to this point the book has been designed to inhibit Christian action! I shall outline a fifth strategy to which I am led by criticism of the four strategies described in the last chapter.

This fifth strategy is not easily labelled, nor is it easily followed. It begins with a complete rejection of the double standard for the Church and state, for personal life and public life. The choices of the Christian as a citizen or as a participant in the economic process are his personal choices. He retains moral responsibility in what he votes for, in what he supports through his part in the development of public opinion, in the policies to which he consents or by which he profits. If he accepts policies which he would not choose to initiate in a world governed by fully Christian standards, he must have reasons for doing that rather than for ultimate resistance even at great sacrifice.

This fifth strategy also rejects the absolute identification of the Christian ethic with the particular policies which the individual believes that he should support. This reserve is an expression of the transcendent character of the Christian ideal which keeps every human program and every human institution under judgment. This reserve is also a consequence of the Christian belief in the universality and persistence of sin. The meaning of this belief in practical terms is that nothing that we do or achieve is likely to be free from distortion by an over-emphasis upon those interests that are closest to us or by the narrowness of our own perspective as we make judgments. If we are aware of these tendencies we can in some measure guard against them and correct them, and so they are not to be regarded fatalistically as definite limits to our achievements. But one of the surest ways of being trapped by them is to assume that now at last we have *the* Christian solution. This reserve is also dictated by regard for the elements of what we may call technical autonomy in most social judgments. We can expect that other Christians will differ from us on the methods by which we propose to solve our problems.

To summarize: this fifth strategy is one that emphasizes the relevance together with the transcendence of the Christian ethic and which takes account of the universality and persistence of sin and the elements of technical autonomy in social policies.

I have said that this strategy is difficult to follow. Indeed it is almost impossible to follow it except within a Christian community that is aware of what is involved. Within the Protestant Churches there has in recent years been an impressive development of thought which is consistent with this strategy. The Oxford Conference on Church, Community and State in 1937, one of the great landmarks in the development of social Christianity, charted a course for the Church along the lines that I have just described. Three of the most influential Christian thinkers who have guided the Church in the past decade can be classified best under this strategy though each has his own emphasis – the late Archbishop of Canterbury, William Temple, Reinhold Niebuhr and Emil Brunner. Of the three, Temple was closest to the Catholic confidence in the possibility of a distinctively Christian society, and Brunner is closest to the Lutheran dualism, whereas Niebuhr holds a central position that seems an equal distance from both of those tendencies, but the thought of all three is within the limits of the general position which I am describing. Temple was impressed particularly by the technical aspects of social problems concerning which there could be no distinctively Christian guidance. Brunner and Niebuhr give more emphasis to the moral ambiguity of all social decisions. All three show awareness of both factors.

Christian ethics must always be seen against the background of Christian faith. The positive content in the Christian ethical standard is the commandment of love, love that knows no barriers, love that is willing to pay the price of the cross. But there is also at the center of the Christian life an attitude of humility before God which is a source of ethical guidance. It is the humility of one who is aware of his weaknesses and sin, who criticizes himself by reference to the commandment of love, who in his hours of worship sees himself under the judgment and mercy of God.

I shall now state five ways in which Christian faith and ethics should guide us in all of our decisions in regard to social policy.

1. *The Christian should be controlled by Christian faith and ethics in the motives that prompt him to make his decisions.* In all life it is difficult to keep such motives from being distorted by pride and self-concern but there is here no necessary difference between private and public life. It is possible for us to be

governed by a disinterested and sensitive concern for those on the other side of every social barrier, for those whose welfare is affected by the policies which we support, even though their interests conflict with ours. The difficulties, outlined in the second chapter, that stand in the way of Christian behavior in the relations between large-scale social groups can be transcended so far as the purposes of individual Christians are concerned. They are no excuse for the failure of any one of us who has become aware of their existence. The Church should be an environment in which Christians are prepared to transcend those difficulties.

Christian love that seeks the welfare of all who are affected by any social policy that is supported, that is willing to subordinate all private interests and all narrow group interests to that purpose, is the actual content of obedience to God. To seek to do the will of God in our concrete situation is to seek the good of all of his children. The relation between grateful and faithful love for God and love for all neighbors as motives for action is much discussed in contemporary theology. Fortunately we do not have to decide in most cases which of these is prior to the other because both reinforce each other in our experience. On the other hand there are times of testing when we are dealing with issues that concern the welfare of neighbors whom we have never seen, neighbors in the mass, neighbors who to all appearances lack the human dignity which in faith we assume that all men possess, neighbors who are difficult opponents or enemies. It is in the face of this ultimate test of our love for men that we realize that such love does depend upon faith in God's love for them. But even at that point we find that when this faith is real it is accompanied by compassion, which works directly without the conscious need of religious support, and that in a society influenced by the Hebrew-Christian tradition there are many people who are servants of such compassion without any background of personal religious faith at all. It is doubtful how far such compassion would reach if there were no indirect influence from religious faith. For our purposes it is enough to say that Christian love even in these hard cases is a reality. It can control the motives which drive us to seek the best available social policy. [. . .]

There are those who see little value in motives governed by Christian love in the complicated problems of public life and insist on enlightened self-interest as a sufficient incentive. It is true that in the relationship between large scale social groups enlightened self-interest does often seem to fit better what is possible for the majority, and to represent a goal so far beyond present achievements, that it would be foolish to ask for more. Also, the statesman who is responsible for public policy can seldom ask for anything that is in conflict with the long run interests of his own nation, even though he may as a Christian have higher goals. If he does have higher goals he is likely to put his emphasis upon self-interest in his appeal to the public or to the legislature.

In the post-war period the administration in Washington, in its attempt to get appropriations from Congress for UNNRA or for rehabilitation loans to other countries, has stressed the argument that such action by Congress would be in the interests of America. It is doubtless important to stress national self-interest as a common denominator that would unite a Congressional majority.

It is fortunately true that when a long view is taken there are many points of correspondence between Christian goals and the real welfare of any one nation or group. America's national interest in world prosperity, the industrialist's interest in a general level of high wages, the worker's interest in the solvency of industry, the interest of every nation in preventing a third world war – these are all promising factors in the contemporary world. But there are limits to the effectiveness of the motive of self-interest even in regard to these areas of mutual interest.

It is so hard to keep self-interest enlightened. Unless there is at least a strong body of opinion in a nation that really cares for the welfare of other peoples, the conception of self-interest will slip until it becomes narrow-minded expediency. It is necessary to have those in public office who share this concern.

Moreover, the enlightened self-interest of a whole nation may demand real sacrifice of interests from individuals or groups within it. There is no simple harmony between the interest of each and the interest of all that does not call for real sacrifices of much-prized advantages from many. Any strong man or corporation or nation may gamble on being able to keep more than its share of privilege without endangering the general conditions of welfare too much for its own good.

The existing conflicts of interest between nations and races and classes, even though they could conceivably be resolved in the interests of all, are so deeply rooted that to overcome them would require a passion for justice and fellowship, not merely a discreet balancing of interests. A minority that shares that passion can be a very important factor, much more important than the size of the minority may suggest. Also, the majority are capable of responding to appeals to conscience when issues are made clear. They may not be consistent or sustained in their sensitivity or compassion but they can rise to meet a concrete need. The Gallup Poll in 1945 and again in 1946 showed that seventy per cent of the American people 'would be willing to go back to food rationing in order to send food to people in other countries.' The nation as a whole was ahead, not of what the Administration wanted, but of what it believed the people wanted. It was ahead of Congress – not, we may hope, ahead of what the majority of members of Congress wanted as individuals, but of what they dared do under pressure from minorities that were assumed to hold the balance of power in particular constituencies.

So, while enlightened self-interest is a strong support for many policies that the Christian can regard as right, and while it may often be the most that can be relied on as a common denominator of motive in a nation, it needs to be supplemented or at times corrected by a passion for justice, by a vision of true human community, by a real interest in the people of other lands, by dedication to God's purpose for the nations.

2. *The Christian may find guidance in making social decisions from the self-criticism that is encouraged by Christian humility.* If love is the central Christian motive, humility is the major corrective of the distortions of judgment to which all men are prone. Christian teaching about the depth, universality and persistence of sin should prepare us to see the ways in which our own ideas and the ideas of our own nation or social group are influenced by narrow interests and one-sided perspectives. Christian teaching about God's transcending of all human purposes and programs should prepare the Christian to avoid the tendency to make absolute even the best that he plans or achieves.

244

This aspect of Christian faith should prevent the Christian from regarding any social system, now or in the future, as beyond criticism. It is a curious quirk of the human mind to become easily credulous concerning the ideal character of some social system. This is the baffling aspect of the devotion of many of our most sensitive and high-minded contemporaries to the Soviet Union. Christians are warned by their own faith never to make the kind of claims for any human achievements that are taken for granted by the Communists and their allies. The literature of Communism fosters just such uncritical enthusiasm for a particular social system within history. Whatever may be said for or against Communism as a form of economic organization, and whatever may be said for or against Russian policy at a given juncture, and whatever may be the policy of the Russian government in relation to Christianity and the Church, there will always be a profound difference between the Christian and the Communist ways of looking at life and history so long as Communists make the institutions and policy of the Soviet Union or of any other part of the earth the supreme objects of trust. [. . .]

The habit of seeing one's nation under God, under what we may regard as God's criticism would take most of the poison out of international relations. It would help to break the vicious circle of self-righteous denunciation between Russia and the Anglo-Saxon nations. [. . .]

In the social conflicts which have become fateful in American life, the first word of Christian guidance must be that Christians begin with their own sins rather than with the sins of their opponents. This will be very difficult. Christian business men will be tempted to stress first of all the sins of organized labor with its new power and aggressiveness and they will be inclined to forget that their own bitter resistance to the Labor Movement in the past, and their own example in acquisitiveness when there were few checks upon them, are the moral background of the contemporary situation. It will also be difficult for Christians in the Labor Movement to make labor self-critical. This is their responsibility. [. . .]

There is one area in which we can see how humility is needed to correct what has been done in the name of love. I refer to the criticism of Christian paternalism. Genuine and even sacrificial

245

concern for the welfare of others has been expressed in paternalistic forms. The Christian ethic has been given this twist in economic and political relationships from the days of St. Paul. Paul himself provides some correctives for it but he did not himself see these full implications for the relations between masters and slaves or between men and women. Slavery, industrial tyranny and imperialism have all been defended by sincere Christians because they believed that they could best serve the interests of less privileged people through the use of power over them. The idea that property was a sign of virtue has died hard among those who possessed it. Christian philanthropy has undercut the interest that Christians might be expected to have in raising others to a position of equality with themselves. As suggested in the first chapter, many factors converge in our time to make the case for paternalism less plausible even to the privileged. Social mobility and the articulateness of exploited races and classes have destroyed static ideas of social hierarchy. Anthropological study of groups that were once regarded as inferior has revealed that there are no such inherent differences among large classes of men to justify permanent divisions among them as superior and inferior. In very different ways the American experiment and the Russian experiment have made possible faith in the so-called 'common man'. But the Christian has one other ground for rejecting paternalistic attitudes toward others – he knows that he cannot himself be trusted with unchecked and uncriticized power over them. Abraham Lincoln saw this truth long before it was generally recognized by the more orthodox spokesmen of the Church when he said: 'no man is good enough to govern another without that other's consent.'

3. *The third way in which Christians should be guided by Christian ethics in dealing with the most difficult social problems is that everything that they do should be kept under the criticism of Christian love.* Rigorous criticism of existing institutions and rigorous criticism of all proposals for change are both essential. The methods that we use should also be subject to the same criticism. Those who criticize should see themselves within the dilemmas that confront the statesmen or others who must make some decision in the actual situation. The critic often dwells in a world of alternatives that do not exist for the man who must act in the present moment. The pacifist critic of the nation during

these last years of war has seen much that was true but he has seldom allowed his mind to dwell on the human consequences of a policy that would have allowed the Axis powers to dominate Europe and Asia. He saw the evil of war with special clarity but he often did not see with the same clarity the evil of totalitarian tyranny on the march. He saw the human consequences of obliteration bombing and what he said about this may have been right, but he seldom put himself in the position of the man who had the responsibility of deciding between the use of this dreadful method of warfare and what may have seemed to him to be a much longer war. The idealistic criticism of the San Francisco Conference and the United Nations Charter has often been vitiated by the same unwillingness to face rigorously the alternatives. [. . .]

What is essential is that we never cease to call any policy by its right name in the light of the Christian standard, that we never attempt to deceive ourselves concerning the real nature of what we do. I have already called attention to some of the differences between Christianity and Communism. Another difference is that, whatever the ultimate ethical aims of Communism may be, its tendency is to justify any means that is deemed necessary without keeping alive a strong sense of moral conflict. Christians in practice have often been guilty of the same thing but their faith, if it is understood, corrects them. The Communist faith even if understood will not correct the Communist at this point. The reason for this difference is that for the Christian every individual person has a status before God which is the source of worth that no political relationship can destroy. When terror is used against political opponents by the Communists, these opponents have already lost any dignity that they might have had, in virtue of being opponents of the Communist purpose or even of the party tactics. To sacrifice the person who is an opponent is to brush off an obstacle. It is only the plan, the goal, the collectivity that is the source of moral obligation. The Kulak, the 'wrecker', the Fascist (a term now used so broadly that it seems to include all opponents of the Communists) is not a person to be redeemed but a thing to be removed. Frederick Schumann, who writes about the Soviet Union with great sympathy, remarks that the Communists in the famine of 1932 appeared less disturbed by dead Kulaks than by dead cows. The former were 'class enemies'. [. . .]

247

[. . .] There are, however, at least two differences between the Christian who sanctions war and the position that is here not unfairly associated with the consistent Communist.

The first is that for Christian ethics there is no collective good that is not embodied in the welfare of concrete individuals. Consequently if individuals are sacrificed as soldiers or as the helpless victims of blockades or bombing, this can only be justified if we are driven by the evidence to the conclusion that any alternative policy would lead to the sacrifice of individual persons on an even greater scale.

Another difference is that at no point will the Christian cease to regard these means, that are destructive of persons, as evil. The enormity of this evil will weigh upon him continually. He will suffer with the victims in this tragic situation. He will never regard them as mere obstacles to be removed. He will be driven by this experience to do everything that is possible to create a new order in which such hateful means will not be required. Doubtless many Communists feel this kind of moral conflict more than many Christians. There have been times when the Church supported persecution of heretics that was similar to this modern terror used against political opponents. In theory, according to the prevailing religious assumptions at the time, such persecution was not inconsistent with the Christian concern for the individual because there was the possibility that it might rescue him from error that would damn his soul; but, where persecution was carried on by the Church to preserve others from the contagion of error, or in the interests of the religious unity of the nation or of ecclesiastical power, it was morally as abhorrent as modern political persecution. Today, while Communism discourages moral sensitivity about means, Christianity creates such sensitivity.

Christian ethics without Christian faith cannot prepare us to bear the burden of this conflict between a sensitized conscience and the evil that one may have to do. It would be particularly difficult to allow oneself to criticize what one does with full honesty. The natural tendency would be to slur over the real nature of our decisions and to make them appear better than they are. Complete honesty depends upon faith in the mercy of God who helps men to bear this kind of moral burden. Here, as

248

in other respects, Christian ethics are not self-sufficient. They lead us to a degree of inner tension that may often be too great for the soul unaided by the grace of God.

4. *The Christian ethic guides us in determining the goals which represent the purpose of God for our time.* These are not absolute and all-inclusive goals but the next steps that our own generation must take. The Kingdom of God in its fullness lies beyond our best achievements in the world but God does have purposes for us that can be realized. To live for them is to live for the Kingdom now. The moral criticism of the means now used makes the search for an order in which better means will be possible all the more imperative.

What are these goals? We can define the nature of them by referring to the idea of 'middle axioms'. The use of that term in this context goes back to the writings of Dr. J. H. Oldham in preparation for the Oxford Conference in 1937. The term may not be a good one but it points to something that is distinctive and I shall use it for convenience. A 'middle axiom' is more concrete than a universal ethical principle and less specific than a program that includes legislation and political strategy. Dr. Oldham says of 'middle axioms': 'They are an attempt to define the directions in which, in a particular state of society, Christian faith must express itself. They are not binding for all time, but are provisional definitions of the type of behavior required of Christians at a given period and in given circumstances.' To agree on these 'middle axioms' will still leave many pressing problems unsolved, but clarity about them will give both the Church and the individual Christian a sense of direction. In order to illustrate this idea of the middle axiom I shall suggest middle axioms in four areas. [*Two only given here.*] [. . .]

(A) Christian teaching concerning economic institutions is clear at the stage of guiding principles but among Protestants there is less agreement on this subject than there is about world order. The report of the Oxford Conference provides the most authoritative statement of guiding principles and I cannot do better than quote five principles from that report in somewhat abbreviated form:

(1) Right fellowship between man and man being a condition of man's fellowship with God, every economic arrangement which frustrates or restricts it must be modified.

(2) Regardless of race or class every child and youth must have opportunities of education suitable for the full development of his particular capacities.

(3) Persons disabled from economic activity, whether by sickness, infirmity, or age, should not be economically penalized on account of their disability, but on the contrary should be the object of particular care.

(4) Labour has intrinsic worth, and dignity, as being designed by God for man's welfare. The duty and the right of men to work should therefore alike be emphasized. In the industrial process labour should never be considered as a mere commodity. In their daily work men should be able to recognize and fulfil a Christian vocation. The workingman, whether in field or factory, is entitled to a living wage, wholesome surroundings and a recognized voice in decisions which affect his welfare as a worker.

(5) The resources of the earth, such as the soil and mineral wealth, should be recognized as gifts of God to the whole human race and used with due and balanced consideration for the needs of the present and future generations.

These principles should be seen against the background of the very drastic criticism of the present economic order in that same report on four counts: that it encourages acquisitiveness, that it creates in some countries 'shocking' and in all countries 'considerable' inequality, that it is characterized by the concentration of irresponsible economic power and that it very generally frustrates the sense of Christian vocation. At least with these criticisms in mind we can gain some idea of the direction in which Christians would have society move.

Today Christian thinking about economic problems is confused by arguments over free enterprise and social planning. The European Churches have come to accept the trend toward planning as inevitable and as having within it a promise of greater justice. The American Churches are split on this issue. I propose two middle axioms that should be a minimum basis for common action by American Christians:

a. That the national community acting through government in cooperation with industry, labor and agriculture has responsibility to maintain full employment.

b. That the national community should prevent all private centers of economic power from becoming stronger than the government.

Those two goals are illustrations of the sort of thing that can be regarded as necessary in our situation but even to mention them is to raise problems that suggest other goals. For example, while the government must take ultimate responsibility to prevent mass unemployment and to prevent any unit of economic power – whether it be a corporation or a labor union – from holding up the community, it is also true that government should be restrained from attempting to absorb all activities. Strong government that can take responsibility when necessary must be combined with the encouragement of non-political centers of initiative and power. There is no universal formula for achieving or preserving this balance. There is no Christian formula for it. This is an example of our constant problem of making our way between opposite dangers. The Christian must have his eye upon both dangers, and he should observe in himself the tendency that is so obvious in others to exploit one or the other danger as a propaganda device, depending on which of them is the more immediate threat to the interests of his own group. There are few people who do not favor government intervention when it is on their side and there are few who do not denounce it as a matter of principle when it goes against them. Some awareness of this situation would make it easier to achieve a balance between governmental and non-political forms of initiative.

(B) One final example of a goal for public life that I shall cite grows out of the relationship of Christian ethics to democracy. There has been in the mind of the Church no necessary connection between political democracy and Christian ethics in the past. The Catholic Church has had a preference for hierarchical forms of society and even the most recent pronouncements of the Pope can be regarded as ambiguous though they give the impression of support for democracy. The great Protestant denominations did not begin as defenders of democratic institutions though Protestantism prepared the soil in which those institutions have been able to grow. Democracy as we know it in America and in western Europe has two poles. One is popular sovereignty involving majority rule with universal suffrage and the other is constitutional protections for the individual and minorities. The first without the second may lead to totalitarian tyranny with a mass base as we have recently learned through tragic experience. This is the weakness of the Communist conception of 'democracy'. The second without the first is likely to lead at best to the relatively restrained and decent rule of an oligarchy that is out of touch with the real needs of the people.

Christian ethics do not make this question easy for us for we cannot say that there is any one form of government that is suited to all nations now. Moreover democracy based upon a one-sided optimism concerning human nature, concerning the common man is inconsistent with the dominant strain in Christian teaching about the sin and frailty of all men.

There are, however, good grounds for seeing democracy in the two-fold sense that I have described as a goal toward which Christians should move. First, there is the faith in the potential dignity of all men as children of God, which is as much a part of Christian doctrine as the recognition of the universality of sin. Second, it is clear that constitutional protections for the individual and for minorities are absolutely necessary to prevent tyranny. Third, there is no group that is disinterested enough to have power over others without the check that is provided by universal suffrage. Reinhold Niebuhr has stated the case for democracy along these lines in an unforgettable epigram: 'Man's capacity for justice makes democracy possible; but man's inclination to injustice makes democracy necessary.' A cynic could not believe in democracy because for him enforced order would be the chief necessity. One who is uncritical of his own class might be tempted to think that if only people of his type had the power, all would be well. Faith in the possibilities of common men combined with rigorous criticism of human pretensions, especially the pretensions of the respectable and the strong, furnish the Christian basis for belief in democracy. It is significant that Karl Barth, who has always stressed the independence and transcendence of Christianity and the sinfulness of man to the point where the relevance of Christian ethics to social policy is endangered, writes about democracy in the following way: 'When I consider the deepest and most central content of the New Testament exhortation, I should say that we are justified, from the point of view of exegesis, in regarding the "democratic conception of the State" as a justifiable expansion of the thought of the New Testament.'

5. *The fifth element in this strategy that I am presenting is the attempt to counteract some of the consequences of what we must do as citizens or in some official capacity by action of another kind.* There is a margin of freedom for Christian action for the individual or for the Church apart from the main line of social policy in which the nation or the community as a whole may be involved. The importance of this non-official corrective action has been made clear to me by Professor Emil Brunner's discussion of the subject in *The Divine Imperative.* He shows that 'we never meet other people merely within the orders', that is, within the limits of our official responsibilities. As Brunner says: 'the "office" only constitutes one aspect of life; it is the first point, but not the last, it is the shell which contains life, but not the life itself.' And then he adds: 'actual life consists in meeting another person in love.' This apparent separation of what one does officially, from love as the motive, is misleading because Brunner rejects a double standard for public and private relationships and regards love as the ultimate motive for what we should do in all spheres of life.

There are two ways in which we find room for this corrective action. One is in face-to-face personal relations. A man does not live and act in only one capacity in relation to others, even in relation to the same people. A man is not just an employer or employee, a soldier or a statesman, a judge or a prosecutor or a policeman, an American citizen or a German citizen. Brunner uses as one of his favorite illustrations the judge who must decide according to the law and not as he might prefer to do in the light of all the extenuating circumstances or of the needs of the concrete case. He says that the judge as a Christian may still allow the accused to know that 'in the spirit of solidarity he bears his guilt with him'. This may be difficult in practice in many cases but one can see how this represents the ultimate demand of Christian love for one who occupies that position. The same is true of anyone called to discipline another on behalf of an institution, whether he be Dean of a college or Warden of a prison. [. . .]

The second way in which we can see how a Christian can counteract in one relationship some of the effects of what he must do in another is the result of his membership in the Church. The fact that I am at the same time both a citizen of a nation and the member of a universal Church is a source of considerable ethical freedom. Even in war, which surrounded us with so many ugly necessities, Christians proved to be free to keep in existence channels of reconciliation that were used as soon as the war ended. In the case of many decisions that limit our action, decisions that mean taking sides for one movement or party against another, membership in the Church furnishes a relationship across the line of conflict that may modify the conflict itself.

At the beginning of this chapter I said that this strategy is not easy to follow. The burden upon the mind and the conscience of the individual Christian is very great for he must finally bring together all of these factors that have been outlined and make his own decision. For the Protestant there is no escape from this burden. Often the decision is an either-or decision with no reservations so far as immediate action is concerned, though there will be reservations in attitude that may influence the quality of the action in some measure and which may affect the possibilities of future action. If the individual Christian were alone, the burden of this responsibility for decision might well become intolerable. As a member of the Church he may find guidance for action and channels for action. [...]

Source: John C. Bennett, *Christian Ethics and Social Policy* (New York:Charles Scribner's Sons 1946), pp. 17–88. It was published in England as *Christian Social Action* (Lutterworth 1954).

c h a p t e r   t e n

J. Philip Wogaman
1932–

Introduction

Brought up in a Methodist manse in the desert region of Arizona, Wogaman witnessed the exploitation of local migrant workers, and racism. Through the formative years of the 1940s, he became increasingly aware of the importance of economic life and its damaging effects on those who were vulnerable. It produced a continuing experiential basis, along with his education and professional career, for his development into one of the foremost Christian social ethicists in the United States. Educated at the University of the Pacific and Boston University, he taught social ethics at the former (1961–66). From there, he moved to Wesley Theological Seminary, Washington, DC, as Professor of Christian Ethics, and Academic Dean (1972–83). He was also president of the Society of Christian Ethics of the USA and Canada (1976–7). He is now Senior Minister at the Foundry United Methodist Church in downtown Washington.

As a teacher, and author of a dozen books, Wogaman's work has evolved through several stages. For example, reflecting the great poverty debate of the 1960s in the United States, his *Guaranteed Annual Income* (1968) brought together his experience and theology, enabling him to link Christian ethics, economics and a concern for the vulnerable. The 1970s and 1980s were a period when he consolidated his theological method (*A Christian Method of Moral Judgement*, 1976) and its elaboration in political and economic affairs (*Christians and the Great Economic Debate*, 1977, and *Christian Perspectives on Politics*, 1988).

Complementing his work in the field of ethics was his

involvement in public life and the Churches. For example, in the 1970s Wogaman chaired the United Methodist Task Force, part of the Churches' involvement in the Nestlé controversy, and served on a government commission to monitor the guidelines for the behaviour of multi-nationals. This took him to Third World countries to examine their problems and theological concerns. Such work with his own Church, and the National Council of Churches, and his relationship with decision-makers in the US Senate, confirmed the strategic value of the Center for Theology and Public Policy, based in his seminary. His lifelong concern for the poor was seen in his move to a downtown church, and in his avowed commitment to democratic socialism.

Wogaman represents the development of social Christianity through the maturing discipline of Christian social ethics. As such, it has continued to be the major influence on church statements on social matters in North America and Britain. He describes this perspective as the mainstream liberal tradition. It reflects on the one hand the development of the progressive orthodoxy of the social gospel and its critical interaction with Christian realism; on the other hand, it indicates its continuing evolution as Christian social reform, through progressive comment on contemporary public affairs.

Central to his contribution is the role of theological method. Although in continuity with the work of theologians like John Bennett, it represents a reformulation to meet the growing complexities and uncertainties of the contemporary context. He therefore creates the tool of Christian moral presumptions, out of the interaction between faith and political economy, arguing that they should only be set aside when Christian and empirical evidence suggests otherwise. Complementing his use of moral presumptions is his employment of ethical surveys of economic and political stances. Wogaman deploys them to identify more adequate ways forward for Christian thought and practice by balancing the strengths and limitations of alternative systems. Both moral presumptions and typologies illustrate his concern to illuminate approaches to ethical thinking rather than construct a systematic treatment of all ethical issues. The cumulative effect of his moral judgements on political and economic affairs suggest a continuing commitment to a responsible society (a concept used by the social Christianity of the ecumenical movement in the late 1940s and 1950s). It is a commitment powerfully supported by his decisive option for political democracy, representing, as it does, his subordination of economic mechanisms to wider social and political concerns, including the poor.

Text 14 reflects this theological consolidation of method and judgement. It is therefore drawn from his work in the 1970s, *A Christian Method of Moral Judgement*, and *Christians and the Great Economic Debate*. Edited into one consecutive argument, it discusses moral presumptions, their use as ideology, and how an appraisal of alternative political and economic models can suggest general guidelines for Christian involvement in society. It is a conclusion that indicates a preference for democratic socialism. Both books were published in the United States and Britain, illustrating the latter's continuing relationship and convergence in the development of social Christianity. A comparison between Bennett, Temple, Wogaman and Preston illustrates this characteristic.

Text 14: Coping with Uncertainty in Politics and Economics

Coping with uncertainty: methodological presumptions

How are we to make moral decisions and judgements in spite of all this uncertainty?

That is not just a problem for us in dealing with economic life. Almost every aspect of human experience is complicated. When we make our decisions morally we can only rarely be *certain* we have done the right thing. Even such 'simple' things as raising children and deciding upon a job leave plenty of room for doubts about the outcome of our decisions. Still, as moral beings we have to make our decisions and live with them. And we had better be able to make them with some self-confidence if we are not to be completely demoralized by them.

One approach to this problem has, in some areas of life, made it possible for people to make decisions with some assurance despite factual uncertainty. That approach is to try to establish where the main presumption should lie, and then require deviations from the presumption to bear the burden of proof. We 'presume' certain things to be good or right or true unless we are given ample reason to believe otherwise. Or, to state this differently, we try to decide what will receive the 'benefit of the doubt' in case there continues to be doubt.

This is the approach used in a criminal court, where the accused person is 'presumed' to be innocent until he is proved, beyond reasonable doubt, to be guilty. This is the approach followed by most executives or administrators who, after all, cannot be expected to have at their command all the factual expertise to arrive at a decision. Such decision-makers tend to seek out information and opinions from the generally acknowledged experts in a particular field, and then to 'presume' the rightness of the information or opinions, unless, after testing the expert, some contrary view is clearly more reasonable. Thus, a medical doctor's opinion will be given the 'presumption' over that of a layman or a quack. This does not mean, of course, that one simply decides in advance of all evidence that every accused person is innocent and that every expert is right. Only a foolish person would fail to examine all the evidence to the best of his or her ability before finally deciding. But if, after examining the evidence carefully, there is still uncertainty, the matter will be decided in accordance with one's initial presumption. One does not, by this method, arrive at certainty. But one does have a way of deciding things with greater assurance.

Later, in Chapter 3, I want to suggest several moral presumptions which, I believe, can serve as a strong basis for judgments having to do with economic life. But for now, several rather simple presumptions which often guide economic policy-making can be mentioned to illustrate the use of presumption in this field. The general presumption of most people in labour-management relations is usually against strikes. All but the most conservative among us support the right of collective bargaining by unions. But we (including most union members and leaders) regard a strike as a weapon of last resort. The burden of proof is against it. It will not be used or approved of unless it seems to have been necessary beyond reasonable doubt (although labour and management will of course disagree as to when, if ever, it is in fact necessary). On the other hand, once a strike has been declared, all union people – whether or not members of the affected union – will have a strong presumption against crossing the picket line. Some make this an absolute, although with most union members it is simply a very strong presumption. One does not cross a picket line unless there are overwhelmingly strong reasons for doing so.

Another illustration: ever since Adam Smith capitalistic economics has usually had a presumption in favour of competition in business. Laws against monopoly were fairly late in coming; but when they did they were an attempt to support what was already a long-standing view that every monopoly enterprise should have to bear the burden of proof. It was assumed that prices would be lower and enterprises would be more efficient if businesses had to compete among themselves for the market. Until forty or fifty years ago this was, in fact, a typical argument used against labour unions, for the latter were considered to be monopolies of a very important commodity – namely, labour. (In the United States legislation was enacted in the 1930s which declared that 'labour is not a commodity'.) In some fields, such as utilities, transportation, and communication, it has become evident that competition often does more harm than good – but this has always had to be established beyond reasonable doubt.

In the United States there has always been a dominant presumption against governmental interference in the economy. When in doubt, according to the presumption, private enterprise should be permitted to do things in its own way. This presumption has been particularly set in the United States against actual public ownership of enterprises, although even here – as in the case of the Tennessee Valley Authority and the postal service – the 'burden of proof' has been met for some kinds of governmental ownership. In the socialist countries, on the other hand, the burden of proof has been against private enterprise. In the Soviet Union, Lenin set out to collectivize the whole of industry only to discover that it would be necessary, at least in the 1920s, to encourage some carefully regulated private enterprises. Some private enterprises and franchises exist throughout the Marxist world today, although these have been permitted only because a doctrinaire refusal to do so would clearly damage the forward movement of the economy.

Of course, some of the most interesting decision-making situations occur when presumptions turn out to be contradictory with each other, and then we have to choose which presumption should be given the real benefit of the doubt. The classic case, referred to above, involves the twin presumptions in favour of full employment and against inflation. Both of these presumptions are important in many Western policy-making circles today. But the moment of truth comes when such policy-makers believe that some more unemployment must be created in order to bring the inflation rate down or when some more inflation must be accepted as the price of fuller employment. By and large, policy-makers will take one action hoping it will in the long run cure both the problem of inflation and that of unemployment. But for the short run, it is often believed that a choice must be made.

Other kinds of presumptions could be listed. Some people have a fairly strong presumption against going into debt and certainly against defaulting on a debt once it has been made. Many people have a presumption in favour of honesty in their business dealings.

I suppose these are not things we think about very much on the conscious level. Yet, if presumptions such as these shape our basic judgements and decisions, then we certainly should try to be as clear as we can about them. At the very least, it will help us to understand ourselves better and, perhaps, to clarify the disagreements among persons who respect one another. Careful examination of our working presumptions in the light of our most basic moral values may even bring us to see that our working presumptions are sometimes a denial of the things we really believe in. And then we may have to change.

The question of ideology
It will be noticed that the particular presumptions, which I cited as illustrations above, depend to a considerable extent upon some overall viewpoint or other as to how economic life

J. Philip Wogaman

ought to be organized. Some suggest a 'capitalist', others a 'socialist' general attitude.

Most of our particular presumptions do reflect such a wider orientation. Despite widespread criticism of the term (I shall examine the criticisms in the next chapter), I believe the right word to describe these general viewpoints is ideology. I have in mind something like Julius Gould's definition of ideology as 'a pattern of beliefs and concepts (both factual and normative) which purport to explain complex social phenomena with a view to directing and simplifying sociopolitical choices facing individuals and groups'. An ideology is a complex weaving together of values and beliefs. It is our (often unconscious) picture of what society ought to be like. We may believe that this picture describes society as it once was, and therefore we seek to return to that 'golden age' of the past. We may think it describes society as it is, in which case we will stoutly resist all change. Or we may think of it as a vision of what has never been but may someday be, in which case we shall be 'progressive' or possibly revolutionary. Whether ideology represents a 'false consciousness' or doctrinaire rigidity will be taken up in the next chapter. But here let it be freely admitted that all ideologies contain some element of value judgement – some conception of the good. Hence, while ideology is not the same thing as religion or philosophy, it may depend upon values and beliefs which have religious and philosophical origin. [. . .]

Source: J.Philip Wogaman, *Christians and the Great Economic Debate* (SCM Press 1977), pp. 7–11.

Ideological formulations

It is beyond the scope of the present book to take up the wide variety of possibly Christian ideological formulations definitively. Throughout, we have had to use such materials only suggestively and illustratively. The meaning of our discussion of Christian ideological formulation should now be tested, however, with reference to more concrete examples of possible ideological thinking. I wish here to consider, only briefly and suggestively, the ideological problems posed by political and economic life. In both of these broad areas, we confront immense difficulties if we are forced (or feel forced) to make

261

judgements as Christians without the benefit of an overall normative conception – an 'ideal model' – of what politics or economics involves and how it should be structured if God's will were truly to be done on earth.

Political ideal models

In the most general sense, political ideology is concerned with the organization of social decision-making at the level of the state. In principle, it entails the activity of everybody within the limits of the state, and in this sense the state can itself best be described as society acting as a whole. Most political theorists would add to this that the state functions through law and that it is invested with the ultimate powers of coercion. The political order potentially affects all of the conditions of human existence. Not surprisingly, the power to determine the policies of the political order is vigorously contested. Political ideologies are mainly concerned with the determination of how that power should be allocated and exercised.

It may be noted quickly that some political ideologies are on the face of it contrary to aspects of Christian faith. The difficulties with traditional monarchy were noted as early as the Old Testament in the dire predictions of Samuel, the last of the pre-monarchical Hebrew judges, who warned of tyrannies and injustices and pointed out that the people would be treated like slaves if they should create a monarchy for themselves. Even under the most benevolent of monarchies, there is a sense in which that is still true. Society is organized paternalistically, which always means, I take it, that 'father knows best'. Such paternalistic authority may seem justified by the ignorance of the people or by the wisdom of some kings and aristocracies. But proper respect cannot, in that kind of system, be shown to the God-given possibilities in human nature. Moreover, proper recognition cannot be given to the human limits and sinfulness of every monarch. Traditional monarchy is, furthermore, an offence to Christian understandings of mutuality, since it creates nearly insuperable class and caste barriers to normal human interaction. Relationships are dominated by the superiority of some and the inferiority of others. Hereditary monarchy and aristocracy tends to heighten this problem, of course.

Political fascism is even more alien to Christian understanding, even though it often appears disguised in the clothing of populist egalitarianism. Monarchy can at least be respectful of individual rights; but fascism swallows up the personhood of its subjects into the absoluteness of the state. As Mussolini stated it, 'fascism conceives of the State as an absolute, in comparison with which all individuals or groups are relative, only to be conceived of in their relation to the State'. The glorification of power in fascism frequently reflects deep social anxieties and the fear of disorder; but it is profoundly idolatrous in its theological implications. The value of the individual as a child of God is transformed into his utility to the state. His freedom is real only in so far as its expression coincides with the will of the state or in so far as it is irrelevant to the state. His life becomes *public* in the most awful sense. In the polarity individual/social, the individual is lost and therefore, also, the social character is perverted. Fascism also tends to be a chauvinistic creed, to disdain peace, to glorify aggressive warfare against 'weak' and 'inferior' peoples. In its particularly virulent Nazi form, fascism was racist. In a word, fascist ideologies run counter to virtually all of the positive, negative, and polar presumptions discussed in this book.

Political anarchism has attracted numerous followers in various forms over the past two centuries. Essentially, it is the view that political power is itself the root expression of evil and should be abolished altogether. Typically, anarchism presupposes a highly optimistic theory of human nature. As we have seen in Chapter 4, Tolstoyan anarchism regards coercive governmental institutions as the source of evil; once the coercive structures have been abolished, man's goodness and creativity will be free to blossom forth spontaneously. By far the most important form of political anarchism is Marxist Communism, which views the 'withering away of the state' as a scientifically predictable outcome of a successful socialist revolution. In the Marxist form, political power is an expression of class exploitation and class conflict. In the classless society which will follow the revolution, there will be no need for the coercive state – only for politically neutral institutions of economic administration. Although the point is not often enough understood, Marxist anarchism also rests upon the assumption of the nearly flawless goodness of human nature when the latter is not alienated by exploitation. Communism, in its political ideology, is often mistaken for a fascist-type totalitarianism primarily because its conception of the state during the period of revolutionary struggle and consolidation makes similar demands upon people and involves similar disregard for individual human rights. Ultimately, however, it is anarchist. The problem with anarchism in its various forms, again, lies in its understanding of human nature. Its conception is contrary to Christian insight into the sinful character of man, but it also appears to deny even human freedom to sin in the ultimate society. As many commentators have noted, these ultimate expectations lead to a blind spot concerning methods to be employed by the party and state during the interval leading up to the classless society.

These major ideological tendencies come in countless forms and variations. Our purpose is not to catalogue them but to illustrate how ideological tendencies can in themselves be contrary to Christian faith. Logically, what this means is that a Christian cannot organize his or her political thinking on the basis of these ideologies and that the Christian will tend to place the burden of proof against particular policies which have as their principal rationale their being an outgrowth of one of these ways of thinking. Christians often have to live and work in situations dominated by such ideological tendencies. But their own point of view must be in serious tension with them.

But Christian political thinking can relate much more positively to some forms of democratic ideology. Let it be noted with care that when speaking of democratic ideology as being a fit framework for Christian thinking, I have in mind the political tradition and not *laissez-faire* economics. Moreover, we are discussing ideal models and not the current institutional practices of any particular country, such as the United States. With these caveats, we can cite four interlocking principles of democratic ideology: the concept of popular sovereignty, equality before the law, majority rule, and secure civil rights and liberties. Each of these is worth a brief commentary in relation to Christian thought.

The idea of popular sovereignty has ancient, non-Christian roots, principally in Stoicism and in Greek experience with the city-state. The Stoic political philosophers held that the ultimate location of political power is in the people of the civil community – not in their rulers. While much Stoic political philosophy was subsequent to the development of Roman Imperium, these philosophers held that even the emperor is not finally sovereign. His powers are delegated to him by the people, if not explicitly then by implication. The civil community is a political and legal covenant. This idea had significance in medieval political thinking and emerged in the modern world through such philosophers as Hobbes, Locke, and Rousseau, each of whom expressed it quite uniquely.

Some Christian social philosophers, such as Jacques Maritain, have been reluctant to speak of popular sovereignty – not because of anti-democratic attitudes but because they consider any human claim of sovereignty to be pretentious. Only God is ultimately sovereign. From a theological standpoint this is a point well taken. But it only raises in different form the question of the human channels through which God's political sovereignty can best be exercised. Christians, in other words, clearly do hold political power to be responsible to a transcendent frame of reference. But the question is, what human beings have this responsibility? Very strong theological reasons exist for considering the old classical idea of popular sovereignty to be more compatible with Christian faith than any alternative. Only popular sovereignty recognizes in political terms the ultimate responsibility which every person has before God. Every other conception of political sovereignty implies that some self-designating persons stand between all others and God. The term 'self-designating' must be used here since those who participate in designating the ruler have a share in sovereignty. The maximum case for 'divine right of kings', such as that of James I of England ('The state of monarchy is the supremest thing upon earth: for kings are not only God's lieutenants upon earth, and sit upon God's throne, but even by God himself they are called Gods'), emphasizes that the king has his powers directly from God and is responsible only to God for their exercise. Similar claims have been made for various forms of theocracy involving rule by priestly castes. All such political ideologies presuppose theologically unacceptable distinctions between those persons who have this *a priori* political relationship to God and those who do not. Popular sovereignty, on the other hand, means that all are called to be citizens as well as

265

subjects, though some will be singled out for the offices of government in some way. The concept of popular sovereignty was well-expressed in the formula of the responsible society by the First Assembly of the World Council of Churches (Amsterdam, 1948): 'A responsible society is one where freedom is the freedom of men who acknowledge responsibility to justice and public order, and where those who hold political authority or economic power are responsible for its exercise to God and the people whose welfare is affected by it. Man must never be made a mere means for political or economic ends . . .'. Here responsibility to God is joined with responsibility to the people, and it is implicitly recognized that no ruling élite can consider itself solely responsible to God or its own conception of justice or truth or human well-being. In our time this obviously calls into question the claims and pretensions of strong-arm dictators who have set aside constitutional electoral systems. But it also raises questions which need to be taken seriously by revolutionary élites who presume to determine the future destiny of an entire society. In evaluating the latter, much depends upon whether or not the revolutionary intent is to establish institutions which genuinely reflect popular sovereignty.

The other three principles of democratic ideology can be described as corollaries of popular sovereignty. Equality before the law is clearly implied by the conception of each person as 'king'. Since political authority is ultimately derived, on the human level, from the whole body politic, all stand equally in relationship to the law of the body politic. Equality before the law must also be seen as a necessary political application of the presumption of equality, which was discussed in theological terms in Chapter 3. Majority rule also follows from this: if all are equal but unanimity of judgement on policy questions is not possible, then the larger number of equal people should carry the presumption over the smaller number. This does not mean that the larger number is necessarily right (G.K. Chesterton once remarked, somewhat cynically, that 'the majority is always wrong'), but only that there is a greater probability of rightness attached to the views of the majority than to those of any given minority.

Some have concluded that democratic ideology stops here. If it does, then nothing is to prevent a majority from running rough-shod over a minority. But the guarantee of civil rights and liberties for all, whether in a majority or minority, is also presumed by democratic ideology. There are some things that a majority can never do as an expression of democratic rule. It can never violate the right of minority persons to exist, to be free to dissent from policies established by the majority, and to be free to express themselves in the market place of ideas. One could add other basic human rights which have come to be accepted in the context of democratic ideology. It is only a metaphorical way of expressing the rationale for this, but I rather like the observation that we enjoy the rights of kings. The king must be free to express his will, to have unlimited access to information needed for governing, to worship as he pleases – and he must be free from arbitrary arrest and harassments of officers of the law who are, after all, *his* officers.

These points concerning democratic ideology do not mean that we have become gods, but only that no human beings should be allowed to be simply the political subjects of the will of others. All should be free to participate in social decision-making, although only some will serve as officers and legislative decision-makers.

When democratic ideology was engaged in the death-struggle with fascism and in the immediate post-war world, these ideas would scarcely have needed vindication among thinking people. Democratic slogans and ideas were dominant everywhere and were evidently the wave of a new humanist future. They had, indeed, considerable importance in the struggle for liberation which swept across Asia and Africa during the course of which a billion people changed their political status. But today the case has to be made again, and from a more defensive posture, among those who regard democratic ideology as a mask for Western socio-economic privilege. I shall turn in a moment to the problem of economic ideology. But before doing so the question must again be put rather sharply: What *political* alternative to democracy is more in harmony with Christian faith and humanistic values? Shall we accept an alternative which does *not* treat all persons as sovereign? which does not function by majority rule (and if not, by what minority are we to be ruled, and how, aside from the barrel of a gun, is this minority to be chosen)? which does not consider equality before the law? which does not respect the civil rights and liberties of the people? Credible arguments can be mustered that democracy is not workable apart from favourable economic relationships. The Watergate scandals established beyond doubt that vast economic power can be translated into gross political inequalities. Experience in smaller countries of the Third World, such as Chile and Guatemala, clearly indicate that foreign economic interests can utterly subvert the democratic political process and deliver the institutions of power into the hands of predatory élites. But these are not arguments against democratic ideology; they are arguments against the subversion of democracy. The use of democratic ideological slogans to mask selfish privilege must be seen first of all as an inauthentic application of democratic ideology – not as its logical consequence.

The overall case for political democracy is impressive enough to make this ideological model a presumptive point of reference. Other things equal, or when in doubt, political decisions ought to be supportive of this ideological perspective. The burden of proof should be against solutions to the problem of political organization which are not consistent with it. If, under particular and extreme circumstances, it should be necessary for a minority to seize control of a society and rule it in disregard for the sovereign rights of all of the people, they must bear the burden of proving that the consequences of their not doing so would be even worse. In some of the African countries following independence the claim was made that small educated élites had to rule their lands through tightly-controlled, one-party governments until more people could be prepared for leadership and tribal rivalries could be brought under control. We cannot here go into the merits of any of these cases; but it seems to me that a Christian should be willing to entertain the possibility of this being a true statement of the political problem. If so, a case could be made that the present élite represents the possibility of future democratic society. But in a doubtful case the presumption should be in favour of efforts to involve all persons within the society in the blessings and responsibilities of self-government. At this writing, the minority white governments of southern Africa show utter disregard for popular sovereignty and equality and basic civil rights in the name of protecting 'civilization'. In such cases it seems quite evident that sufficient proof could not be brought forth to justify such a deviation from democratic ideology.

Similarly, revolutionary movements, which are not in themselves democratically organized, must bear the burden of proof that their present methods are necessary for the sake of a future democratic possibility. It can never be assumed that the possibility will automatically be fulfilled unless there is already a deep commitment to it.

In the United States much judicial attention has been given to the meaning and limitations to be placed upon items in the Bill of Rights. Are freedom of speech and press and religion to be considered absolutes, and if so how far do they extend? If they are not absolutes, then what can justify limitations placed upon them? In the main, the courts have given the rights great presumptive weight without treating them quite as absolutes. Civil liberties are, for example, to be respected fully unless their exercise is inadvisable because of a 'clear and present danger'. Freedom of speech is to be respected unless it inordinately violates the desired peace and quiet and other rights of others. Freedom of the press is to be protected zealously unless by its exercise innocent persons are libelled, etc. In such instances, the presumption is properly placed in favour of the implications of democratic ideology, whether or not one regards the burden of proof as having been met sufficiently to justify exceptions.

Economic ideal models

Economic ideologies are concerned with the systems of production and distribution of scarce values. In the main, economic life involves material needs and wants, although some scarce values (such as theatrical entertainment and copyrights) are not exactly material. On the other hand, some material things, such as air and sunlight are plentiful enough not to be described as 'scarce' values in the economic sense under most circumstances.

Much social controversy over the past two hundred years has involved the mutually exclusive claims of competing economic ideologies – of which there have been a bewildering number. One recalls the traditionalist defences of slavery and feudalism, mercantilism, the emergence of private enterprise and free market capitalism, and the various reformist and revolutionary kinds of socialism, including nineteenth-century utopias, syndicalism, the single tax movement, Fabianism, and Marxism. Such economic ideologies embody an organizing conception of the facts of economic life and a more or less clear attitude toward the moral values which the ideologies purport to protect or advance. Strong vestiges of traditionalist economic organization remain in the modern world, with feudalism and even slavery still existing here and there. When put in ideological form, such traditionalist economic systems tend to be paternalistic and to place great emphasis upon fixed and inherited social stations. Invariably they are offensive to conceptions of equality. Their models of mutuality are paternalistic, involving the mutual 'loyalties' of authority and subject. Often they are highly restrictive of the freedom and opportunity of the subject classes. While some of the language of the New Testament tends to support such ideological conceptions ('slaves obey your masters', etc.), these are the points in New Testament teaching which seem most bound to the technological and cultural situation of an age now past. It is difficult to reconcile the paternalistic ideological assumptions of a St Paul in his concrete teaching on specific socio-economic and political questions with St Paul's own deeper insights on grace and freedom (as contained, for instance, in Galatians and Romans). Some of the older natural law conceptions in the Thomistic tradition tended to support this kind of ideological paternalism in economics. But traditionalist economic ideology, the defence of the *ancien regime*, is now everywhere very much on the defensive.

The great watershed in twentieth-century economic ideology still lies between *laissez-faire* capitalism and socialism. Few people are either all for one or the other. But these two ideological frameworks represent the assumptions which people tend to accept and on the basis of which actual decisions are made.

According to *laissez-faire* ideology, the economic role of government should be restricted to the protection of property and the adoption of regulations guaranteeing fair competition. Economic enterprise is fundamentally a private thing and should be kept so. Individuals should be free to invent, to produce, to invest, to buy and sell in a free market without interference. Competition among those who produce and sell will ensure maximum efficiency in both production and

270

distribution because buyers will select the best products at the lowest prices. People will be motivated to work hard and to produce creatively because they will themselves benefit from this productivity. In a free-enterprise economic system, as Adam Smith remarked, each person's vigorous pursuit of his own selfish interests will, 'by an invisible hand', redound to the greater good for all – because only by producing and selling goods and services needed and wanted by others under favourable terms will each person be able to serve his own selfish interests. Under free-enterprise capitalism everybody who is willing to work will find it possible to earn a livelihood and mankind will be assured of continuing material progress and prosperity. Or so the ideology holds.

In its Western ideological form, *laissez-faire* capitalism has been supported by what is loosely termed the 'Protestant ethic', an individualistic work ethic emphasizing work (in relation to one's calling) and thrift (in relation to 'stewardship'). It was summarized by John Wesley's 'Gain all you can. Save all you can. Give all you can.' But in its economic ideological form, the 'give all you can' is to be replaced by an 'accumulate all you can' – it being understood that accumulation is not idle wealth but the development of capital enterprise for the production of still further wealth. Not that ideology is altogether opposed to giving. Persons of substantial wealth should be benefactors of mankind through their endowment of libraries, and universities, and museums, and art galleries. Indeed, by their acquisition of wealth, such persons will have demonstrated their greater capacity to determine which institutions of culture are most deserving of such philanthropy. But the hallmark of the 'Protestant ethic' is its emphasis upon work and its judgement that, economically speaking, we tend to get what we deserve, whether wealth or poverty.

In assessing the influence of this *laissez-faire* ideology we should be reminded again that the influence persists despite the fact that no present-day economy is a pure example of its logic. To be consequential, an ideology need only shape the consciousness and with it the judgements of people who believe in it. American business and labour interests may both compromise away the purity of *laissez-faire* capitalism when their concrete interests are at stake, but both have often enough demonstrated their mental captivity to the ideology itself. It is something like sinning against our ideals when practicality and self-interest seem to require it, but continuing to espouse the ideals and to put them into practice whenever we consider it feasible. We should also remember that the ideological emphasis upon work in *laissez-faire* capitalism is by no means unique to that ideology. Where, for instance, could one find a greater emphasis upon an ascetic work ethic than in contemporary China?

John C. Bennett, who is himself critical of capitalism, points to three of its advantages which should not be lost to our thinking:

> The first is that it has always taken seriously the problem of incentive.... Second, capitalism as a method of economic organization has the advantage of encouraging many independent centers of economic initiative.... A third advantage is that capitalism stands for the value of having at least segments of the economy let to impersonal and automatic forms of regulation instead of attempting to include all economic processes in one vast plan at the center. Christian realism about the sin and finiteness of man provides warning against the attempt to plan everything. Such pretentious planning involves too great concentration of power.

While agreeing with Bennett as to the importance of these values, it seems more than questionable whether *laissez-faire* capitalism, as an ideological frame of reference, can serve as vehicle for Christian moral judgement. Bennett refers to major points of conflict between capitalism and Christian faith, as enumerated by the Oxford Conference on Life and Work in 1937:

> (1) the tendency of economic institutions to enhance the acquisitiveness of men, (2) the shocking inequalities in economic opportunities and in access to the conditions on which the welfare of all depends, (3) the irresponsible possession of economic power, (4) the difficulty of finding ways of making a living that do not conflict with one's sense of Christian vocation.

While these criticisms seem pointed more at actual practice in the countries most influenced by capitalism than they are at *laissez-faire* ideology as such, a strong case can be made that these flaws are almost bound to result wherever the ideology is taken seriously. The enhancement of acquisitiveness is the full intention of the ideology. That is what is supposed to lead to the cornucopia of benefits for society as a whole. Inequality likewise is absolutely implicit in the capitalist scheme of incentives. Indeed, the ideology proclaims the great value of 'getting ahead', presumably of others. Thus, we are led to value ourselves in proportion to our material superiority over others. It takes little analysis of the real world to discern that the reverse is more likely to be the case: wealth is more likely to correlate with sin than with righteousness. Even the desire to be superior to others is in itself a sin against God's intended human community of love and brotherhood. Even were this not so, the materialism of this acquisitiveness should be a serious flaw from a Christian standpoint. And even were *this* not so, *laissez-faire* leaves to chance and the 'invisible hand' what should be the first objective of every economic system: serving the economic needs of persons in community. The theory is that all will be best if cared for in this way and that those who are not well cared for (the poor) will in fact have deserved their poverty through their own moral inadequacies. But it is not so in the real world. Only as Western capitalistic countries have moved away from the pure ideology through adoption of more liberal social welfare programmes have the needs of helpless and innocent poor people been met. In the United States these programmes have been strung together illogically and often wastefully precisely because they have been hampered by the confines of *laissez-faire* ideology. Welfare programmes have had to be constructed half-apologetically, the meeting of needs being supplanted by irrelevant formulas for self-reliance (irrelevant because the vast majority of poor people could not under any circumstances become fully self-sufficient economically). The problems of *laissez-faire* are compounded by international exploitation of the raw materials and labour of poorer countries by the wealthier ones. In sum, *laissez-faire* capitalism is principled selfishness and irresponsibility when it is implemented seriously.

The other main contemporary economic ideology is socialism in its now numerous variations. Joseph A. Schumpeter's definition of socialism is satisfactory up to a point. He speaks of it as 'that organization of society in which the means of production are controlled, and the decisions on how and what to produce and on who is to get what, are made by public authority instead of by privately-owned and privately managed firms'. As an ideology, socialism also contains both practical and ethical rationales. The main point is that economic power is formally responsible to the whole of society, through the state, and not simply to those who hold it as private wealth. Accordingly, economic decisions are much more likely to be made in such a way as directly to benefit everybody and not simply those who own the instruments of production. Marx's theory of industrial crisis makes this point in moral terms if not in the scientific sense he imagined. According to Marx, industrial crisis and economic depression occurs when there is no longer enough purchasing power in the market to absorb the products of industrial production. In such a situation, industry no longer has any incentive or economic capability to continue to produce since it is owned privately and must make a profit. *Laissez-faire* ideology might assert that this loss of market demand reflects consumer disinterest in the products of industry. But to Marxist analysis, the same phenomenon is better accounted for by the fact that workers always receive less in wages than the market value of what is produced – the balance being kept by the capitalist as surplus value. In the long run (usually every ten years or so) production catches up with and passes the available purchasing power of wage workers. One after another, industries are forced to cut back on production. More and more workers are thrown out of work, thus losing the wages needed for purchasing power. A vicious circle thus develops in which unemployment constricts the market of industry's products, leading to further unemployment and economic depression. Whether or not this account of economic crisis has been rendered obsolete by subsequent economic theories (especially those of John Maynard Keynes), the ethical point has a certain validity. Under capitalism, economic decisions will always be made for the benefit of investors, even if the decisions that have to be made lead straight into public economic disaster. Under socialism decisions can at least be based on social, not private, objectives. There is no need for the scandal of unused plant capacity and stockpiles of products and food rotting because of the lack of private purchasing power. There is no obstacle to full production and full employment since nobody has to make a private profit for production to occur. Inequalities may exist in fact, but unlike capitalism there are no inequalities in principle. The incentive for planned obsolescence is removed.

In the abstract, the case for socialism seems indisputable. In actuality there are also problems with socialism which the Christian should note. The most important is the problem of power: who is to control economic power when it is a state monopoly? Private economic power centres are irresponsible in very large measure, but at least there is some accountability to the market (diluted as that accountability may be by private monopoly conditions and saturation advertising). Where political and economic power are united, however, the latter will be no more responsible than the former. Socialism combined with any political system other than democracy will be no more responsible than the political system – a point which most of the Marxist socialist countries have demonstrated too well. Even combined with democracy, socialism could tend towards the corruption of the political institutions by placing too much power in the hands of office holders – power which could be used to perpetuate officials in office and generally contribute to corruption. Socialism, while meeting rather well the test of the positive moral presumptions, needs to be checked rather carefully in relation to the negative ones. Does it offer enough hedge against man's sinful tendency to seize and use power selfishly?

The other main problem with socialism is that it may weaken individual initiative and diminish the responsiveness of the open market. While these points are sometimes offered as definitive objections to socialism, they are merely points where socialism is sometimes undeveloped. In principle (that is, in the ideology) there is no reason why the market mechanism cannot be used nor why individual initiative cannot be stimulated in a socialist economy. Even within the American civil service there are instances of great initiative and creativity (such as in programmes of the National Institutes of Health, the Public Health Service, and the US Forest Service). Meanwhile, most of the socialist countries, including the Marxist ones, employ a market system of sorts without doing violence to their ideological purity. Some, such as Yugoslavia, even encourage development of new economic initiatives in the form of co-operatives.

From this brief discussion there may emerge the rudiments of an economic ideology which is more or less compatible with Christian faith. It would, I believe, be a form of democratic socialism. Its economic institutions would be responsible to government, and government would be responsible to the people. In the development of both governmental and economic institutions care would be taken to keep too much power from becoming concentrated in a few hands. Economic initiative would be encouraged and rewarded, although a truly 'humanized' society would be one in which the grateful recognition of service rendered would be sufficient reward. The presumption in the distribution of economic benefits would be for equality. Use of incentives creating inequalities would be kept to the minimum required by the general condition of human sinfulness. Small-scale business activities, including what Robert Theobald calls 'consentives', would be consistent with this. Major industries and, in the long run, intermediate industries should, however, be publicly capitalized and owned.

An important component in Christian ideological thinking about economics must be the question of social welfare. I refer to the provision of certain services to the public at minimal or no charge – including health care, education, public transportation, and a basic income guarantee. Such welfare provisions can be provided under welfare capitalism, of course. In a system of welfare capitalism, business and industry are permitted to function more or less without restraint, but they are then taxed heavily enough by government to finance generous welfare provisions for the whole society. This continues to place too much emphasis upon selfishness as an economic motive and to concentrate too much power in private hands, although it is a great improvement over pure *laissez-faire*. Welfare capitalism acknowledges the responsibility of all economic endeavour to the whole community, but it continues to permit great inequality and large concentrations of potentially irresponsible economic power. An equally important reservation concerning welfare capitalism is that it often continues to lodge the burden of proof against further needed extensions of the welfare principle. The presumption continues to favour private wealth-building. One of the worst things about *laissez-faire* ideology is that it puts a quite irrational burden of proof against public expenditures of all kinds, including those for the arts and other culturally-enriching and community-building activities. Historically, only those public expenditures which clearly expedite private economic activity – such as the building of railways, highways, and airports – have not had to confront an initial negative prejudice of great magnitude. Education serves economic activity in this way, but even so it is probably fortuitous that the emergence of common schools and the concept of universal free state school education preceded the full ascendancy of *laissez-faire* in America. Otherwise state school education would almost certainly have faced the resistance with which universal health care proposals have been greeted in recent years. Military expenditures have not usually had to face much resistance in recent years in this country, but this is readily interpreted in terms of the defence of existing institutions of private economic activity.

In recent years, both capitalism and socialism have been challenged by the wastefulness and ecological irresponsibility of modern technology. Polluted rivers and smoggy air can exist under either form of ideological sponsorship, and government presumably requires higher standards under either system. *Laissez-faire* probably has the greater blind spot at this point, however. It is a good deal easier for a private corporation to dump its refuse on to the public and to regard this as a good bargain than it is for a publicly controlled enterprise to do so. In the former case, the business is likely to increase its profits by lowering its costs. In the latter, the public disposal of pollutants must be entered into the ledger as a cost and dealt with responsibly. The steady, predictable resistance to environmental control measures by private industries in the United States illustrates the point. But concern for ecology belongs in a Christian economic ideology as one of the givens, and it cannot be said that socialism has always made this a prominent concern.

Some Christians would go even further and argue that Christian economic thought should establish a presumption against modern, large-scale technology as such. That is clearly the tendency of some of the work of Jacques Ellul on this subject and many Christians who are responsive to the ecology movement concur. I believe it is too late to advance the outright dismantling of modern technology as a serious proposition. In balance, the benefits of technology in liberating human beings from heavy physical toil and the uncertainties of climate and season and food supply probably outweigh the problems of technological civilization. Even were this not so, it is doubtful whether any substantially lesser technological base could adequately feed, clothe, and shelter the present world population. The most promising solutions to the problems posed by modern technology may turn out to be those which involve further technological development. For example, the harnessing of the power of the sun and the development of safer forms of nuclear energy might be ways of solving some of the problems of contemporary technology.

In a widely quoted and in many ways very sensible book, the British economist E. F. Schumacher proposes a sweeping change of current attitudes toward large-scale technology. His interest is partly one of reversing the present ruinous rate of exploitation of the earth's finite resources and partly one of restoring a human sense of proportion to economic activity. His proposals for small-scale technology and his economic analysis are worthy of deeper study and stand as a reminder that many of the further technological developments of which I have spoken need to be in the direction of smaller-scale activities. It is difficult to relate Schumacher's work to any of the traditional options in economic ideology, and he may have significant things to say to all of them.

Conclusion

These ideological illustrations cannot be treated here in greater detail. That is an important continuing task for Christian ethics and, indeed, for every responsible Christian. I have intended by their use to suggest how the basic presumptions of Christians can be translated into broader conceptions of what society ought to be. Such ideal models of social organization cannot usually be judged by their immediate practicality, although we should question the adequacy of any model which is on the face of it impractical. Ideological thinking helps us to organize our moral judgements even when confronted by the illusiveness of our noblest conceptions of the good. By accepting the presumptive validity of our ideal models of society, we at least know what a compromise is when it is forced upon us. We can at least require deviations or exceptions to bear the burden of proof.

We must remind ourselves yet once again that no ideology is to be regarded as an ultimate in itself. All ideal models gain their value from their adequacy in reflecting God's loving purposes for human existence. Since none of us is God, we cannot expect to have perfect models even in our heads, much less in the actual world.

Source: J.Philip Wogaman, *A Christian Method of Moral Judgement* (SCM Press 1976), pp. 196–215.

Liberation Theology

Ulrich Duchrow
1935–

Introduction

Brought up in Germany, Duchrow followed a traditional route for education and church life, in a Lutheranism that was still conservative despite its Confessing Church tradition. To be ordained and pursue an academic career in theology was even more restrictive, although Duchrow's work on the Lutheran doctrine of the two kingdoms revealed the possibilities of a more radical reinterpretation of a tradition. In the 1970s he worked in Geneva as Director of Studies of the Lutheran World Federation. During a visit to Brazil, Duchrow encountered the enormous problem of Third World poverty that existed side by side with a small ruling élite living in First World affluence. His contact with Franz Hinkelammert introduced him to the dependency theory as an explanation of social divisions, and as a key tool in liberationist analysis. Rethinking his theology now became his great concern, focused on the global market economy, on what he regarded as the core of the great challenge facing the contemporary world. It led him to combine academic life, as Professor of Systematic Theology at the University of Heidelberg, with Secretary for Mission and Ecumenism of the Evangelical Church of Baden.

One of Duchrow's aims has been to develop an awareness of economic issues in regional churches, through the pressure of local discipleship groups. This has linked to his involvement in the growing networks of grassroot organizations in Europe which oppose the harmful effects of the market economy in the West. His latest work with *Kairos Europa – Towards a Europe for Justice*, epitomizes this struggle. Never accepted as a major influence in his own more conservative denomination, the opposite has been the case with the World Council of Churches (WCC). His contact with liberationist groups in the Third World, and his promotion of such a perspective in the West, has given him a major role in the WCC. As consultant following the Vancouver Assembly (1983) for the conciliar commitment to justice, peace, and the integrity of creation, his influence has extended to the Canberra Assembly (1991) through his involvement with the Commission on the Churches' Participation in Development (CCPD).

All Duchrow's involvements are held together by a deep personal commitment to God at work in the world's economy. It is powerfully reflected in his own lifestyle. In a remarkable way he brings together key features of this debate over today's global market economy, from its German heartland to the ecumenical movement's standing alongside the oppressed of the Third World. His overriding conviction is that capitalism is heretical because it worships capital rather than meeting the basic needs of the world's peoples and environment. He therefore regards it as a credal issue for the Churches, of the same order of importance as apartheid and nuclear war. The task is much more doctrinal than ethical, particularly when the latter means Christian social reform as a responsible society. It requires a committed reading of the Bible. It involves encountering the God of liberation standing against the oppression of the poor by the market economy, and for a biblical economy meeting the needs of people and creation. It requires the conversion of the Church through small discipleship groups.

Text 15 is an edited address given to an international consultation, organized by the West European Network, on work, unemployment and the Churches, held in the Ruhr in 1988. As such, it indicates Duchrow's involvement with Western groups in their struggle against the global market economy. He regards it as a complement to the struggles against it in the Third World. The conference participants therefore represented a wide variety of groups, denominations and nations working on employment and church issues. The text uses the Church and socialist concepts of theses to develop its analysis of capitalism, its theological critique, and interpretation of the Church's role in economic life. There are clear resonances with liberation theology's militant reading of the Bible, its concept of the national security state, and its use of the dependency theory. It therefore reflects much in the social Christianity tradition of radical Christian socialism, but in intimate dialogue with the new movement of liberation theology.

Text 15: The Witness of the Church in Contrast to the Prevailing Ideologies of the Market Economy

Western European Christians who have been drawn into the concern for economic justice by the cry of the poor and by the message of the Bible have been looking with envy to the fact that in the USA not only individuals but also Churches have issued impressive statements and developed practical programmes to cope with the life and death issues involved. Let me just mention the Roman Catholic Bishops' economic pastoral, the paper of the Presbyterian Church 'Christian Faith and Economic Justice', and the Study Paper of the United Church of Christ 'Christian Faith and Economic Life'. In Western Europe we are far behind, although the Federation of Protestant Churches in France already in 1971 raised the question of 'The Church and the Powers' and the Anglican Church in Great Britain recently published its 'Faith in the City'.

Most of all these pronouncements from the 'One-Third World' of the industrialized wealthy nations, however, remain in the traditional Western approach of the post-Constantinian majority churches which expect change from the powerful and, therefore, addresses prophetic appeals to them. Thus changes are designated from within the system, although there are some elements transcending this approach. On the contrary churches and theologies from the situation of the 'Two-Thirds World' of the impoverished nations base their primary starting point in the empowerment of the poor on the basis of God's action in history as revealed in the Bible. Thus from this perspective the predominant systems today are being challenged more basically and more drastic transformations are being called for.

In this situation it seems important to me to identify more clearly the factors in the whole economic system that create the present situation and that would have to be changed in order to create an economic system that would sustain all inhabitants of the earth and the earth itself which the present system does not. Liberal and even more social democratic strategies have mostly concentrated on the sphere of distribution. Marxism has concentrated on the sphere of production, particularly on the ownership of the means of production. However, today it seems especially important to look at the monetary side of economy including its influence on the sphere of consumption, particularly the needs being served. It is on this aspect of the monetary system in the context of the debt crisis that I wish to concentrate. Let me first briefly outline the three models of capitalist market economy, in the context of which the modern monetary system has developed.

I. The concepts of the capitalist market economy

Thesis 1
The problems of the present-day debt crisis cannot be looked at separately from the socio-economic and political concepts of the total system within which they have developed. In the course of history and the present, the system of the capitalist market economy has gone through several predominating stages. A first classic concept is *'laissez-faire'* capitalism. This has two main theoretical variants. According to the one, it is morally good because it furthers the well-being of all (Adam Smith). According to the other it is autonomous (a law unto itself) like a law of nature (in the sense of the rational model of classical physics), without connection either to morals or ethics (Max Weber).

In the context of early capitalism in England in the late eighteenth century with his work, *An Enquiry Into the Nature and Causes of the Wealth of Nations*, Adam Smith founded classic Liberalism. If free individuals pursue their economic self-advantage a common benefit ensues, namely common prosperity. 'As if guided by an unseen hand' this mechanism is controlled by the competition of individuals in a free, open market, especially through the setting of prices.

Several (unproven) assumptions are contained in this theory:

1) economic growth brings about general prosperity; and 2) the market and competition achieve a just distribution by acting as a harmonizing mechanism.

Over a century later Max Weber describes liberal capitalism in much less euphoristic terms. Rather, it is, in its autonomy, a fateful force. According to Weber its decisive hallmark is its rationality, in the sense given to the word in modern science, i.e. morally indifferent and therefore in a state of tension with ethics and religion. [. . .]

Looked at from a theological point of view, this interpretation has – since Friedrich Neumann – become bound up with the so-called new Lutheran, 'Two Kingdom Doctrine' as well as with a particular kind of calvinist election doctrine. And this interpretation has its effect in all bourgeois churches on a broad front in the popularized form of slogans such as 'Politics doesn't belong in the church'. In this way one simply allows the 'unbridled slavery' of the market to happen.

Thesis 2

In the face of the crisis of *laissez-faire* capitalism and its actual negative social consequences a second concept has been developed which is called 'Welfare capitalism'. This assigns a regulating role to the state in the 'property owning market society'. Here too there are two main variants: Keynes' state-interventionist concept which lays stress on a state employment policy and regulation of the money supply by the state: on the other side there is the 'social market economy', in which the state supervises the legal framework for competition and influences the distribution of income through its social policies.

Both concepts neglect to acknowledge the structures of international injustice. [. . .]

The fact that the market economy has wolfish characteristics is the reason why the 'pure' market where work, capital and land become simple commodities has never been able to assert itself. When, in the middle of the last century an attempt in this direction was made in England, opposing forces arose to protect the people affected, amongst which, apart from the state, the worker movement should be mentioned. [. . .]

After the great world economic crisis at the end of the twenties and beginning of the thirties in this century various attempts were programmatically undertaken to make capitalism more secure from crisis and to limit its social consequences. John Maynard Keynes became the best known, [...] In his major work on the theories of full employment (*The General Theory of Employment, Interest and Money*, 1936) Keynes departed from Adam Smith's belief in the balancing role of the state. He examines the dynamics of upswing and depression or recession of economic phases and the possibility of avoiding their negative consequences through a state employment policy (public investment) and regulation of the money supply.

For the German Federal Republic and other West European countries such as Holland a different model became decisive, the 'social market economy'. Apart from Ludwig Erhardt, Alfred Muller-Armack is a classic representative of this position. According to its proponents 'the purpose of the social market economy is to unite the principle of freedom with social equality'. [...]

From a theological point of view Welfare capitalism finds the greatest approval in the large churches of Western Europe. It is generally thought that the negative side of the market economy can be held in check by the opposing controls of state and unions. However, certain questions are here ignored: 1) the ecological consequences of the growth economy; 2) the assumptions in the world economy for increased production (e.g. cheap raw materials and labour by exploiting the two-thirds world), above all, however, the fact is overlooked that since the worldwide turn to monetarism social welfare elements have been constantly reduced in favour of the pure market.

Thesis 3
If one confines the role of the state to making the money supply available for the economic process and furthermore declares that social responsibility is really the task of private charity, one is then in the ideological position of monetarism. The socially explosive situation which results in the dependent, marginal countries of Asia, Africa and Latin America is held in check by a massive increase in the resources of the Military and of the Secret Service (from which the armaments industry can profit yet again). The increase in social tension in the central countries is controlled by an increase in police surveillance but above all

by control of the media. For this reason, the present phase, which is reducing social welfare even in the industrial countries, is called the phase of National Security Industrial capitalism.

The ideological position of monetarism was developed primarily by Milton Friedman of the Chicago School of Economics and put into practice by Pinochet in Chile, Margaret Thatcher in England, and Reagan in the USA.

From there it has continued to affect the whole Western system and even the socialist East has allowed itself to become involved in this development, all of which has a bearing on indebtedness to and dependence on the IMF as well as ideological aspects. However, I cannot develop that here.

From an economic point of view the central basis and decisive direction of this phase is the transitionalization of capital. The world is only a system in which transnational financial and industrial capital uses the various political, cultural, social and military conditions for the most profitable investment possible. I will pass over for the moment the effects of the uninhibited economic market on peoples and societies in the various regions of the world.

Looked at ideologically, monetarism is concerned with the systematic reduction of all forces opposing the developing monopolistic market. [...]

Nevertheless even here there are those who would offer a theological justification. Best known is the letter of the American Lay Commission, 'Towards the Future – Catholic Social Thoughts and the US Economy', which was a counter to the Pastoral Letter of the US bishops. Here too certain misuses in the Market Economy are admitted but only as random isolated mistakes. For the rest, the thesis is represented, that the free Market Economy corresponds exactly to the encouragement of Matthew 25, i.e. that profiteering with the talents leads to the feeding of the poor, on the basis of which Jesus will question us on the Last Day (preamble, p. 209). Thus the creation of the new kingdom is decisive, and this is made possible essentially through a spirit of enterprise, which according to this 'creation theology' is to be seen as the first and most important image of God (Genesis 1: 26–28). The word capitalism is derived from 'caput' – head, intelligence, according to the Lay letter (ch. 1, p. 3, 1235). Thus intelligent enterprise is co-creator with God (ibid., and ch. 2, p. 1, L249ff.). It increases the wealth of creation and then benefits the poor.

However much the three models of the capitalist market economy may differ from each other in detail, their practical result is more or less clearly the same: developing division between rich and poor as well as the endangering of the natural bases of life on earth. This fact cannot be ignored worldwide. Within the rich industrial countries it is clearer than ever, even in those which for some time have sought to cushion this dynamic for a period of time by means of welfare capitalism (at other peoples' cost).

One must keep in view the practical results and not only the theoretical concepts of the capitalist market economy if one is to apply oneself to a theological critique of it.

II. Theological critique of the concepts of the capitalist market economy

Thesis 4

According to biblical testimony God enters history and reveals himself in that God frees the Hebrews who were marginalized and oppressed by the advanced civilizations (Exodus 3). This is the way God acts throughout the whole of biblical history.

God's justice consists in saving the poor, the weak, the oppressed, where necessary by overcoming the strong, the oppressors. As against this, false gods, idols, oppress.

As a counter to the power structure of the other nations Jahweh's nation of freed slaves, Israel, is to develop an alternative social order in which there are no slaves, no poor. If anyone does become poor he is not to be robbed of the basis of his existence through, amongst other things, the imposition of interest on loans (Exodus 22:25). After Israel conformed to the advanced nations with negative results, God sends his prophets. Antidotes to impoverishment such as the Year of Jubilee are developed (Leviticus 25). Jesus presents the nation on the verge of God's kingdom with the alternative – God or Mammon. His disciples are gathered, above all, from people who have been pushed to the margins of society, and they shall form alternative communities.

Processes of accumulation which allow the few to become rich and powerful and the many to become poor and dependent have not existed only since society based on the capitalist market economy. They began, rather, over ten thousand years ago with the transition of small communities to cultivation of the land, founding towns, cultivating the valleys and large states. Thus then with the transition to 'large' societies, advanced civilizations, the division of labour, exchange and monetary economies, legal and ruling structures render relationships between people anonymous. They create power levers which some can use at the cost of others. As a counter to this development there arises in Israel the belief in Jahweh the God of love and justice and in Greece the rational political philosophy of Plato and Aristotle.

In biblical terms justice (Heb. ṣᵉdaqah) is a notion of relationship. It means 'a way of acting in harmony with the community'. When all relationships (between God, man and Creation) are whole, peace reigns – shalom (Isaiah 32:17). In practice, community relationships are destroyed or endangered by sin, especially the structures of the accumulation of power in advanced societies. In this situation God's judging (shaphaṭ) and judgement (mishpaṭ) signify the re-establishment of justice and of 'shalom', so that God in his mercy hears the cries of the oppressed and frees them (Miranda). Faced by the sinful structures of the imbalance of power, justice becomes a battle cry. If the oppressors do not repent, God's judgement becomes chastisement.

The classic example of God's justice: Jahweh frees the Hebrews (i.e. the outcasts of early established societies) (Exodus 2ff.) from slavery. The nation freed by God shall act like God himself and build an alternative just society. Therefore God gives them 'mishpaṭim' precepts amongst which it is forbidden to practise usury (cf. Exodus 21–23:19 and Exodus 20 1ff.). When Israel itself becomes a monarchy (I Sam.8) which serves the false gods of power (1 Kings 18) and breaks up into rich and poor (1 Kings 21) God sends prophets, who call for justice (Amos 5:25). Helping the poor and weak to gain their just rights, is identical with the acknowledgement of Jahweh (Jer.22:16). After the collapse of the monarchy there arises the hope of God's kingdom. Jesus brings this kingdom and its justice and is experienced as the messiah.

The poor are encouraged (Lk.4:16ff.) and small communities based on the new justice spread (Mt.5:13ff.) (Acts 4:32) and reject unjust power structures (Mk.10:42ff.). Jesus' resurrection is the proof of God's power so that through suffering and dying for the sake of justice, life is brought forth. Paul sees God's justice, in the fact that God, through the Holy Spirit, calls on the nations of the whole of creation and enables them to turn from injustice and corruption in order to serve justice and gain eternal life. [. . .]

Even from this short survey of the biblical view of God's justice as a counter to the structures of socio-economic and political injustice it becomes clear that it is devious, to want to make acceptable according to the Bible or theology, that egoism should be regarded as a basis for economic activity. In the same way it is completely untenable to maintain that the mechanisms of the economy have nothing to do with being Christian or with the Church but that they are autonomous. But before we can formulate these criticisms in a different way we must understand more precisely the mechanisms of accumulation and impoverishment in the different phases of their development.

Thesis 5
Aristotle, who was fundamental for the Middle Ages, the Reformation and even for Karl Marx, analyses the difference between acquiring food, household management, and an economy based on increasing the money supply. Hunting, tilling the fields, raising cattle, craft skills or exchange (which includes the use of money as a means of exchange) on which the first two are based have as their aim the satisfying of daily needs, especially the providing of food necessary to life and are therefore in accordance with nature. The last, an economy based on increasing the money supply and on the taking of interest – usury, as well as price speculation through the building of monopolies has no limited goal but desires the increase and growth of wealth and monetary profit for their own sake and is against nature. For, with its unlimited desire to live with the aid of unlimited means of increasing money it does not achieve the good life, i.e. living in community with others. As against that Aristotle sets the twofold virtue of justice – a sharing justice (distributive) and (through exchange) an equalising justice (commutative).

Ulrich Duchrow

This brilliant analysis by Aristotle in his work *Politikōn* (on the affairs of the community, or in short Politics) Book I, Chapters 8–13, is important for us both historically and systematically for various reasons. It is fundamental that Aristotle sees the aim of the economy (Oikonomia) of household management and of acquiring natural goods as being the creation of the means necessary for the satisfaction of the basic needs of the householder man or woman. That means that the overwhelming aim of the natural economy is the satisfaction of the basic needs of mankind. This unites the biblical argument directly with that of Aristotle up to the fourth plea of the Our Father for daily bread. One might also say that possessions and goods are means to life (Lebens-Mittel), meant to be used.

The distinction between two kinds of acquiring and with them two ways of using money is also important. For on the one hand I can collect those goods found in nature and those goods developed from the materials found in nature, transform them and exchange them (and in the larger trade area use money as the means of exchange) or I can strive for money for its own sake, that is for limitless wealth by means of money which keeps re-creating itself (in Greek 'Tokos' means both interest (financial) and the male child). This is 'the art of acquiring money' (Chremastike). By increasing money for its own sake I snatch from others their share of profit.

The theological interpretation of this desire for infinity through self-generating money will occupy us later. At the moment it is important to see only, that for the well-being of the community of the Polis, Aristotle rejects the increase of money for its own sake as destructive. [. . .]

The same differentiation is to be applied to the Middle Ages. After the demise of the Roman Empire the Economy based on the transport of goods receded and the natural-based economy of feudalism predominated. Already in the high Middle Ages, however, a town-based culture developed anew, manufactured goods appeared but above all the great trading and banking houses arose – what is called early capitalism.

In this situation Scholarly and Canon Law held true to the principles of the biblical and classical tradition in prohibiting usury and monopoly building, although ever more loopholes were developed to facilitate the practice of the charging of interest. In rough outline this, then, was the starting point at the beginning of the era of the Reformation.

Thesis 6

Martin Luther rejects the early capitalist system (and not only individual transactions) as idolatry and as contrary to the first commandment (the Great Catechism). On the basis of faith and charity the Christian should allow himself to let go, should give willingly and should lend freely without charge. On the grounds of charity and practical reason consumer credit with interest in cases of necessity, as well as the formation of monopolies, should be strictly rejected by the church under threat of punishment. In so saying Luther already recognizes, that the added value, hidden in the charging of interest, is exploitation of another's work and another's life. In principle John Calvin, too, stands in this tradition. Moreover, both Luther and Calvin had early thoughts about, what in contemporary economics is called, Productive Credit, but recognize that it should have severe, strict guidelines. This offers an interesting perspective even for modern times. [. . .]

Thesis 7

Karl Marx deciphers the 'secret of surplus profit', in economic development up to the era of capitalism through three fundamental principles. 1) He brings us to understand the quality of idolatry in this system through his analysis of the fetish of commodity, the fetish of gold and the fetish of capital. All the regulations and institutions of the system, while remaining invisible yet at the same time playing a vital role for people and the environment, ultimately serve the accumulation of capital, and as such are considered as sacrosanct. 2) In so doing he refines the aristotelian differentiation between money as money (in the sense of its being a means of exchange for the value of commodities in the satisfaction of basic needs in consumption), and money as capital (in the sense of the unlimited increase of money for its own sake). 3) He also provides the basic analysis of what was indicated by Luther, that the increase and accumulation of capital either as merchant capital or as industrial or interest-bearing capital, the added value contained in them, then, is created only by the exploitation of other people's labour. Thus he sees that only that proportion of profit is invested in reproducing the labour force as is minimally necessary for its maintenance. People and human needs which go beyond this minimal reproduction of the labour force, as well as the environment itself, hold no interest for the accumulation of capital. This is the reason for the processes which impoverish mankind and destroy the environment. [. . .]

In our search for a theological critique of capitalist concepts of the market economy, Marxist analysis remains of greatest importance independently of that critique. Far from making an application of a theological critique of a pre-capitalist economy to a capitalist one more doubtful, Marxist analysis confirms and strengthens the arguments. What biblical tradition rejected for the sake of God and mankind, what Aristotle rejected for the sake of the Polis, what Luther described as idolatry and as capital devouring more and more of the world, has according to Marx's analysis, been raised to the level of an all-embracing system. What then are the individual consequences for a theological critique?

Thesis 8
The heart of *'laissez-faire'* and monetarist concepts of the capitalist market economy has revealed itself to be an ideological and even fetishist illusion, namely the thesis, that economic growth within a capitalist framework can be synonymous with the spread of wealth and welfare within a whole nation or for all those who take part in the economic process. Rather it is an idolatrous increase in the wealth of the few at the cost of the life of the majority and of the earth itself. Because of this, all classical theological arguments against the charging of interest and the forming of monopolies apply to these concepts with renewed force. This means that they should be rejected by the Church in principle as the worship of idols and the destruction of life. The concepts of welfare capitalism such as the Social Market Economy must answer the question, how, under present economic and political circumstances, they can make oppositional political forces and the counter balance of the

Trade Unions so strong as to be in a position to force trans-national and increasingly monopolized capital to turn away from death dealing mechanisms for the increase of money and to turn to a life affirming fulfilling of basic needs in all parts of the world.

If it is correct that *'laissez-faire'* capitalism and monetarist capitalism of national security are, in principle, the worship of idols and lead to an increase of wealth and power for the few at the cost of the lives of many, the church is presented not only with an ethical question but a question of faith. This is even more so when attempts are made at a theological justification of these death dealing mechanisms. Confronted by a totalitarian fascist state Dietrich Bonhoeffer established two criteria for a church confronted by a question of faith, a 'status confessionis' where the church must give a clear answer, 'yes' or 'no', and when she must become a confessing church (eine bekennende Kirche):

1. When a socio-political institution notoriously fails to fulfil its God-given duty,
2. When it tries 'too much' to be and to do, i.e. when it becomes absolute.

The first argument against the capitalist economic order is that the economy systematically fails to fulfil its mandate, which is the satisfying of the basic needs of all its people. The second argument is that the economy aimed solely at the increase of money and which destroys people and the environment describes itself as autonomous and seeks its own theological justification. The consequence is that each church must, according to its own tradition, examine the economic structures and in the case of results similar to those related here, must repudiate them in the strongest possible form at its disposal, both theoretically and in practice. [. . .]

Now we touch upon the central question of today, that industrial and finance capital have become fully transnationalised whereas political institutions remain organized as before, on a national basis and are becoming ever more powerless. Here lie the main causes of the worldwide debt crisis and the difficulty of overcoming them. For that reason in this last section we turn to the question of the responsibility of the church in this situation.

III. Inferences for the debt crisis and the church

Thesis 9

The debt crisis is not a unique problem, but rather the clearest, world-economic expression of a social system where, in an all powerful market, the few seek an increase in money for its own sake at the cost of the lives of the majority of people and of the earth itself. In this system money grows like a cancer and destroys the life of the whole body. The main actors in this catastrophic development are, of course, the transnational banks and firms, the governments of the Western industrial nations and their international instruments, such as the IMF, but as consumers, savers and voters we all bear a responsibility as partakers in the process. In the short term attempts might be made within the framework of the system to influence the political and economic powers for the benefit of the poor and the environment. From a long term point of view, the only thing that will help is to overcome the system geared to the increase of money through an orientation of the economy towards the true economic value of its products and to meeting the basic needs of all people within ecologically responsible limits of growth (on the basis of a decentralized subsistence economy). [. . .]

Certainly, those who bear the main responsibility for the present crisis are the transnational banks and companies, and the governments of the Western industrial nations, who determine the actual regulations for the deathly game of the international division of labour. There are, too, those international institutions such as GATT and the IMF which are dominated by them.

There is, surely, some purpose in reminding them of their responsibility at a time when the effects of their system are increasingly rebounding on the industrialized societies in the form of unemployment, reductions in social welfare and ecological crisis. Basically, however, it is a question of overcoming the whole system, for within it – as Max Weber has so rightly maintained – no ethical principle takes hold – and that means today that there is no principle of survival. Change ... but in what direction?

We must try to gather together here the insights of the ecology movement, of the women's movement, of the solidarity and freedom movements of the two-thirds world, of all the new socio-ecological movements, because the 'white-man's' European civilization model, against which they are all turning, rests upon the exploitation of the colonies which is connected with the continuing exploitation of nature (including one's own body), the exploitation of women, of labour and of the two-thirds world. This means, too, that we must go beyond a socialism, which, as it exists, is equally consumer goods oriented.

One can formulate the following basic principles for a new orientation. 1) The whole analysis of critiques and aims must occur 'from below'. 2) The alternative must be aware of the limits imposed by a creature-based creation. 3) We must reject radically the development of one area at the cost of others. 4) The criterion of participation must be introduced also for basic economic decisions. 5) Labour must no longer be used for the accumulation of capital but must be directed towards a human life standard for all. 6) The dominance of unlimited needs, which are, in reality, addictions, must be broken and replaced in the economy by the criterion of basic need.

The practical results of these basic principles would mean, both economically and politically, that an economic system would have to be developed, not only in the countries of the two-thirds world, but also in the industrial countries, which had, as a basis, a new independent decentralized, ecologically sympathetic system of self-provision (subsistence economy) in order to satisfy basic needs. Originally, an economy centred on increasing the money supply formed only part of the overall economy with the result that one was able to resist it and its effects, as for example Luther did in his time. In the meantime, however, the money economy has extinguished almost the subsistence (self-provisioning) elements in the economy or made them dependent. It is worth recovering them. The meeting of basic needs must be independent of the world market in order to get out of the spiral of the accumulation of capital and an increase in the production of goods relative to purchasing power. Producer/consumer co-operatives would be an important starting point for an economy related to need. The market could be freed from a compulsion to accumulate capital and thus serve genuine exchange.

It remains to be examined how money might regain the role as a means of exchange. The theoreticians of a capitalist market economy certainly have to answer the question what they would do when, for ecological or other reasons, economic growth tended towards zero. For, according to their own assumptions, interest is only legitimate as a function of economic growth and ought, therefore, to approach zero when the growth curve does so.

What should happen beyond the level of regional exchange, at world market level, must be examined with regard to basic principles. The present deep crisis should be understood as an opportunity. 'It is not for the first time in history, that grass has grown on the ruins of empire and that corn has been sown again.'

Real allies in this process of reform are not only the women, whom Maria Mies has called on to form 'a movement for a consumer free society', but also the small farmers and tradesmen, as well as the workers who see themselves threatened by mass dismissal through the process of rationalization demanded by the processes of the accumulation of capital, or who have fallen sacrifice to it already. In this way, a worldwide coalition could be formed by those who have been 'colonized' and by those who have been marginalized by the process of capital accumulation, in order to form a front for a just, participating society which is capable of survival.

As far as the rich countries are concerned, the processes of marginalization have been felt only by minorities. The majority are (still) profiting from the system. It can hardly be expected that an alternative policy could gain support of the majority. What is the role of the church in this situation?

Thesis 10
In this situation it is the task of the church to turn to God, for God loves mankind and all creation and, therefore, justice, peace and life. This means a fundamental turning away from the false gods of a life-destroying cancerous-like growth in the accumulation of capital. In the short term the church may certainly appeal to the sense of responsibility of the powerful members of the present system. More important, however, is the nature of the church, as the image of God in its liturgy, its

confessing, its diaconate and community and its support for alternative models of the economy. Amongst other things this could have the following consequences:

1. In co-operation with the marginalized, churches, parishes and Christian groups could start a basic education programme in economic affairs ('learning about the economy in church communities').

2. They could take part not only in the 'consumer free movement' and 'consumer/producer co-operatives', but also change their own ways of using money.

3. A first step could be a different approach to interest on investment. They could withdraw their money from normal commercial banks and invest it in alternative banks such as 'the ecumenical development bank' (EDCS). Furthermore, with the interest which they (still) receive from normal commercial banks they could set up an 'ecumenical fund for combatting slavery to debt and unemployment'. All this presents no triumphal way for the church but a way in the joy of the crucified and risen Messiah, Jesus of Nazareth, the initiator and perfector of the new humanity. [. . .]

In the traditional model the mainstream churches restrain the social and political powers by, on the one hand, sharing in their power and, on the other, by exercising their prophetic critical role. In principle this is a legitimate option (if only the prophetic role were acknowledged). The above mentioned efforts of the church are to be supported only in so far as they foster a cancellation of the debt of the poor countries in line with the biblical Year of Jubilee, as well as co-determination for these countries in the IMF, a strengthening of political control over the financial institutions and a strengthening of the political vis à vis the economy in general. Every inch of territory won on behalf of the poor and the environment and every change in relationship in their favour is also one on behalf of God's justice and love.

However, if the church were content only with such appeals it would be to avoid the main question. Not only is it obvious to everyone that in the long term these fatal problems which arise from the modern growth economy will not be solved by appeals. But above all the church would be avoiding the two basic questions it faces: 1) Is the present economic system to be reconciled with God's will given biblical and church theological tradition and the present level of ecumenical discussion? 2) Can collaboration with the economic system be reconciled with the essential nature of the church?

It would be wrong to treat this only as a theoretical question and embark on endless discussions. It affects people and the world itself and concerns the church's faithfulness or lack of it. Therefore as well as attempting to influence as far as possible those in positions of responsibility, the church can and must begin to free itself from the economic and social structures and to work towards alternatives both for itself and society at large. Here, the mainstream churches can learn from the attempts of the peace and liberation churches to fulfil their role as church.

It is of utmost importance that the church does not seek to act differently only within its social framework. If the economic question affects the church in the very nature of its being then all its dimensions are affected: liturgy, the spirituality of its prayer and eucharist; its understanding of the Bible and its acknowledgement of the lordship of Christ over all powers and idols; its learning to live in alternative, sharing community; the diaconate in all its political, social aspects from declaring as unlawful all irresponsible institutions, to its refusal to co-operate with blatant wrong-doing, up to active sharing in the building up of a counterforce (countervailing power) in co-operation with 'people's movements'.

Source: Ulrich Duchrow, 'The Witness of the Church in Contrast to the Ideologies of the Market Economy', in *Poverty and Polarisation: A Call to Commitment* (The William Temple Foundation 1988).

chapter twelve

Gustavo Gutiérrez
1928–

Introduction

Brought up in a poor mestizo family in Lima, Peru, Gutiérrez embarked on a medical course at San Marcos University. He never completed it, because of a call to the priesthood. He then followed the traditional route for promising ordinands, through graduate study in Europe, first at Louvain (1951–5) and then at Lyons (1955–9). There he befriended Camilo Torres, the guerrilla priest killed in 1966, and Juan Segundo, another leader of liberation theology. Gutiérrez was ordained priest in 1959. A part-time teaching post at the Catholic University in Lima was then complemented by pastoral work in Rimac, one of the oldest Lima slums.

He has remained there to this day, in what is now the Bartolomé de Las Casas centre. It was this involvement with the poor that began his re-education. Understanding the devastating effects of poverty, its causes, and people's struggles against it, became the place where Gutiérrez encountered the living God. It compelled him to reject European theology, however progressive, and to develop what became a theology of liberation. The latter evolved into the classic book of that name (1971), and played an increasingly important part in church conferences, particularly at Medellín (1968); Gutiérrez drafted its key section on peace with its rejection of institutionalized violence against the poor. He was a major participant at the conference 'Christians for Socialism' in Chile in 1973, and has had a close relationship with socialist groups, including the United Left (a coalition of Marxist parties) in Peru. This has complemented his influential role in the development of liber-

ation theology in Latin America, and its growing contacts with
liberationist movements throughout the world. Not surprisingly, his involvements have led to serious conflicts with Rome.
The Truth Shall Make You Free (1990) contains his magisterial
defence. He has travelled widely to great acclaim, in the United
States, Britain and France, among other places.

Gutiérrez is certainly a seminal theologian and a leader with
outstanding spiritual gifts, yet he is pre-eminently a pastor,
working from his base in Rimac, and sharing in the life and
struggles of the poor. It is out of this context that his theology
has emerged, as a by-product of conflict rather than a meticu-
lous academic exercise in a university. As a result of years of
intimate involvement with the poor and his assiduous note-
taking, he has been able to capture what the poor think about
their involvement in struggle, and to relate biblical insights to it.
Praxis became the concept coined to describe this interaction
between people living out and reflecting on their commitments.
Gutiérrez regarded this as the primary act of faith; liberation
theology, as the secondary act, was to reflect on it, in the light of
the word of God. It was to become a rich explosive mixture
bringing together political engagement, including through
socialist analysis and organization, church life as official
Churches and base communities, spirituality as encountering
God in the poor and living life accordingly, and interpreting the
Bible from the underside of history as a militant reading of the
gospel. Not surprisingly, it constituted a comprehensive challenge to established interests in society, Church and theology.
The poor have continued to be the basis of all his Christian
social thought and practice. Ideology, however valuable in the
struggles of the poor, is always subordinate to this priority.

Text 16 provides an important entry point into liberation
theology. The book itself is Gutiérrez's magnum opus, and is
generally regarded as the greatest produced by the movement.
It reflects a context of revolutionary ferment in the Latin
America of the early 1960s, and Gutiérrez's attempts to fashion
a theology speaking to and through these times. The process of
its evolution illustrates the collaborative nature of such theology, and its relationship with church conferences. Beginning at
a consultation in Brazil in 1964, Gutiérrez tested out the
understanding of theology as reflection on praxis. Further

clarifications were gained at the Chimbote and Medellín conferences in 1968, and at a SODEPAX meeting in Switzerland in
1969. The book was published in Spanish in 1971, and in
English in 1973. Its task was to bring together into a systematic
whole, experiences and reflections from a broad spectrum of
dialogues with the poor and other liberation theologians in the
1960s. Yet, as Gutiérrez acknowledges, liberation theology is a
changing response to the changing reality of the poor. It is
therefore fitting that this text is from the 1988 edition of the
book, and from the new extended introduction. In it, Gutiérrez
sets out the theological developments that have occurred since
the first edition. For example, he acknowledges that the dependency theory is no longer a sufficient explanation of Third World
poverty. More important, it provides a clear concise summary
of liberation theology.

Text 16: Developing a Theology of Liberation

Expanding the view

In 1968 the Latin American bishops wrote this description of
the new phase of history that was dawning among us:

> Latin America is obviously under the sign of transformation
> and development; a transformation that, besides taking place
> with extraordinary speed, has come to touch and influence
> every level of human activity, from the economic to the
> religious.
>
> This indicates that we are on the threshold of a new epoch
> in this history of Latin America. It appears to be a time of
> zeal for full emancipation, of liberation from every form of
> servitude, of personal maturity and of collective integration
> (Medellín, 'Introduction').

This was a vision of a new historical era to be characterized by a
radical aspiration for integral liberation. However painful the

Latin American situation is (and it was painful in 1968), the vision is still valid. During the intervening years much has happened to change the history of the region and bring it across the threshold of which the bishops spoke and into an ever-accelerating process. [. . .]

The passage of time has caused essentials to become clearer. Secondary elements have lost the importance they seemed to have at an earlier period. A process of maturation has been under way. But the *temporal* factor is not the only one affecting the course of liberation theology during these years. There has also been a *spatial* extension. Within the different Christian confessions and their respective traditions, thinkers have adopted the liberation perspective suggested by the message of God's reign. In this development, theological influences (which in some cases were evidently nonexistent at the beginning) have played a less important role than the impulse given by a situation of fundamental oppression and marginalization that the Christian conscience rejects and in response to which it proclaims the total gospel in all its radicalness.

Black, Hispanic, and Amerindian theologies in the United States, theologies arising in the complex contexts of Africa, Asia, and the South Pacific, and the especially fruitful thinking of those who have adopted the feminist perspective – all these have meant that for the first time in many centuries theology is being done outside the customary European and North American centers. The result in the so-called First World has been a new kind of dialogue between traditional thinking and new thinking. In addition, outside the Christian sphere efforts are underway to develop liberation theologies from Jewish and Muslim perspectives.

We are thus in the presence of a complex phenomenon developing on every side and representing a great treasure for the Christian churches and for their dialogue with other religions. The clarification I mentioned earlier is thus not limited to the Latin American context but affects a process and a search that are being conducted on a very broad front today.

These considerations should not make us forget, however, that we are not dealing here solely with an intellectual pursuit. Behind liberation theology are Christian communities, religious groups, and peoples, who are becoming increasingly conscious that the oppression and neglect from which they suffer are incompatible with their faith in Jesus Christ (or, speaking more generally, with their religious faith). These concrete, real-life movements are what give this theology its distinctive character; in liberation theology, faith and life are inseparable. This unity accounts for its prophetic vigor and its potentialities.

It is not possible, when speaking of liberation theology, to pass over in silence this broad movement of Christian and religious experiments and commitments that feed reflection. In these pages I must nonetheless deal especially with the Latin American world, for it is the world closest to me and the one in which I have made my own contribution and experienced my own development. [. . .]

The 'new epoch in the history of Latin America', of which Medellín spoke, continues to be our vital context. In the language of the Bible, we are in a *kairos*, a propitious and demanding time in which the Lord challenges us and we are called upon to bear a very specific witness. During this *kairos* Latin American Christians are experiencing a tense and intense period of *solidarity*, *reflection*, and *martyrdom*. This direct, real-life setting enables me to go more deeply into the three points that I have for some time regarded as basic to liberation theology and have also been the primary ones in the chronological development of this theology: the viewpoint of the poor; theological work; and the proclamation of the kingdom of life. I should like to explain here what is permanent in each of these, the enrichments each has received, the development and maturation that time has effected, and the resultant evolution of ideas in the theological perspective that I have adopted.

A new presence

What we have often called the 'major fact' in the life of the Latin American church – the participation of Christians in the process of liberation – is simply an expression of a far-reaching historical event: *the irruption of the poor*. Our time bears the imprint of the new presence of those who in fact used to be 'absent' from our society and from the church. By 'absent' I mean: of little or no importance, and without the opportunity to give expression themselves to their sufferings, their camaraderies, their plans, their hopes.

This state of affairs began to change in Latin America in recent decades, as a result of a broad historical process. But it also began to change in Africa (new nations) and Asia (old nations obtaining their independence), and among racial minorities (blacks, Hispanics, Amerindians, Arabs, Asiatics) living in the rich countries and in the poor countries as well (including Latin American countries). There has been a further important and diversified movement: the new presence of women, whom Puebla described as 'doubly oppressed and marginalized' (1134, note) among the poor of Latin America. [. . .]

Liberation theology is closely bound up with this new presence of those who in the past were always absent from our history. They have gradually been turning into active agents of their own destiny and beginning a resolute process that is changing the condition of the poor and oppressed of this world. Liberation theology (which is an expression of the right of the poor to think out their own faith) has not been an automatic result of this situation and the changes it has undergone. It represents rather an attempt to accept the invitation of Pope John XXIII and the Second Vatican Council and interpret this sign of the times by reflecting on it critically in the light of God's word. This theology should lead us to a serious discernment of the values and limitations of this sign of the times.

A complex world

'Dominated peoples', 'exploited social classes', 'despised races', and 'marginalized cultures' were formulas often used in speaking of the poor in the context of liberation theology (there was repeated reference also to discrimination against women). The point of these formulas was to make it clear that the poor have a social dimension. But the turbulent situation in Latin America has caused many to place an almost exclusive emphasis on the social and economic aspect of poverty (this was a departure from the original insight). I am indeed convinced that it is still necessary to call attention to this dimension of poverty if we are to do more than touch the surface of the real situation of the poor, but I also insist that we must be attentive to other aspects of poverty as well.

As a matter of fact, the increasingly numerous commitments being made to the poor have given us a better understanding of how very complex their world is. For myself, this has been the most important (and even crushing) experience of these past years. The world of the poor is a universe in which the socio-economic aspect is basic but not all-inclusive. In the final analysis, poverty means death: lack of food and housing, the inability to attend properly to health and education needs, the exploitation of workers, permanent unemployment, the lack of respect for one's human dignity, and unjust limitations placed on personal freedom in the areas of self-expression, politics, and religion. Poverty is a situation that destroys peoples, families, and individuals; Medellín and Puebla called it 'institutionalized violence' (to which must be added the equally unacceptable violence of terrorism and repression).

At the same time, it is important to realize that being poor is a way of living, thinking, loving, praying, believing, and hoping, spending leisure time, and struggling for a livelihood. Being poor today is also increasingly coming to mean being involved in the struggle for justice and peace, defending one's life and freedom, seeking a more democratic participation in the decisions made by society, organizing 'to live their faith in an integral way' (Puebla, 1137), and being committed to the liberation of every human being.

All this, I repeat, goes to make up the complex world of the poor. The fact that misery and oppression lead to a cruel, inhuman death, and are therefore contrary to the will of the God of Christian revelation who wants us to live, should not keep us from seeing the other aspects of poverty that I have mentioned. They reveal a human depth and a toughness that are a promise of life. This perception represents one of the most profound changes in our way of seeing the reality of poverty and consequently in the overall judgment we pass on it. [. . .]

All this takes us far from the simplistic position we were perhaps in danger of initially adopting in analyzing the situation of poverty. A fundamental point has become clear: it is not enough to describe the situation; its *causes* must also be determined. Medellín, Puebla, and John Paul II in his encyclical on work and, more recently, on social concerns, as well as in other writings, have made a forceful analysis of these causes. Structural analysis has thus played an important part in building up the picture of the world to which liberation theology addresses itself. The use of this analysis has had its price, for although the privileged of this world can accept the existence of human poverty on a massive scale and not be overawed by it (after all, it is something that cannot be hidden away in our time), problems begin when the *causes* of this poverty are pointed out to them. Once causes are determined, then there is talk of 'social injustice', and the privileged begin to resist. This is especially true when to structural analysis there is added a concrete historical perspective in which personal responsibilities come to light. But it is the conscientization and resultant organization of poor sectors that rouse the greatest fears and the strongest resistance.

The tools used in this analysis vary with time and according to their proven effectiveness for gaining knowledge of social reality and finding solutions for social problems. Science is by its nature critical of its own presuppositions and achievements; it moves on to new interpretive hypotheses. It is clear, for example, that the theory of dependence, which was so extensively used in the early years of our encounter with the Latin American world, is now an inadequate tool, because it does not take sufficient account of the internal dynamics of each country or of the vast dimensions of the world of the poor. In addition, Latin American social scientists are increasingly alert to factors of which they were not conscious earlier and which show that the world economy has evolved.

Problems like unpayable foreign debt, to give but one example, are drawing attention, sharpening awareness of what lies behind them, and refining the available analytical tools (it is worth mentioning here that Medellín in 1968 called attention to the dangers of foreign indebtedness; see 'Peace', 9d). It is in fact impossible to deal effectively with the poverty experienced in Latin America without following the development of the most urgent problems and without attending to factors that enable us to locate these problems in a broad and complex international context.

All this requires that we refine our analytical tools and develop new ones. The socio-economic dimension is very important but we must go beyond it. In recent years there has been an insistent emphasis, and rightly so, on the contrast between a Northern world developed and wealthy (whether it be capitalist or socialist) and a Southern world underdeveloped and poor.

This approach yields a different view of the world scene, one in which it is not enough to focus on ideological confrontations or give a narrow interpretation of opposition between social classes. It also brings out the radical opposition that is the setting for the confrontation of East and West. Diverse factors are making us aware of the different kinds of opposition and social conflict that exist in the modern world.

As far as poverty is concerned, an important transformation is undoubtedly taking place in the social analysis on which liberation theology depends to some extent. The change has led liberation theology to incorporate beneficial perspectives and new sources of knowledge from the human sciences (psychology, ethnology, anthropology) for its study of a reality that is intricate and shifting. To incorporate does not mean simply to add on without interrelating. Attention to cultural factors will help us to enter into mentalities and basic attitudes that explain important aspects of the reality with which we are faced. The economic dimension itself will take on a new character once we see things from the cultural point of view; the converse will also certainly be true.

There is no question of choosing among the tools to be used; poverty is a complex human condition, and its causes must also be complex. The use of a variety of tools does not mean sacrificing depth of analysis; the point is only not to be simplistic but rather to insist on getting at the deepest causes of the situation, for this is what it means to be truly radical. Responsiveness to new challenges requires changes in our approach to the paths to be followed in really overcoming the social conflicts mentioned earlier and in building a just and fraternal world, as the gospel calls upon us to do.

If we were simply to adopt the traditional approach, we would be taking the course that has always been taken in the social sciences in their contribution to analysis. But we also know that the sciences and, for a number of reasons, the social sciences in particular, are not neutral. They carry with them ideological baggage requiring discernment; for this reason the use of the sciences can never be uncritical (see the Introduction of *Libertatis Nuntius*). In consequence, both the scientific outlook itself and the Christian conception of the world call for a rigorous discernment of scientific data – discernment, but not fear of the contributions of the human disciplines. We need to make an unruffled but critical use of mediations that can help us to understand better where and how the Lord is challenging us as we face the life (and death) of our brothers and sisters.

Opting for the God of Jesus

Important though it is to acquire a substantial knowledge of the poverty in which the vast majority of Latin Americans live and of the causes from which it springs, theological work proper begins when we try to interpret this reality in the light of Christian revelation.

The meaning given to poverty in the Bible is therefore a cornerstone of liberation theology. The problem of poverty is an ancient one in Christian thought, but the new presence of the poor to which I have referred gives it a new urgency. An essential clue to the understanding of poverty in liberation theology is the distinction, made in the Medellín document 'Poverty of the Church', between three meanings of the term 'poverty': real poverty as an evil – that is something that God does not want; spiritual poverty, in the sense of a readiness to do God's will; and solidarity with the poor, along with protest against the conditions under which they suffer.

This is the context of a theme that is central in liberation theology and has now been widely accepted in the universal church: the preferential option for the poor. Medellín had already spoken of giving 'preference to the poorest and the most needy sectors and to those segregated for any cause whatsoever' ('Poverty', 9). The very word 'preference' denies all exclusiveness and seeks rather to call attention to those who are the first – though not the only ones – with whom we should be in solidarity. In the interests of truth and personal honesty I want to say that from the very beginning of liberation theology, as many of my writings show, I insisted that the great challenge was to maintain both the universality of God's love and God's predilection for those on the lowest rung of the ladder of history. To focus exclusively on the one or the other is to mutilate the Christian message. Therefore every attempt at such an exclusive emphasis must be rejected.

During the difficult decade of the 1970s this attitude gave rise to many experiences and resultant theological reflections in the

Latin American church. In the process, formulas intended to express commitment to the poor and oppressed proliferated. This became clear at Puebla, which chose the formula 'preferential option for the poor' (see the Puebla Final Document, part 4, chapter 1). It was a formula that theologians in Latin America had already begun to use in preceding years. The Puebla Conference thus gave it a major endorsement and importance.

The term 'option' has not always been correctly understood. Like every term, it has its limitations; the intention in using it is to emphasize the freedom and commitment expressed in a decision. The commitment to the poor is not 'optional' in the sense that a Christian is free to make or not make this option, or commitment, to the poor, just as the love we owe to all human beings without exception is not 'optional'. Neither, on the other hand, does the term 'option' suppose that those making it do not themselves belong to the world of the poor. In very many instances, of course, they do not, but it must be said at the same time that the poor too have an obligation to make this option. [. . .]

In the final analysis, an option for the poor is an option for the God of the kingdom whom Jesus proclaims to us; this is a point that I myself have developed and discussed in depth on various occasions. The entire Bible, beginning with the story of Cain and Abel, mirrors God's predilection for the weak and abused of human history. This preference brings out the gratuitous or unmerited character of God's love. The same revelation is given in the evangelical Beatitudes, for they tell us with the utmost simplicity that God's predilection for the poor, the hungry, and the suffering is based on God's unmerited goodness to us.

The ultimate reason for commitment to the poor and oppressed is not to be found in the social analysis we use, or in human compassion, or in any direct experience we ourselves may have of poverty. These are all doubtless valid motives that play an important part in our commitment. As Christians, however, our commitment is grounded, in the final analysis, in the God of our faith. It is a theocentric, prophetic option that has its roots in the unmerited love of God and is demanded by this love. Bartolomé de Las Casas, who had direct experience of the terrible poverty and decimation of Latin American Amerindians, explained it by saying: 'God has the freshest and keenest memory of the least and most forgotten.' The Bible has much to say to us about this divine remembering, as the works of J. Dupont, among others, have made clear to us.

This same perception was confirmed by the experience of the Christian communities of Latin America and reached Puebla via the document that the Peruvian bishops prepared for the CELAM meeting. Puebla asserted that simply because of God's love for them as manifested in Christ 'the poor merit preferential attention, whatever may be the moral or personal situation in which they find themselves' (no. 1142). In other words, the poor deserve preference not because they are morally or religiously better than others, but because God is God, in whose eyes 'the last are first'. This statement clashes with our narrow understanding of justice; this very preference reminds us, therefore, that God's ways are not ours (see Isa. 55:8).

There have certainly been misunderstandings of the preferential option for the poor, as well as tendencies, sociological and spiritualist, to play it down, and this on the part both of those who claim to favor it and those who are expressly opposed to it. It can be said, nonetheless, that the option is now an essential element in the understanding that the church as a whole has of its task in the present world. This new approach is pregnant with consequences; it is also, we must say, only in its beginnings.

The role of reflection

The rich, troubled, and creative life that the Latin American church is living as it tries to respond to the challenge set for it by the new presence of the poor calls for a deeper understanding of its own faith in the Lord Jesus. For a long time, as a result of a Latin American cultural tradition imposed by colonization, theology as practiced among us simply echoed the theology developed in Europe. Latin American theologians had recourse to European theology without any reference to its intellectual and historical context, with the result that their theology easily became a set of abstract propositions. Or else they made a painful effort to adapt European theology to a new reality, but were unable to explain the reasons for its themes and priorities or for the development of this kind of thinking, as long as the effort was undertaken in a North Atlantic framework.

The quest for models or guidelines outside itself was long characteristic of Latin American thinking, and indeed still is in some circles. But the urgency and rich resources of the commitment that many Christians were beginning to make to the process of popular liberation during the 1960s raised new questions based on Latin American reality, and they pointed to new and fruitful ways for theological discourse. Liberation theology is one manifestation of the adulthood that Latin American society, and the church as part of it, began to achieve in recent decades. Medellín took note of this coming of age and in turn made a major contribution to its historical significance and importance.

All this reminds us that this theological perspective is explicable only when seen in close conjunction with the life and commitments of Christian communities. This connection was present at the historical beginnings of liberation theology in the 1960s and is still fully operative today. It is the basis for the familiar distinction between the two phases of theological work: Christian life and reflection in the strict sense. The way in which a people lives its faith and hope and puts its love to work is the most important thing in God's eyes and is also, or ought to be, the most important in discourse about God and God's saving will.

I have already pointed out the important role played in Christian consciousness by the irruption of the poor into our history. In the development of liberation theology our awareness of this new presence has made us aware that our partners in dialogue are the poor, those who are 'nonpersons' – that is, those who are not considered to be human beings with full rights, beginning with the right to life and to freedom in various spheres. Elsewhere, on the other hand, the best modern theology has been sensitive rather to the challenge posed by the mentality that asserted itself at the European Enlightenment; it is therefore responsive to the challenges posed by the nonbeliever or by Christians under the sway of modernity.

The distinction between these two approaches is not an attempt to juxtapose two theological perspectives. It tries only to be clear on their respective starting points, to see their difference, and then correctly to define relationships between the two. If we follow this line, we will avoid yielding to a tendency found in some academic settings: the tendency to regard liberation theology as the radical, political wing of European progressive theology. Such a view of liberation theology is clearly a caricature for anyone with a good knowledge of the subject. It is true, of course, that in a world of increasingly rapid communication it is not possible to do theology in a manner free of all contacts and influences; it is, however, both possible and necessary to be clear on the perduring basis and inspiration of our theological thinking. Only on that condition can there be dialogue among the various theologies that share a concern to speak of God in our day.

The life of a people

One of the first statements of my way of understanding the theological task was that liberation theology is 'a critical reflection on Christian praxis in light of the word of God'. The point of this was not to try to reduce the riches of a quest to a short definition, but rather to point out a path to be followed.

In many and very different ways the Bible shows us that the doing of God's will is the main demand placed on believers. Karl Barth echoed this thought when he said that 'the true hearer of the word is the one who puts it into practice'. In liberation theology I accepted this traditional datum of Christian revelation because I was moved by the witness of those who were beginning to commit themselves ever more fully to the process of freeing the poor from the various servitudes from which they suffer.

This commitment reflected the experience of the oppressed themselves, who were beginning to become the agents of their own destiny. During the 1950s and 60s we saw the first steps being taken in conscientization, and we saw the poor beginning to organize themselves in the defense of their right to life, in the struggle for dignity and social justice, and in a commitment to their own liberation. As a result, they were beginning to play a major active role that would become stronger with the passing years and that is still intensifying today amid advances and regressions. Many Christians played a part in this process. It is therefore wrong to say that theological thinking on liberation originated in the middle classes and that only years later did it open itself to the experience of the poor themselves. No, this experience played its part from the outset – at the level it had reached at that time. To be ignorant of this is to be mistaken about what happened at that time or even to give an explicitly false picture of it; the facts reject any such interpretation.

The praxis on which liberation theology reflects is a praxis of solidarity in the interests of liberation and is inspired by the gospel. It is the activity of 'peacemakers' – that is, those who are forging shalom. Western languages translate this Hebrew word as 'peace' but in doing so, diminish its meaning. Shalom in fact refers to the whole of life and, as part of this, to the need of establishing justice and peace. Consequently, a praxis motivated by evangelical values embraces to some extent every effort to bring about authentic fellowship and authentic justice. For faith shows us that in this commitment the grace of Christ plays its part, whether or not those who practice are aware of this fact.

This liberating praxis endeavors to transform history in the light of the reign of God. It accepts the reign now, even though knowing that it will arrive in its fullness only at the end of time. In this practice of love, social aspects have an important place on a continent in which socio-economic structures are in the service of the powerful and work against the weak of society. But in my understanding of it, 'praxis' is not reducible to 'social aspects' in this narrow sense. The complexity of the world of the poor and lowly compels us to attend to other dimensions of Christian practice if it is to meet the requirements of a total love of God.

In saying this I am not trying to make the Christian commitment less demanding and radical, but only to bring out the breadth of vision and the courage needed if we are to enter into the world of the poor and respond to their varied aspirations for justice and freely given friendship. As I have traveled this road, I have learned much in recent years; various experiences of being a part of the world of the poor have brought me to a less theoretical knowledge of that world and to a greater awareness of simple but profoundly human aspects of it, apart from which there is no truly liberating commitment. The struggles of those who reject racism and machismo (two attitudes so deeply rooted in the culture and custom of peoples and individuals), as well as of those who oppose the marginalization of the elderly, children, and other 'unimportant' persons in our society, have made me see, for example, the importance of gestures and ways of 'being with' that some may regard as having little political effectiveness.

In addition, the experience of these years has shown me that generous solidarity with the poor is not exempted from the temptation of imposing on them categories foreign to them and from the risk of dealing with them in an impersonal way. Sensitivity to these and other dangers is part of a human and Christian praxis whose truly liberating effects extend to those also who are trying to carry on such a praxis for the benefit of the poor and exploited. If there is no friendship with them and no sharing of the life of the poor, then there is no authentic commitment to liberation, because love exists only among equals. Any talk of liberation necessarily refers to a comprehensive process, one that embraces everyone. This is an insight that has been repeated again and again since the beginnings of liberation theology and that in my own case has become much more firmly established and has acquired a much greater importance with the passage of the years.

Christian life is commitment in the form of an acceptance of the gift of the reign of God. It is also, necessarily, prayer. There is no life of faith that does not have its contemplative dimension. The Latin Americans who are struggling for justice are also persons who believe and hope. They are oppressed persons, but also Christians who, like Mary in her Magnificat, remember their obligations of thankfulness and of surrender to God in prayer.

This outlook is characteristic of the faith of our Latin Americans. They cultivate a form of prayer that the modern mind is likely to regard as primitive if not downright superstitious. But, although it is true that various factors play a part in this way of living the faith, it would be a serious mistake to stop at a superficial analysis and not to discern the profound sense of God that this prayer manifests in ways that are perhaps not very enlightened but that are not therefore any less legitimate. Deeply rooted as it is in this popular devotion, while also drawing nourishment from the wellspring of protest against repression and the demand for freedom, the prayer life of the Christian communities that are engaged in the process of liberation possesses great creativity and depth. Those who have claimed from time to time that Latin America has been losing the spirit of prayer have shown only that they themselves are remote from the everyday life of the poor and committed sectors of our peoples.

Those working at a theology of liberation in the Asian context have likewise tried to bring out the deeply contemplative side of that continent on which ancient and magnificent religions of the human race have left such a profound imprint. Aloysius Pieris, theologian of Sri Lanka, describes the Asian peoples as both poor and religious. Both of these conditions point the way to a radical and complete liberation. Meanwhile, black theology in the United States has drawn fruitfully on the liberating and religious perspectives that find expression in black music. Theology done in the African context has likewise always been open to the cultural riches of the African people; religion is an essential element of this cultural treasure.

Prayer is a privileged way of being in communion with Christ and of 'keeping all these things in our heart', as his mother did (see Luke 2:51). The Gospels tell us of various occasions when the Lord went apart to pray. Contemplation was an essential part of his life. At one of the most difficult times in his experience, he rebuked his disciples for having been unable to persevere with him during his final prayer, which had turned into a difficult struggle for him. Luke tells us that he was 'in an agony' as he struggled for his life, so that his sweat 'became like great drops of blood' (22:44–45). Our communion with the prayer of Jesus must reach this point of 'agony' – that is, of combat (that is what the Greek word *agōnia* means). But this requirement is not difficult for those to understand who are putting their own lives on the line as they share the lot of the stripped and impoverished of Latin America.

Those, therefore, who adopt the liberation perspective must have the sensitivity that is needed for understanding and cultivating the celebratory and contemplative dimension of peoples who find in the God of their faith the source of their demand for life and dignity. Nothing could be further from my mind, however, than to defend in this context the kind of spiritualism that serves as a refuge from the troubles and sufferings of daily life. I am referring rather to the desire and determination to live simultaneously, and to the reciprocal

318

enrichment of each, two pursuits that the Western mind often
separates. The Western mind persistently applies this dichotomy in interpreting both the more spontaneously unified
behavior of other peoples and cultures, and the theological
efforts made in that context.

I am, of course, not speaking of syntheses that are fully
successful and without defects, but rather of a process whereby
one achieves a diversified presence that is open to a variety of
experiences and that progresses only amid setbacks; that develops gradually and deploys creativity. It is a matter of honesty
to recognize this fact, as well as of respect for those who bear
this witness. We find ourselves, then, in the presence of a
process that locates us at a point at which it is impossible to
separate solidarity with the poor *and* prayer. This means that we
are disciples of Christ, who is both God and a human being.

What we see here is an authentic spirituality – that is, a way of
being Christian. It is from this rich experience of the following
of Jesus that liberation theology emerges; the following constitutes the practice – at once commitment and prayer – on which
liberation theology reflects. The increasing number of Latin
American theological works on spirituality in recent years are
not as it were an appendix to works on other themes; they
represent rather a deeper penetration of the very wellspring
from which this kind of theological thinking flows.

The work done on spirituality will help to develop, more than
has hitherto been done, a traditional aspect of theology (one
whose existence was acknowledged at an early date in the
perspective I am adopting here) – namely, its function as
wisdom. Discourse on faith is knowledge that brings with it a
taste of its object; it is a spiritual tasting of the word of the Lord,
and, as such, it nourishes our life and is the source of our joy.

In liberation theology the way to rational talk of God is
located within a broader and more challenging course of action:
the following of Jesus. Talk of God supposes that we are living
in depth our condition as disciples of him who said in so many
words that he is the Way (see John 14:6). This fact has led me to
the position that in the final analysis the method for talking of
God is supplied by our spirituality. In other words, the distinction of two phases in theological work is not simply an academic
question; it is, above all, a matter of lifestyle, a way of living the

faith. Being part of the life of our people, sharing their sufferings and joys, their concerns and their struggles, as well as the faith and hope that they live as a Christian community – all this is not a formality required if one is to do theology; it is a requirement for being a Christian. For that reason, it also feeds the very roots of a reflection that seeks to explain the God of life when death is all around.

The locus of reflection
The historical womb from which liberation theology has emerged is the life of the poor and, in particular, of the Christian communities that have arisen within the bosom of the present-day Latin American church. This experience is the setting in which liberation theology tries to read the word of God and be alert to the challenges that faith issues to the historical process in which that people is engaged. Revelation and history, faith in Christ and the life of a people, eschatology and praxis: these are the factors that, when set in motion, give rise to what has been called the hermeneutical circle. The aim is to enter more deeply into faith in a God who became one of us, and to do so on the basis of the faith-filled experience and commitment of those who acknowledge this God as their liberator.

The major challenges to which theology must respond will come, therefore, from the demands of the gospel as seen today in the development of an oppressed but Christian people. Since liberation theology is a critical reflection on the word of God received in the church, it will make explicit the values of faith, hope, and love that inspire the praxis of Christians. But it will also have to help in correcting possible deviations on the part of those who reject the demands for participation in history and the promotion of justice that follow from faith in the God of life, and also on the part of those who run the risk of forgetting central aspects of Christian life, because they are caught up in the demands of immediate political activity.

Because liberation theology takes a critical approach, it refuses to serve as a Christian justification of positions already taken. It seeks to show that unless we make an ongoing commitment to the poor, who are the privileged members of the reign of God, we are far removed from the Christian message. It also wants to help make the commitment to liberation increasingly evangelical, effective, and integral. Theology is at the service of the evangelizing mission of the Christian community; it develops therefore as an ecclesial function. Its task is one that locates it within the church, for it is there that it receives revelation and there that it is nourished by the charisms of prophecy, government, and teaching that reside in the church and guide its efforts.

It is clear from what I have been saying that when I call reflection in the strict sense a *second* stage of theological work, I am by no means saying that is *secondary*. Discourse about God comes second because faith comes first and is the source of theology; in the formula of St. Anselm, we believe in order that we may understand (*credo ut intelligam*). For the same reason, the effort at reflection has an irreplaceable role, but one that is always subordinate to a faith that is lived and receives guidance within the communion of the church.

The first stage or phase of theological work is the lived faith that finds expression in prayer and commitment. To live the faith means to put into practice, in the light of the demands of the reign of God, these fundamental elements of Christian existence. Faith is here lived 'in the church' and geared to the communication of the Lord's message. The second act of theology, that of reflection in the proper sense of the term, has for its purpose to read this complex praxis in the light of God's word. There is need of discernment in regard to the concrete forms that Christian commitment takes, and this discernment is accomplished through recourse to the sources of revelation. The ultimate norms of judgment come from the revealed truth that we accept by faith and not from praxis itself. But the 'deposit of faith' is not a set of indifferent, catalogued truths; on the contrary, it lives in the church, where it rouses Christians to commitments in accordance with God's will and also provides criteria for judging them in the light of God's word.

For all these reasons, a principal task of 'reflection on praxis in the light of faith' will be to strengthen the necessary and fruitful links between orthopraxis and orthodoxy. The necessity of this circular relationship between the two is a point frequently underscored in liberation theology; as is always the case in dealing with essential dimensions of one and the same reality, it is not possible to accept the one and belittle the other. More than that, any attempt to focus on only one means the loss of both; orthopraxis and orthodoxy need one another, and each is adversely affected when sight is lost of the other. The polemical manner in which this subject is sometimes treated (whether for or against the union of orthopraxis and orthodoxy) should not make one forget that fidelity to the message of Jesus requires one not to impoverish or mutilate it by choosing where no choice is possible. In a key passage of Mark's Gospel (8:27–33) he speaks in an incisive way of the necessity of this enriching circular relationship. Theology as critical reflection must make its contribution to this profound unity.

Starting from Christian praxis (commitment and prayer), theology seeks to provide a language for speaking about God. It deals with a faith that is inseparable from the concrete conditions in which the vast majority and, in a sense, even all the inhabitants of Latin America live. Among us the great pastoral, and therefore theological, question is: How is it possible to tell the poor, who are forced to live in conditions that embody a denial of love, that God loves them? This is equivalent to asking: How can we find a way of talking about God amid the suffering and oppression that is the experience of the Latin American poor? How is it possible to do theology 'while Ayacucho lasts'? As the church, the assembly of the disciples of Jesus, we must proclaim his resurrection to a continent scarred by 'inhuman' (Medellín, 'Poverty', 1) and 'antievangelical' (Puebla, 1159) poverty. As I said earlier, in the final analysis poverty means death. Liberation theology had its origin in the contrast between the urgent task of proclaiming the life of the risen Jesus and the conditions of death in which the poor of Latin America were living.

Theology done in such a setting has something in common with all theology: dialogue with the prevailing culture or, in our case, with the various cultures to be found in Latin America. This dialogue has barely begun, and it has a long way to go. In conducting it, we will be greatly helped if we adopt the view of theology as wisdom, which I mentioned above – that is, if we see theology as knowledge shot through with the 'savored' experience first of God but then also of the people and culture to which we belong. In the contributions that I myself have been able to make to liberation theology, my frequent references to

Felipe Guamán Poma de Ayala, César Vallejo, José Carlos Mariátegui and José Maria Arguedas, among others, have had the purpose precisely of communicating some of this 'savor'. These men are all Peruvians who have experienced their own time in depth; they have been deeply involved in the sufferings and hopes of our peoples and have been able to express, as few others have, the soul of the nation, its Amerindians and mestizos. But, I repeat, this is an area in which far more remains to be done than has so far been accomplished.

This approach makes it urgent that we acquire a better understanding of our history. A people that knows the past that lies behind its sufferings and hopes is in a better position to face and reflect on the present. Furthermore, we must learn from the attempts made to understand the faith by Christians who are able to face up intensely to their times and to appeal to the gospel with clarity and courage. These men and women try to see clearly amid the changes of history and, in many cases, try to oppose the interests of the powerful. I am thinking here of the witness given by many sixteenth-century missionaries who did not forget the demands of the kingdom of life when they were faced with cruel exploitation and death being inflicted on the Amerindians. Among those missionaries, Bartolomé de Las Casas was perhaps the one who saw most deeply into the situation and best articulated a theological reflection based on it. He was, however, only *primus inter pares*, for he had many companions who shared his commitment and his hope. The witness of all those persons should feed the life of the Christian community today, for it is one tributary of the great ecclesial tradition within which every sound theology is located.

Although theology is a language for communicating God, in every place it must display the inflections given it by those who formulate it and those to whom it is directed. Every language has a number of dialects. The language of Jesus the Nazarene (like that of Peter, his disciple, to whom they said: 'Your accent betrays you': Matt. 26:73) undoubtedly showed him to be a native of Galilee and seemed odd to the inhabitants of Jerusalem. Our theological language is subject to the same rule; it takes its coloring from our peoples, cultures, and racial groupings, and yet we use it in an attempt to proclaim the universality of God's love. This accent may not be to the liking of those who until now have regarded themselves the proprietors of theology and are not conscious of their own accent (to which, of course, they have every right) when they speak of God.

This dialogue between faith and culture in Latin America is accompanied by another, which is different in character but highly important and derives its tone from the first. I am referring to the encounter in recent years of theologies springing from human contexts unlike our own. I mentioned earlier the dialogue between the theologies of the Third World, in which the theologies emerging from minorities in different countries all participate on an equal footing. But this further dialogue does not stop at the borders of the Third World. There have also been very profitable meetings with representatives of types of theological thinking that originate in Europe and North America. Then there is the encounter with the feminist perspective in theology and with the new and challenging contribution this is making. My impression is that the deeper importance of this dialogue is to be found, not in the coming together of theologians, but in the communication established among Christian communities and their respective historical, social, and cultural contexts, for these communities are the real subjects who are actively engaged in these discourses of faith.

In my view, the fact that any understanding of the faith has its roots in the particularity of a given situation should not cause us to neglect the comparison of what we are doing with efforts being made at the level of the universal church. Particularity does not mean isolation. It is true, of course, that each type of theological thinking cannot, and ought not, be applied mechanically to situations different from that in which it arose; whence the foolishness of attempts to do just that with liberation theology, as if it resembled a pharmaceutical prescription. But it is no less true that any theology is discourse about a universal message. For this reason, and to the extent that it springs from an experience that is both deeply human and deeply Christian, every theology also has a universal significance; or, to put it more accurately, every theology is a question and challenge for believers living other human situations.

Authentic universality does not consist in speaking precisely the same language but rather in achieving a full understanding within the setting of each language. The book of the Acts of the

Apostles tells us that the reason for the astonishment felt by the speakers of different languages who were gathered in Jerusalem on Pentecost was not that the apostles all spoke in a unique tongue but that 'we hear, all of us in *our own native language*' (Acts 2:6–8). The goal, then, is not uniformity but a profound unity, a communion or *koinōnia*. One element in this Christian *koinōnia* (which extends far beyond mere intellectual dialogue) is the understanding that the various forms of theology exist within a profound ecclesial communion and give a richly diversified expression to the truth proclaimed by the Only Son.

Friends of life

Christians are witnesses of the risen Christ. It is this testimony that calls us together in a permanent way as the church and at the same time is the very heart of the church's mission. The realization that life and not death has the final say about history is the source of the joy of believers, who experience thereby God's unmerited love for them. To evangelize is to communicate this joy; it is to transmit, individually and as a community, the good news of God's love that has transformed our lives.

Theology is at the service of this proclamation of the reign of love and justice. Nothing human falls outside the purview of the reign, which is present in history and is transforming it, while also leading it beyond itself. Liberation theology made this perspective its starting point as it attempted to show the meaning of the proclamation of the gospel for the history of Latin America. This is indeed the most important point in this type of theological thinking – namely, that its major concern is with the proclamation of the gospel to the peoples of Latin America. This concern gave birth to it and continues to nourish its efforts.

The major achievement of the Latin American church from 1968 to 1988 was that it renewed with unwonted energy its mission of evangelization and, ultimately, of liberation. It is in this context that we must understand what the preferential option for the poor means. As a result, throughout Latin America (including sectors that used to regard themselves as estranged from the church) and on the international stage, the church has acquired a presence it never had before. Various factors have played a part in producing this result (which is in fact an ongoing process); one of them is liberation theology, which has in large measure articulated the way in which the Latin American Christian community now proclaims its message.

The witness given by Christians has, of course, inevitably elicited resistance and painful hostility. One thing is nonetheless certain: the commitment made by a church that is conscious of the necessity of proclaiming and building a peace based on justice for all, but especially for those who today suffer more from despoliation and mistreatment, has left its mark on the history of Latin America during these years. The Latin American church has made this commitment in many forms throughout the length and breadth of the region, and it has even begun to make its voice heard outside its own borders. Echoing the gospel itself, the Second Vatican Council called on the entire church to make such a commitment. It is the special characteristic of the Christian community that it goes out into the world to 'make disciples of all nations' (Matt. 28:20) and is therefore never satisfied with successes already obtained. It must continually go out of itself and look forward in expectation of the Lord's coming.

To liberate = to give life

The historical process in which Latin America has been involved, and the experiences of many Christians in this process, led liberation theology to speak of salvation in Christ in terms of liberation. This approach meant listening to the 'muted cry [that] wells up from millions of human beings, pleading with their pastors for a liberation that is nowhere to be found in their case' (Medellín, 'Poverty', 2). Puebla added that this cry 'might well have seemed muted back then' but today it is 'loud and clear, increasing in volume and intensity, and at times full of menace' (no. 89). In speaking thus, the two episcopal conferences were displaying a manifest fidelity to the message of the God who acts in history to save a people by liberating it from every kind of servitude. Continuing in the line of Medellín and Puebla, Pope John Paul II addressed these strong and sensitive words to the bishops of Brazil: 'The poor of this country, whose pastors you are, and the poor of this continent are the first to feel the urgent need of this *gospel* of radical and integral *liberation*.

To conceal it would be to cheat them and let them down' (letter of April 1986; emphasis added).

The combination of these two factors – the message that is at the heart of biblical revelation, and the profound longing of the Latin American peoples – led us to speak of liberation in Christ and to make this the essential content of evangelization. Something similar has been happening in other sectors of the human race and in the Christian churches present in their midst. There is a longing for liberation that wells up from the inmost hearts of the poor and oppressed of this world and opens them to receive the saving love of God. This longing is a sign of the active presence of the Spirit. The various theologies of liberation to which I have referred are meeting the challenge and giving expression to the experience and its potentialities.

From the outset, liberation was seen as something comprehensive, an integral reality from which nothing is excluded, because only such an idea of it explains the work of him in whom all the promises are fulfilled (see 2 Cor. 1:20). For that reason I distinguished three levels or dimensions of liberation in Christ, and Puebla made the distinction its own (nos. 321–29). First, there is liberation from social situations of oppression and marginalization that force many (and indeed all in one or another way) to live in conditions contrary to God's will for their life. But it is not enough that we be liberated from oppressive socio-economic structures; also needed is a personal transformation by which we live with profound inner freedom in the face of every kind of servitude, and this is the second dimension or level of liberation.

Finally, there is liberation from sin, which attacks the deepest root of all servitude; for sin is the breaking of friendship with God and with other human beings, and therefore cannot be eradicated except by the unmerited redemptive love of the Lord whom we receive by faith and in communion with one another. Theological analysis (and not social or philosophical analysis) leads to the position that only liberation from sin gets to the very source of social injustice and other forms of human oppression and reconciles us with God and our fellow human beings.

This idea of total liberation was inspired by that of integral development that Paul VI set down in *Populorum Progressio* (no. 21). With the help of this concept the pope showed how it is possible, without confusing the various levels, to affirm the deeper unity of a process leading from less human to more human conditions. Amongst the 'more human' conditions he listed 'finally and above all: faith, a gift of God accepted by human good will, and unity in the charity of Christ, who calls us all to share as offspring in the life of the living God, the Father of all human beings.' The pope was obviously speaking of human possibilities in a broad sense, not disregarding the gratuitousness of faith and love.

There is no slightest tinge of immanentism in this approach to integral liberation. But if any expression I have used may have given the impression that there is, I want to say here as forcefully as I can that any interpretation along those lines is incompatible with my position. Moreover, my repeated emphasis (in my writings) on the gratuitousness of God's love as the first and last word in biblical revelation is reliable evidence for this claim. The saving, all-embracing love of God is what leads me to speak of history as profoundly one (in saying this, I am not forgetting the distinctions also to be found within history). What I want to say when I speak of history has been expressed with all desirable exactness by the Peruvian bishops:

> If we mean by the 'history of salvation' not only those actions that are properly divine – creation, incarnation, redemption – but the actions of human beings as they respond to divine initiatives (either accepting them or rejecting them), then there is in fact only one history, for the uncertain endeavors of human beings, whether they like it or not, whether they even know it or not, have their place in the divine plan (*Documento sobre teología de la liberación*, October 1984).

History is, after all, the field where human beings attain to fulfillment as persons and in which, in the final analysis, they freely say yes or no to God's saving will.

Liberation theology is thus intended as a theology of salvation. Salvation is God's unmerited action in history, which God leads beyond itself. It is God's gift of definitive life to God's children, given in a history in which we must build fellowship. Filiation and fellowship are both a grace and a task to be carried out; these two aspects must be distinguished without being separated, just as, in accordance with the faith of the church as definitively settled at the Council of Chalcedon, we distinguish in Christ a divine condition and a human condition, but we do not separate the two.

This christological truth enables us to determine what gives unity and what creates duality in the process of liberation – that is, in the saving work that God calls us to share. Puebla makes the distinction in carefully worded language at the end of its lengthy section on the three dimensions or levels of liberation:

> We are liberated by our participation in the new life brought to us by Jesus Christ, and by communion with him in the mystery of his death and resurrection. But this is true only on condition that we live out this mystery on the three planes described above, without focusing exclusively on any one of them. Only in this way will we avoid reducing the mystery to the verticalism of a disembodied spiritual union with God, or to the merely existential personalism of individual or small-group ties, or to one or another form of social, economic, or political horizontalism (no. 329).

The very complexity of the concept of liberation prevents us from reducing it to only one of its aspects.

In this view of the matter, a key point – not always assigned its proper value – is consideration of the 'second level', that of human liberation. I myself have always emphasized its necessity in my writings. This emphasis reflected an effort to avoid the narrow approach taken to liberation when only two levels, the political and the religious, are distinguished. The political and the religious are certainly basic aspects of liberation, but exclusive attention to them often led to a simple juxtaposition of them, thus impoverishing both, or else to an identification of the two, thus perverting the meaning of both. From the theological standpoint, emphasis on the mediation of aspects of the human that are not reducible to the socio-political made it easier to think of the unity of all the aspects without confusing them; it also made it possible to speak of God's saving action as all-embracing and unmerited, without reducing it to a purely human set of activities, as well as to interrelate the political and the religious dimensions while also incorporating the needed ethical perspective. Inertia, however, caused some to interpret the three dimensions distinguished by liberation theology and later by Puebla in the more common, but theologically different, perspective: the relationship between only two of the levels or dimensions.

In his Apostolic Exhortation *Evangelii Nuntiandi* Paul VI made this very careful statement:

> We must ... say the following about the liberation that evangelization proclaims and endeavors to bring about:
> a) It cannot be limited purely and simply to the economic, social, and cultural spheres but must concern the whole person in all dimensions, including the relationship to an 'absolute' and even to *the* Absolute, which is God.
> b) It is based, therefore, on *a conception of human nature*, an anthropology, which can never be sacrificed to the requirements of some strategy or other, or to practice, or to short-term effectiveness.

As a matter of fact, in the measure that we acquire a more complete vision of the process of liberation, its humblest level – the second – helps us understand better the process in the light of faith.

All that has been said shows that liberation, understood as an integral whole (as it is in liberation theology and in the Medellín documents), is the central theme of evangelization. It is at the heart of the Lord's saving work and of the kingdom of life; it is what the God of the kingdom seeks.

Source: Gustavo Gutiérrez, *A Theology of Liberation* (SCM Press 1988 edition, with new introduction), pp.xvii-xl.

part three

Christian Conservatism

c h a p t e r   t h i r t e e n

John Bird Sumner
1780–1862

Introduction

Sumner was born into a clerical family in Kenilworth, and educated at King's College, Cambridge, where he won the Hulsean Prize (1801), and became a Fellow. After ordination in the Church of England in 1803, he became an assistant master at Eton and pursued an unobtrusive career in teaching and theological scholarship. All this was changed when he entered the competition for the rich Burnett prize, with his *Treatise on the Records of the Creation* (1816), a remarkable combination of theological and economic insights. Although he only came second, the rewards turned out to be enormous. He quickly became a Fellow at Eton, a prebend of Durham Cathedral, and then Bishop of Chester (1828). The latter was a heavy responsibility, including as it did the great new industrial areas of Liverpool and Manchester.

Yet, in the midst of overseeing the building of over two hundred schools and churches, mostly in poorer areas, Sumner was also able to publish biblical studies, sermons and visitation charges. In 1848 he became Archbishop of Canterbury. Besides being a church leader, he was also deeply involved in public life. Although he was a firm supporter of a *laissez-faire* economy, including the Poor Law Reform Act of 1834, it was with the progressive intention of promoting a prosperous economy and the relief of poverty. He therefore supported the Factory Acts, Corn Law reform and the Public Health Bill because they benefited the poor even though they interfered in the free market.

Even though Sumner held the highest office in the Church of

England, he remained a teacher and pastor, and was known for his piety and simplicity of life. His important contribution to Christian social thought emerged from his unusual ability to link theological insights and the new discipline of modern economics. In this, and in other respects, he predates social Christianity's use of the social sciences, but to quite different effect. Always an evangelical, his theology was characterized by the reasoned moderation of Anglicanism. Rejecting Calvinism as morally repugnant, he integrated natural theology and the Christian dispensation. The result was that he was able to regard the development of the modern free market economy as a beneficent indication of God's purposes for human well-being. It was a synthesis that enabled him to engage creatively with economists like Malthus, Ricardo and Stewart (he was a respected member of their select Political Economy Club).

Out of this interdisciplinary experience, Sumner focused on the central economic problem of scarcity, and illustrated how it could contribute, through the free market, to the improvement of the human lot in general, and of the poor in particular. It was a thesis pervaded by a strong sense of achievable progress. As a result, it went some way to counterbalancing the gloom shed by early Malthusian political economy, with its advocacy of war and famine as the solution of the scarcity problem.

Text 17 is taken from *The Records of the Creation*, an influential and popular book which was soon into its seventh edition. It became the principal means by which churchmen in the early nineteenth century discovered the ideas of Malthus and political economy. As such, it helped to establish the ideological dominance of Christian political economy in the nineteenth century. It therefore contributed to the context that provoked the development of social Christianity.

The shape of the book is governed by the terms of the competition for the Burnett prize. Volume one addresses the existence of God, and volume two, the wisdom and goodness of God. The text covers this more important second volume, parts two and three. In part two, on 'the wisdom of the Creator', Sumner takes the bold step of using Malthus's principle of population to show how necessary inequalities of wealth, intellect and virtue contribute to human betterment through the free market. In part three, on 'the goodness of the Creator', he recognizes the inevitability of poverty in the midst of the wealth of a free market system. Yet he then examines how it can be remedied through the market economy, public education for all, accident and sickness insurance, financial institutions to utilize the savings of the poor, and private charity as a last resort. He therefore illustrates many of the arguments and insights used by Christian conservatism throughout the nineteenth and twentieth centuries.

Text 17: Reconciling Inequality and God's Purposes in the Free Market

Part II On the wisdom of the Creator

Chapter V

> *On the Principle of Population, and its Effects: intended to show that Man is inevitably placed in that Condition which is most calculated to improve his Faculties, and afford Opportunities for the exercise of Virtue.*

I am willing to suppose it has appeared from the foregoing discussion, that a state of society, consisting of various ranks and conditions, is the state best suited to excite the industry and display the most valuable faculties of mankind. Taking, therefore, into consideration the object of man's existence upon earth, it might naturally be expected that the Creator would devise a mean which would inevitably tend to bring the human race, for the most part, into such a situation.

And this, in fact, I believe to be the final cause of that 'principle of population', with whose powerful agency we have recently been made acquainted; the final cause, in other words, of that instinctive propensity in human nature, under all governments, and in every stage of civilization, to multiply up to the means of subsistence, and even to press, by increase of numbers, upon the limits of the food assigned them. The consequence of this universal tendency is, to render an inequality of fortunes, and a consequent division of ranks, no less general; not as a matter of agreement or expediency in which mankind have a liberty of option; but as a matter of imperious necessity, growing out of the established constitution of their nature.

The existence of this principle was first remarked by political economists in the concluding half of the last century, and allusions to it may be found in the writings of Wallace, Hume, Franklin, Smith, and particularly of Mr. Townsend, who in the course of his travels through Spain had an opportunity of illustrating its influence and effects in every valley and opening of the mountains, many of which in that country are in a manner insulated from the rest of the world. The human race, he observes, however at first, and while their numbers are limited, they may rejoice in affluence, will go on increasing, till they balance their quantity of food. From that period, two appetites will combine to regulate their numbers. But the merit of establishing the fact, that, notwithstanding the checks to population, both from natural and moral causes, which exist, more or less, in every country, mankind *do* every where increase their numbers, till their multiplication is restrained by the difficulty of procuring subsistence, and the consequent poverty of some part of the society: this merit is justly due to the comprehensive treatise, in which Mr. Malthus has unfolded this important branch of human history. The work to which I allude, is too well known to justify any abridgement of its leading doctrines, and too well digested to allow any material addition to its statements.*

* *I would be understood to speak here of the facts established by Mr. Malthus, as to the different ratio of increase of mankind and their support: in saying which, I do not allude to the arithmetical and geometrical ratios, as if they were established laws of nature, but to the universal tendency of the species to increase faster than subsistence can be supplied. With the hypothetical ratios which open the subject in Mr. Malthus's work, I have no immediate concern. Even though as abstract facts they may be undeniable, the general argument of Mr. Malthus is independent of them: and the propositions he brings forward would stand as well even if the introductory statement could be overthrown. Whatever exceptions may be urged against the mode in which Mr. Malthus has introduced his arguments, or to some of*

the particular consequences he has deduced from them, on which, of course, even the surest premises leave just room for difference of opinion; it is impossible to rise from his treatise without a conviction, that there is a tendency in mankind under all known circumstances, to pass the limits of their actual supply. It may, however, naturally be asked, how a treatise, which admits the justice of Mr. Malthus's premises, and even takes them as a basis, should represent the effects of the principle of population upon mankind, under such a different aspect? This will admit of very satisfactory explanation. It was the object of Mr. M. to show the strength of that principle. Its strength was to be proved by a circumstantial detail of the checks which retard or diminish population in every country of the world, notwithstanding and in spite of which, no country has actually any food to spare. Those checks are, moral restraint, vice, and misery. Of these three, moral restraint, i.e. restraint upon marriage from prudential considerations, is incalculably the most universal and effectual, and is distinctly stated as such by Mr. M. vol.ii. p. 75. But it is a silent and an unseen check, and, comparatively, makes no figure in the account; whereas the vices and the natural evils to which mankind are liable, wear a tremendous appearance when collected into a small space to prove a particular point. That there was much poverty, much vice, much misery in the world, was well known before; but it was lost in the more evident appearance of industry, plenty, and content, till all the checks to population were brought together in the aggregate, to point out to us the vigorous operation of the law of increase. For this reason, Mr. Malthus's first volume, though none of its main facts can be disproved, is not to be taken as a representation of the actual state of human nature, but of the disorders to which it is liable. The human constitution is not to be judged of from a system of nosology; nor the state of society in England from Mr. Colquhoun's View of the Police of the Metropolis.

The fact stands thus. An instinctive principle in our nature, forcibly urgent, wherever it meets with no discouragement from the difficulty of providing for a family, mutually attaches the sexes to each other. Where this desired and desirable union is unrestrained, and its offspring subject to no premature mortality, the increase which attends it is so rapid, as to double the original population in twelve or fifteen years. And, not to insist upon extreme cases, the increase in countries to a certain degree civilized and widely extended, is known to proceed in a geometrical ratio, i.e. to double the population in twenty-five years, as long as it continues possible, by the employment of skill and labour on a surface of unoccupied land, to find a plentiful subsistence for this growing population. [. . .]

A survey of the different conditions in which we find mankind collected; whether the hunting state, the pastoral, the agricultural, or the commercial; will satisfactorily prove, that by a principle inherent in their constitution, mankind invariably press against, and have a tendency to surpass their actual and available supply of food. [. . .]

With regard to the more crowded commercial countries of Europe, the most advanced we know in point of absolute civilization, we have only to look around us in order to be satisfied whether the people do not increase up to the means of support; i.e. whether those who have no other maintenance than the daily wages of their labour, do not increase till that labour earns barely sufficient to support their families. The result of such observation cannot fail to be, that in every department of national industry there are more claimants for employ than employers; that the demand is for labour rather than for labourers; that there are somewhat more manufacturers, more artificers, more agriculturalists, than can be usefully or profit-ably, under the existing circumstances, kept in activity by the funds destined for their maintenance. And as labour is the only claim to support which the lowest classes can urge; to be without employ, is to be without support; and to multiply beyond the demand for labour, is to multiply beyond the available supply of subsistence. [. . .]

Such then is the established fact, that, according to the attachments and instincts of our common nature, the human race continues to increase, till the population presses upon the actual supply of food; so that there will always be in every inhabited country as many persons existing as it will support at all, and always more than it can support well. And having merely stated this undeniable truth, it becomes my object more particularly to consider its effects upon the moral and political state of mankind.

I. The primary result of this universal tendency to increase, is the division of property. The property of first necessity to every man, is his supply of food. Whilst this is plentiful, he is careless about it. Its value originates with its scarcity. If the fruits of the earth were supplied from a source as regular and inexhaustible as the water of the ocean, there could be no occasion, and there would, probably, be no thought, of their appropriation. If every family, like the Israelites in the wilder-ness, could supply their wants without the necessity of labour or the fear of deficiency, no one would think of setting bounds to the demand of any claimant, or grudge his neighbour his share of the superabundance.

By the constitution of things, however, it appears, that abundance, even if it exists for a while, can never be of long duration. It defeats itself. Wherever it is found, the number of claimants is daily increasing in proportion, and will soon require an addition to the supply of food, which can only be procured by labour; and as soon as it demands labour, becomes valuable.*

* *I need hardly observe, that I do not state this as the mode in which we have been uniformly led to the division of property; the case is only put hypothetically, to prove that even under the most favourable circumstances the pressure of population would soon either render such division inevitable, or leave the inhabitants in the most wretched and stationary condition, if they refused to comply with the intentions of Providence for their comfort and improvement.*

The hypothesis, however, has so much justification in fact, that it is very nearly a representation of the case of Abraham and Lot. 'The land was not able to bear them, that they might dwell together; for their substance was so great, so that they could not dwell together. And there was a strife between the herdmen of Abraham's cattle, and the herdmen of Lot's cattle. And Abraham said unto Lot, Let there be no strife, I pray thee, between me and thee, and between my herdmen and thy herdmen; for we are brethren. Is not the whole land before thee? separate thyself, I pray thee, from me; and if thou wilt take the left hand, then I will go to the right hand; or if thou depart to the right hand, then I will go to the left. Thus Lot chose him all the plain of Jordan; and Lot journeyed east, and they separated themselves one from another' (Gen.xiii). [. . .]

II. The first effect, it has appeared, of the natural law which uniformly presses the population against the means of subsistence, is the *division of property*. Its second effect, springing inevitably from the former, is the division of ranks. [. . .]

It has thus appeared, from a brief statement of the laws which regulate population, that the instinctive principle which attaches the sexes to one another, and rears a family, keeps the inhabited districts of the world so continually full, as to call into action all their resources, and oblige them to economize the means of subsistence, by making them the reward of individual exertion. I have also traced the progress by which this principle necessarily leads to an inequality of ranks and fortunes, which effect, indeed, it has constantly and universally produced in a greater or less degree, from the earliest date of history. For the primary agent is all along to be found in that original law, which multiplies the consumers of the fruits of the earth faster than the ·fruits themselves. The difference of men's habits and powers would signify nothing, if food were so plentiful that it could be procured without a return of labour. Were it the law of the universe, no matter how brought into execution, that every man born into the world should find himself heir to indolence and plenty, then there need be no division of property, since no one could possibly, according to the supposition, possess what his neighbour wanted, or require what his neighbour had. Or if it had been appointed that all mankind should possess the same genius, the same powers of mind and body, and be exempt from physical evils, the division of property would not necessarily have been accompanied by inequality. But since the fact is ordained otherwise, and, for reasons already shown, wisely ordained; since men are born with various capacities of mind, and different degrees of bodily strength; since the necessaries of life can only be produced by labour; and since there are, in all countries, more claimants for the necessaries of life than can be easily or plentifully supplied with them; it must inevitably follow that possessions shall be *appropriated and unequally divided*; and that the conveniencies of life shall belong, in the greatest abundance, to the head which is most fertile in resources, or the hand which is the most industrious in exertion.

If then the wisdom is to be estimated by the fitness of the design to its purpose, and the habitual exercise of the energies of mankind is allowed to be that purpose, enough has been said to confirm the original proposition. The Deity has provided, that by the operation of an instinctive principle in our nature, the human race should be uniformly brought into a state in which they are forced to exert and improve their powers: the lowest rank, to obtain support; the one next in order, to escape from the difficulties immediately beneath it; and all the classes upward, either to keep their level, while they are pressed on each side by rival industry, or to raise themselves above the standard of their birth by useful exertions of their activity, or by successful cultivation of their natural powers. If, indeed, it were possible, that the stimulus arising from this principle should be suddenly removed, it is not easy to determine what life would be except a dreary blank, or the world except an uncultivated waste. Every exertion to which civilization can be traced, proceeds directly or indirectly from its effects; either from the actual desire of having a family, or the pressing obligation of providing for one, or from the necessity of rivalling the efforts produced by the operation of these motives in others. [. . .]

It appears, then, that the principle of population, prescribed by the Deity as an instrument for peopling the world with a successive stock of intelligent inhabitants, and keeping it in that state which was most agreeable to his plan in its formation, not only fills but civilizes the globe, and contains in itself a provision for diffusing the beneficial effects which it originally generates. To trace the power of such a principle, and to discover, on inquiry, that an object so extensive as the replenishment and civilization of the globe is accomplished by the silent operation of a single natural law, empowers us to pronounce that the designs of the Creator are carried into execution with infinite wisdom. Neither should it be forgotten, that the law itself, by which these ends are attained, is neither harsh nor coercive, but forms an important part of our earthly happiness: it is not written in characters of severity, but promulgated by the gentle voice of persuasion. [. . .] To enlarge, however, upon this head, would be to encroach on a subject more properly belonging to that part of this work which treats of the goodness of the Creator. I shall accordingly conclude the present chapter, by a concise recapitulation of the general argument.

It appeared then, first, to be the design of the Creator to people the world with rational and improvable beings, placed there, it should seem, in a state preparatory to some higher sphere of existence, into which they might hereafter be removed. With this view, he implanted in the first progenitors of the species a passion transmitted by them to their descendants; which in the outset prompts the finest feelings of the mind, and leads to that close union of interests and pursuits, by which the domestic comfort and harmony of the human race is most effectually promoted. The operation of this principle, filling the world with competitors for support, enforces labour and encourages industry, by the advantages it gives to the industrious and laborious at the expense of the indolent and extravagant. The ultimate effect of it is, to foster those arts and improvements which most dignify the character and refine the mind of man; and lastly, to place mankind in that situation which best enables them to improve their natural faculties, and at the same time best exercises, and most clearly displays, their virtues.

The collateral benefits derived from the same principles were shown to be the promotion of universal comfort, by ensuring the most effective disposition of labour and skill: and the diffusion of the civilization thus attained, by a gradual and steady progress, throughout the various regions of the habitable globe.

Such is the view of the omniscience and comprehensive wisdom of the Creator, deducible from the facts respecting population, and its tendency to a quicker increase than the supply of food can keep pace with, which have been first explained to the present generation, and added to the stock of physical truths unfolded by modern inquiry. The particular effects of the multiplication of the species, which the object Mr. Malthus had in view obliged him to illustrate and enlarge upon, are so unprepossessing, that many persons have forcibly shut their eyes against the completeness of the induction, and the extent of the evidence by which the force of the principle is indisputably proved. Others, unable to withstand conviction, have been inclined to class this among the 'boisterous doubts and sturdy objections, wherewith, in philosophy, as well as in divinity, the unhappiness of our knowledge too nearly acquaints us'. They have considered it as an anomaly in the system of divine administration; a provision for entailing upon mankind much laborious poverty, and some painful indigence. The antidote, however, is commonly found to grow within reach of the poison. The instinctive principle by which every country in the world is replenished with inhabitants so fast as its fertility allows, when more generally understood, and more fully reflected upon, will be appealed to as a proof, that as our knowledge and researches extend, they discover to us, in the moral as well as in the natural world, new proofs of most comprehensive wisdom in the Creator. It is, in fact, the mighty engine, which, operating constantly and uniformly, keeps our world in that state which is most agreeable to the design of the creation, and renders mankind the spontaneous instrument of their Maker, in filling and civilizing the habitable globe. We may not, perhaps, be able to discover all the bearings, or follow all the consequences of a principle which is undoubtedly the primary, though secret agent, in producing all the boundless varieties of the human condition. It ought, however, to satisfy us, if, as our inquiries penetrate farther into the general laws of the animate and inanimate creation, we clearly discover a wonderful subserviency of appointed means to the accomplishment of some uniform design: affording, even where the design is but partially understood, such testimony of wisdom in the means, as obliges us to rely in humble acquiescence upon the Supreme Disposer of both.

Part III On the goodness of the Creator

Chapter V
On the Capabilities of Improvement in the State of advanced Civilization.
It may be plausibly argued, that speculations on the nature of happiness, however satisfactory in the closet, are often decisively contradicted by the realities of life; and that the appearance of our own society, which meets every eye, is a standing argument against my conclusions. It furnishes us with an example of great public prosperity; of all the mechanical improvements and refinements of art, which the combination of skill and capital, and an industrious population, can produce: yet what is the result? Indigence and pauperism; and in the very heart of opulence, and industry, and intelligence, considerably more than a tenth part of the population relieved by public charity.

It is very soothing to our indolence and self-satisfaction, to charge upon the constitution of the world, that is, upon the ordinances of the Deity, the various evils of poverty and ignorance which confront us on every side. But it would be more reasonable as well as more decorous, to inquire in the first place, how far such evils arise necessarily from the law of nature, and how far, on the other hand, they admit of easy mitigation, and only need that care and attention which the Christian religion enjoins every man to bestow upon his neighbour. When a South American Indian is seized with an infectious disorder, he is shut up in a solitary hovel, and abandoned to his fate. In our improved state of society, the sufferer under a similar calamity experiences the benefit of skill and care, and is probably recovered. But we must not be Europeans in our treatment of bodily maladies, and treat the minds and morals of our fellow creatures with barbarian indifference. The Author of our existence, when he did not exempt us from the civil or physical disorders of an imperfect state, ordained also that each should have their alleviations; without which mankind would live miserably or perish prematurely. Those alleviations, indeed, are not definitely pointed out or prescribed. Neither was it possible they should be; inasmuch as they depend on circumstances varying at every point of civilization, varying in every climate and country, and even in the same country according to its progress towards opulence. The human race, whose faculties are infinitely improved by a state of advanced civilization, is bound to employ them in discovering and applying the remedies of those evils which peculiarly belong to each condition of society. It is a part of the system by which the Deity acts universally, to render man a free and spontaneous, but not a necessary instrument of his own welfare. [. . .] This is as true of the moral as of the natural world. Neither soil can dispense with cultivation, although both are so constituted as to be capable of excellent produce. Let that only be undertaken, which in our advanced stage of civilization is within the reach of practicable accomplishment, and the general state of society, like the country it cultivates, would on every side be full of 'beauty to the eye and music to the ear'.

I. The fundamental cause of the greatest evils of the poor is ignorance. Ignorance, however, is not only the mere incapacity to write or read; experience often teaches us, that these acquirements, however desirable, are by no means indispensable; and that though they are wanting, there may be much intellect, a quick sense of the ways and means of individual advantage, and an accurate knowledge of moral good and evil. The ignorance arising from the want of intercourse with minds superior to their own, possessed of wider information, and having therefore different views of interest and duty; this, together with the scantiness of religious knowledge, is the ignorance which most generally and most hurtfully besets the lower classes.

It cannot be argued, that either of these sorts of ignorance is unavoidable. They were not, even in former days; but in our own, the improvements so happily introduced into education, have brought the first rudiments of learning within reach of the poorest rank. And they have done more: for it is one of the principal advantages of the Madras system, that it sharpens the faculties and exercises the minds of those subject to it so successfully, as to render them, comparatively, different beings from the scholar of a former age. So that the drilled and practised soldier does not show a greater change from the slovenly and awkward follower of the plough, than the child thus educated from the tenant of some remote hamlet or neglected waste, which population has found out, but none of its advantages have reached.

An indefinite capability of improvement opens before us, when the human mind is thus put in motion. But, that the soil may give all its produce, the skill of the agriculturist must be superadded to the labour of the peasant. A right direction, as well as a stimulus, must be applied to the mind, by the superintendence and occasional intercourse of the superior ranks. Where this intercourse is not wanting, to obviate any mischief which the system of competition might introduce, and counteract wrong impressions; when the good seed of religion is sown upon the soil prepared by education, to remind the growing generation that the object of the care bestowed upon them is not to raise them above their allotted condition, but to fit them for performing more adequately their duties both to God and man; then we have a prospect of general improvement, not chimerical and visionary, but approved by judgement and realized by experience. [. . .]

Ignorance, therefore, is not the inevitable lot of the majority of our community; and with ignorance a host of evils disappear. Of all obstacles to improvement, ignorance is the most formidable, because the only true secret of assisting the poor is to make them agents in bettering their own condition, and to supply them, not with a temporary stimulus, but with a permanent energy. As fast as the standard of intelligence is raised, the poor become more and more able to co-operate in any plan proposed for their advantage, more likely to listen to any reasonable suggestion, more able to understand, and therefore more willing

345

to pursue it. Hence it follows, that when gross ignorance is once removed, and right principles are introduced, a great advantage has been already gained against squalid poverty. Many avenues to an improved condition are opened to one whose faculties are enlarged and exercised; he sees his own interest more clearly, he pursues it more steadily, he does not study immediate gratification at the expense of bitter and late repentance, or mortgage the labour of his future life without an adequate return. Indigence, therefore, will rarely be found in company with good education.

II. In the case, however, of its unavoidable occurrence, a remedy is already provided by the state. The Poor Laws possess this advantage among many objections, that we are not haunted with the idea of unalleviated distresses: if nature is worn down with age or sickness, if labour yields no support, and family assistance fails, the indigent member of society has at least a shelter to which he may retire, and either take refuge from the pelting of the storm, or be enabled to weather it by temporary assistance.

This provision, like other human institutions, contains a mixture of good and evil. Unquestionably, local charity, well directed, might supply small and particular districts much more comfortably and much less expensively than the operation of any laws; but much good sense, and leisure, and benevolence, are requisite to perform this business in an impartial manner. Many may be expected to doubt whether irremediable poverty, and the helplessness of sickness, infancy, and old age, can ever be safely left, in a large and fully peopled community, to the care of that spontaneous charity on which they must devolve in the absence of all legislative provision. In the mean time it is some satisfaction to reflect that an infant family, deserted by profligate parents, or left orphans by the visitation of God, are not abandoned as if human life was of no value; and that the disabled or decrepit labourer has a sure resource, and is not condemned to elicit casual sustenance from door to door. But the system, though professing to remedy the evils of human nature, would be in fact more innocent if human nature were more perfect; so that none should receive its aid except the objects really deserving such interference, nor any depend upon its support except in failure of all other resources. The injury does not fall upon the contributor to the rates, as is commonly

346

supposed, who, if he did not pay these, would pay much more in the enhanced price of every article from the augmented wages of labour: the principal mischief is done to the moral character of the receiver, who is extravagant, in confidence of a sure support: or, if he is not positively taught improvidence, at least does not learn prudence.

The Friendly Societies, which include nearly a million of labouring members of our own community, in some measure diminish the evils resulting from the system of Poor Laws: and the eagerness with which they have been incorporated, is an evidence that the lower classes are not unwilling to avail themselves of any intelligible plan for the improvement of their condition, or to fortify themselves against the uncertainties of life by forethought and frugality. But Friendly Societies, though good, are not the best possible provision; because they assist only old age and personal sickness; whereas a labourer, through the afflictions of his family or temporary loss of employ, may be seriously distressed without positive illness: and the evil at last requires a cure, which seasonable relief might have prevented from existing. [. . .]

The present state of our civilization has suggested a more unexceptionable plan for the melioration of the condition of the poor; which it is the more necessary to point out, because it shows that the peculiar evils and their appropriate remedies lie near together, in every stage of society. An advanced state of public opulence does not seem at first sight the most desirable air for a poor man to breathe. Of necessity, its population is dense, and the reward of labour scanty; and every road to preferment so choked [*sic*] with rival adventurers, that he has little prospect of surpassing or even overtaking them in the race. But, on the other hand, the same circumstances of society afford opportunities, which no other can, of deriving the greatest possible advantage from every farthing which labour can obtain. The demand for capital, occasioned by universal industry, the ease of communication, the general intelligence to foresee, and public credit to ensure every profitable opportunity, are a set-off, if a proper use were made of them, against the evils of low wages and contending labourers. An American peasant with four shillings a day is not richer, if comfort is riches, than an English peasant with two, and has little other superiority than the questionable one of being more independent of his employer.

The security of capital in this country, the ease with which it is turned to the best use, the quick and ready communication of labour and the produce of labour throughout the whole kingdom, afford inestimable facilities to what ought to be the first consideration of public and private men, the improvement of the state of the mass of the community. I do not mean to insinuate that this subject has been neglected in Great Britain. The eminence which our country has reached by her charities is no less remarkable than that to which she has been raised by the superiority of her arms and opulence. But something still remains to be done. The poor man requires to be taught prudence, by seeing its advantage clearly before him. There are few situations in which the labouring classes might not save, in the season of their strength, a provision for the season of infirmity: but as things are, there are still fewer, where they can place out their savings at all, or, if at all, with security. A great commercial establishment cannot stop its machinery to receive weekly shillings from a hundred or a thousand individuals. If it could, or would, the melancholy instability of country banks, often built upon no other foundation than the credulity of the neighbourhood, is a powerful objection to their becoming, without an especial guarantee, the depositaries of petty savings. No bankruptcy among these establishments takes place, which does not heap ruin on the heads of hundreds of the most deserving members of the community: those who by laborious industry and long self-denial have laid up their twenty, or fifty, or hundred pounds, as a support to a future family or their own declining years; and now find themselves by a sudden blow deprived of the hard earned produce of a life of labour. Neither does the evil stop with the immediate sufferers. The bursting of a single dam inundates a widely-extended level. Is this the fruit of frugality? Why should we hoard up, that others may squander our savings? This reasoning is too obvious, not to be unanswerable in the view of youth, and irresistible when backed by inclination.

The difficulty admits of easy remedy, though it is really the greatest of which our labouring poor can complain. If some of the more intelligent inhabitants of a district, or the principal landholders of a county, would bestow their attention upon this subject, as they have with great advantage upon Insurance Societies and other general interests, they would deserve the gratitude of the age, and receive the most satisfactory applause, the improvement of public welfare. In a small district, or a single village, an individual might effect something, by vesting a certain sum in the hands of trustees as a security to his poorer neighbours; and by devoting a few hours in every week or month to receiving their small savings, he might render them most effectual service, without the least risk to himself, by allowing the 4 per cent. for their little capital. But the system, to be useful, ought to be general; and, if general, could not be well managed without the regularity of habits of business and skill in the employment of capital. The establishment of county banks, with such security as should be satisfactory to the superintendents of the scheme, would be both desirable, and easily practicable; and might soon be made so far advantageous as at least to defray the expenses of management, since the customer would have just reason to be satisfied, if he could obtain without risk even 4 per cent. for his money. The security of the capital is of much more consequence than the rate of interest; and its insecurity, according to any mode already within reach of the poor of employing their savings, is one great reason why so little is at present saved.

It is a benevolent appointment of Providence, that judicious charity is twice blessed, and redounds to the advantage of the giver, sometimes not to his moral only, but temporal advantage. If a system of this kind should ever be universally established, its promoters will find the poor-rates diminished, which now oppress landed property so heavily, not only by the amount of the sum thus annually saved from dissipation, but by all the habits which the constant custom of frugality and thoughtfulness would generate; and parish support will only be what it ought to be, the resource of irremediable misfortune, of orphan infancy or friendless age. Such a system seems alone to be wanting, in order to render this country the happiest as well as the most intelligent of the world; it would form a natural union with the general education now diffused among the poor; it derives an evident facility from the state of public debt; and is peculiarly demanded by the sudden variations of prices which our present condition seems likely to entail upon us, as well as to correct the improvident habits which the existence of a Poor Law has introduced among our peasantry.

It certainly cannot be pretended that these and similar advantages of an opulent state, spring up spontaneously, like the produce of the golden age: intelligence must be exerted to descry, and philanthropy to direct them. But it might form a serious objection against the divine goodness, if it were supposed that the condition of the majority of the community must always be deteriorated, as the community itself advanced in opulence. That this highest point of civilization is still capable of such a measure of general happiness, as belongs to an imperfect and preparatory state, is all that I undertake to prove. Should any one think the universal establishment or application of such beneficial plans impracticable, it will be easy to show that the impossibility does not lie in the nature of things. There can be no harm in building an Utopia on a Christian foundation. There is positive good, when the question regards the benevolence of the Creator; who, when he placed within the reach of man the means of general happiness, Christian doctrines, Christian precepts, and Christian intelligence, justly demands on man's part that he should stretch out his hand to obtain them. [. . .]

Shall I be asked, whether I look forward in earnest to any such melioration of society, or that it should generally present this aspect to the observer? I can only answer, that there is nothing in the nature of things to make it impossible; there is wealth enough, and intelligence enough; the difficulty arises not from the inability, but the unwillingness of mankind. We have no right to reject an obvious remedy, and then complain that the disease is incurable. Let every one in his station do his duty, and there will be little room for murmuring against the condition of the human race. This is all, I repeat, with which the vindicator of the divine goodness is concerned: the right performance of these duties is the trial of man's virtue; and if they are faithfully performed, public welfare is his immediate reward. There are at this moment many districts which furnish examples of the practicability of such improvement; where a large majority of the population display in their conduct the excellence of the religion they profess; where the rising generation is so educated as to be useful in their respective stations; where regular contributions provide Bibles and clothing, and other articles of use and comfort; where the elder members of the society are associated for the purpose of visiting the sick, instructing the ignorant, comforting the afflicted, and reporting cases of distress. If there are any such parishes now, there is no reason why there should not be more; nay, there is no necessary obstacle to their becoming universal. The prevalence of religious knowledge, education, and frugality, does not defeat its own object, or tend, like indeterminate or indiscreet charities, to encourage a redundant population.

There are mistakes on this head, which demand correction. It has been urged, that our improved knowledge on the subject of population is unfavourable to charity; and even inconsistent with Christianity which enjoins it. This may be an easy shelter to the selfish and extravagant, who lull their consciences with the belief, that, in spending sumptuously instead of giving prudently, they are practising political economy. But the most rigorous precept of Scripture might be followed in the most literal exactness, without any danger of injuring the community or any violation of general rules: 'Turn not your face from any poor man'; but inquire into the circumstances of his distress, and point out to him the mode in which the prudent regulations of society have directed that it should be relieved. The subdivision of labour, which is peculiar to a large and intelligent community is applicable to charity, as well as to literature and the arts, and renders it very possible to bestow attention on the wants and distresses of every individual.

There is something in this mutual dependence and connection of the different members of society on one another, which is both pleasing in contemplation, and eminently suited to the situation of mankind as the children of one common parent, and the heirs of one common immortality. A state of civilization, which supposes opulence, competency, and poverty, in all their various degrees, is far more suitable, when thus improved, to the purposes of man's being, than any condition of uniform equality could become, even if we depart from experience in framing it, and indulge the imagination with an ideal picture. That there should be room for the exercise of benevolence, a disposition of the mind, which, in fact, contains within itself

351

many virtues, was undoubtedly in the contemplation of the Creator. The contrast of condition which arises from the unequal distribution of wealth, is well fitted to excite this; and a crowd of Christian graces follow in its train: the humility which visits the cottager, encourages his industry or cheers his distress; the denial of selfish gratification, for the purpose of raising laborious poverty; the prudence which with-holds relief from the clamorous, to give it, though at the expense of time and trouble, to unobtrusive merit; the reciprocal emotions of gratitude and goodwill; and 'all the charities' of neighbour, friend, and patron, have their origin in the just exercise of benevolence. When man is in a more perfect state, he will stand in no need of these opportunities, which are, in effect, trials: but no *preparatory* dispensation could be more consistent with the divine goodness, than that which makes the general well-being of the members of society depend upon their right performance of their respective duties.

Source: John Bird Sumner, *A Treatise on the Records of the Creation and on the Moral Attributes of the Creator; with particular reference to the Jewish history, and to the consistency of the principle of population with the wisdom and goodness of the Deity* (London, J. Hatchard and Son, 187 Piccadilly, 1833, 5th edition), Volume 2, pp. 113–202, 328–67.

Brian Griffiths
1941–

Introduction

Griffiths is a classic convert. Born into a Welsh working-class family, he was educated at the Dynever Grammar School, and the London School of Economics. From there, he moved into academic life as lecturer (1968–77) and then Professor of Banking and International Finance, and Dean, at the City University Business School, London (1977–85). He became a non-executive director of the Bank of England in 1984. His political transformation complemented his professional development. Brought up in a socialist environment, with a concern for justice and the poor, the Labour government's mishandling of the economy in the 1960s provoked his conversion to free market economics and monetarism. His tract for the times, *Monetarism and Morality: A Response to the Bishops* (1985), sets out these views.

In 1985 Mrs Thatcher made Griffiths head of her Policy Unit, until her resignation as prime minister in 1990. As Lord Griffiths, he continues to play a major part in the Conservative government's educational policies. Undergirding all these changes was Griffiths's religious development from the closed ranks of the Plymouth Brethren to the established Church of England (1978). He has played a prominent role in his local church as churchwarden and lay preacher, and in the national Church's Industrial and Economic Affairs Committee. He remains a committed evangelical.

Griffiths is the leading Christian moralist of the market-place in Britain. Through his impressive involvement in economic and political life, he has constructed a way of holding together Christian convictions and the market economy. The result is no crude evangelical justification of neoconservatism, but rather a reasoned case for the market economy in a Christian framework. He achieves this on the basis of biblical evidence, from which he deduces seven guidelines for a Christian political economy: the positive mandate to create wealth; the need for private property rather than state or collective ownership; each family holding a permanent stake in the economy; the community relieving poverty rather than promoting equality; the government remedying economic injustice; guarding against materialism; and accountability and judgement forming integral parts of economic life. Pursuing such a Christianized market economy places him in strong opposition to Marxist socialism, but also to the secular capitalism of libertarians like F. A. Hayek and Milton Friedman. It also ensures his commitment to the reform of capitalism, given its disturbing record on unemployment and poverty, by restoring its basis in Christian values. He is clear that the very survival of the market economy depends on such a programme.

Text 18, taken from his *Morality and the Market Place* (1984), comprises the 1980 London lectures in contemporary Christianity. As such, they sought to address the context of the 1970s, and their domination by the crisis of capitalism. The text illustrates Griffiths's theological method, and particularly his use of the Bible. His development of a biblically based conservative political economy contrasts sharply with the conclusions of liberation theology and its use of the Bible. It also brings him into conflict with the indirect method of Bennett, Preston and Wogaman. The content of his argument relates to the development of Christian guidelines for the reform of capitalism. In the later sections of the book, he elaborates their implications for government, corporations and trade unions. What is of particular interest is that it was such guidelines that informed the major policy changes of Thatcherism in the 1980s. Griffiths describes these achievements in *The Conservative Quadrilateral* (1990), and shows how they were connected to Christian insights into the individual and community, choice and responsibility, markets and welfare, and wealth creation and trusteeship (the Christian conservative quadrilateral).

Text 18: Christianizing the Market

Is Christianity relevant?

At the beginning of this book we observed the global conflict which exists today between socialism and capitalism. We looked at the remarkable record of capitalism in creating wealth and contrasted it with the present malaise which now seems to infect most economies of the Western world. We argued that the sickness or crisis of capitalism was not at heart a technical matter, but a lack of legitimacy with respect to the system itself. We explored various explanations of the present situation – such as Schumpeter's analysis, the growth of government and the role of technology as an autonomous and primary force – and concluded that the root of the problem lay in a basic tension within humanism (the prevailing philosophy today in the Western world) namely between the desire to control and the desire to be free. This resulted in the inability of humanism as a philosophy to place adequate constraints on the exercise of freedom and also its inability to generate that set of values which is necessary if capitalism is to work. As a result we argued that the so-called 'crisis' of capitalism results from a prevailing set of cultural values, which are alien to those required if the market economy is to survive, typified by a counterculture which eschews the traditional distinction between good and evil and right and wrong, and which is committed to establishing an egalitarian economic system.

Next we considered the major alternative form of economic system, namely a socialism based on Marxism. We argued that Marxism could be broken up into three elements: a philosophy of history, a theory of economics and a view of the state and revolution. We then considered its claim to be scientific,

355

humanistic and atheistic; concluding that it was more accurate to describe it as an ideology than a science, that its humanitarianism was very real yet flawed, and that its atheism was fundamental to an understanding of the ideology. We noted that in practice there was a connection between two triads – the Marxist commitment to abolish the family, private property and religion and the seeming inevitability of economic inefficiency, religious persecution and political terror. Because Marxism like humanism is also the product of an Enlightenment view of the world, the practical problems of both capitalism and communism are seen to have a common origin – namely the inability of humanism as a philosophy to resolve the basic tension between freedom and control. Capitalism suffers from inflation, instability, pollution and injustice because of inadequate limits on the exercise of freedom. Communism suffers from the direction of capital and labour and state control of the family, religion, education and the arts, because of inadequate limits on the urge to dominate.

In other words the root of the problems with both systems is a religious one. It is the irreconcilable contradiction inevitable in humanism because of its false assumptions in constructing a world-view. The tragedy, however, is that neither system recognizes the true cause of its problem. From a Christian point of view therefore the root cause of the crisis of capitalism is not bigger government *or* more complex technology *or* even defects in the system of property rights, but certain false values on which it is based. Similarly Marxism is wrong in seeing the problems of modernity as exclusively the result of the capitalist system and attempting to account for the behaviour of a Stalin or a Khruschev [*sic*], or a Mao Tse-tung or a Hoxha in terms of the cult of personality while at the same time ignoring the lack of moral constraints on the exercise of power in modern Marxist states.

Accepting, therefore, that the inadequacies of both capitalism and Marxism are inextricably connected with religion, has Christianity anything to offer? Is Christianity relevant to matters of political economy? Does it have anything to say about economic values and institutions? Can it point us as a nation in certain directions? Can it help Third World countries as they are forced to choose between capitalism and Marxism both of which seem to have unattractive features? If I did not believe that the answer to these questions was in each case a resounding yes I would have found it very difficult to give these lectures. I believe that the Christian faith provides us with a unique perspective on matters of political economy which is not confined to issues of personal honesty and motivation, but which is also related to the basic institutions and goals of our societies.

Common approaches to economics and Christianity

Before, however, I examine in more detail my own personal views on this subject I would like to set them against the background of alternative approaches.

The first assertion I would like to discuss is that the connection between the Christian faith and economic matters is indirect. It is an approach which is developed at some length by Professor Ronald H. Preston. 'We cannot move directly to particular fixed ethical conclusions from either the Bible or Natural Law.' Although the traditional approach is precisely this, Professor Preston argues that it is no longer adequate because of the effects of secularization on Western society. Traditional teaching is relative rather than fixed because of our greater understanding of the limits imposed by culture. The decline of religion and the growth of the scientific world-view have meant that 'Both the natural sciences and the social sciences have succeeded in gaining a proper autonomy from ecclesiastical control.' Nevertheless anyone who wishes to say something in this area must draw on the results of research undertaken by the social sciences and so must accept their autonomy. Using this approach he attacks in particular those theologians earlier in the century who criticized capitalism and who equated the Kingdom of God with socialism.

While I think he is right to criticize those who propounded a social gospel earlier in the century he does so for the wrong reason. The theology of the social gospel was inadequate because of its neglect of the importance of personal salvation and its neglect of the importance of sin in considering the structures of society. It should not however be criticized because of its attempt to relate the gospel as directly as possible to the world in

357

which we live. The problem with Professor Preston's method is his assumption that the social sciences have a legitimate independence from Christian theology. To the extent that the Church no longer dominates Western thought this is of course correct. But because modern social science is itself the result of an Enlightenment view of the world I believe that the task of the Christian is to question the validity of such autonomy. As Christians we must not be intimidated by secularization: if we are, we have nothing distinctive to say. In fact if we took this argument to its logical conclusion we would of course be forced to reject Christianity itself, which in its fundamentals is a premodern view of the world. The wide acceptance of secularization is not a strong enough reason for us to cease applying biblical social teaching as directly as possible to the world in which we live. To the extent that Professor Preston is warning us of the dangers of oversimplification and bad hermeneutics then we do well to listen to him.

A second approach is to argue that the Christian faith is something intensely personal, concerned with individual spirituality and not something which has a social dimension concerned with the affairs of this world. Based on the idea that the service of God is incompatible with the service of Mammon and that true spirituality involves the renunciation of the material world, this view produces a dualism in which one set of principles applies at the level of personal relationships and an altogether different set to the affairs of the world. Taken to an extreme view it results in monasticism and the creation of Christian communes. I believe it to be a defective understanding of the Christian doctrine of creation and also as we shall see later, of the social dimension of the gospel.

A third approach which grows out of the Latin American situation is the 'Theology of Liberation'. The twin starting points for this view are the widespread injustice and oppression which exist today in Latin America and which are then analysed sociologically with a Marxist framework, together with the fact that in the Incarnation God has declared his intention to liberate all people from every kind of slavery and injustice. The perspective of liberation theology is historical. History is the process by which the liberation which Christ proclaimed will be made effective for the whole world. Because therefore God is working within the sphere of history, great emphasis is made of the 'primacy of action'. For example, Gutiérrez can say that:

To work, to transform this world, is to become a man and to build the human community; it is also to save. Likewise, to struggle against misery and exploitation and to build a just society is already to be part of the saving action, which is moving towards its complete fulfilment. All this means that building the temporal city is not simply a stage of 'humanization' or 'pre-evangelization' as was held up until a few years ago. Rather it is to become part of a saving process which embraces the whole of man and all human history. Any theological reflection on human work and social praxis ought to be rooted in this fundamental affirmation.

I find two critical problems with this approach; its epistemology and its soteriology. By emphasizing the 'primacy of action' what these theologians are really saying is that we do not know – indeed we cannot obtain knowledge except through praxis. The only valid starting point is the situation. This is precisely the method of the Marxist. Miguez Bonino sums up their views on this point as follows:

They are saying in fact that there is no truth outside or beyond the concrete historical events in which men are involved as agents [and] there is therefore no knowledge except in action itself, in the process of transforming the world through participating in history.

I believe that this view is explicitly a rejection of the importance of the biblical revelation.

Next there is these theologians' view of salvation. Salvation is viewed purely in temporal terms. It is synonymous with the quest for justice. As the quote from Gutiérrez shows, the struggle to build a just society is itself part of the process of salvation. Another Latin American writer, José P. Miranda, goes even further and argues that God 'is knowable exclusively in the cry of the poor and the weak who seek justice'. This is a far cry from our Lord's proclamation of the good news in which salvation is primarily spiritual and moral, not political and social, and in which the act of deliverance *itself* is wholly unrelated to the reform of social and political institutions even though it should have an implication in that area.

The Bible and the elements of a biblical input

It is against this background therefore that I would like to state what I see as the relevance of Christianity to political economy. In so doing I lay great emphasis on the Biblical text because I consider the Scriptures to be our ultimate authority in matters of doctrine and life. This is in no sense an attempt to deny the importance of church tradition or the use of human reason. But when there is a conflict between the Bible and either tradition or the assumption of theology I believe we should assert the supremacy of the written Word if for no other reason than that our Lord adopted precisely this approach with respect to the Old Testament. He regarded the Old Testament text as an accurate historical record, as authoritative in matters of doctrine and ethics, and as inspired of God. In the matter of relating Christianity to economics this is a vitally important assumption because we face great cultural and intellectual pressure as Christians to adopt a form of dualism in which we substitute Smith or Marx or Friedman or Hayek for the divine revelation as the ultimate authority in this area of life. To the extent that we do this I believe we are guilty of a modern form of syncretism which is of necessity unsatisfactory.

For many of those who do take the text seriously however, Christian teaching on the subject of wealth is summed up *either* by one of the easily remembered phrases from the Gospels such as 'Sell all that you have and distribute to the poor, and you will have treasure in heaven' (Lk 18:22) or 'You cannot serve God and Mammon' (Lk 16:13) or that 'It is easier for a camel to go through the eye of a needle than for a rich man to enter the Kingdom of God' (Lk 18:25) *or* by the way in which the members of the Jerusalem Church as recorded in Acts of the Apostles shared their wealth according to the principle 'From each according to his ability, to each according to his need'.

The problem with extracting one of the sayings of Jesus or using the example of the Jerusalem Church as a model for contemporary society is that the whole of the Old Testament is neglected. Professor Gordon Dunstan is correct in arguing that 'The fundamentals of Christian social doctrine are written in the Old Testament – the Gospel had a different purpose.' It is impossible to understand the New Testament and the teachings of Jesus without understanding the Old Testament.

The Old Testament lays down the fundamentals of a Christian social ethic in three major ways. *First*, it explains the nature and purpose of creation, which has implications for our view of the physical universe, our attitude to work and the objects of economic life. *Second*, the cataclysmic effects of the Fall introduce us to the problem of scarcity and imbalance in the world as well as the impossibility of creating some economic Utopia. And *third*, the various laws which make up the Mosaic Code as part of God's covenant with the Hebrew nation, set the framework for a system of political economy. These laws are quite explicit and cover such issues as property rights, the regulation of the capital market, monopolistic price and wage setting, taxation and the redistribution of income and wealth. Although they are enunciated in the Old Testament in the context of a primitive agricultural society they nevertheless embody principles of lasting value. By contrast the New Testament is a record of the Incarnation and the establishment of the Kingdom of God, and as such is concerned primarily with the ethics of those claiming citizenship in the new Koinonia and the quality of their life there.

By using the text of Scripture I believe there are five major elements which enter into a Christian view of political economy – the understanding of Creation and Fall, the political economy of Israel, the coming of the Kingdom and the teaching of Jesus, the life of the Early Church and the eschatological hope. [*The first element alone is given below.*]

Creation and Fall

The starting point for any Christian view of economic life is our view of the physical world. To the Christian the natural world is not the result of some accident or chance event but of a deliberate act of creation. It is the intended consequence of a conscious act. In the words of Genesis, God said 'Let there be ... ' and there was. In fact when God created this world he is described as working (Genesis 2:13), and frequently the world is said to be the work of his hands.

The Creator is revealed to us as a rational, moral, feeling person, capable of making choices. Although independent of his creation he is nevertheless continually involved in its maintenance. The creation therefore is not like some frictionless machine, which once set in motion carries on until stopped, but something which is dependent on the continuing work of its Creator. This is important because according to Genesis, man alone of the created world is made in the image of God. This gives man great dignity. God's image in man implies that he too is a rational, moral, feeling person capable of making choices. Not only that but part of his very *raison d'être*, like that of his Creator, is to work. The fourth commandment is very explicit that six days of every week are for work and one for rest. In a Christian view, therefore, work is not just necessary in order to live but the result of an irrepressible drive which is rewarding in its own right. I am never surprised when after a holiday a colleague or neighbour tells me 'I had a very nice holiday but I must say it's nice to get back to work'. The Christian view is that work is as natural a part of our lives as food, sex, worship and leisure.

There is, however, another side of the picture which derives from the Fall. The tragedy of man is that he declares himself autonomous of God and in consequence is condemned to live East of Eden. Part of the judgement is that the whole productive process is fractured and that in particular work now assumes an element of drudgery and toil, regardless of whether that work is manual, non-manual, skilled, unskilled, managerial or professional. While it would be quite wrong to use this as a justification for the existence of certain exceptionally laborious jobs, it is also quite wrong to regard stress, tedium and alienation simply as the result of advanced technology and modern capitalism and to hope with the Marxist that by changing certain structures we can achieve some Utopia. The Fall not only affects work: it also affects our preferences, appetites and wants. It introduces, to use the biblical expression, covetousness. In other words the Fall affects ends as well as means. It is not too strong to say that the ultimate economic problem – choice under conditions of scarcity – results from this radical rupture in the natural world and in human personality.

The context in which man is created to work is controlled by a specific mandate. The Genesis account is again very clear: 'And God blessed them, and God said unto them, Be fruitful, and multiply, and replenish the earth, and subdue it; and have dominion ... over every living thing' (Gen. 1:28) and is repeated to Noah (after the Flood) in a virtually identical form. In Psalm 8 a similar theme emerges. After considering the mystery of creation, the Psalmist writes of man: 'Thou madest him to have domination over the works of thy hands; thou hast put all things under his feet.' These verses suggest very clearly that God created the physical world for our use and pleasure, with sufficient resources for our needs and with the specific commission to harness the resources of the natural world for our benefit. In terms of man's relationship to nature the key idea here is that of dominion. Man has dominion over the natural world. It is important to notice that he is not granted sovereighty. He cannot do just as he pleases. He has no mandate to violate and transgress the natural world. He must respect it, recognizing that it is God's creation and that he exercises dominion as a trustee but does not possess exclusive proprietory rights as owner.

If we accept therefore that man is created with a desire to work, subject to a charge to control and harness the earth, it follows that the process of wealth creation is something intrinsic to a Christian view of the world. It is interesting in this respect to compare the Christian view with that of other religions. The two key features of a Christian view are that there is no essential dichotomy between the physical world and the spiritual world and that man is given authority over nature. Consider the Greek philosophers. In the Greek philosophy the physical world had the status of a deity to be feared and worshipped, which not surprisingly was a great constraint to the development of technology and the exercise of dominion over nature. More recently, in many primitive societies, where animism has been practised, it would have been considered sacrilege to bring nature under control. Even in India today, where certain animals are considered sacred and where the life of the spirit and contemplation take precedence over the development of the material world, this is an important handicap to the development of the Indian economy. It is no accident that the rise of science and technology and subsequently industrialization and the process of wealth creation followed the acceptance of an explicitly biblical view of the world in which manual work was not considered contemptible and in which man was delegated the task of managing the world's resources for his benefit. [. . .]

Christian guidelines for economic life

Having outlined the key elements in a biblical view of economic life, the next question is how are these put together? How do we attempt to deduce some general guidelines from its history and teaching which are of relevance for us today? I believe that this is a critical question. We start from the Biblical revelation, having a high regard for the text. We want to address ourselves to concrete problems in today's world. In attempting to do this, the intermediate step by which we attempt to develop certain guidelines is crucial. Incidentally it is just at this point that I find many theologians who enter this field particularly weak; mainly because what they deduce from a biblical view is so general (and sometimes even vague) that it is of little practical help in choosing between the main alternatives of the world today. I would like to emphasize the following guidelines:

First, there is a positive mandate to create wealth. The Christian has a distinctive view of the physical world. It is neither sacred nor magic. It is God's intention that we cultivate it, improve it and harness its resources for our own use. Man has been created to have dominion in this world. The urge to control, direct and manage the resources of this world is part and parcel of man's nature and vocation. Idleness is at root alien to human personality. It was never part of God's intention that poverty should be the norm for economic life. Prosperity, not poverty, is God's intention for his world, though we must be careful to distinguish prosperity from luxury. In the Bible, therefore, economic life has a legitimacy which derives from the nature of the created world. There is nothing inherently grubby, dirty or second rate about the whole business of getting and spending. This positive mandate to create wealth however is in the context of our fiduciary responsibilities. This world is God's world not ours. We are invested with the responsibilities of trusteeship. We are not free to deface and destroy the natural world. We are accountable to the Creator. In this as in other areas the ends can never justify the means. The order to create wealth can never justify permanent damage to the balance of nature.

Second, private property rather than state, social or collective ownership is the Christian norm for society. God alone has total and unconditional ownership of property. 'The absolute and transcendental title to property is the Lord's; the present and historical title to property is man's.' Throughout the Bible private property is the normal and accepted form of ownership and there is no conflict between trusteeship and private property rights. This was the form of property rights used when the land was parcelled out among families in Israel. Even though the idea of community was so strong in the Pentateuch and even though society was organized along tribal lines, it is important to notice that property rights were not communal, they were private. This was not accidental. The justification of private property rights in a Judaeo-Christian world-view is rooted in creation. Man was created as a responsible being. But freedom presupposes the ability to make choices concerning those things over which persons have control. In the material area of life this can be guaranteed only by the existence of private property rights. As a result, in the Eighth Commandment, God protects private property. 'Thou shalt not steal.' Emil Brunner, the Swiss theologian, argues the case forcefully as follows:

> The man who has nothing at his disposal cannot act freely. He is dependent on the permission of others for every step he takes, and if they so wish they can make it impossible for him to carry on any concrete activity. Without property there is no free personal life. Without property there is no power to act ... And the word 'property' must be taken literally as ownership or, as we say today, private property. Without private property there is no freedom.

Contrast this with a Marxist view of property rights. The logic of the Marxist argument is as follows: men are created equal; private property is theft; such injustice can only be removed by state ownership. But an economic system without the freedom established by property rights results in the direction of labour and capital – something described so powerfully by Solzhenitsyn as the Gulag Archipelago. A hundred years ago Professor Charles Hodge, a Princeton theologian, put it very clearly in his systematic theology:

> The foundation of the right to property is the will of God ... This doctrine of the divine right of property is the only security for the individual or for society. If it be made to rest

on any other foundation it is insecure and unstable. It is only by making property sacred, guarded by the fiery sword of divine justice that it can be safe from the dangers to which it is everywhere and always exposed.

This is precisely what the Eighth Commandment does when it says 'Thou shalt not steal'.

I believe that when Milton Friedman defends capitalism as a necessary but not sufficient condition to ensure a free society, it is not capitalism as an ideology to which he refers, but the guarantee by the state to respect private property rights.

But one thing needs to be made clear. The Christian view of private property rights is different from the Roman or Justinian view which derived ownership from the concept of natural right. In a Roman view ownership meant the unconditional and exclusive use of property by the individual. He was free to choose (subject of course to the law of contract) exactly how he wished to use that property. By contrast a Judaeo-Christian view places emphasis on duties as well as rights – think of the poor-tithe, the gleaning laws and the legislation of a zero rate of interest in the Pentateuch economy.

Third, each family should have a permanent stake in economic life. The basic unit for society is and always has been the family. Because of this the Judaeo-Christian world-view recognizes the need to create political and economic structures which ensure that the family is not debarred from a permanent interest in economic life. In a simple agricultural community, such as that at the time of the Pentateuch, this meant each family being able to own land. The principle which underlay the concept of Jubilee (that all land alienated during the preceding fifty years was to be returned to its original owner or his descendants) was that each family should not find itself in a position in which it was permanently barred from owning land, the vital productive asset in that economy. As a result of industrialization land has been replaced by capital as the most important means of production and in the process, real wages or, expressed differently the value of human capital, has increased as well. In my judgement therefore the equivalent of this principle today is the right of each family to home ownership, the need for more diffused and direct ownership of equity capital and the opportunity not just for a formal education but for retraining and post-experience training in later life.

There is also the other side to this particular coin. In the Judaeo-Christian view, while the state has the responsibility for ensuring that the family is an on-going economic concern, the family has the responsibility to look after itself and the welfare of its members.

Fourth, the relief and elimination of poverty rather than the pursuit of economic equality should be a Christian concern. The concept of equality has dominated the twentieth century. The Bible teaches clearly that all men are created equal in the sight of God. God knows, values and loves each one of his creatures. The American Declaration of Independence declared as self-evident truths 'that all men are created equal, that they are endowed by the Creator with certain inalienable Rights: that among these are Life, Liberty and the pursuit of Happiness'. The recognition that all men are equal in the sight of God is fundamental to liberty as we know it in modern Western societies. Equality before God leads of necessity to equality before the law. It is an essential characteristic of a Christian society. By the seventh and eighth centuries BC Israel had become quite wealthy. Alongside wealth had come materialism and with it injustice, the oppression of the poor, bribery and corruption and the abuse of the legal system by the wealthy – with one law for the rich and another for the poor. Such inequality was roundly condemned by the Old Testament prophets.

But there is all the difference in the world between people created as equal before God, having equal access to the law, and the way in which equality is used so frequently today: not as equality of opportunity but as equality of outcome. Economic justice, so it is claimed, demands economic equality – defined as an equalized after-tax real income. But this concept is quite alien to Scripture. As we saw earlier there were various mechanisms built into the Hebrew economic system to prevent perman-ent and substantial economic inequality from developing. But there is never a suggestion in Scripture that economic justice implies economic equality. Indeed as we have seen economic equality in society could only be achieved under two kinds of circumstances – *one* through the use of coercion in which case it is incompatible with freedom and the *other* in a situation in which people do not respond or even care about material rewards.

The authentic Christian concern is not in creating equality but in relieving poverty. Three major causes of poverty can be distinguished in the Bible: *first*, oppression and exploitation – the typical situation being that of an employer using monopoly power or the use of fraud and violence in order to pay low wages; *second*, misfortune, such as the position of widows, orphans, or as a result of accident and injury; *third*, laziness. In the first case the appropriate response is to remove the cause of the poverty; in the second to meet the needs of those who are deprived; and in the third to do nothing. The Old Testament however is not just a clinical analysis of poverty. When God instructs his people Israel to care for the poor, the appeal is invariably on the basis of what he has done for them.

> You shall not wrong a stranger or oppress him, for you were strangers in the land of Egypt. You shall not afflict any widow or orphan. If you do afflict them, and they cry out to me, I will surely hear their cry; and my wrath will burn, and I will kill you with the sword, and your wives shall become widows and your children fatherless – (Exod. 22:21–4).

Fifth, economic injustice is to be remedied. In Biblical times injustice resulted from the exploitation of monopoly power in grain, corn, food and in the employment of labour. Injustice in this sense is not measured by the level of wages but the extent of oppression, exploitation, cheating and forced labour: something all too familiar in the early stages of industrialization in the UK and in certain American countries today, not to mention the labour camps of the Soviet Union.

Listen to the prophetic note throughout Scripture:

> Jer.22:13–17 'And woe to you, King Jehoiakim, for you are building your great palace with forced labour. By not paying wages you are building injustice into its walls and oppression into the door-frames and ceilings.
>
> 'Why did your father Josiah reign so long? Because he was just and fair in all his dealing that is why God blessed him. He saw to it that justice

368

and help were given to the poor and the needy and all went well for him. This is how a man lives close to God. But you! You are full of selfish greed and all dishonesty! You murder the innocent, oppress the poor and reign with ruthlessness.'

Lev.19:13 'You shall not rob nor oppress anyone and you shall pay your hired workers promptly. If something is due to them, don't even keep it overnight.'

James 5:4 'Hear the cries of the field workers whom you have cheated of their pay.'

Malachi 3:5 'At that time my punishments will be quick and certain: I will move swiftly against wicked men who trick the innocent, against adulterers, and liars, against all those who cheat their hired hands or oppress widows and orphans, or defraud strangers and do not fear me.'

Apart from condemning the abuse of economic power, the Bible has little to say in a positive sense as to what constitutes fair and just wages and prices. The notion of what constitutes a just wage and a just price has in consequence been a much debated question in the history of the Church. In my judgement it is difficult to improve on a genuinely competitive wage or price. That is, most of the grounds of injustice in this area stem from the presence of monopoly power and the disregard of a law. I find it difficult to believe that we can improve on trying to establish competitive markets within the framework of a rule of law.

Sixth, there is the constant warning of materialism. Money, wealth and profit have a legitimacy in a Christian world-view: but they also carry a danger. The Tenth Commandment, 'Thou shalt not covet thy neighbour's house', recognizes that the quite legitimate desire for prosperity and ownership may be misdirected. Instead of being an act of service, making money and owning things can become purely selfish activities; and it is in this sense that our Lord issues the warning that 'you cannot serve both God and Mammon', and tells the story of the very prosperous farmer who is destroyed by his self-indulgence. In an age which has become dominated by the Gross National Product and the Dow-Jones Index, the level of interest rates and the state of the pound, the money supply and the Public

Sector Deficit, and at a more mundane level, the Sunday colour supplements offering a world of gourmet food and package holidays in the sun, it is a warning which is easily muffled by our culture.

Seventh, accountability and judgement are an integral part of economic life. The Christian has a high view of man. Although part of nature in that he is made from dust, he is nevertheless created in the image of God and as such possesses many of the qualities of Godhead: mind, will, emotions, conscience. He is the supreme achievement of God's creation. Yet despite this he is created in a relationship of accountability to God and the sphere of his accountability includes the economic. He is accountable as a steward of the earth's resources; he is accountable for his own particular talents; and he is accountable for the way in which he acquires and disposes of his wealth.

It is within this context that we have to come to terms with the Christian view of judgement which is arguably the most unfashionable biblical doctrine of the twentieth century. Judgement is frequently thought of in a retributive and future context. It is the verdict passed on those who choose self rather than God. An unprejudiced reading of the New Testament certainly suggests that to be true. The successful farmer of Luke and the story of the rich man and Lazarus are sufficient evidence of that. But judgement can be present as well as future. The process of sowing and reaping is evidenced now. Actions have consequences. Throughout the Old Testament God actively judges people and nations. In this context we may well ask whether we are not living in an age when God is judging our Western civilization – whether the inflation of the Western world is a judgement on materialism, or the rising unemployment a judgement on militant trade unionism or the crisis of capitalism a judgement on the secular humanism of our age.

So far, we have considered some key principles derivative from a Christian world-view which are relevant to issues of political economy. But in conclusion I should like to emphasize that Christianity places emphasis not only on structures but also on personal obedience. The structures of the Pentateuch were good but a stable and wealthy economic society could only flourish to the extent that Israel was obedient to the whole of the law and its commandment. In this sense a set of Christian guidelines must never be interpreted as an attempt to legislate the Gospel. Proper structures are desirable in themselves but by themselves they are never a substitute for that vital Christian life which comes from personal commitment to follow Jesus Christ. The New Testament has a good deal to say with respect to church administration. But a biblically constituted Church is no guarantee that it will be a community of life, growth and love. Similarly, just economic structures are I believe a part of God's intention for human society. But we must never forget that the good news of the Incarnation is that God's supreme revelation is of personal liberation which we can all experience in Jesus Christ which in turn will help to shape and mould those structures which we have considered.

Source: Brian Griffiths, *Morality and the Market Place: Christian Alternatives to Capitalism and Socialism* (Hodder & Stoughton 1982 edition), pp. 71–99.

Michael Novak
1933–

Introduction

Novak was born in Johnstown, Pennsylvania, in 1933. His grandparents came from the hill-farming communities of Eastern Slovakia, and settled in the small industrial towns of Pennsylvania and Connecticut in the United States. These family experiences influenced greatly Novak's early appreciation of Roman Catholic communitarianism and of Christian socialism. They are also revealed in his study of the massacre of striking miners in 1897 in Pennsylvania, *The Guns of Lattimer* (1978).

Originally destined for the priesthood, he was educated at Stonehill College, Massachusetts, and then at the Gregorian University, Rome. He then studied at the Catholic University and at Harvard, deciding to pursue a richly varied intellectual life rather than the ordained ministry. Much of his life was then spent in academic posts at Harvard, Stanford University, the Rockefeller Foundation, Syracuse University, and the University of Notre Dame. Yet his move to join without tenure that 'extraordinary fraternity' of the American Enterprise Institute in 1978, as Resident Scholar and then Professor in Religion and Public Policy, provided a much better base for the radical conservatism and plurality of his philosophy and social involvements. The latter included journalism through the *National Review*, *Christian Century* and *Christianity and Crisis*, and contributions to public life as speech writer for the Democratic Vice-Presidential candidate in the early 1970s, as a member of the Presidential Task Force Project on Economic Justice (1985), and as ambassador to the Conference on Security and Cooperation in Europe (1986). He remains a committed Roman Catholic layman, serving as vice-chair of the Lay Commission on Catholic Social Teaching and the United States Economy (1984). He is a prolific author, covering a wide field from sport to liberation theology, and from novels to historical studies. He has been a frequent traveller to Latin America, Eastern Europe, Hong Kong, Italy, and the United Kingdom.

In so many ways, Novak's life epitomizes a growing awareness and articulation of American identity as democratic capitalism. Moving from a background of Christian socialism and the traditional anti-democratic capitalist communitarianism of Roman Catholic teaching, he came to a deep appreciation of the material and spiritual benefits of democratic capitalism. In particular, he has emphasized its tripartite plural nature as political democracy, market economy, and moral-cultural values and institutions. His change of mind and heart has also brought him into strong conflict with Western theological and ecclesiastical establishments, with their liberal suspicions of democratic capitalism, and equally ill-informed support for socialism. His founding and directing of the Institute of Religion and Democracy (1981), symbolizes these commitments, and his powerful moral concern to raise the wealth of nations in order to benefit the poor.

Text 19 reflects his vocation to make theologically articulate what he, with Niebuhr, regards as the inarticulate wisdom of democratic capitalism. It is drawn principally from his *The Spirit of Democratic Capitalism*, one of those rare books which 'actually change the way things are'. Begun at the end of the 1970s, when American policies and values were under strong attack, it represents a vigorous criticism of the ideals and practice of socialism, and an equally vigorous promotion of the virtues of what he came to call democratic capitalism. The tonal quality of the book came as a shock to the liberal and radical establishments of theology and Church. Its strongly apologetic character and relationship to the organized neoconservatism of the 1970s and 1980s is reflected in its publication by the American Enterprise Institute in the United States, and the Institute of Economic Affairs in the United Kingdom, two leading neoconservative think tanks. It has been translated into numerous languages. The text, like the book, is divided into three parts:

1. A definition and elaboration of the plural nature and spirit of democratic capitalism, as democracy, market economy, and moral-cultural institutions and values. For the sake of brevity, this section is taken from the pamphlet, *The American Vision. An Essay on the Future of Democratic Capitalism* (1978) which acted as a trailer for the book.
2. A criticism of Marxist and democratic socialism.
3. A development of a theology of economics, focused on six doctrines: the Trinity, the Incarnation, competition, original sin, the separation of realms, and caritas. He argued later for the addition of creation as invention. He concentrates on economics, because he regards theological comment on it as quite inadequate. The Christian promotion of democratic capitalism needs to correct this deficiency, given the central importance of the market economy.

Text 19: The Spirit of Democratic Capitalism

What is democratic capitalism?

I designate our system by the name 'democratic capitalism' in order to stress its tripartite nature. It is not an *economic* system only, but a *political* and *cultural* system as well. The name 'democratic capitalism' suggests clearly the political and economic structure of our ideals. It suggests as well, although less directly, a commitment to those cultural ideals that might be expressed by some such locution as 'a liberal civilization' – a civilization whose aims include an open society, respect for the rights and dignity of individuals, and the vision of justice and equity that has been developing in Western society since earliest times.

Ours is not a system of 'free enterprise' only, nor of 'private property', nor of 'individual liberties', nor of 'limited government' alone. These are locutions proper to a preoccupation with the economic sphere, and they seem to be favored by writers and speakers whose interests are mainly those of economics and business. They will not suffice as descriptions of our system as a whole, as it actually is experienced. They will not command the full loyalties, nor express the full interests, of all who enjoy the fruits of our system. Thus, most available defenses of our system spring from a base too narrow both in the interests to which they appeal and in the intellectual grounds on which they stand. The designation 'democratic capitalism' is intended to go beyond a description of the economic system merely, and to include the political system and the cultural system, too.

Strengths of democratic capitalism
Many of the critics of democratic capitalism discuss its economic system wholly in terms of its alleged 'expropriation' and 'pollution' of nature's resources. Yet Marx held that the capitalist stage was essential to the emergence of socialism, because it alone could enrich the world and build an economic base for a vision of plenty. In a world of inevitable scarcity, equality is not imaginable. Only in a world of plenty can there emerge a vision of equal distribution, with enough of everything for everyone.

More to the point, the emergence of democratic capitalism did not take place everywhere in the world at once. As a system of economic organization, it was invented rather late in human history and, at first, only in a few centers of activity: in Great Britain, in Flanders, in Germany – in short, in northwestern Europe. This late emergence led Max Weber to speculate upon the importance to the development of the capitalist idea of Protestant (especially Calvinist) culture. Not only was culture significant from the first; so also was politics. The development of capitalism in economics was accompanied in a few places by the emergence of democracy in politics. In a few nations, economic habits and political habits reinforced one another in the daily practices of citizens. From the beginning, then, the trinitarian and interdependent nature of the system – the concomitant development of economic, political, and cultural ideals – has been in evidence.

Capitalism and wealth. Those who have experienced the growing power of this tripartite system have experienced the first of its often overlooked advantages: its *wealth-conferring* character. The earth has long been rich in oil, copper, iron ore, rubber, and countless other resources. But for millennia, many of these resources went unknown, neglected, or unused. The imagination and enterprise unleashed by democratic capitalism brought recognition of the actual wealth lying fallow in the bosom of nature; invented new uses for these resources; and conferred wealth on many regions of the world that the inhabitants of those regions did not know they possessed. As an instance, consider how oil lay unknown and unused under the deserts of Araby. Only with the development of the piston engine was a use for that heretofore useless stuff invented.

Many of us saw evidence of the wealth-conferring nature of our system during the bicentennial celebrations in many American towns and cities in 1976. At the turn of the century, in the year 1900, most of America shared a poverty normal to humankind. In bicentennial parades, one watched the implements, tools, and artifacts of preceding generations pass by on floats. In towns in Iowa (themselves barely a century old), one saw vividly that within the lifetimes of our own grandparents the United States was what we would now call an 'underdeveloped country'. Farm implements were made of wood and the most primitive ores; power came through the muscles of men and animals. The laws of erosion and crop rotation, of soil and water management, and other scientific agricultural skills were then largely unknown. The rise of democratic capitalism conferred enormous wealth upon the citizens of such towns within some seventy-six years, a very short period of human history.

Efficiencies. If democratic capitalism has conferred enormous wealth upon the world, a wealth never before even envisaged except in a few places, for a very few, and unsteadily, it has also proven to be the most *efficient* system ever devised by human beings. Whatever its faults – and these are many – no other system even comes close to it in inventiveness, production, and widespread distribution. Socialist systems have proved to be less successful. (Since the Communist Revolution of 1917, the Soviet Union, once capable of being the breadbasket of large sections of the world, has had sixty years of 'poor weather'.) It is not necessary to make this point invidiously. There are serious flaws in the sort of efficiency generated by democratic capitalism. Unplanned and unguided, our system permits shortages in some areas and unnecessary abundance and wastage in others, until the market corrects them; and in some areas the market does not work well. But the very idea that plenty is attainable – that there might be a material abundance to be equitably distributed – is singularly founded upon the enormous wealth produced by such a system.

Capitalism and democracy. There is a third advantage gained by a democratic capitalist system, an advantage that looks to the political rather than to the economic sphere. Capitalism may flourish without democracy, but democracy apart from capitalism is very difficult to achieve. Between capitalism and democracy there is an underlying system of mutual reinforcement, an internal harmony. There are examples of welfare states (they are more properly called socialist), that are democratic – Great Britain, Sweden, Israel, among others. But in all of these, underlying traditions owe much to a liberal capitalist past. Those nations that have leaped straight into socialism, which they insist upon describing as 'democratic', manifest strong centralized governments, without checks and balances, and deficient institutions for the defense of individual rights. Traditions of private property and individual rights grew up in the capitalist orbit. An economic order built upon respect for the decisions of the individual in the marketplace; upon rights to property which the state may not abridge; and upon limiting the activities of the central state, are at the very least harmonious with the habits of mind required for a functioning democratic political order.

There are several examples in recent history of capitalist authoritarian regimes moving in the direction of a democratic political order. There are no examples of socialist regimes doing so. In theory, perhaps, there is no contradiction between democracy and socialism. In practice, clearly there is.

Habits of mind. My fourth observation concerns the cultural sphere. Democratic capitalism depends upon a unique human type. Three habits of mind, in particular, must be highly developed if democratic capitalism is to function. These habits of mind are not wholly virtuous; they include, as we will shortly notice, certain important deficiencies. They are, nevertheless, both distinctive and admirable. They represent three forms of spiritual enrichment uniquely available in our culture.

• The first of these is an *empirical* habit of mind. Whatever the traditional way of doing things, whatever the conventions, whatever the prevailing theories, the system of democratic capitalism rewards a systematic skepticism and a basic trust in experience. It encourages citizens to invent new ways better in tune with experience. Our culture teaches us to be heedless of theory and to look with fresh eyes at the facts. In one sense, of course, the suggestion box found so often in factories and schools is an invitation to theoretical thinking, to imagination, to ideas. But what it teaches, above all, is that we should keep our eyes upon our own experiences, that we should be taught by what we actually encounter rather than by what someone else laid down from a distance. My father-in-law, a lawyer from Iowa, used to instruct me: 'Michael, if you can't do it, teach it.' Priority is given to the man of action; the man of theory is viewed with a certain skepticism. This empirical habit of mind, despite obvious weaknesses, is a source of considerable intellectual and cultural power.

• The second habit of mind is related to the first: It is the habit of *pragmatism*. No matter what theories may dictate, this habit of mind instructs us to observe: *How does it work in practice?* Our culture encourages a pervasive recognition of the limits of theory and of the intractability of the real world. We have trained ourselves to find intellectual excitement in the task of solving concrete problems. By contrast, the solution of conceptual puzzles seems rather like a form of diversion. In the academic world, many of the most promising intellects soon find greater satisfaction in the challenges of administration than at their tame and safely protected desks.

Our businessmen prize doing rather than theorizing. They are, by and large, indifferent to the need to conceptualize their tasks, to theorize about them, or to get straight all the ideological implications of what they do. They would rather build a plant for Pepsi Cola or Ford in Leningrad than argue with party apparatchiks about the relative merits of capitalism. They seem to believe that if only they build a better mousetrap, the world will come to their door. It is not necessary to succeed on the plane of theory, they hold, if one can excel every day in the realm of practice. In these days, of course, the side made to seem attractive in the media can ride roughshod over facts, experience, and reality. Pragmatism is not enough. But it has its clear rewards.

Marx wrote that changing the world is more important than understanding it correctly. In this light, the pragmatism of our civilization may come to seem more highly developed than that of the Marxist world. Our pragmatists, at least, are not burdened by the official blinders of the Marxist state and party apparatus. They travel with so much less ideological baggage that Schumpeter was led to theorize that they might in the long run prove spineless against the onslaught upon them by a more theoretical and principled socialism. So our pragmatism hurts us both by depriving us of an ideological offensive, and by leaving us weaponless in defense.

● The third habit of mind nourished in our civilization is the habit of *practical compromise*. In order to sign a commercial contract, or in order to pass a bill through our legislatures, we do not consider it necessary to reach agreement on all the metaphysical, religious, or intellectual implications that may be involved. We train ourselves to be rather studiously nonideological and 'nonprincipled', and to accept the best concrete compromise we can attain. We try not to insist upon total ideological harmony. We agree to disagree, even while signing on the dotted line to provide the specified limited services. In order to accomplish something, we have been well tutored, it is not necessary to agree about everything.

The world of action is not the same as the world of faith, or vision, or theory, or ideal. Our vision of history is not, in that sense, simple or absolutist. We recognize that different parties may cherish different visions, and that our opponents, rather than we, may perhaps in the long run prove to be correct. We are satisfied with modest incremental steps forward. This willingness to compromise is one of the main propellants of this nation's social dynamism. More romantic persons, who insist upon pure devotion to their own clear ideals, strike us as quixotic and, in the end, self-destructive.

We half admire them, but we do not believe that history works as they seem to assume. We are rather systematically modest about the capacity of systems of ideals to match the real complexities of history. Almost uniquely among the peoples of the world, we prefer to be tutored slowly by actual experience, step by step, experiment by experiment. This intellectual modesty, this willingness to compromise, is a national strength. But it, too, has its own inherent dangers and flaws. [. . .]

Source: Michael Novak, *The American Vision. An Essay on the Future of Democratic Capitalism* (Washington DC: American Enterprise Institute 1978), pp. 7–12.

The rejection of socialism

Marxism has been the greatest fantasy of our century. . . . The influence that Marxism has achieved, far from being the result or proof of its scientific character, is almost entirely due to its prophetic, fantastic, and irrational elements. . . . At present, Marxism neither interprets the world nor changes it: it is merely a repertoire of slogans serving to organize various interests.

– Leszek Kolakowski, *Main Currents of Marxism*

Socialist movements continue to grow around the world, particularly in Africa and Latin America. Yet it is not easy today to state what socialists stand for. This difficulty arises less from the fact that socialists are divided in their views, although they are, than from the fact that socialists are embarrassed by the totalitarianism of existing socialist states. So far as intellectual content goes, the word 'socialism' appears to designate – in the West, at least – two vague and shifting sets of attitudes: first, idealism about equality; secondly, hostility toward democratic capitalism.

In its central historical vision, whether Marxist or non-Marxist, socialism was once presented, negatively, as a way of analyzing the deficiencies of democratic capitalism. Positively, socialism once meant the abolition of private property; state ownership of the means of production through the nationalization of industries; state control over all aspects of the economy; the abolition of 'bourgeois democracy' through the creation of a classless society; and an international order based upon a class analysis transcending national, cultural, and linguistic frontiers. Socialism meant the banishing of the profit motive, which was judged to be the root cause of the exploitation of labor. It also meant the abolition of imperialism, since capital and the profit motive were judged to be the root of empire. Socialism promised a social structure which would end competition between person and person and give to each according to need while taking from each according to ability, a social structure which would thus effect a change in what earlier generations had erroneously regarded as 'human nature'. Socialism, it was confidently predicted, would bring about a new type of human being, 'socialist man'. Such a human being would act from motives of human solidarity, community, cooperation, and comradeliness.

Socialism has many intellectual roots, including pre-Marxist traditions of religious socialism. Socialism, some said, is the practice of which Christianity is the religion. Others, like Marx and Engels, rejected 'soft' socialism. Such Marxists emphasized that socialism could only come about through violence, since the owners of the instruments of production could not be expected to give up their power and privileges without a struggle. But not all socialists have been Marxists.

In the 133 years since *The Communist Manifesto* and in the 64 years since the Bolshevik revolution, several important lessons have been learned by virtually all socialists. First, the socialist dream has sometimes resulted in a nightmare of oppression, totalitarian control, and ruthless imperialism. Second, national and ethnic loyalties have proved to be stronger than class loyalties. Thus as early as World War I, workers, even socialist workers, manufactured the munitions used by soldiers, even socialist soldiers, in each of the national armies. Since that time, socialist nations have declared war on one another, invaded one another, and publicly and emotionally denounced and threatened one another.

Furthermore, specific elements in socialist doctrine have been shown to be deficient in practice. Nationalized industries do not prevent low wages to workers, do not conspicuously improve working conditions, do not diminish environmental damage, and do not raise levels of efficiency, material progress, and humane attitudes in the work force. On the other side, those small portions of agriculture allowed by socialist regimes to remain in private hands have outperformed collectivized state agriculture by factors as high as 30 to 1, despite far higher concentrations of resources (machinery, fertilizers, roads, etc.) devoted to state collectives. Again, administered prices and wages have been shown to be far less intelligent, efficient, and rational than the market mechanism. In the economic sphere, therefore, nearly every central socialist doctrine has been shown to be in need of critical transformation.

In the political sphere, the central administrative state has proved to be a more thorough instrument of oppression and exploitation than the democratic capitalist state.

In the moral-cultural sphere, no fully socialist state has yet shown that it can tolerate the broad range of dissent, human liberties, and human rights achieved by democratic capitalist states.

Dogmatism and sectarianism bedevil socialist cultures, perhaps precisely because of their claim to represent science rather than opinion. In sum, the socialist frame of mind and socialist practice have been shown to be far less humane than Marx and non-Marxist socialists had expected.

Solzhenitsyn and others have testified that no one behind the Iron Curtain can bear to discuss socialism without at least a sardonic smile. For individuals, the creed is empty, even though it still functions as a powerful instrument of legitimation for Soviet domestic repression and international empire.

Outside the self-declared socialist nations of the Soviet bloc and China, socialists have also been transformed. Few today point to the Soviet Union or to China as models they would wish to emulate. Although some try to place the best face they can upon existing socialist experiments elsewhere, and continue to greet new ones with fresh hope, most insist upon distinguishing what *they* mean by socialism from what occurs within existing socialist states. In this sense, socialism has lost its grip on concrete reality. Most Western and Third World socialists try to rescue the dream from the manifest horrors of actual experimentation. Even as a doctrine, socialism has been revised in almost every part. Thus, for example, the leading socialist social scientist in the United States, C. Wright Mills, took pains in one essay to list the key propositions of socialism, and to show how each of them has been proved by history to be false or misleading.

In the real world, socialism has acquired two decisive centers of gravity. On the one hand, its doctrines legitimate the extension of the empire of the Soviet Union. On the other, among the Western bourgeoisie, it is a catch-all for many types of utopianism and radical individualism, a substitute religion. On both counts, it has precipitated strong intellectual and popular revulsion. This loss of faith is most widespread within the Soviet orbit and, outside it, among formerly socialist intellectuals. [. . .]

A theology of economics for democratic capitalism

The importance of ideals

The ideals a system is designed to serve, especially if they are transcendent ideals, stimulate each new generation to advance the work of its forebears. Building a humane social order is not a task for one generation merely. It is a journey of a thousand years. For democratic capitalism, barely two hundred have been traversed. To know its ideals is to be restless under the status quo and to wish to do better in the future.

It is important to grasp the ideals of a system clearly for another reason. There are many on the democratic left in the United States who interpret their own experience, judge the system in which they live, and try to direct its development, according to the ideals of socialism. Democratic capitalism, which is exceedingly flexible and experimental, has learned much from their efforts. Yet in the end, it is surely better for them and for the American system to be clear about each other. Insofar as socialism is a unitary system, dominated in all its parts by a state apparatus, socialism is not an improvement upon democratic capitalism but a relapse into the tyrannical unities from which the latter has emerged. A unitary, dominant, central state authority has been tried before. The enforcement of high moral ideals by coercion of law has been tried before.

Insofar as democratic socialism has given up the classic positions of Marxism and the collectivized state, it may now be no more than a left-wing variant of democratic capitalism. Insofar as it separates the moral-cultural system from the state, and also separates the economy (in some degree) from the state, it preserves the pluralist structure of democratic capitalism intact. In practice, of course, the political, economic, and moral-cultural programs of democratic socialists do not run helter-skelter. Running through them is a consistent thread of statism. In general, the left wishes to strengthen the political system at the expense of the economic system and the moral-cultural system.

It is the role of socialists on the Democratic left, as Michael Harrington and Irving Howe, the editor of *Dissent*, instruct their readers, to become the 'conscience' of the Democratic Party. But this conscience is *not* the conscience of democratic capitalism. It is the conscience of the socialist system they wish America yet to become.

My reasons for not wishing to march into the cold with them have already been given. Here I would like merely to summarize some of the important doctrines of Christianity (of which there are analogues in Judaism and other major religions) which helped to supply the ideas through which democratic capitalism has emerged in history.

It is no accident that democratic capitalism arose first in Jewish-Christian lands (or that it is imitable only in analogous cultures). Apart from certain specific views of human life and human hope, neither a democratic polity nor a market economy makes sense. If those who live under democratic capitalism lose sight of the moral foundations of the system, a loss of morale is likely to occur. Moral ignorance will bring moral paralysis. Necessary reforms and advances cannot be attempted when individuals within the system have lost sight of its proper ideals.

Some theologians may be dismayed that I do not more often cite Scripture in what follows. A host of texts is at my disposal. The economy of biblical nations in the Near Eastern basin was, after all, an economy of caravans and traders, a desert crossroads of active commercial life. Nonetheless, writers of the biblical era did not envisage questions of political economy such as those we face today. The revelation of God which Christians and Jews (and Muslims) hold to have been given through these writings was intended for all human beings universally, in all conceivable systems, even in systems of slavery (which have dominated world history) as well as in societies of hunters, in agricultural societies, in urban societies, in primitive societies, in modern societies, in future societies. For all such contexts, Scripture has words of universal power. It is a mistake, I believe, to try to bind the cogency of Scripture to one system merely. The Word of God is transcendent. It judges each and every system, and finds each gravely wanting. Liberation theologians in the Third World today err in binding Scripture to a socialist political economy, and I do not wish to indulge in a parallel mistake.

For candor's sake, I must add that the emphasis upon Scripture studies during the past generation does not seem to have effected, as its sponsors hoped, the revitalization of Christian life and practice. There is a great gap between the Word of God and systems of economic, political, social, and cultural thought in modern societies. The human mind requires a powerful set of philosophical and theological concepts in order to relate the pure and simple Word of Scripture to the complex body of modern thought. By trying to take a shortcut around systematic philosophical and theological reflection, and by ignoring intellectual and social history, too many contemporary clergymen, theologians, and devout lay-persons have ensnared themselves in pious simplicities which falsify reality. Quoting Scripture, they do not manage to relate the Word of God *incarnationally* to every fiber of modern civilization. They fail to understand that Scripture applied to the real world without exact intellectual analysis echoes emptily. Those who would apply Scripture to public policy cannot take shortcuts.

On this terrain, there can scarcely be certainty. Perhaps they are right who believe that 'Christianity is the religion of which socialism is the practice'. I do not think they are right, and I have tried to set forth reasons for this judgment. For my part, I do not claim that democratic capitalism is the practice of which Christianity and Judaism are the religions. That is not my view. Both Christianity and Judaism have flourished, or at least survived, in every sort of social system known to humankind. If democratic capitalism were to perish during the next fifty years, as well it may, Christianity and Judaism could still survive; according to God's promise, they will survive to the end of time. It is essential, then, not to confuse the transcendence of Christianity and Judaism with the survival of democratic capitalism. If democratic capitalism were to perish from the earth, humankind would decline into relative darkness and Jews and Christians would suffer under regimes far more hostile to their liberties and their capacities. Yet Judaism and Christianity do not *require* democratic capitalism. It is only that without it they would be poorer and less free. Among political economies, there may be something better than self-correcting democratic capitalism. If so, it is not yet in sight.

It is, therefore, a sad commentary on the sociology of knowledge in the Christian churches that so few theologians or religious leaders understand economics, industry, manufacturing, trade, and finance. Many seem trapped in pre-capitalist modes of thought. Few understand the laws of development, growth, and production. Many swiftly reduce all morality to the morality of distribution. They demand jobs without comprehending how jobs are created. They demand the distribution of the world's goods without insight into how the store of the world's goods may be expanded. They desire ends without critical knowledge about means. They claim to be leaders without having mastered the techniques of human progress. Their ignorance deprives them of authority. Their good intentions would be more easily honored if supported by evidence of diligent intelligence in economics.

Yet it is not economics that is our proper subject here. Our task is to cite, if all too briefly, religious doctrines which have been powerful in leading humanity, slowly and fitfully, to those formulations of institutional practices which have made economic development, political liberty, and a moral-cultural commitment to progress on earth emerge in history as a realistic force. I judge six such doctrines most important, and will address them in their Christian form.

Six theological doctrines

[Three only are included below.]
1. *The Trinity.* The first of these is the symbol of the Trinity. No one has seen God. What we know of God can only be inferred from our experience and from what God has chosen to reveal of Himself. These are the two sources of our knowledge:

what we learn from the works of the Creator and the Lord of History, and what we learn from his self-revelation. Characteristically, therefore, humans develop a language about God, inadequate as they recognize it to be, based upon what they most value in their own experience. They seek signs of the godly in everything. 'Grace,' George Bernanos tells us, 'is everywhere.'

The one God of Christians is also plural; appropriately, then, the mind becomes accustomed to seeing pluralism-in-unity throughout creation, even in social systems.

Some Protestants fear that any knowledge of God which arises from human experience is bound to be flawed and distorted – to be, in the final measure, idolatrous compared to God as he knows himself. Yet in this matter experience and Scripture are at one: community is essential to our notion of God. Jesus described himself as the Son, one with the Father, and one as well with the Holy Spirit of love whom the Father would send. These are dark words. But they do suggest that even God is not best thought of as the Aristotelian *Nous*, a lonely individual in solitariness. A plural God, yet one?

No one sees God or comprehends what can be intended in speaking of God as Three-in-one. Yet it is at least clear that God is more to be conceived as a kind of community than as a solitary individual. From human experience, human beings have learned to place highest value upon communities of love, however humble and flawed. The image of the solitary loner, however noble and heroic, however brave in facing the darkness alone, somehow rings false as a representation of the highest of human experiences. What is most valued among humans is that community within which individuality is not lost. To build such community is to share God's life. (It is through this strong sense of community that Judaism supplies an analogous way to God.)

I do not think it wrong to hold that this lesson of experience is consistent with the teaching of Scripture. Experience and Scripture alike suggest that what is most real in human life, of highest value, most godlike, is a community of persons. Thus the creation images the Creator, and the creature is made to be in God's image, through community. When Jesus says, 'Forsake all and follow me' (Matthew 16:24), he is giving his life for the entire human community. So must we all.

It is true that socialism aims at community. It is less clear that its institutional arrangements effect, or can effect, the survival of individuality. This deficiency makes the community socialism builds suspect. In practice, it exhibits itself more as collective than as community.

The problem posed for political economy by the doctrine of the Trinity is how to build human community without damage to human individuality. How can there be one and yet many? How can all humans be united as one, yet retain personal liberty in insight and choice? This is the systemic problem which democratic capitalism has set out to solve. Its solution is remote from being perfect. Democratic capitalism is by no means the Kingdom of God. It remains in partial bondage to the world, the flesh, and the devil. Yet St. Patrick saw a metaphor for the Trinity in a shamrock. St. Augustine saw a metaphor for God in the procession of an insight (the Word) from an active intelligence (the Father), and in the procession of the choice of love (the Spirit) from both. These metaphors do not represent God adequately. They are merely arrows shot, as it were, in God's direction and fated from the beginning to fall short. Yet they do direct our attention in the direction of awe, silence, and wonder. Metaphors taken from silent nature and from the inner life of the human person are dangerous. Those taken from political economy may be even more so. Yet analogy is the air the Catholic mind breathes.

In everything I have been taught to seek God's presence. Thus also in political economy. I find attractive – and resonant with dark illumination – a political economy differentiated and yet one. Each of its component systems has a certain autonomy from the others; each system is interdependent with the others. Each has its distinctive operations, methods, rules. Each tames and corrects and enhances the others.

Moreover, this systemic differentiation is designed to permit many other sorts of communities to flourish. To be sure, the *forms* of each of these communities – families, neighborhoods, local agencies, interest groups, voluntary associations, churches, unions, corporations, guilds, societies, schools – are transformed under democratic capitalism into modalities unfamiliar in previous history. Less and less are they rooted in kith and kin, blood and status, propinquity and immobility. They have become more voluntary, fluid, mobile. They are nonetheless communities for that. Further, for too long the philosophers of democratic capitalism have neglected them, being hypnotized by the two dominant historical emergences, the *individual* and the *state*. Yet in fact, even if insufficiently studied in theory, these 'mediating communities' make the life of individuals and the life of states possible. In Poland, for example, the clumsy state apparatus is the despair of millions, who derive their real sustenance from their families, neighbors, friends, churches, and other social institutions. Strong individuals need strong mediating structures both in order to become what they are and in order to act effectively in the world. States need strong mediating structures in order to accomplish more cheaply and efficiently and with greater love what the state either cannot do at all or can do only at prohibitive expense and badly. When mediating communities suffer and are broken, both individuals and states are crippled.

Under democratic capitalism, the individual is freer than under any other political economy ever experienced by the human race, and this fact has led some scholars to speak of anomie, alienation, fragmentation. Such abstractions move us when we imagine others as strange, discrete objects separate from ourselves. Yet the scholars who write of such things do not appear to be particularly anomic, alienated, or fragmented; nor do their readers; nor our own families, loved ones, and mediating communities. In all societies, one meets lost souls, but there is no evidence that their number increases under conditions of modernity. It is obviously true that *old* forms of community die and that *all* forms of community become subtly different. It is also obvious that new forms bring their own pains, doubts, and uncertainties. But under democratic capitalism mediating communities multiply and thrive, become subject to choice, and afford enormous variety and possibility.

Under democratic capitalism, each individual participates in many vital communities. The social life of each is not exhausted by the state or controlled by the state. The federal government alone presently has at its disposal an annual budget reaching $452 billion, excluding intergovernmental transfer payments. State and local governments spend another $381 billion. This communal spending averages out for a population of 225 million

389

to about $3,072 for every man, woman and child. It does not include the communal spending of private associations, churches, guilds, unions, art leagues, schools, sporting activities, and other social institutions. In terms of money alone, the social vitalities of democratic capitalism are significant.

It may seem blasphemous to some to go from the Trinity to communal patterns of monetary expenditures. Yet in the patterns of its communal and individual life, a society does reveal its highest ideals, if darkly. Ideals of community oblige it constantly to do better. [. . .]

2. *Original sin.* The [second] doctrine is original sin, which we have already explored under a more general heading in Part One. The force of the word 'original' may, however, need exposition. Its effect is to deflate human pretensions of unambiguous virtue.

Some among the Greeks, some rationalists of the Enlightenment, and some socialists and other utopians seem ready to imagine healthy, normal, moral, reasonable human beings coming into existence somewhere or someday under stipulated favorable conditions. This is either because they think that the evils and inconstancies of the human heart are superable, or because they think that individuals are evil only through living within evil structures. In the latter case, they try to imagine a new society which will enable men to stand taller, achieve a nobility never before achieved, give spontaneous expression to altruistic and creative impulses, and, for good measure, have only pure and reasonable thoughts.

The force of the doctrine of original sin is to steel the gullible mind against such illusions. Human liberty is subject to evil expression as well as to good. Human intelligence is not only limited but often biased and distorted. The human passions are subject to common disorders. Those who believe in original sin believe that it is cruel, in such circumstances, to expect too much of other human beings. They believe, furthermore, that the root of evil does not lie in our systems but in ourselves.

Every form of political economy necessarily begins (even if unconsciously) with a theory of sin. For every system is designed *against* something, as well as in *favor* of something. Every system nourishes, every system inhibits. That is why some types of persons do particularly well within one system, others within another. The system of democratic capitalism, believing itself to be the natural system of liberty and the system which, so far in history, is best designed to meet the premises of original sin, is designed against tyranny. Its chief aim is to fragment and to check power, but not to repress sin. Within it every human vice flourishes. Entrepreneurs from around the world, it appears, flock to it and teach it new cultural speci-alities, of vice as well as of virtue, of indelicacy as well as of delicacy. *Nil humanum mihi alienum,* such a system might well say: 'Nothing from the world's cultures is alien to me.' Out-siders like Solzhenitsyn are often shocked by such a nation's public immoralities: massage parlors, pornography shops, pick-pockets, winos, prostitutes, pushers, punk rock, chambers for group sex – you name it, democratic capitalism tolerates it and someone makes a living from it.

One can imagine a form of democratic capitalist society which would put an end to public vice. The United States used to be stricter than it now is. Halfhearted measures in this direction are still sometimes made. But the heart of most citizens is clearly not in the wholesale legal repression of all sinful behavior. Socialist societies repress sin much more effectively. They begin by repressing economic activities.

If there is to be reform concerning the public exhibition of vice in the modern United States, such reform will probably have to emanate from the moral-cultural system rather than from the political system. But the present ethos is still in an anti-bourgeois phase, in which some forms of decadence are not only not ridiculed, but are admired as 'liberation'. The wheel may turn again, more than once. The denizens of *Playboy* eventually inspire a 'moral majority', whose own errors and decline are inevitable. Sin is where the majority is. Its fashions change from time to time.

A free society can tolerate the public display of vice because it has confidence in the basic decency of human beings, even under the burden of sin. The concept of original sin does not entail that each person is in all ways depraved, only that each person sometimes sins. Belief in original sin is consistent with guarded trust in the better side of human nature. Under an appropriate set of checks and balances, the vast majority of human beings will respond to daily challenges with decency, generosity, common sense, and even, on occasion, moral heroism.

3. *The separation of realms.* The classic text is: 'Give to Caesar the things that are Caesar's, and to God the things that are God's' (Mt. 22:21). In earlier chapters, we have already explored the importance of structural pluralism to democratic capitalism. This pluralism renders the mission of Christianity uniquely difficult. Some traditional societies imposed Christianity upon their citizens. Some socialist societies could conceivably do so. Under pluralism, no democratic capitalist society has a right to do so.

This means that the political system of democratic capitalism cannot, in principle, be a Christian system. Clearly, it cannot be a confessional system. But it cannot even be presumed to be, in an *obligatory way*, suffused with Christian values and purposes. Individual Christians and their organized bodies may legitimately work through democratic means to shape the will of the majority; but they must also observe the rights of others and, more than that, heed practical wisdom by respecting the consciences of others even more than law alone might demand. On the question of abortion, for example, no one is likely ever to be satisfied with the law, but all might be well advised not to demand in law all that their own conscience commands.

Dietrich Bonhoeffer has written about the impossibility of a Christian economy. For one thing, a market system must be open to all regardless of their religious faith. Economic liberty means that all must be permitted to establish their own values and priorities. The churches and other moral-cultural institutions may seek to persuade persons to avoid some actions and to take others. Public authority properly forbids some practices, regulates others, commands others. Nonetheless, a wide range of economic liberties remains. This liberty is valued as the atmosphere most favorable to invention, creativity, and economic activism. To repress it is to invite stagnation.

For another thing, Christian values in their purity command a high level of charity that is not of this world. Christians are urged to moral behavior that seems counter-natural: to love enemies; to do good to those that hate them; when struck, to turn the other cheek. Such counsels are high standards by which to fault even our best daily practice. They are not rules cut to the expected behavior of most persons most of the time. Again, it is said: 'Love your neighbor as yourself' (Lev. 19:18). It is not easy to love oneself. Escape from too much self often affords sorely needed relief. Often it is easier to love the poor and the oppressed than to love one's nextdoor neighbor. Part of the attraction of Christianity derives from the moral heroism to which such counsels call. Christianity in this sense is like a mountain peak. There is danger in such mountains. Christians who are not alpinists easily deceive themselves about their virtue.

No intelligent human order – not even within a church bureaucracy – can be run according to the counsels of Christianity. Not even saints in company assembled can bear such a regimen. Monasteries are designed for sinners, beginners, and backsliders. In the world at large, moreover, the consciences of all Christians are not identical. An economy based upon the consciences of some would offend the consciences of others. A free economy cannot – for all these reasons – be a Christian economy. To try to run an economy by the highest Christian principles is certain to destroy both the economy and the reputation of Christianity. Each Christian can and should follow his or her conscience, and cooperate in coalitions where consensus may be reached.

Liberty is a critical good in the economic sphere as well as in the sphere of conscience. Yet the guardians of the moral-cultural system are typically less concerned about liberty in the economic system than about their own liberty. Intellectuals insist upon a free market for their own work, but easily endorse infringements upon the liberty of economic activists. Journalists are quick to resist enchroachments upon the laws which protect their own liberties; they are slow to protest – if they do not themselves encourage – infringements upon the liberties of industry and commerce. So it is and always was.

These different interests and different concerns illustrate the systematic distortions in human perception to which the doctrine of original sin draws attention. The perception of each of us is regularly more self-centered than our ideal selves can plausibly commend. We are not often as objective as we would like to be. That is why the separation of systems is appropriate to our weakness. At the heart of Judaism and Christianity is the recognition of sin, as at the heart of democratic capitalism is a differentiation of systems designed to squeeze some good from sinful tendencies. [...]

Under God

All things considered, democratic capitalism will carry a heavy burden to Judgment Day. Its fundamental structure has proved to be productive, its liberties are broad; consequently, its responsibilities are many. Had the experiment failed, had the United States remained a primitive country, badly governed, surly and anarchic, the world might love it more. If the United States were unable to govern itself, the world could scarcely look to it for leadership. If the United States were still poor, no others could blame it for their own poverty. A former colony like other former colonies, it might be eligible for help from the World Bank.

But the United States is not stricken weak with poverty. Its system has been productive beyond compare. Its experiment has (so far) worked. Its people are free. Its burden of responsibility is, therefore, higher.

In this book, I have not been concerned to pass judgment on the practice of capitalism. I have been concerned to grasp the ideals latent in its practice. This procedure seems to me legitimate. There are hundreds of books about the ideals of socialism, many of them written before there was even a single instance of socialist practice, many others written by ignoring socialist practice. If it is legitimate for socialists to dream and to state their ideals, it is also legitimate for democratic capitalists to dream and to state our ideals. One must compare ideals with ideals, practice with practice.

Some will retort that the real world of democratic capitalism is harsher and more evil than I describe. The question is, By which standards should we judge harshness and evil? In order to judge the practice of democratic capitalism severely but fairly, the first step is to judge it in the light of its own ideals. These must first be stated. They are latent in its own practice; they do not have to be pulled out of the sky.

To say that democratic capitalism does not meet the ideals of socialism is plainly inadequate. It does not even attempt to do so. It has its own ideals. Whether in *practice* it achieves, as well, the *ideals* of socialism – and does so better than any extant socialist state – is an empirical question. Someone should assemble the evidence to answer it.

Nor does it suffice to say that democratic capitalism does not measure up to the full standards of Jewish and Christian visions of the Kingdom of God. It does not pretend to do so. No political economy dares to pretend that it measures up to that Kingdom. Yet democratic capitalism does welcome judgment under that Kingdom's clear light. For it is a system designed to be constantly reformed and transformed, and it alone of all known systems has within it resources for transformation through peaceful means.

In the light of its own ideals, criticism of democratic capitalism is both possible and necessary. Undoubtedly, the system has failed its own ideals, in large ways and in small. It is designed to be a free system within which individuals, interest groups, and moral minorities may try to direct it according to their lights. 'Many things,' Shakespeare writes in *Henry V*, 'may work contrariously.'

Almighty God did not make creation coercive, but designed it as an arena of liberty. Within that arena, God has called for individuals and peoples to live according to his law and inspiration. Democratic capitalism has been designed to permit them, sinners all, to follow this free pattern. It creates a noncoercive society as an arena of liberty, within which individuals and peoples are called to realize, through democratic methods, the vocations to which they believe they are called.

Under God, they may expect to meet exact and just judgment.

Source: Michael Novak, *The Spirit of Democratic Capitalism* (New York: American Enterprise Institute/Simon & Schuster 1982), pp. 189–92, 333–60.

BIBLIOGRAPHY

There are many publications in the fields of social Christianity, liberation theology and Christian conservatism. The following bibliography is therefore necessarily selective, particularly with regard to such major contributors as Maurice, Temple, Gladden and Niebuhr. Between them, these writers produced hundreds of books and thousands of articles. However, their major publications are included here, along with important background books. I hope my comments will assist those approaching the subject for the first time.

General

Cort, J. C., *Christian Socialism: An Informal History* (New York: Orbis Books 1988). Covers the Bible, the Fathers, the Middle Ages, England and Europe, the United States, and liberation theology. Useful on the modern Roman Catholic contribution. Popular style of writing.

Dorrien, G. J., *Reconstructing the Common Good: Theology and the Social Order* (New York: Orbis Books 1990). Strong sections on Rauschenbusch, Gutiérrez, Bonino, and Segundo. Also comments on the religious socialism of Tillich and Moltmann.

Ford, D. F., ed., *The Modern Theologians: An Introduction to Christian Theology in the Twentieth Century*, vol. 2 (Oxford: Basil Blackwell 1989). Short sections on British, North American, and liberation theology.

Christian socialism in England

Avis, P., *Gore: Construction and Conflict* (Worthing: Churchman Publishing 1988).

Bettany, F. G., *Stewart Headlam: A Biography* (London: John Murray 1926).

Binyon, G. C., *The Christian Socialist Movement in England: An Introduction to the Study of its History* (London: SPCK 1931). A more general survey.

Christensen, T., *Origin and History of Christian Socialism, 1848–54* (Universitetforlaget Aarhus 1962). Best detailed study of the first stage of English Christian socialism.

Edwards, D. L., *Leaders of the Church of England, 1828–1978* (Oxford:

Oxford University Press 1971 and Hodder & Stoughton 1978). Includes introductions to Maurice, Westcott, Gore, and Temple.

Engels, F., *The Condition of the Working Class in England* (London: Panther Books 1969, introduction by Eric Hobsbawm; first German edition, Leipzig 1845).

Fletcher, J., *William Temple* (New York: Seebury 1953).

Gore, C., *Christ and Society* (London: George Allen & Unwin 1928).

Headlam, S., *Christian Socialism: Fabian Tract No. 42* (London: The Fabian Society 1892).

Iremonger, F. A., *William Temple, Archbishop of Canterbury: His Life and Letters* (Oxford: Oxford University Press 1948).

Jones, P.d'A., *The Christian Socialist Revival, 1877–1914: Religion, Class and Social Conscience in Late-Victorian England* (New York: Princeton University Press 1968). The best detailed examination of the second stage of English Christian socialism.

Kent, J., *William Temple. Church, State and Society in Britain, 1880–1950* (Cambridge: Cambridge University Press 1992).

Maurice, F. D., *The Kingdom of Christ: or Hints to a Quaker, Respecting the Principles, Constitution, and Ordinances of the Catholic Church* (London: J.G.F. and J. Rivington, second edition 1842). His major theological study.

——, *The Lord's Prayer. Nine Sermons Preached in the Chapel of Lincoln's Inn in the Months of February, March, April* (London: John W. Parker 1848). Includes reflections on the revolutionary events of 1848. Compare to Rauschenbusch on the Lord's Prayer in *For God and the People*.

——, *Theological Essays* (London: Macmillan 1853).

——, *Learning and Working. Six Lectures delivered in Wallis's Rooms, London, in June and July 1854: The Religion of Rome and its influence on Modern Civilization, December 1854 at Edinburgh* (London: Macmillan 1855). Develops his aims and philosophy for the Working Men's College.

——, *The Workman and the Franchise. Chapters from English History on the Representation and Education of the People* (London: Alexander Strahan 1866).

——, *Social Morality. Twenty one Lectures delivered in the University of Cambridge* (London: Macmillan, second edition 1872).

Mayor, S., *The Churches and the Labour Movement* (London: Independent Press 1967). Draws particularly on the contemporary church press, from the early nineteenth century to 1960.

McClain, F., *Maurice, Man and Moralist* (London: SPCK 1972). An imaginative interpretation.

Norman, E. R., *Church and Society in England, 1770–1970* (Oxford: Clarendon 1976). Long, better on the earlier periods.

——, *The Victorian Christian Socialists* (Cambridge: Cambridge University Press 1987). Concise but detailed introductions to Maurice, Kingsley, Ludlow, Hughes, Headlam, Ruskin, and Westcott.

Oliver, J., *The Church and Social Order: Social Thought in the Church of England, 1918–1939* (Oxford: Mowbrays 1958). Important material for stage three of English Christian socialism.

Preston, R. H., *Religion and the Persistence of Capitalism* (London: SCM Press 1979). Use first four chapters, and Chapter 5 on R. H. Tawney.

——, *Explorations in Theology 9* (London: SCM Press 1981). Papers on ecumenical social ethics, transnationals, and middle axioms.

——, *Church and Society in the Late Twentieth Century: The Economic and Political Task* (London: SCM Press 1983). Chapter 1 surveys the history of English Christian socialism; Chapter 3 surveys early Christian conservatism; Chapter 4 surveys liberation theology. Appendix 2 is a detailed examination of middle axioms.

——, *The Future of Christian Ethics* (London: SCM Press 1987).

——, *Religion and the Ambiguities of Capitalism* (London: SCM Press 1991). Coming to terms with the collapse of command economies.

Ramsey, A. M., *From Gore to Temple: The Development of Anglican Theology between Lux Mundi and the Second World War, 1889–1939* (London: Longmans 1962). Important theological survey of incarnational theology, central to stages two and three of English Christian socialism.

Reardon, B. M. G., *From Coleridge to Gore: A Century of Religious Thought in Britain* (London: Longmans 1971). Useful theological discussion of Maurice and Gore.

Reckitt, M. B., *Maurice to Temple: A Century of the Social Movement in the Church of England* (London: Faber 1947). Lively account of English Christian socialism. Useful for insights into the Christendom movement.

Suggate, A. M., *William Temple and Christian Social Ethics Today* (Edinburgh: T. & T. Clark 1987). Best introduction to Temple's social thought.

Tawney, R. H., *The Acquisitive Society* (London: Bell 1921). The first of his great moral tracts for the times, followed by the second:

——, *Equality* (London: George Allen & Unwin 1931. Revised with new chapter, fourth edition 1952; 1964 edition with introduction by R. M. Titmuss).

——, *Religion and the Rise of Capitalism* (London: John Murray 1926; New York: Harcourt Brace 1926). Seminal study, continued by R. H. Preston into the present.

——, *The Attack and Other Papers* (London: George Allen & Unwin 1953). The final chapter is an adaptation of his paper for the 1937 Oxford Conference.

——, *The Radical Tradition* (ed. by R. Hinden. London: George Allen & Unwin 1964).

——, *The American Labour Movement and Other Essays* (ed. by J. M. Winter. Brighton: Harvester Press 1979). The main essay reflects Tawney's 'diplomatic' work in America in 1941–2. It also includes 'Poverty as an Industrial Problem' (1913).

Temple, W., *Christianity and the State* (London: Macmillan 1928).

Bibliography

—, *Christianity and Social Order* (London: first published by Penguin Books 1942. Shepheard-Walwyn and SPCK 1976 edition, with introduction by R. H. Preston).

Terrill, R., *R. H. Tawney and His Times: Socialism as Fellowship* (London: Andre Deutsch 1974; New York: Harvard University Press 1976).

Vidler, A., *The Theology of F. D. Maurice* (London: SCM Press 1948). Short, but clear, introduction.

Wagner, D. O., *The Church of England and Social Reform since 1854* (New York: Columbia University Press 1930). Useful on social Christianity and the official churches including 1914–26.

Westcott, B. F., *Social Aspects of Christianity* (London: Macmillan 1887). Detailed argument that lies behind the following:

—, *Socialism* (London: Guild of St Matthew 1890).

Winter, J. M., *Socialism and the Challenge of War: Ideas and Politics in Britain, 1912–18* (London: Routledge & Kegan Paul 1974). Sensitive interpretation of Tawney in Chapters 3 and 6.

Winter, J. M., and Joslin, D. M., eds, *R. H. Tawney's Commonplace Book* (Cambridge: Cambridge University Press 1972). Tawney's diary, 1912–14.

Wright, A., *R. H. Tawney* (Manchester: Manchester University Press 1987). Good short introduction to Tawney's intellectual development.

The social gospel and beyond in the United States

Bennett, J. C., *Social Salvation* (New York: Charles Scribner's Sons 1935). After a more conservative development, he returned to this more critical perspective in his *The Radical Imperative*.

—, *Christian Realism* (New York: Charles Scribner's Sons 1941).

—, *Christian Ethics and Social Policy* (New York: Charles Scribner's Sons 1946; London: Lutterworth 1954, published as *Christian Social Action*). A short classic – elaborating theological method for Christian social policy-making.

—, *Christianity and Communism Today* (New York: Association Press 1948, revised edition 1960). Theological realism at its most influential.

—, *Christian Values and Economic Life* (New York: Harper & Row 1954, co-author). Summarizes the output of the major study by the Federal Council of Churches into economic life.

—, *The Radical Imperative: From Theology to Social Ethics* (Philadelphia: Westminster Press 1975). Theological realism coming to terms with liberation theology.

Buckham, J. W., *Progressive Religious Thought in America: A Survey of the Enlarging Pilgrim Faith* (Boston: Houghton Mifflin & Co. 1919).

Bibliography

The importance of the relationship between liberal theology and social Christianity. Buckham was a friend of Gladden.

Carter, A., *The Decline and Revival of the Social Gospel: Social and Political Liberalism in American Protestant Churches, 1920–1940* (Ithaca, New York: Cornell University Press 1956).

Cauthen, K., *The Impact of American Religious Liberalism* (New York: Harper & Row 1962).

Dombrowski, J., *The Early Days of Christian Socialism in America* (New York: Columbia University Press 1936). Pioneer study; valuable comment on the radical strand, including Herron.

Dorn, J. H., *Washington Gladden: Prophet of the Social Gospel* (New York: Ohio State University Press 1967). Detailed study of a key representative figure of the social gospel.

Ely, R. T., *Social Aspects of Christianity and Other Essays* (New York: 1889). Early economist and lay theologian.

Fox, R., *Reinhold Niebuhr: A Biography* (New York: Pantheon Books 1985). Essential reading.

Gladden, W., *Working People and their Employers* (New York: Funk & Wagnalls Co. 1894, second edition. First edition, Boston 1876). The book that began the social gospel.

——, *Applied Christianity: Moral Aspects of Social Questions* (Boston: Houghton, Mifflin & Co. 1886).

——, *Tools and the Man: Property and Industry under the Christian Law* (Boston: Houghton, Mifflin & Co. 1893).

——, *Recollections* (Boston: Houghton, Mifflin & Co. 1909). Essential account of the first two stages of the social gospel.

Handy, R. T., ed., *The Social Gospel in America* (New York: Oxford University Press 1966). The most accessible introduction and reader, covering Gladden, Ely and Rauschenbusch.

Harland, G., *The Thought of Reinhold Niebuhr* (New York: Oxford University Press 1960).

Harries, R., ed., *Reinhold Niebuhr and the Issues of our Times* (Oxford: Mowbrays 1986). Good articles by Fox, Gustafson, Preston, and Gilkey.

Hopkins, C. H., *The Rise of the Social Gospel in American Protestantism 1865–1915* (New York: Yale University Press 1940). Most complete, and favourable, account.

Kegley, C., and Bretall, R.W., eds, *Reinhold Niebuhr: His Religious, Social and Political Thought* (New York: Macmillan 1956. Revised and expanded second edition, ed. by C. Kegley, New York: Pilgrim Press 1984).

Lee, R., *The Promise of Bennett* (Philadelphia and New York: J. B. Lippincott Company 1969). Brief, clear exposition of what is also a summary of theological realism's contribution to Christian social ethics.

Mathews, S., *The Social Teachings of Jesus* (New York: Macmillan 1897).

Bibliography

——, *The Social Gospel* (Philadelphia: Griffith and Rowland Press 1910).

May, H. F., *Protestant Churches and Industrial America* (New York: Harper & Bros. 1949). To be read with Hopkins.

Meyer, D. B., *The Protestant Search for Political Realism, 1919–1941* (New York: University of California Press 1960). Creative interpretation of theological realism, particularly through the contributions of Niebuhr and Bennett, and in the context of comment on Rauschenbusch.

Miller, R. M., *American Protestantism and Social Issues, 1919–1939* (New York: Chapel Hill, University of North Carolina Press 1958).

Minus, P. M., *Walter Rauschenbusch: American Reformer* (New York: Macmillan 1988).

Niebuhr, H. R., *The Kingdom of God in America* (Chicago: Wilett, Clark & Co. 1937).

Niebuhr, R., *Moral Man and Immoral Society: A Study in Ethics and Politics* (New York: Charles Scribner's Sons 1932. First British edition, London: SCM Press 1963). Essential reading.

——, *An Interpretation of Christian Ethics* (New York: Harper & Bros. 1935; London: SCM Press 1941).

——, *The Nature and Destiny of Man* (two volumes; New York: Charles Scribner's Sons 1941, 1943).

——, *The Children of Light and the Children of Darkness: A Vindication of Democracy and a Critique of its Traditional Defense* (New York: Charles Scribner's Sons 1944). The character of Niebuhr's apologetic at its best.

——, *Christian Realism and Political Problems* (New York: Charles Scribner's Sons 1953).

Rasmussen, L., *Reinhold Niebuhr: Theologian of Public Life* (New York and London: Collins/Harper & Row 1989). Valuable introductory essay, and selection of Niebuhr texts.

Rauschenbusch, W., *Christianity and the Social Crisis* (Boston: Pilgrim Press 1907). The classic of the social gospel.

——, *For God and the People: Prayers of the Social Awakening* (Boston: Pilgrim Press 1910; London: SCM Press 1927).

——, *Christianizing the Social Order* (New York: Macmillan 1912).

——, *A Theology for the Social Gospel* (New York: Macmillan 1918).

Sharpe, D. R., *Walter Rauschenbusch* (New York: Macmillan 1942).

Stackhouse, M. L., *Public Theology and Political Economy* (Grand Rapids, MI: Eerdmans 1987). See Chapters 3 and 4 on the social gospel.

Stone, R. H., ed., *Faith and Politics: A Commentary on Religious, Social and Political Thought in a Technological Age* (New York: George Braziller 1968). Important collection of Niebuhr's essays, including on Christian pragmatism.

Strong, J., *Our Country: Its Possible Future and Present Crisis* (New York: Baker & Taylor 1885). As innovatory and influential as the early Gladden, but instead on urbanization.

Bibliography

Wogaman, J. P., *Guaranteed Annual Income: The Moral Issues* (Nashville: Abingdon 1968).
——, *A Christian Method of Moral Judgement* (Philadelphia: Fortress Press; London: SCM Press 1976).
——, *Christians and the Great Economic Debate* (Philadelphia: Fortress Press; London: SCM Press 1977). Typology of economic systems.
——, *Economics and Ethics: A Christian Enquiry* (Philadelphia: Fortress Press; London: SCM Press 1986).
——, *A Christian Perspective on Politics* (Philadelphia: Fortress Press; London: SCM Press 1988). Typology of Christian responses to politics, and an elaboration of the mainstream liberal tradition.

Liberation theology

Boff, C., *Theology and Praxis: Epistemological Foundations* (New York: Orbis Books 1987). The most detailed exposition of praxis as liberationist methodology.
Boff, L., *Jesus Christ Liberator* (New York: Orbis Books; London: SPCK 1978). The implications of liberation theology for christology.
——, *Church, Charism and Power: Liberation Theology and the Institutional Church* (New York: Crossroad Publishing Co.; London: SCM Press 1985). The critical consequences of liberationism for traditional ecclesiastical authority structures.
——, *Ecclesiogenesis: The Base Communities Reinvent the Church* (New York: Orbis Books and Collins Liturgical 1986).
Bonino, J. M., *Doing Theology in a Revolutionary Situation* (Philadelphia: Fortress Press; London: SPCK 1975). The major work of liberation theology by a Protestant theologian.
——, *Toward a Christian Political Ethics* (Philadelphia: Fortress Press; London: SCM Press 1983).
Duchrow, U., *Global Economy: A Confessional Issue for the Churches?* (Geneva: World Council of Churches Publications 1987). On confessional theology and economics, out of the Lutheran tradition, and including interpretations of Luther and Bonhoeffer.
——, 'The Witness of the Church in Contrast to the Prevailing Ideologies of the Market Economy', in *Poverty and Polarisation: A Call to Commitment* (Manchester: William Temple Foundation 1988).
——, 'Political and Economic Wellbeing and Justice: A Global View', in Franklin, R., ed., *Studies in Christian Ethics, Vol.3, No.1.* (Edinburgh: T. & T. Clark 1990).
Ferm, D. W., *Third World Liberation Theologies: A Reader* (New York: Orbis Books 1986).
Gibellini, R., ed., *New Frontiers of Theology in Latin America* (New York: Orbis Books 1979; London: SCM Press 1980).

402

——, *The Liberation Theology Debate* (London: SCM Press 1987). Clear, short introduction, covering history, method, Christian symbols, international networks, and the Roman Catholic debate.

Gutiérrez, G., *A Theology of Liberation* (New York: Orbis Books 1973; London: SCM Press 1974; 1988 edition with new introduction).

——, *The Power of the Poor in History* (New York: Orbis Books; London: SCM Press 1983). Draws on material from 1969–79, and includes theology from the underside of history.

——, *We Drink from our Own Wells: The Spiritual Journey of a People* (New York: Orbis Books; London: SCM Press 1984).

Hennelly, A. T., ed., *Liberation Theology: A Documentary History* (New York: Orbis Books 1990). Includes Moltmann, J., 'On Latin American Liberation Theology: An Open Letter to José Míguez Bonino'. European Christian socialist criticism of liberation theology.

Hinkelammert, F. J., *The Ideological Weapons of Death: A Theological Critique of Capitalism* (New York: Orbis Books 1986). Use of dependency theory, and influences Duchrow.

McAfee Brown, R., *Gustavo Gutiérrez: An Introduction to Liberation Theology* (New York: Orbis Books 1990).

McCann, D. P., *Christian Realism and Liberation Theology: Practical Theologies in Creative Conflict* (New York: Orbis Books 1980).

Miranda, J. P., *Marx and the Bible: A Critique of the Philosophy of Oppression* (New York: Orbis Books 1974).

Segundo, J. L., *The Liberation of Theology* (New York: Orbis Books 1976; Dublin: Gill & Macmillan 1977). On theological method as the hermeneutic circle.

Sobrino, J., *Christology at the Crossroads* (New York: Orbis Books; London: SCM Press 1978).

Christian conservatism

Benne, R., *The Ethic of Democratic Capitalism: A Moral Reassessment* (Philadelphia: Fortress Press 1981).

Berger, P., *The Capitalist Revolution: Fifty Propositions about Prosperity, Equality and Liberty* (New York: Basic Books 1986; London: Wildwood House 1987).

Brown, S. J., *Thomas Chalmers and the Godly Commonwealth in Scotland* (Oxford: Oxford University Press 1982).

Griffiths, B., *Morality and the Market Place: Christian Alternatives to Capitalism and Socialism* (London: Hodder & Stoughton 1982). The clearest introduction to Christian conservatism, including the development of theological method.

——, *The Creation of Wealth* (London: Hodder & Stoughton 1984).

——, *Monetarism and Morality: A Response to the Bishops* (London: Centre for Policy Studies 1985). Short pamphlet. Better on the technical interpretation of monetarism than as an ethical interpretation.

——, 'The Conservative Quadrilateral', in Alison, M., and Edwards, D.L., eds., *Christianity and Conservatism: Are Christianity and Conservatism Compatible?* (London: Hodder & Stoughton 1990). Christian defence of Thatcherite policies in the 1980s.

Hilton, B., *The Age of Atonement: The Influence of Evangelicalism on Social and Economic Thought, 1785–1865* (Oxford: Clarendon 1988). Important complement to Waterman's study of Christian political economy. Includes observations on the rise of the incarnational theology of social Christianity.

Hole, R., *Pulpits, Politics and Public Order in England, 1760–1832* (Cambridge: Cambridge University Press 1989).

Malthus, T. R., *An Essay on the Principle of Population, as it affects the future improvement of society. With remarks on the speculations of Mr. Godwin, M. Condorcet, and other writers* (London: Johnson 1798; London: Penguin Books 1970, with introduction by A. Flew).

McVickar, J., *Outlines of Political Economy* (New York: 1825).

Neuhaus, R. J., *The Naked Public Square: Religion and Democracy in America* (Grand Rapids, MI: Wm B. Eerdmans 1984).

Novak, M., *The Spirit of Democratic Capitalism* (New York: American Enterprise Institute/Simon & Schuster 1982). Classic American argument for Christian conservatism. Includes Chapter 19 on Reinhold Niebuhr. New edition (London: The Institute of Economic Affairs, Health and Welfare Unit 1991; Maryland: Madison Books 1991). Contains a new Afterword by Novak.

Sumner, J.B., *A Treatise on the Records of the Creation and on the Moral Attributes of the Creator; with particular reference to the Jewish History, and the consistency of the principle of population with the Wisdom and Goodness of the Deity* (London: Hatchard 1816, 2 volumes).

Waterman, A. M. C., *Revolution, Economics and Religion: Christian Political Economy, 1798–1833* (Cambridge: Cambridge University Press 1991). The major study of Christian political economy.

Whateley, R., *Introductory Lectures in Political Economy* (London: Fellowes 1832. Second edition, including lecture 9, and other additions, London: Fellowes; New York: Kelly 1966). Important early distinction between positive and normative economics.

INDEX

Abrecht, Paul   9n, 129
Althaus, Paul   239
American Economic
    Association   25
Amsterdam conference   8, 146,
    197, 225, 266
Anabaptists   204, 235
Anselm, St   321
Aquinas, St Thomas   137, 270
Aristotle   201, 203, 233, 291–5,
    389
Assmann, Hugo   36, 48n

baptism   16
Barth, Karl   20, 151, 233, 252,
    315
base communities   39, 303
Becker, Gary   134
Beecher, Henry Ward   22, 46n
Benne, Robert   41
Bennett, John C.   1, 6–9n, 20–1,
    23, 28–31, 129–31, 146, 256–7,
    272, 354; on problems of *social*
    ethics   227–32; on four
    Christian social strategies
    232–9; on a fifth strategy
    239–54
Berger, Peter   41
Bliss, William D. P.   27
Boff, Clodovis   36
Boff, Leonardo   36, 38–9, 48n
Bonino, José Miguez   36, 48n,
    359
Bonhoeffer, Dietrich   296, 392
Brotherhood of the
    Kingdom   28, 171, 173
Brunner, Emil   20, 230, 241, 253,
    365
Burke, Edmund   199
Bush, George   41
Bushnell, Horace   24
Butler, Joseph   202

capitalism   6, 11, 14, 20–1, 27,
    31–3, 42, 112–13, 130, 141,
    143, 159, 161–7, 172, 175–81,
    184, 215, 225, 237, 259, 261,
    270–5, 284, 293–6, 309, 348–9,
    355–7, 362, 366, 370, 394; *see*
    also democratic capitalism;
    economy, market
Chartists   13, 14
Chetham's Library   10
Chicago   23, 26
Chimbote conference   36, 304
Christendom Group   20
Christian political ecomomy   2,
    6, 43–5, 114, 334
Christian (theological)
    realism   20, 28–32, 42, 89,
    130, 172, 197, 198–9, 213–24,
    226, 256
Christian Social Union   18–19,
    23, 25, 46n, 79–80
Christian Socialist
    Fellowship   27
Christian symbols   30, 37–8, 44,
    198
Church Association for the
    Advancement of the Interests
    of Labor   25
Church social statements   4, 7,
    20–1, 26, 28, 31, 36, 39, 42, 80,
    130, 144–7, 148, 151, 232–3,
    256, 285, 300, 306–30 *passim*
Church Socialist League   17
communism   21, 32, 42, 68–9,
    130, 198, 215, 221–3, 226, 233,
    236, 245, 247–8, 252, 263–4,
    356; *see also* Marx; marxism
competition   15, 18, 25, 32, 40,
    59, 64, 66–8, 81, 116, 137, 161,
    175–6, 184, 259, 270, 286–7,
    374, 381
Conference on Politics,
    Economics and Citizenship   7,
    8, 11, 20, 88, 112–13
conflict, industrial   23–5, 59, 62,
    88, 90, 115, 129, 158, 161–70
    passim, 177, 187–8, 258–9

405